Forms of Verse

BRITISH AND AMERICAN

Genius in art is probably only the intuitive knowledge of form. KARL SHAPIRO

Forms of Verse

BRITISH AND AMERICAN

Sara deFord
Clarinda Harriss Lott
GOUCHER COLLEGE

APPLETON-CENTURY-CROFTS
EDUCATIONAL DIVISION
New York MEREDITH CORPORATION

7110-1

Library of Congress Card Number: 77-94257

PRINTED IN THE UNITED STATES OF AMERICA

390-26000-2

ACKNOWLEDGMENTS

The following publishers and other copyright holders kindly granted permission to reprint the poems and passages here listed.

ESTATE OF R. P. BLACKMUR. "Mr. Virtue and the Three Bears" by R. P. Blackmur, first published in *Poetry*, December 1951, vol. 79, no. 3, copyright 1951, The Modern Poetry Association. Reprinted by permission of the Editor of *Poetry* and the Estate of R. P. Blackmur.

CITY LIGHTS BOOKS. "A Supermarket in California" from *Howl* by Allen Ginsberg. Copyright © 1956, 1959 by Allen Ginsberg. Reprinted by permission of City Lights Books.

COLLINS-KNOWLTON-WING, INC. "A Frosty Night" from *Collected Poems 1955* by Robert Graves. Reprinted by permission of Collins-Knowlton-Wing, Inc. Copyright © 1955 by Robert Graves.

THE CRESSET PRESS LIMITED. "To a Fat Lady Seen from a Train" from *Collected Poems* by Frances Cornford, The Cresset Press Limited, 1954.

THE LITERARY TRUSTEES OF WALTER DE LA MARE. "Silver" by Walter de la Mare, reprinted by permission of The Literary Trustees of Walter de la Mare and The Society of Authors as their representative.

WALT DISNEY MUSIC COMPANY. Excerpt from "The Ballad of Davy Crockett," lyrics by Tom Blackburn. Used by permission of the publisher Walt Disney Music Company, Glendale, Calif.

DODD, MEAD & COMPANY, INC. "The Soldier" reprinted from *The Collected Poems of Rupert Brooke* by permission of Dodd, Mead & Company, Inc. Copyright 1915 by Dodd, Mead and Company; copyright renewed 1943 by Edward Marsh.

DOUBLEDAY & COMPANY, INC. "The Waking," copyright 1953 by Theodore Roethke, from *The Collected Poems of Theodore Roethke*. Reprinted by permission of Doubleday & Company, Inc.

NORMA MILLAY ELLIS. "What lips my lips have kissed" from *Collected Poems* by Edna St. Vincent Millay, Harper & Row. Copyright 1923, 1951 by Edna St. Vincent Millay and Norma Millay Ellis.

FARRAR, STRAUS & GIROUX, INC. "The Public Garden" reprinted from *For the Union Dead* by Robert Lowell, by permission of Farrar, Straus & Giroux, Inc. Copyright © 1962 by Robert Lowell.

GROSSMAN PUBLISHERS, INC. Ode (Bk. I, 9) from *The Odes of Horace: The Centennial Hymn*, trans. by James Michie. Reprinted by permission of Grossman Publishers, Inc.

GROVE PRESS, INC. "Heat" and "Pear Tree" by H. D. Reprinted by permission of Grove Press, Inc. Copyright © 1957 by Norman Holmes Pearson.

HARCOURT BRACE JOVANOVICH, INC. "conceive a man, should he have anything" and "mOOn Over tOwns mOOn," copyright, 1935, by E. E. Cummings; renewed, 1963, by Marion Morehouse Cummings. "what freedom's not some under's mere above," copyright, 1940, by E. E. Cummings. "if i have made, my lady, intricate," copyright, 1926, by Horace Liveright, renewed, 1954, by E. E. Cummings. "All in green went my love riding," copyright, 1923, 1951, by E. E. Cummings. All five poems reprinted from E. E. Cummings, *Poems 1923–1954*, by permission of Harcourt Brace Jovanovich, Inc. – "Morning at the Window" and "The Love Song of J. Alfred Prufrock" from *Collected Poems 1909–1962* by T. S. Eliot, copyright, 1936, by Harcourt, Brace & World, Inc.; copyright, © 1963, 1964, by T. S. Eliot. – "Between the Porch and the Altar: III, Katherine's Dream" (excerpt), "France," and "The Soldier" from *Lord Weary's Castle* by Robert Lowell, copyright, 1944, 1946, by Robert Lowell. – Excerpt from "Still, Citizen Sparrow" in *Ceremony and Other Poems* by Richard Wilbur, copyright, 1948, 1949, 1950, by Richard Wilbur. – Excerpts from Virginia Woolf, *The Waves*, 1931. – All reprinted by permission of Harcourt Brace Jovanovich, Inc.

HARVARD UNIVERSITY PRESS. "I taste a liquor never brewed," "I'm Nobody," "The Murmur of a Bee," "A word is dead," and "I felt a Funeral, in my Brain" reprinted by permission of the publishers and the Trustees of Amherst College from Thomas H. Johnson, Editor, *The Poems of Emily Dickinson*, Cambridge, Mass.: The Belknap Press of Harvard University Press, Copyright, 1951, 1955, by The President and Fellows of Harvard College. The scholarly work of Mabel Loomis Todd and Millicent Todd Bingham has been of great value to this edition.

DAVID HIGHAM ASSOCIATES, LTD. "Solo for Ear-Trumpet" in *The Wooden Pegasus* by Edith Sitwell, Blackwell & Mott, 1920. Reprinted by permission of the Executors and their agent, David Higham Associates, Ltd.

THE HOKUSEIDO PRESS. "Wild persimmons" by Issa from *Haiku* (4 vols.), ed. and trans. by R. H. Blyth. Reprinted by permission of The Hokuseido Press, Tokyo.

HOLT, RINEHART AND WINSTON, INC. "The Ballad of William Sycamore" from *Ballads and Poems: 1915–1930* by Stephen Vincent Benét. Copyright 1931 by Stephen Vincent Benét. Copyright © 1959 by Rosemary Carr Benét. – "Moon Compasses," "A Considerable Speck," and "Birches" (excerpt), copyright 1916 by Holt, Rinehart and Winston, Inc.; copyright 1936, 1942, 1944 by Robert Frost; copyright © 1964, 1970 by Lesley Frost Ballantine. "Blue-Butterfly Day" (excerpt), "The Planners," and "The Night Light," copyright 1923, 1947 by Holt, Rinehart and Winston, Inc.; copyright 1951 by Robert Frost. "Once by the Pacific," "Any Size We Please," "A Soldier," and "The Master Speed," copyright 1928, 1947 by Holt, Rinehart and Winston, Inc.; copyright 1936, © 1956 by Robert Frost; copyright © 1964, 1970 by Lesley Frost Ballantine. "The Pasture," copyright 1939, © 1967 by Holt, Rinehart and Winston, Inc. "The Gift Outright," copyright 1942 by Robert Frost. All twelve poems from *Complete Poems of Robert Frost*. – "On Wenlock Edge" and "Is my team ploughing" from "A Shropshire Lad" (Authorised Edition) from *The Collected Poems of A. E. Housman*. Copyright 1939, 1940, © 1959 by Holt, Rinehart and Winston, Inc. Copyright © 1967 by Robert E. Symons. – "The weeping Pleiads wester" and "The rainy Pleiads wester" from *The Collected Poems of A. E. Housman*. Copyright 1936 by Barclays Bank Ltd. Copyright © 1964 by Robert E. Symons. – Excerpt from "Fog" from *Chicago Poems* by Carl Sandburg. Copyright 1916 by Holt, Rinehart and Winston, Inc. Copyright 1944 by Carl Sandburg. "Grass" and excerpt from "Prayers of Steel" from *Cornhuskers* by Carl Sandburg. Copyright 1918 by Holt, Rinehart and Winston, Inc. Copyright 1946 by Carl Sandburg. – All reprinted by permission of Holt, Rinehart and Winston, Inc.

HOUGHTON MIFFLIN COMPANY. "A Miracle for Breakfast" from *Poems North and South* by Elizabeth Bishop. – "Lilacs" (excerpt) and "A Decade" by Amy Lowell. – "Ars Poetica" and "The Silent Slain" by Archibald MacLeisch. – Excerpt from Preface to *Some Imagist Poets*, 1915. – Used by permission of the publisher, Houghton Mifflin Company.

BRUCE HUMPHRIES, PUBLISHERS. "Evening" by Richard Aldington. Reprinted by permission of Bruce Humphries, Publishers, Boston, Mass. 02116.

MRS. RANDALL JARRELL. "The Death of the Ball Turret Gunner" by Randall Jarrell. Permission to reprint granted by Mrs. Randall Jarrell.

ALFRED A. KNOPF, INC. "Cinquain: A Warning." Copyright 1922 by Algernon S. Crapsey and renewed 1950 by The Adelaide Crapsey Foundation. Reprinted from *Verse* by Adelaide Crapsey. – "A High-Toned Old Christian Woman." Copyright 1923 and renewed 1951 by Wallace Stevens. Reprinted from *Collected Poems of Wallace Stevens*. – "August" and "Puritan Sonnet" (last 14 lines of "Wild Peaches"). Copyright 1921 by Alfred A. Knopf, Inc. and renewed 1949 by William Rose Benét. Reprinted from *Collected Poems of Elinor Wylie*. – All reprinted by permission of Alfred A. Knopf, Inc.

LITTLE, BROWN AND COMPANY. "My Dream" from *Marriage Lines* by Ogden Nash, by permission of Little, Brown and Co. Copyright, 1954, by Ogden Nash. The poem originally appeared in *The New Yorker.*

LIVERIGHT PUBLISHING CORPORATION. Excerpt from "For the Marriage of Faustus and Helen" in *The Collected Poems of Hart Crane.* By permission of Liveright, Publishers, N.Y. Copyright © renewed, 1961, by Liveright Publishing Corp.

THE STERLING LORD AGENCY. Excerpt from "One Night Stand" by LeRoi Jones. Copyright © 1960 by LeRoi Jones. Reprinted by permission of The Sterling Lord Agency.

THE MACMILLAN COMPANY. "Winter in Durnover Field" from *The Collected Poems of Thomas Hardy,* copyright 1925 by The Macmillan Company. – Excerpt from "The Fish" reprinted from *Collected Poems* by Marianne Moore. Copyright 1935 by Marianne Moore, renewed 1963 by Marianne Moore and T. S. Eliot. – Excerpt from *The Man Against the Sky* by E. A. Robinson. Copyright The Macmillan Company, 1916, renewed 1944 by Ruth Nivison. – Excerpt from *Lancelot* by E. A. Robinson. Copyright 1920 by E. A. Robinson. – "A Crazed Girl" and "High Talk," copyright 1940 by Georgie Yeats. "Leda and the Swan" and excerpt from "Among School Children," copyright 1928 by The Macmillan Company, renewed 1956 by Georgie Yeats. "The Folly of Being Comforted," copyright 1903 by The Macmillan Company, renewed 1931 by W. B. Yeats. Excerpt from "The Ballad of Father Gilligan," copyright 1906 by The Macmillan Company, renewed 1934 by W. B. Yeats. All six poems reprinted from *Collected Poems* by W. B. Yeats. – "Colonel Martin" reprinted from *Last Poems and Plays* by W. B. Yeats. Copyright 1940 by Georgie Yeats. – All reprinted with permission of The Macmillan Company.

HAROLD MATSON COMPANY, INC. "The Conflict" by C. Day Lewis. Copyright 1935 by C. Day Lewis. Renewed 1962. Reprinted by permission of Harold Matson Company, Inc. – Draft of "The Express" by Stephen Spender in The Poetry Collection of the Lockwood Memorial Library, State University of New York at Buffalo. Reprinted by permission of the author, the Curator of the Lockwood Memorial Library, and the Harold Matson Company, Inc.

WILLIAM MORROW AND COMPANY, INC. Excerpt from "Love Poem" in *The Iron Pastoral* by John Frederick Nims. Published by William Sloane Associates, Inc. Copyright 1947 by John Frederick Nims. Reprinted by permission of William Morrow and Company, Inc.

NEW DIRECTIONS PUBLISHING CORPORATION. Excerpt from "Marriage" in Gregory Corso, *The Happy Birthday of Death.* Copyright © 1960 by New Directions Publishing Corporation. – "Dove sta amore" from Lawrence Ferlinghetti, *A Coney Island of the Mind.* Copyright © 1958 by Lawrence Ferlinghetti. – Excerpts from "Arms and the Boy" and "From My Diary" from Wilfred Owen, *Collected Poems.* Copyright Chatto & Windus Ltd. 1946, © 1963. – "Alba," "Ballad of the Goodly Fere," "In a Station of the Metro," and "A Virginal" from Ezra Pound, *Personae.* Copyright 1926 by Ezra Pound. – "And death shall have no dominion" (excerpt), "Ballad of the Long-Legged Bait," "Do not go gentle into that good night," "The force that through the green fuse drives the flower" (excerpt), and "When all my five and country senses see" from Dylan Thomas, *Collected Poems.* Copyright 1939, 1943 by New Directions Publishing Corporation. Copyright 1952 by Dylan Thomas. – "The Red Wheelbarrow" from William Carlos Williams, *Collected Earlier Poems.* Copyright 1938 by William Carlos Williams. – All reprinted by permission of New Directions Publishing Corporation.

OXFORD UNIVERSITY PRESS, INC. "No worst, there is none," "Felix Randal," "Pied Beauty," and excerpt from "God's Grandeur" from *Poems of Gerard Manley Hopkins,* 3rd ed., edited by W. H. Gardner. Copyright 1948 by Oxford University Press, Inc. Reprinted by permission.

G. P. PUTNAM'S SONS. "In Flanders Fields" reprinted by permission of G. P. Putnam's Sons from *In Flanders Fields and Other Poems* by John McCrae. Copyright 1919 by G. P. Putnam's Sons.

RANDOM HOUSE, INC. "Petition" and excerpt from "The strings' excitement" (*Poems*), copyright 1934 and renewed 1961 by W. H. Auden, reprinted from *The Collected Poetry of W. H. Auden.* "Time can say nothing but I told you so," copyright 1941 by W. H. Auden, reprinted from *Selected Poetry of W. H. Auden.* "The Presumptuous" (*The Double Man*), copyright 1941 by W. H. Auden, reprinted from *The Collected Poetry of W. H. Auden.* "Adolescence" and "Far from the heart of culture he was used" (Sonnet XVIII of "In Time of War"), copyright 1945 by W. H. Auden, reprinted from *The Collected Poetry of W. H. Auden.* "Hearing of harvests rotting in the valleys," copyright 1937 and renewed 1964 by W. H. Auden, reprinted from *On This Island* by W. H. Auden. – "Buick" (*Person, Place and Thing*), copyright 1941 by Karl Shapiro. "The Fly" (*Person,*

Place and Thing), copyright 1942 by Karl Shapiro. "Recapitulations" (*Trial of a Poet and Other Poems*), copyright 1943, 1946, 1947 by Karl Shapiro. All three poems reprinted from *Poems 1940–1953* by Karl Shapiro. – "The Express" (*Poems*), copyright 1934 and renewed 1961 by Stephen Spender, reprinted from *Collected Poems 1928–1953* by Stephen Spender. – All reprinted by permission of Random House, Inc.

FLORENCE DUNBAR ROBERTSON. "Disillusion" by Florence French Dunbar, reprinted from *Mount Holyoke College Verse*, II, ed. by Ada L. F. Snell, Oxford University Press, 1937, by permission of Florence Dunbar Robertson.

CHARLES SCRIBNER'S SONS. "A Gift of Great Value" from *For Love* by Robert Creeley. Copyright © 1962 Robert Creeley. – Excerpt from "A Letter from a Girl to Her Own Old Age" by Alice Meynell. – "Reuben Bright," "The House on the Hill," and "Octave #2" from *The Children of the Night* by E. A. Robinson. – "Ode to the Confederate Dead" from *Poems* by Allen Tate. Copyright 1931, 1932, 1937, 1948 Charles Scribner's Sons; renewal copyright © 1959, 1960, 1965 Allen Tate. – All reprinted with the permission of Charles Scribner's Sons.

PETER VIERECK. "Kilroy" from *New and Selected Poems, 1932–1967*, by Peter Viereck, Bobbs-Merrill, New York, 1967, copyrighted by the author; previously printed in his *Terror and Decorum*, New York, 1948.

THE VIKING PRESS, INC. "A White Blossom" and excerpt from "Piano" from *The Complete Poems of D. H. Lawrence*, vol. I, ed. by Vivian de Sola Pinto and F. Warren Roberts. Copyright 1920 by B. W. Huebsch, Inc., renewed 1948 by Frieda Lawrence. Reprinted by permission of The Viking Press, Inc.

WESLEYAN UNIVERSITY PRESS. "Death of a Vermont Farm Woman" from *Light and Dark* by Barbara Howes. Copyright © 1959 by Barbara Howes. Reprinted by permission of Wesleyan University Press.

This book is dedicated to my students,
my co-author among them,
who taught me how to write it,
and, before them all, to my teacher Ada Laura Fonda Snell,
Professor Emeritus of English at Mount Holyoke College,
who taught me, long ago, her course in versification.

S. deF.

Preface

This book, a study of the techniques of verse, is designed to facilitate the appreciation of poetry as a formal art. The method is the use of exercises in analysis of "classic" passages in the standard, basic forms of English verse. At the end of each group of exercises in a standard form—in blank verse, for example—the student is asked to write in that form as a means of furthering his understanding and appreciation of verse writing. This method is not an attempt to teach creative writing or the writing of poetry; students who may be frightened by the idea of versifying are advised that the possession of an ordinary vocabulary and the ability to count to five (for basic pentameter) on the fingers are the only skills necessary for the writing of competent verse. The parallel between this exercise and the newspaper crossword puzzle indicates that both involve filling an arbitrary number of spaces with verbal equivalents of meaning. The exercises in writing verse are designed as a kind of laboratory or studio experience in the science and art of versification. Similar exercises are undertaken in elementary courses in music theory and in the fine arts as a means of comprehending these media.

For the purposes of instruction and the development of critical judgment, the exercises in writing round off a period of discovering by close analysis flaws in the achievements of major practitioners of the form. An attempt to write in the form usually persuades even the most adversely critical student that Pope did have skills that the student cannot claim: the student's couplet either says what he wishes to say, in appropriate diction, *or* it observes the rules of

Pope. Unless both teacher and student are unusually fortunate, a first attempt at epigrammatic heroic couplet will probably be a failure on one or both counts.

In the plan of the book we have followed the procedure used in a course offered since 1948 at Goucher College to sophomore and junior students. The procedure has proved exceptionally useful to English majors at the beginning of the concentration in English literature. Each one of the basic poetic forms is explained in a preliminary essay, which is followed by famous examples of these forms in English poetry from Chaucer to the present. Exercises in the analysis of these forms are based on the passages given. Major documents in the history of English poetry—for example, Milton's statement on "The Verse" of *Paradise Lost*—are included.

The book does not attempt to carry the student beyond a knowledge of standard forms, though some examples of both early and modern experimentation—the lyrics of Wyatt, quantitative verse, syllable-counting verse, contemporary adaptations of stress verse, etc.—have been included. The book opens with a study of the rhythmical prose of the 1611 Bible and the *Areopagitica*; it closes with samples of free verse, from Whitman to current poets, illustrating the use of rhythm and diction for an effect quite different from that achieved through meter and rhyme.

The glossary, which supplements the text, has been compiled primarily for use in studying the craft of poetry. Hence, with the exception of certain staples, such as "metaphysical conceit" and "pastoral," it omits most terminology belonging exclusively, or almost exclusively, to literary history. On the other hand, it describes and exemplifies a number of the foreign verse forms practiced in English, since we believe that the student can attain both discipline and flexibility by experimentation with a wide variety of forms. The definitions are as businesslike, concrete, and unfanciful as we could make them. While we have excluded certain terms to avoid complicating the subject unnecessarily, we have included many not utilized in the text as an aid to understanding critical discussions of poetry or attempting additional experimentation.

This book has been written and rewritten with the constant help of the students at Goucher College who have studied versification with us since 1948. The completed manuscript has been greatly improved by the skillful corrections of Mary Taylor Hesky of Goucher College, and both we and the publishers have reason to be grateful for the accurate typing of Mrs. Kathryn Cornell. The errors of whatever kind are, of course, our own.

S. deF., C. H. L.

Contents

VII

The Development of Tetrameter and Four-Stress Verse 172

VIII

The Sonnet 195

A Note to the Student

In the analysis of each of the major, basic types of English versification, you will find suggestions for written exercises. These exercises should be done carefully, since development of skill in the technical analysis of verse depends on practice. A comparison of your work with that of other students will undoubtedly show a number of different answers to many of the questions. Rarely is there a single right answer, although some may be absolutely wrong ones. The exercises are designed to be cumulative in progression and in difficulty; hence failure to work out Exercise 1 or 2, for example, will probably result in serious problems in working out Exercise 3. *Keep all exercises, when corrected, for further study and review*. The exercises on blank verse will be used for a cumulative study on the historical development of that form.

It will facilitate the reading and correcting of the exercises, both for you and for the teacher, if you follow these directions:

1. In scansion exercises, always copy the passage to be analyzed, and make sure that you have copied accurately; do *not* do your exercises in the book itself.
2. Write or type on standard $8\frac{1}{2}$ by 11 paper.
3. Use double space when typing.
4. For handwritten work, use lined paper with wide lines—*i.e.*, regular theme paper rather than notebook paper with narrow lines and punched holes. Write on every *other* line.

5. Never write or type on the back of the paper.
6. For technical markings use blue or black ink. The markings should go directly over the syllables. Neat and clear work is less apt to be marked incorrect.
7. Where it is necessary to divide a word by syllables, consult a dictionary for correct division and mark the division with a short straight line, perpendicular to the line of the passage; do not use slanted lines unless directed to do so.

Forms of Verse

BRITISH AND AMERICAN

I

Rhythm and Meter

STRESSED AND UNSTRESSED SYLLABLES

Attempts to set up distinctions between verse and prose are to be found in numerous studies. As a brief and practical introduction to the problem, let us say that most of the prose in use, whether written or spoken, is not, nor is it intended to be, an artistic form. In "practical" prose, therefore, the occurrence of RHYTHM* can be taken as probably coincidental, and the student who is undertaking an analysis of artistic prose for the first time has probably not been conscious of the existence and handling of rhythmical design in prose. Even the untrained student may, however, have been aware of pleasure in certain arrangements of prose sentences and displeasure in other arrangements of the same sentences. The term "arrangements" is used in order to distinguish the effects achieved by sequences of stressed and unstressed syllables (see ACCENT) from those obtained by changes in the words themselves. Thus, had the translators of the 1611 Bible written,

> M˘y shépher˘d i˘s th˘e Lórd,

there would be *three* light, unstressed syllables between the two stressed, and no unstressed syllable at the end. The arrangement of stressed and unstressed syllables is obviously different, although the words are not. To choose, however, the American Revised,

> J˘ehóv˘ah i˘s m˘y shépher˘d,

or the Moffatt,

> Th˘e Ĕtérn˘al shépher˘ds mé,

* Words printed in SMALL CAPITALS are defined in the Glossary. See p. 307 for a list of the prosodic symbols used in this book.

not only varies the rhythmical pattern but offers words with quite different meanings and connotations as alternatives for the "Lord."

Rhythm may be defined as a recognizable pattern of stressed and unstressed syllables, with roughly equivalent time intervals between the stresses. A pattern will be repeated, perhaps with slight variations, but it is usually not continued in prose more than three times. Consider the Lord's Prayer (Revised Standard Version):

> Th́y kíngdŏm cóme,
> Th́y wíll bĕ dóne . . .

In each of these clauses, there are three stresses; moreover, "-dom" and "be" form an approximately equal time interval. In the next line of the Prayer, however, a different rhythmical pattern occurs:

> On eárth as it ís in héaven,

a sequence which approximates the rhythm of the opening,

> Our Fáther who árt in héaven.

Rhythm as an arrangement of stressed and unstressed syllables that is repeated, sometimes with slight variations, gives to the reader the pleasure of recognition of sound pattern and the pleasure of expectation of the recurrence of this pattern. The departures from it that may occur—for instance, the addition of an extra light syllable, or the omission of one, as in the opening line of Psalm 23, cited on p. 5—may be recognized as pleasing variations. Moreover, because of the human tendency to find or create pattern, the slight variation of "shepherd" may be hurried, in reading aloud, so that it is nearly equivalent in time to the stressed "want" with a pause after it. The reader's pleasure in rhythmical prose is similar to the pleasure of a trained musician in the variations on the themes in symphonic music. The patterns are there, but they may be varied in many ways. Thus the short patterns of the opening line of Psalm 23 are altered by the new patterns of

> He máketh me . . . he léadeth me . . .

in long clauses. These, too, are broken off by the five stresses of

> Yéa, though I wálk through the válley of the shádow of déath,

before still another pattern is adopted in

> I will féar no évil.

Anyone who reads aloud or listens to the reading of this Psalm will discover that the common reading

> for thóu art wíth me

is surely the result of the "creation" of a pattern, since there is no logical stress on "with."

It is not our task to examine minutely the use of rhythm in prose, in which it is a beautiful and highly complex art. Our concern is with rhythm as a fundamental element of verse, one which appears in English verse since Chaucer as a basic pattern, or series of patterns, of stressed and unstressed syllables. Although most students are aware of rhythm in verse and can find pleasure in highly complex patterns, extended or syncopated, specialists in technical studies of versification have found it difficult to construct a definition or description of rhythm that is accurate when applied to particular passages easily recognized by the ear as rhythmical. Since poetry from time immemorial has been composed for recitation, the problem lies in the time intervals between the stresses, which may look quite different, but which the reader (always reading aloud) converts into equivalent or nearly equivalent time intervals as he reads slowly or hastily, or inserts pauses to occupy the needed time.

ANALYZING RHYTHMICAL PROSE

As an example of one reading of the rhythmical patterns of seventeenth-century prose, note the concluding sentence of Sir Walter Raleigh's *History of the World.* The single slanted lines indicate a brief pause, the end of a CADENCE; the double slanted lines indicate a long pause, also the end of a cadence. The syllables stressed indicate one reader's interpretation in an oral reading of the passage:

> O eloquent,/ just,/ and mighty Death!// whom none could advise,/ thou hast persuaded;// what none hath dared,/ thou hast done;// and whom all the world hath flattered,/ thou only hast cast out of the world and despised;// thou hast drawn together all the far-stretched greatness,/ all the pride,/ cruelty,/ and ambition of man,/ and covered it all over with these two narrow words,/ *Hic jacet**!//

According to this reading the following similar patterns can be observed:

1. O eloquent
2. just
1. and mighty
2. Death
3. whom none could advise
3. what none hath dared
4. thou hast persuaded
4. thou hast done
5. thou hast drawn together
5. and covered it all over
6. all the far-stretched greatness
6. all the pride, cruelty, and ambition
7. with these two
7. narrow words
7. *Hic jacet*

* These words are pronounced "hick yáhket" and mean "here lies."

Note that a pattern is often used twice, sometimes three times, but not more than that, and, in pattern No. 7, the third use is considerably varied. In each pattern, the number of stresses is the same, but the time intervals between the stresses are sometimes longer or differently arranged. Note especially the two-stress pattern of No. 7. The passage begins and ends with short cadences, Nos. 1, 2, and 7, while longer cadences are used in the middle, which describes the power of Death. Dealing with an abstraction, death, the passage utilizes the figure of speech PERSONIFICATION and, since Raleigh addresses the personified Death, the rhetorical figure of APOSTROPHE.

EXERCISE 1

Following the example of the analysis of the passage from Raleigh, analyze Psalm 23 and the passage from the *Areopagitica*, according to the directions given below.

THE TWENTY-THIRD PSALM

The Lord is my shepherd; I shall not want.
He maketh me to lie down in green pastures: he leadeth me beside the still waters.
He restoreth my soul: he leadeth me in the paths of righteousness for his name's sake.
Yea, though I walk through the valley of the shadow of death, I will fear no evil: for thou art with me; thy rod and thy staff they comfort me.
Thou preparest a table before me in the presence of mine enemies: thou anointest my head with oil; my cup runneth over.
Surely goodness and mercy shall follow me all the days of my life: and I will dwell in the house of the Lord for ever.

1611 Bible

I cannot praise a fugitive and cloistered virtue, unexercised and unbreathed, that never sallies out and sees her adversary, but slinks out of the race, where that immortal garland is to be run for, not without dust and heat. Assuredly we bring not innocence into the world, we bring impurity much rather; that which purifies us is trial and trial is by what is contrary.

From JOHN MILTON, *Areopagitica*, 1644

1. Read both passages aloud slowly and thoughtfully several times.
2. Be sure that you understand the meaning.
3. Decide which syllables you stress. In making this decision, remember that there are only two choices: either you stress the syllable or you do not. If you seem to stress a syllable orally at all, it should be so marked. Ordinarily main verbs and their subjects and objects require some stress;

prepositions and articles, on the other hand, are usually unstressed. Mark the stress in ink directly above the syllable.*

4. Count the number of words in each passage, since they are of different lengths.
5. List the CONCRETE NOUNS in each passage. If the same word is used more than once, list it each time it appears.
6. List the ABSTRACT NOUNS in each passage.
7. List the words which contain three or more syllables in each passage.
8. List the FIGURES OF SPEECH—specifically examples of METAPHOR, SIMILE, and PERSONIFICATION—in each passage and identify them.
9. For each passage consider what you believe to be the intended effect, intellectually and emotionally, on the reader.
10. Using the information gained in answering the questions above, write a short essay on the use of the various devices in contributing to, or detracting from, what you believe to be the intended effect of the passages. Take into account the difference in length of the passages. For example: what is the effect, in the selection from the *Areopagitica*, of the use of a larger number of polysyllabic words (words of three or more syllables) in proportion to the total number of words in the passage? In concluding your essay, decide which passage is more effective for its purpose, in your opinion. Why?

EXERCISE 2

The sun had not yet risen. The sea was indistinguishable from the sky, except that the sea was slightly creased as if a cloth had wrinkles in it. Gradually as the sky whitened a dark line lay on the horizon dividing the sea from the sky and the grey cloth became barred with thick strokes moving, one after another, beneath the surface, following each other, pursuing each other, perpetually.

From VIRGINIA WOOLF, *The Waves* (Harcourt, 1931), p. 7

The sun rose higher. Blue waves, green waves swept a quick fan over the beach, circling the spike of sea-holly and leaving shallow pools of light here and there on the sand. A faint black rim was left behind them. The rocks which had been misty and soft hardened and were marked with red clefts.

Ibid., p. 29

The sun rose. Bars of yellow and green fell on the shore gilding the ribs of the eaten-out boat and making the sea-holly and its mailed leaves gleam blue as steel. Light almost pierced the thin swift waves as they raced fan-shaped over the beach.

Ibid., p. 73

* Be sure to copy the passages accurately before putting down any markings. See Note to the Student, p. xv.

As an alternate, or in addition, to Exercise 1, consider the three passages given above from a modern novel. Follow the directions given for Exercise 1, with the following changes: examine all *three* passages in answering the questions. Omit Questions 5 and 6, since nearly all nouns in these passages are concrete; omit Question 8—these passages are description only and make limited use of figures (note in the first passage, "as if a cloth," in the third, "blue as steel"). Instead of extended analysis of figures, consider the IMAGES. List these by types. After you have completed your technical analysis, answer Question 10.

FEET AND METER

In moving from an examination of rhythm as it exists in prose to a study of rhythm in formal, patterned verse, the student should consider METER as a subdivision of rhythm. All meter is a particular form of rhythm, one more strictly organized than prose rhythms into patterns that are usually shorter and more regularly repeated in sequence. Meter, as the name suggests, may be "measured." Rhythm, on the other hand, in its broad, general sense, includes elaborate patterns, freely and widely varied, which are difficult if not impossible to measure with precision. Thus, though all meter is rhythmical, all rhythm is not metrical. Rhythm may exist in prose and verse, but meter is not used in prose.

Meter may be defined as the organization of rhythm into regular or measurable groupings of stressed and unstressed syllables occupying nearly equivalent time intervals. Variations in metrical pattern occur, though they are fewer and less noticeable than those in rhythm, which we have described as having "roughly equivalent" time intervals. The time intervals in meter cannot accurately be said to be "precisely equivalent," though they are, to the ear, clearly more regular than those of rhythmical prose. Each of these time intervals is called a FOOT; in conventional English verse, the foot constitutes the basic metrical unit, which will be repeated in a regular pattern. The commonest foot in English is the IAMB, ◡ ′, and the metrical pattern of many poems can be described as iambic, despite frequent variations from the iambic foot.

The terminology for analyzing and describing English meter and, indeed, English prosody in general is unsatisfactory, since it is borrowed from classical prosody and from French, Italian, and other languages. Although attempts have been made from time to time to develop a new vocabulary of terms for the sound patterns of English, none of these has gained general recognition or acceptance. We shall, therefore, use the traditional terminology, with the understanding, always, that just as Latin is not English, a Latin iambic foot does not have the same effect as an English iambic foot on the sound of the verse in which it is used. A clear illustration of this difference is in the great classical meter, the *dactylic hexameter* (see under CLASSICAL PROSODY), used by Virgil in the *Aeneid*. Various attempts have been made to use this meter for similar purposes in English (including, of course, a number of translations of the *Aeneid*). It is indicative, however, of the metrical difficulty that the most memorable English poem in this meter is Longfellow's *Evangeline*. Compare the opening lines of the Latin and the English poem:

Ārmă vĭ|rūmquĕ că|nō Trō|iae quī | prīmŭs ăb | ōrīs|

Thís ĭs thĕ | fórĕst prĭ|mévăl, thĕ | múrmŭrĭng | pínes ănd thĕ | hémlŏcks|

It is notable also that Milton rejected classical precedent and chose for his major English epic the unrhymed iambic pentameter, BLANK VERSE, which he called "English heroic verse":

Thrŏugh É|dĕn tóok | thĕir sól|ĭtár|y̆ wáy.|

In addition to specifying the type of foot used, a designation of meter usually includes a notation of the number of feet used in the lines. Thus the *Aeneid* is described as "dactylic hexameter" (six feet to the line), and *Paradise Lost* as "iambic pentameter" (five feet to the line). Here, too, an inconsistency in the terminology occurs, in that a poem described as "pentameter" can be expected to be consistently written in lines of five feet, but a poem described as "iambic" may have a very large number of other types of feet substituted for the iambic. By this time, the student will have arrived correctly at the conclusion that "prosody, the science of English verse," is very far from scientific precision, although it attempts to describe the sound patterns heard in the structure of a poem.

Meters in which whole poems have been successfully written are four: iambic, trochaic, anapestic, and dactylic (see FOOT). There are, however, two additional feet used for variation and for other effects in English: the pyrrhus and the spondee. These two terms, which have their origin in classical prosody, are difficult to define as used in English verse, which is based primarily on stress. It might be possible to describe the spondee (— —, in the conventional marking) as a foot consisting of two stressed syllables. But as we know from our brief examination of rhythm and meter, English verse, in addition to stress, also makes use of time intervals. The time interval of an unstressed syllable is brief; English prosodists have always believed that the time interval of a stressed syllable is long, so that the use of stress automatically adds length; hence the prosodic symbol ⏗. The true spondee, however, presents two *long* syllables, long in the duration of time required for enunciation, but without stress:

Ghōsts wālk.

EXERCISE 3

Sample lines.

1. Pure iambic:

   The cur|few tolls | the knell | of part|ing day,|

   From THOMAS GRAY, *Elegy Written in a Country Churchyard*

2. Pure trochaic:

   One to | show a | woman | when he | loves her!|

   From ROBERT BROWNING, *One Word More*

   Trochaic with CATALEXIS:

   Bird thou | never | wert,

   From PERCY BYSSHE SHELLEY, *To a Skylark*

3. Pure anapestic:

   The Assyr|ian came down | like the wolf | on the fold,|
   And his co|horts were gleam|ing in pur|ple and gold;|

   From LORD BYRON, *The Destruction of Sennacherib*

4. Pure dactylic:

   Out of the | kingdom of | Christ shall be | gathered by | angels o'er |
   Satan vic|torious,|

   Quoted by Goold Brown in *The Grammar of English Grammars*, 1851, p. 853

Using the examples given above as models, write original lines in each of the forms: pure iambic, pure trochaic, trochaic with catalexis, pure dactylic, dactylic with catalexis, pure anapestic. A satisfactory procedure is to write the sample line, or at least its accents, *above* the line in which you intend to write your own. Then fill in words which fulfill the requirements of stress. After you have completed your own line, read it aloud with appropriate emphasis, correct any mistakes or misplaced stresses, and mark on your final copy the stresses you believe to be there when the line is properly read.

EXERCISE 4

Draft A

THE EXPRESS

After the first powerful plain manifesto,
The ~~clear~~ black statement of pistons, without more fuss
But gliding like a queen ~~?~~ she leaves the station:
Without bowing and with restrained unconcern
She ~~notices~~ passes the houses humbly which crowd~~ing~~ outside
And then the gasworks and at last the ~~printed~~ psalm
Of death ~~written~~ printed by gravestones in the cemetery.
Beyond the town lies the open country
Where, gathering speed, she acquires mystery
~~Like~~ ~~t~~The luminous self-possession ~~possession~~ of ships on ocean.
It is ~~then~~ now she begins to sing—at first low
And then loud and at last with mad joy—
The ~~strange~~ song of her whistle screaming round corners,
~~And~~ ~~o~~Of drums in tunnels, ~~and~~ of her innumerable bolts,
~~And~~ ~~a~~A swaying melody of tearing speed:
And always light, ariel, under~~neath~~ this
Is the tapping metre of her wheels.
We travel further than Edinburgh or Rome
~~For we~~ ~~r~~Reach/ing new eras of ~~insane~~ wild happiness
When night falls

Explore new areas of happiness }
„ „ eras of wild happiness } ?

STEPHEN SPENDER (1909–)

7, 9. cemetery, mystery: Spender is a British poet; hence "ter-ry," the usual American pronunciation of the ending, is inappropriate. Look up the pronunciation of these words in a British dictionary; also look up "aerial" (A, line 16; G, line 15).

Draft G: Final form

THE EXPRESS

After the first powerful plain manifesto
The black statement of pistons, without more fuss
But gliding like a queen, she leaves the station.
Without bowing and with restrained unconcern
She passes the houses which humbly crowd outside,
The gasworks, and at last the heavy page
Of death, printed by gravestones in the cemetery.
Beyond the town, there lies the open country
Where, gathering speed, she acquires mystery,
The luminous self-possession of ships on ocean.
It is now she begins to sing—at first quite low
Then loud, and at last with a jazzy madness—
The song of her whistle screaming at curves,
Of deafening tunnels, brakes, innumerable bolts.
And always light, aerial, underneath,
Retreats the elate metre of her wheels.
Steaming through metal landscape on her lines,
She plunges new eras of white happiness
Where speed throws up strange shapes, broad curves
And parallels clean like trajectories from guns.
At last, further than Edinburgh or Rome,
[Beyond the crest of the world, she reaches night
Where only a low stream-line brightness
Of phosphorus on the tossing hills is light.
Ah, like a comet through flame, she moves entranced,
Wrapt in her music no bird song, no, nor bough
Breaking with honey buds, shall ever equal.]*

STEPHEN SPENDER (1909–)

Put accent marks on the A and G drafts of Spender's *The Express*. Can you identify a "normal foot" and a "normal line length" for the passage? If so, what are they? Comment on the most significant feet in each passage, and compare changes in the rhythm and meter between the two passages. Discuss changes in DICTION and FIGURES (metaphor, simile, personification) that occur between A and G. What poetic effect do you think Spender is attempting to achieve? In what way do alterations in the G draft change the effect?

* Disregard the bracketed final lines in your detailed comparison between the two versions.

II

Diction and Poetic Diction

THE CHOICE OF WORDS

The term "diction" has several meanings as defined in a dictionary. In the study of poetry, as we shall use the term, diction means simply the choice of words used in a poem. A student asked to evaluate a poem should always consider the diction, since a poem is written in words, and an understanding of the choice of words is essential to valid criticism of the poem. Before any reader comes upon the poem, however, the poet has already made *his* choice of the words for the poem. The poet's choices may have been made without conscious evaluations, and (had he been asked) he might have been unable to account for the choices he made, or to explain, in a poem which has been revised, why he preferred one version to another.

Whether or not the poet is conscious of his reasons for selecting certain words rather than others, he makes his choice in accordance with certain concepts he has about the values of words, especially their meaning—not only their DENOTATION but their CONNOTATION—and their sound. He may have to decide, for example, which is the more appropriate in a given place, "brotherly" or "fraternal," two forms identical in denotation but quite different in connotation. And the questions may arise: From what language is the word derived? Does it carry special associations of meaning because of the language of its origin? As to sound, what kind of consonants and vowels does it have? How will the arrangement of sounds fit in with the total sound pattern of the poem? How many syllables does the word have and where do its normal stresses occur? If it is to be used for rhyme, are there suitable rhymes to match it?

These two considerations, meaning and sound, are basic to the choice of words in a poem. The poet who consistently mistakes the appropriate meaning and/or the appropriate sound for his writing fails, since words are his medium and their values and limitations must be respected. The student who also consistently mistakes or misunderstands the meanings and sounds of a completed poem will be unable to evaluate it properly. In *Dover Beach*, Matthew Arnold speaks of the "drear / And naked shingles of the world." In British English, a shingle is a pebbly beach. The reader who slides past this line in Arnold's poem with a vague idea that a shingle is a haircut, a roofing material, or a nervous disease can get no clear idea of the coherence of the poem. The result of this misreading is at best inaccurate and at worst ridiculous.

Discussions of the use of words in poetry are surely as old as the art of poetry itself, but we shall concern ourselves here with two major writers, Pope and Wordsworth, who represent two major opinions about the use of diction. We begin, chronologically, with Pope, whose name is always associated with the term POETIC DICTION as opposed to "diction." Poetic diction takes its origin not in language, but in subject matter: the idea that only certain subjects are appropriate for poetry. For the characteristic eighteenth-century poets, these subjects tended to be narrowly limited to the attractive or beautiful, to the formal, whether in nature or society, to edification in philosophy, religion, or criticism, to the artificial rather than the natural. For example, it is useful to consider the titles of some of the major poems of the century: Pope's *The Rape of the Lock, An Essay on Man, An Essay on Criticism*; Johnson's *The Vanity of Human Wishes*; Goldsmith's *The Deserted Village*; Gray's *Elegy Written in a Country Churchyard.* The last two might be treated in several ways, but, in fact, they are treated formally with numerous generalizations, with all the squalor of earlier seventeenth-century and later romantic poetry tactfully omitted.

"ELEGANT VARIATION"

Beginning with the careful choice of a limited subject matter, the practitioners of poetic diction adapted the available language to their conception of an appropriate treatment of the subject; they limited their vocabulary, as they did their subject matter, to the attractive, the formal, and the artificial. There is in poetic diction a frequent use of general terms, plural forms, abstractions or the personification of abstractions, and of elaborate terminology, the kind which Fowler's *Modern English Usage* has decried as "elegant variation," but which was long ago bluntly described as "never calling a spade a spade."

Examples of the use of general terms and plural forms are easy to find in Augustan eighteenth-century poetry:

Their name, their years, spelt by th'unletter'd muse,
The place of fame and elegy supply:
And many a holy text around she strews
That teach the rustic moralist to die.

From Thomas Gray, *Elegy Written in a Country Churchyard*, 1750

The good or bad the gifts of fortune gain;
But these less taste them, as they worse obtain.

From Alexander Pope, *An Essay on Man*, 1734, IV, 83–84

Abstractions and personifications are readily found:

How nations sink, by darling schemes oppress'd,
When vengeance listens to the fool's request.

From Samuel Johnson, *The Vanity of Human Wishes*, 1749

O sister meek of Truth,
To my admiring youth,
Thy sober aid and native charms infuse!
The flow'rs that sweetest breathe,
Tho' Beauty cull'd the wreath,
Still ask thy hand to range their order'd hues.

From William Collins, *Ode to Simplicity*, 1746

The matter of elegant terminology is more difficult to clarify. Sometimes it is used for ironic effect. Here is an extreme example:

For lo! the board with cups and spoons is crown'd,
The berries crackle, and the mill turns round;
On shining altars of Japan they raise
The silver lamp; the fiery spirits blaze:
From silver spouts the grateful liquors glide,
While China's earth receives the smoking tide.

From Alexander Pope, *The Rape of the Lock*, 1712 (rev. 1714), Canto III

The scene is a coffee party: the making and pouring of the coffee are described. To translate the poetic diction into common vocabulary the following glossary is supplied:

board: table
crown'd: spread or covered
shining altars of Japan: japanned (lacquered) trays

silver lamp: spirit lamp
fiery spirits blaze: the lamp is lighted, it burns
silver spouts: coffeepots
grateful liquors: coffee
China's earth: porcelain cups imported from China
smoking tide: steaming coffee

Ingenuity as well as an extensive vocabulary is obviously required for this type of poetic diction; it is practiced less by other eighteenth-century poets than by Pope, who was a master of this highly technical skill.

Illustrative Excerpts from Alexander Pope

After Shakespeare, the largest number of quotations in Bartlett's *Familiar Quotations* is taken from the works of Pope. The epigrammatic style and the platitudinous content of his couplets make them memorable, even to speakers who may not know the origin of the quotations. The following are typical passages from Pope:

A little learning is a dangerous thing;
Drink deep, or taste not the Pierian spring.

From *An Essay on Criticism*, II, 215–216

True wit is nature to advantage dress'd;
What oft was thought, but ne'er so well express'd.

Ibid., II, 297–298

True ease in writing comes from art, not chance,
As those move easiest who have learn'd to dance.

Ibid., II, 362–363

Hope springs eternal in the human breast;
Man never is, but always to be, blest.

From *An Essay on Man*, I, 95–96

All nature is but art, unknown to thee;
All chance, direction, which thou canst not see;
All discord, harmony not understood;
All partial evil, universal good:
And, spite of pride, in erring reason's spite,
One truth is clear, whatever is, is right.

Ibid., I, 289–294

Know then thyself, presume not God to scan,
The proper study of mankind is man.

Ibid., II, 1–2

That reason, passion, answer one great aim;
That true self-love and social are the same;
That virtue only makes our bliss below;
And all our knowledge is, ourselves to know.

Ibid., IV, 395–398

A description of a dressing table:

From each she nicely culls with curious toil,
And decks the goddess with the glitt'ring spoil.
This casket India's glowing gems unlocks,
And all Arabia breathes from yonder box.
The tortoise here and elephant unite,
Transform'd to combs, the speckled and the white.
Here files of pins extend their shining rows,
Puffs, powders, patches, bibles, billets-doux.
Now awful beauty puts on all its arms;
The fair each moment rises in her charms,
Repairs her smiles, awakens every grace,
And calls forth all the wonders of her face;
Sees by degrees a purer blush arise,
And keener lightnings quicken in her eyes.
The busy sylphs surround their darling care,
These set the head, and those divide the hair,
Some fold the sleeve, whilst others plait the gown;
And Betty's prais'd for labours not her own.

From *The Rape of the Lock*, 1712 (rev. 1714), Canto I

A description of the grief over the actual loss (by cutting off) of the lock of hair:

"Was it for this you took such constant care
The bodkin, comb, and essence to prepare?
For this your locks in paper durance bound,
For this with torturing irons wreathed around?
For this with fillets strain'd your tender head,
And bravely bore the double loads of lead?
Gods! shall the ravisher display your hair,
While the fops envy and the ladies stare!
Honour forbid! at whose unrivall'd shrine
Ease, pleasure, virtue, all, our sex resign.
Methinks already I your tears survey,
Already hear the horrid things they say,
Already see you a degraded toast,
And all your honour in a whisper lost!
How shall I, then, your helpless fame defend?

'Twill then be infamy to seem your friend!
And shall this prize, th'inestimable prize,
Exposed through crystal to the gazing eyes,
And heighten'd by the diamond's circling rays,
On that rapacious hand for ever blaze?
Sooner shall grass in Hyde Park Circus grow,
And wits take lodgings in the sound of Bow;
Sooner let earth, air, sea, to chaos fall,
Men, monkeys, lap dogs, parrots, perish all!"

Ibid., Canto IV

In the following excerpts from *An Essay on Criticism*, Pope illustrates not only his characteristic style but the critical concepts on which this style is based.

'Tis hard to say, if greater want of skill
Appear in writing or in judging ill;
But, of the two, less dangerous is th'offence
To tire our patience, than mislead our sense.
Some few in that, but numbers err in this,
Ten censure wrong, for one who writes amiss;
A fool might once himself alone expose,
Now one in verse makes many more in prose.
'Tis with our judgments as our watches, none
Go just alike, yet each believes his own.
In poets as true genius is but rare,
True taste as seldom is the critic's share;
Both must alike from Heav'n derive their light,
These born to judge, as well as those to write.
Let such teach others who themselves excel,
And censure freely who have written well.
Authors are partial to their wit, 'tis true,
But are not critics to their judgment too?
Yet if we look more closely, we shall find
Most have the seeds of judgment in their mind:
Nature affords at least a glimm'ring light;
The lines, though touch'd but faintly, are drawn right.
But as the slightest sketch, if justly traced,
Is by ill col'ring but the more disgraced,
So by false learning is good sense defaced:
Some are bewilder'd in the maze of schools,

117. Hyde Park Circus: a circular drive worn by heavy carriage traffic. **118. Bow:** within the hearing of the bells of Bow Church, in Cheapside, London, where the Cockney accent, spoken by the lower classes, has traditionally been heard.
17. wit: see Glossary.

And some made coxcombs Nature meant but fools.
In search of wit these lose their common sense,
And then turn critics in their own defence:
Each burns alike, who can, or cannot write,
Or with a rival's, or an eunuch's spite.
All fools have still an itching to deride,
And fain would be upon the laughing side.
If Maevius scribble in Apollo's spite,
There are who judge still worse than he can write.
  Some have at first for wits, then poets pass'd,
Turn'd critics next, and prov'd plain fools at last.
Some neither can for wits nor critics pass,
As heavy mules are neither horse nor ass.
Those half-learn'd witlings, numerous in our isle,
As half-form'd insects on the banks of Nile;
Unfinish'd things, one knows not what to call,
Their generation's so equivocal:
To tell 'em, would a hundred tongues require,
Or one vain wit's, that might a hundred tire.
  But you who seek to give and merit fame,
And justly bear a critic's noble name,
Be sure yourself and your own reach to know,
How far your genius, taste, and learning go;
Launch not beyond your depth, but be discreet,
And mark that point where sense and dullness meet.
  Nature to all things fix'd the limits fit,
And wisely curb'd proud man's pretending wit.
As on the land while here the ocean gains,
In other parts it leaves wide sandy plains;
Thus in the soul while memory prevails,
The solid power of understanding fails;
Where beams of warm imagination play,
The memory's soft figures melt away.
One science only will one genius fit;
So vast is art, so narrow human wit:
Not only bounded to peculiar arts,
But oft in those confin'd to single parts.
Like kings we lose the conquests gain'd before,
By vain ambition still to make them more;
. . .
  First follow Nature, and your judgment frame
By her just standard, which is still the same:

34. Maevius: a minor Roman poet.

Unerring Nature, still divinely bright,
One clear, unchanged, and universal light,
Life, force, and beauty, must to all impart,
At once the source, and end, and test of art.
Art from that fund each just supply provides,
Works without show, and without pomp presides:
In some fair body thus th'informing soul
With spirits feeds, with vigour fills the whole,
Each motion guides, and every nerve sustains;
Itself unseen, but in th'effects remains.
Some, to whom Heav'n in wit has been profuse,
Want as much more to turn it to its use;
For wit and judgment often are at strife,
Though meant each other's aid, like man and wife.
'Tis more to guide, than spur the Muse's steed;
Restrain his fury, than provoke his speed;
The wingèd courser, like a gen'rous horse,
Shows most true mettle when you check his course.
  Those rules of old discover'd, not devised,
Are Nature still, but Nature methodized:
Nature, like liberty, is but restrain'd
By the same laws which first herself ordain'd.
. . .
Some on the leaves of ancient authors prey,
Nor time nor months e'er spoil'd so much as they.
Some drily plain, without invention's aid,
Write dull receipts how poems may be made.
These leave the sense, their learning to display,
And those explain the meaning quite away.
  You then whose judgment the right course would steer,
Know well each ancient's proper character;
His fable, subject, scope in every page;
Religion, country, genius of his age:
Without all these at once before your eyes,
Cavil you may, but never criticise.
Be Homer's works your study and delight,
Read them by day, and meditate by night;
Thence form your judgment, thence your maxims bring,
And trace the Muses upward to their spring.
Still with itself compared, his text peruse;
And let your comment be the Mantuan Muse.
  When first young Maro in his boundless mind

129. Mantuan Muse: Virgil, the author of the Roman epic *The Aeneid.* **130. Maro:** Virgil.

A work t'outlast immortal Rome design'd,
Perhaps he seem'd above the critic's law,
And but from Nature's fountains scorn'd to draw:
But when t'examine ev'ry part he came,
Nature and Homer were, he found, the same.
Convinced, amazed, he checks the bold design;
And rules as strict his labour'd work confine,
As if the Stagirite o'erlook'd each line.
Learn hence for ancient rules a just esteem;
To copy Nature is to copy them.
Some beauties yet no precepts can declare,
For there's a happiness as well as care.
Music resembles poetry, in each
Are nameless graces which no methods teach,
And which a master-hand alone can reach.
If, where the rules not far enough extend
(Since rules were made but to promote their end),
Some lucky license answer to the full
Th'intent proposed, that license is a rule.
Thus Pegasus, a nearer way to take,
May boldly deviate from the common track;
From vulgar bounds with brave disorder part,
And snatch a grace beyond the reach of art,
Which, without passing through the judgment, gains
The heart, and all its end at once attains.
In prospects thus, some objects please our eyes,
Which out of Nature's common order rise,
The shapeless rock, or hanging precipice.
Great wits sometimes may gloriously offend,
And rise to faults true critics dare not mend.
But though the ancients thus their rules invade
(As kings dispense with laws themselves have made),
Moderns, beware! or if you must offend
Against the precept, ne'er transgress its end;
Let it be seldom, and compell'd by need;
And have, at least, their precedent to plead.
The critic else proceeds without remorse,
Seizes your fame, and puts his laws in force.

From *An Essay on Criticism*, 1711, I

A perfect judge will read each work of wit
With the same spirit that its author writ:

138. the Stagirite: Aristotle.

Survey the whole, nor seek slight faults to find
Where Nature moves, and rapture warms the mind;
Nor lose, for that malignant dull delight,
The gen'rous pleasure to be charm'd with wit.
But in such lays as neither ebb, nor flow,
Correctly cold, and regularly low,
That shunning faults, one quiet tenor keep,
We cannot blame indeed—but we may sleep.
In wit, as Nature, what affects our hearts
Is not th'exactness of peculiar parts;
'Tis not a lip, or eye, we beauty call,
But the joint force and full result of all.
Thus when we view some well-proportion'd dome
(The world's just wonder, and ev'n thine, O Rome!)
No single parts unequally surprise,
All comes united to th'admiring eyes;
No monstrous height, or breadth, or length appear;
The whole at once is bold, and regular.
  Whoever thinks a faultless piece to see,
Thinks what ne'er was, nor is, nor e'er shall be.
In every work regard the writer's end,
Since none can compass more than they intend;
And if the means be just, the conduct true,
Applause, in spite of trivial faults, is due.
As men of breeding, sometimes men of wit,
T'avoid great errors, must the less commit:
Neglect the rules each verbal critic lays,
For not to know some trifles, is a praise.
Most critics, fond of some subservient art,
Still make the whole depend upon a part:
They talk of principles, but notions prize,
And all to one lov'd folly sacrifice.
. . .

Ibid., II

"THE LANGUAGE REALLY USED BY MEN"

During much of the eighteenth century Pope was the acknowledged dictator and major practitioner of poetic style, but a reaction was bound to come. Already discernible in the writings of a number of lesser poets of the time, the new trend in the use of language in poetry was clearly marked by the appearance of the *Lyrical Ballads* of William Wordsworth and Samuel Taylor

Coleridge, published in 1798, and reissued with an expanded preface in 1800. Wordsworth advocated "the language really used by men" but, not intending a monotonous transcription of any and all language actually in use, qualified and limited this statement by specifying "men in a state of vivid sensation." As had been true of the practitioners of poetic diction, Wordsworth and his followers developed a theory of appropriate language for poetry from a concept of appropriate subject matter. They proposed, as Wordsworth wrote in the Preface to the second edition of *Lyrical Ballads*, "to choose incidents and situations from common life."

> Humble and rustic life was generally chosen, because, in that condition, the essential passions of the heart find a better soil in which they can attain their maturity . . . ; because in that condition of life our elementary feelings co-exist in a state of great simplicity, and, consequently, may be more accurately contemplated . . . ; because the manners of rural life germinate from those elementary feelings, and, from the necessary character of rural occupations, are more easily comprehended, and are more durable; and, lastly, because in that condition the passions of men are incorporated with the beautiful and permanent forms of nature.

A glance at the titles of some of the poems included in the *Lyrical Ballads* will indicate the great difference between these poems and those characteristic of the Augustan poets of the eighteenth century: *Anecdote for Fathers*, *We Are Seven*, *The Idiot Boy*, *The Waterfall*, and *The Eglantine*. Favorite subjects are drawn from direct and precise observation of nature, from children, especially country children, and shepherds (*Michael*).

Wordsworth's Preface to "Lyrical Ballads"

The Preface to the second edition of *Lyrical Ballads* (1800, 1802) is given here in its entirety,* so that the student can compare it with Pope's critical theory in *An Essay on Criticism*.

The first volume of these poems has already been submitted to general perusal. It was published as an experiment, which, I hoped, might be of some use to ascertain how far, by fitting to metrical arrangement a selection of the real language of men in a state of vivid sensation,[1] that sort of pleasure and that quantity of pleasure may be imparted, which a poet may rationally endeavour to impart.

I had formed no very inaccurate estimate of the probable effect of those poems:

* The notes are taken from *Wordsworth and Coleridge: Selected Critical Essays*, ed. Thomas M. Raysor (New York: Appleton-Century-Crofts, 1958).

[1] **a selection . . . sensation:** the language of conversation in the middle and lower classes of society ("Advertisement" to first edition, 1798).

I flattered myself that they who should be pleased with them would read them with more than common pleasure; and, on the other hand, I was well aware, that by those who should dislike them they would be read with more than common dislike. The result has differed from my expectation in this only, that a greater number have been pleased than I ventured to hope I should please.

Several of my friends are anxious for the success of these poems, from a belief that, if the views with which they were composed were indeed realized, a class of poetry would be produced, well adapted to interest mankind permanently, and not unimportant in the quality and in the multiplicity of its moral relations: and on this account they have advised me to prefix a systematic defence of the theory upon which the poems were written. But I was unwilling to undertake the task, knowing that on this occasion the reader would look coldly upon my arguments, since I might be suspected of having been principally influenced by the selfish and foolish hope of *reasoning* him into an approbation of these particular poems: and I was still more unwilling to undertake the task, because adequately to display the opinions, and fully to enforce the arguments, would require a space wholly disproportionate to a preface. For, to treat the subject with the clearness and coherence of which it is susceptible, it would be necessary to give a full account of the present state of the public taste in this country, and to determine how far this taste is healthy or depraved; which, again, could not be determined without pointing out in what manner language and the human mind act and re-act on each other, and without retracing the revolutions, not of literature alone, but likewise of society itself. I have therefore altogether declined to enter regularly upon this defence; yet I am sensible that there would be something like impropriety in abruptly obtruding upon the public, without a few words of introduction, poems so materially different from those upon which general approbation is at present bestowed.

It is supposed that by the act of writing in verse an author makes a formal engagement that he will gratify certain known habits of association; that he not only thus apprises the reader that certain classes of ideas and expressions will be found in his book, but that others will be carefully excluded. This exponent or symbol held forth by metrical language must in different eras of literature have excited very different expectations: for example, in the age of Catullus, Terence, and Lucretius, and that of Statius or Claudian; and in our own country, in the age of Shakespeare and Beaumont and Fletcher, and that of Donne and Cowley, or Dryden, or Pope. I will not take upon me to determine the exact import of the promise which, by the act of writing in verse, an author in the present day makes to his reader; but it will undoubtedly appear to many persons that I have not fulfilled the terms of an engagement thus voluntarily contracted. They who have been accustomed to the gaudiness and inane phraseology of many modern writers, if they persist in reading this book to its conclusion, will, no doubt, frequently have to struggle with feelings of strangeness and awkwardness: they will look round for poetry, and will be induced to inquire by what species of courtesy these attempts can be permitted to assume that title. I hope, therefore, the reader will not censure me for attempting to state what I have proposed to myself to perform; and also (as far as the limits of a preface will permit) to explain some of the chief reasons which have determined me in the choice of my purpose: that at least he may be spared any unpleasant feeling of disappointment, and that I myself may be protected from one of the most dishonourable accusations which can be brought against an author; namely, that of an indolence which prevents him from endeavouring to ascertain what is his duty, or, when his duty is ascertained, prevents him from performing it.

The principal object, then, proposed in these poems was to choose incidents and situations from common life, and to relate or describe them throughout, as far as was possible, in a selection of language really used by men, and, at the same time, to throw over them a certain colouring of imagination, whereby ordinary things should be presented to the mind in an unusual aspect; and further, and above all, to make these incidents and situations interesting by tracing in them, truly though not ostentatiously, the primary laws of our nature: chiefly, as far as regards the manner in which we associate ideas in a state of excitement. Humble and rustic life was generally chosen, because in that condition the essential passions of the heart find a better soil in which they can attain their maturity, are less under restraint, and speak a plainer and more emphatic language; because in that condition of life our elementary feelings co-exist in a state of greater simplicity, and, consequently, may be more accurately contemplated, and more forcibly communicated; because the manners of rural life germinate from those elementary feelings, and, from the necessary character of rural occupations, are more easily comprehended, and are more durable; and, lastly, because in that condition the passions of men are incorporated with the beautiful and permanent forms of nature. The language, too, of these men has been adopted (purified indeed from what appear to be its real defects, from all lasting and rational causes of dislike or disgust), because such men hourly communicate with the best objects from which the best part of language is originally derived; and because, from their rank in society and the sameness and narrow circle of their intercourse, being less under the influence of social vanity, they convey their feelings and notions in simple and unelaborated expressions. Accordingly, such a language, arising out of repeated experience and regular feelings, is a more permanent, and a far more philosophical language than that which is frequently substituted for it by poets, who think that they are conferring honour upon themselves and their art in proportion as they separate themselves from the sympathies of men, and indulge in arbitrary and capricious habits of expression, in order to furnish food for fickle tastes and fickle appetites of their own creation.[2]

I cannot, however, be insensible to the present outcry against the triviality and meanness, both of thought and language, which some of my contemporaries have occasionally introduced into their metrical compositions; and I acknowledge that this defect, where it exists, is more dishonourable to the writer's own character than false refinement or arbitrary innovation, though I should contend at the same time that it is far less pernicious in the sum of its consequences. From such verses the poems in these volumes will be found distinguished at least by one mark of difference, that each of them has a worthy *purpose*. Not that I always began to write with a distinct purpose formally conceived, but habits of meditation have, I trust, so prompted and regulated my feelings,

[2] It is worth while here to observe, that the affecting parts of Chaucer are almost always expressed in language pure and universally intelligible even to this day (W.'s note).

that my descriptions of such objects as strongly excite those feelings will be found to carry along with them a *purpose*. If this opinion be erroneous, I can have little right to the name of a poet. For all good poetry is the spontaneous overflow of powerful feelings: and though this be true, poems to which any value can be attached were never produced on any variety of subjects but by a man who, being possessed of more than usual organic sensibility, had also thought long and deeply. For our continued influxes of feeling are modified and directed by our thoughts, which are indeed the representatives of all our past feelings; and as, by contemplating the relation of these general representatives to each other, we discover what is really important to men, so, by the repetition and continuance of this act, our feelings will be connected with important subjects, till at length, if we be originally possessed of much sensibility, such habits of mind will be produced that, by obeying blindly and mechanically the impulses of those habits, we shall describe objects, and utter sentiments, of such a nature, and in such connection with each other, that the understanding of the reader must necessarily be in some degree enlightened, and his affections strengthened and purified.

It has been said that each of these poems has a purpose. Another circumstance must be mentioned which distinguishes these poems from the popular poetry of the day; it is this, that the feeling therein developed gives importance to the action and situation, and not the action and situation to the feeling.

A sense of false modesty shall not prevent me from asserting that the reader's attention is pointed to this mark of distinction, far less for the sake of these particular poems than from the general importance of the subject. The subject is indeed important! For the human mind is capable of being excited without the application of gross and violent stimulants; and he must have a very faint perception of its beauty and dignity who does not know this, and who does not further know, that one being is elevated above another in proportion as he possesses this capability. It has therefore appeared to me, that to endeavour to produce or enlarge this capability is one of the best services in which, at any period, a writer can be engaged; but this service, excellent at all times, is especially so at the present day. For a multitude of causes, unknown to former times, are now acting with a combined force to blunt the discriminating powers of the mind, and, unfitting it for all voluntary exertion, to reduce it to a state of almost savage torpor. The most effective of these causes are the great national events which are daily taking place, and the increasing accumulation of men in cities, where the uniformity of their occupations produces a craving for extraordinary incident which the rapid communication of intelligence hourly gratifies. To this tendency of life and manners the literature and theatrical exhibitions of the country have conformed themselves. The invaluable works of our elder writers, I had almost said the works of Shakespeare and Milton, are driven into neglect by frantic novels, sickly and stupid German tragedies, and deluges of idle and extravagant stories in verse.—When I think upon this degrading thirst after outrageous stimulation, I am almost ashamed to have spoken of the feeble endeavour made in these volumes to counteract it; and, reflecting upon the magnitude of the general evil, I should be oppressed with no dishonourable melancholy, had I not a deep impression of certain inherent and indestructible qualities of the human mind, and likewise of certain powers in the great and permanent objects that act upon it, which are equally inherent and indestructible; and were there not added to this impression a belief that the time is approaching when the evil will be systematically opposed by men of greater powers, and with far more distinguished success.

Having dwelt thus long on the subjects and aim of these poems, I shall request the reader's permission to apprise him of a few circumstances relating to their *style*, in order, among other reasons, that he may not censure me for not having performed what I never attempted. The reader will find that personifications of abstract ideas rarely occur in these volumes, and are utterly rejected as an ordinary device to elevate the style and raise it above prose. My purpose was to imitate, and, as far as is possible, to adopt the very language of men; and assuredly such personifications do not make any natural or regular part of that language. They are, indeed, a figure of speech occasionally prompted by passion, and I have made use of them as such; but have endeavoured utterly to reject them as a mechanical device of style, or as a family language which writers in metre seem to lay claim to by prescription. I have wished to keep the reader in the company of flesh and blood, persuaded that by so doing I shall interest him. Others who pursue a different track will interest him likewise; I do not interfere with their claim, but wish to prefer a claim of my own. There will also be found in these volumes little of what is usually called poetic diction; as much pains has been taken to avoid it as is ordinarily taken to produce it; this has been done for the reason already alleged, to bring my language near to the language of men; and further, because the pleasure which I have proposed to myself to impart is of a kind very different from that which is supposed by many persons to be the proper object of poetry. Without being culpably particular, I do not know how to give my reader a more exact notion of the style in which it was my wish and intention to write, than by informing him that I have at all times endeavoured to look steadily at my subject; consequently there is, I hope, in these poems little falsehood of description, and my ideas are expressed in language fitted to their respective importance. Something must have been gained by this practice, as it is friendly to one property of all good poetry, namely, good sense: but it has necessarily cut me off from a large portion of phrases and figures of speech which from father to son have long been regarded as the common inheritance of poets. I have also thought it expedient to restrict myself still further, having abstained from the use of many expressions, in themselves proper and beautiful, but which have been foolishly repeated by bad poets, till such feelings of disgust are connected with them as it is scarcely possible by any art of association to overpower.

If in a poem there should be found a series of lines, or even a single line, in which the language, though naturally arranged, and according to the strict laws of metre, does not differ from that of prose, there is a numerous class of critics who, when they stumble upon these prosaisms, as they call them, imagine that they have made a notable discovery, and exult over the poet as over a man ignorant of his own profession. Now these men would establish a canon of criticism which the reader will conclude he must utterly reject, if he wishes to be pleased with these volumes. And it would be a most easy task to prove to him that not only the language of a large portion of every good poem, even of the most elevated character, must necessarily, except with reference to the metre, in no respect differ from that of good prose, but likewise that some of the most interesting parts of the best poems will be found to be strictly the language of prose when prose is well written. The truth of this assertion might be demonstrated by innumerable passages from almost all the poetical writings, even of Milton himself. To illustrate the subject in a general manner, I will here adduce a short composition of Gray, who was at the head of those who, by their reasonings, have attempted to widen the space of separation betwixt prose and metrical composition, and was more than any other man curiously elaborate in the structure of his own poetic diction.

In vain to me the smiling mornings shine,
And reddening Phoebus lifts his golden fire:
The birds in vain their amorous descant join,
Or cheerful fields resume their green attire.
These ears, alas! for other notes repine;
A different object do these eyes require;
My lonely anguish melts no heart but mine;
And in my breast the imperfect joys expire;
Yet morning smiles the busy race to cheer,
And new-born pleasure brings to happier men;
The fields to all their wonted tribute bear;
To warm their little loves the birds complain.
I fruitless mourn to him that cannot hear,
And weep the more because I weep in vain.[3]

It will easily be perceived, that the only part of this sonnet which is of any value is the lines printed in italics; it is equally obvious that, except in the rhyme and in the use of the single word "fruitless" for fruitlessly, which is so far a defect, the language of these lines does in no respect differ from that of prose.

By the foregoing quotation it has been shown that the language of prose may yet be well adapted to poetry; and it was previously asserted that a large portion of the language of every good poem can in no respect differ from that of good prose. We will go further. It may be safely affirmed that there neither is, nor can be, any *essential* difference between the language of prose and metrical composition. We are fond of tracing the resemblance between poetry and painting, and, accordingly, we call them sisters: but where shall we find bonds of connection sufficiently strict to typify the affinity betwixt metrical and prose composition? They both speak by and to the same organs; the bodies in which both of them are clothed may be said to be of the same substance, their affections are kindred, and almost identical, not necessarily differing even in degree; poetry[4] sheds no tears "such as angels weep,"[5] but natural and human tears; she can boast of no celestial

[3] **vain:** *Sonnet on the Death of Richard West.*
[4] I here use the word "poetry" (though against my own judgment) as opposed to the word "prose," and synonymous with metrical composition. But much confusion has been introduced into criticism by this contradistinction of poetry and prose, instead of the more philosophical one of poetry and matter of fact, or science. The only strict antithesis to prose is metre; nor is this, in truth, a *strict* antithesis, because lines and passages of metre so naturally occur in writing prose, that it would be scarcely possible to avoid them, even were it desirable. (W.'s note, based probably on an article by William Enfield in the *Monthly Magazine*, July, 1796. Enfield opposes poetry to philosophy. See Aristotle's distinction of poetry and history, *Poetics*, ch. IX. These theoretical distinctions are all far too important for a footnote. See Abrams, *The Mirror and the Lamp*, ch. XI.)
[5] **weep:** Milton's *Paradise Lost*, I, 619.

ichor that distinguishes her vital juices from those of prose; the same human blood circulates through the veins of them both.

If it be affirmed that rhyme and metrical arrangement of themselves constitute a distinction which overturns what has just been said on the strict affinity of metrical language with that of prose, and paves the way for other artificial distinctions which the mind voluntarily admits, I answer that the[6] language of such poetry as is here recommended is, as far as is possible, a selection of the language really spoken by men; that this selection, wherever it is made with true taste and feeling, will of itself form a distinction far greater than would at first be imagined, and will entirely separate the composition from the vulgarity and meanness of ordinary life; and, if metre be superadded thereto, I believe that a dissimilitude will be produced altogether sufficient for the gratification of a rational mind. What other distinction would we have? Whence is it to come? And where is it to exist? Not, surely, where the poet speaks through the mouths of his characters: it cannot be necessary here, either for elevation of style, or any of its supposed ornaments; for, if the poet's subject be judiciously chosen, it will naturally, and upon fit occasion, lead him to passions the language of which, if selected truly and judiciously, must necessarily be dignified and variegated, and alive with metaphors and figures. I forbear to speak of an incongruity which would shock the intelligent reader, should the poet interweave any foreign splendour of his own with that which the passion naturally suggests: it is sufficient to say that such addition is unnecessary. And, surely, it is more probable that those passages which with propriety abound with metaphors and figures, will have their due effect if, upon other occasions where the passions are of a milder character, the style also be subdued and temperate.

But, as the pleasure which I hope to give by the poems now presented to the reader must depend entirely on just notions upon this subject, and as it is in itself of high importance to our taste and moral feelings, I cannot content myself with these detached remarks. And if, in what I am about to say, it shall appear to some that my labour is unnecessary, and that I am like a man fighting a battle without enemies, such persons may be reminded that, whatever be the language outwardly holden by men, a practical faith in the opinions which I am wishing to establish is almost unknown. If my conclusions are admitted, and carried as far as they must be carried if admitted at all, our judgments concerning the works of the greatest poets, both ancient and modern, will be far different from what they are at present, both when we praise and when we censure: and our moral feelings influencing and influenced by these judgments will, I believe, be corrected and purified.

Taking up the subject, then, upon general grounds, let me ask, what is meant by

[6] **the:** first word of a long addition to the Preface made in 1802. The 1800 text resumes on p. 32. See n. 10. Including the Appendix, the text of 1802 is approximately twice as long as the Preface of 1800; and the additions indicate an important change of emphasis in Wordsworth's poetic theory. His naturalistic emphasis in defending poetry of rustic life in rustic speech now changes to an expressionist emphasis on the poet himself. W. argues that he expresses his own passions even in dramatic poems, since he has identified himself with the passions of his characters. This argument still limits the poet's own creative contribution to his poems, and forces W. to slip into several naturalistic admissions of the superiority of nature to the dramatic art of narrative poetry. But at least he makes clearer his conception of poetry as the expression of passion.

the word poet? What is a poet? To whom does he address himself? And what language is to be expected from him?—He is a man speaking to men: a man, it is true, endowed with more lively sensibility, more enthusiasm and tenderness, who has a greater knowledge of human nature, and a more comprehensive soul, than are supposed to be common among mankind; a man pleased with his own passions and volitions, and who rejoices more than other men in the spirit of life that is in him; delighting to contemplate similar volitions and passions as manifested in the goings-on of the universe, and habitually impelled to create them where he does not find them. To these qualities he has added a disposition to be affected more than other men by absent things as if they were present; an ability of conjuring up in himself passions, which are indeed far from being the same as those produced by real events, yet (especially in those parts of the general sympathy which are pleasing and delightful) do more nearly resemble the passions produced by real events than anything which, from the motions of their own minds merely, other men are accustomed to feel in themselves:—whence, and from practice, he has acquired a greater readiness and power in expressing what he thinks and feels, and especially those thoughts and feelings which, by his own choice, or from the structure of his own mind, arise in him without immediate external excitement.

But whatever portion of this faculty we may suppose even the greatest poet to possess, there cannot be a doubt that the language which it will suggest to him must often, in liveliness and truth, fall short of that which is uttered by men in real life under the actual pressure of those passions, certain shadows of which the poet thus produces, or feels to be produced, in himself.

However exalted a notion we would wish to cherish of the character of a poet, it is obvious that, while he describes and imitates passions, his employment is in some degree mechanical, compared with the freedom and power of real and substantial action and suffering. So that it will be the wish of the poet to bring his feelings near to those of the persons whose feelings he describes, nay, for short spaces of time, perhaps, to let himself slip into an entire delusion, and even confound and identify his own feelings with theirs; modifying only the language which is thus suggested to him by a consideration that he describes for a particular purpose, that of giving pleasure. Here, then, he will apply the principle of selection which has been already insisted upon. He will depend upon this for removing what would otherwise be painful or disgusting in the passion; he will feel that there is no necessity to trick out or to elevate nature: and the more industriously he applies this principle, the deeper will be his faith that no words which *his* fancy or imagination can suggest, will be to be compared with those which are the emanations of reality and truth.

But it may be said by those who do not object to the general spirit of these remarks, that, as it is impossible for the poet to produce upon all occasions language as exquisitely fitted for the passion as that which the real passion itself suggests, it is proper that he should consider himself as in the situation of a translator, who does not scruple to substitute excellences of another kind for those which are unattainable by him; and endeavours occasionally to surpass his original, in order to make some amends for the general inferiority to which he feels that he must submit. But this would be to encourage idleness and unmanly despair. Further, it is the language of men who speak of what they do not understand; who talk of poetry as of a matter of amusement and idle pleasure; who will converse with us as gravely about a *taste* for poetry, as they express it, as if it were a thing as indifferent as a taste for rope-dancing, or Frontiniac or Sherry. Aristotle, I have been told, has said, that poetry is the most philosophic[7] of all writing: it is so: its object is truth, not individual and local, but general and operative; not standing upon external testimony, but carried alive into the heart by passion; truth which is its own testimony, which gives competence and confidence to the tribunal to which it appeals, and receives them from the same tribunal. Poetry is the image of man and nature. The obstacles which stand in the way of the fidelity of the biographer and historian, and of their consequent utility, are incalculably greater than those which are to be encountered by the poet who comprehends the dignity of his art. The poet writes under one restriction only, namely, the necessity of giving immediate pleasure to a human being possessed of that information which may be expected from him, not as a lawyer, a physician, a mariner, an astronomer, or a natural philosopher, but as a man. Except this one restriction, there is no object standing between the poet and the image of things; between this, and the biographer and historian, there are a thousand.

Nor let this necessity of producing immediate pleasure be considered as a degradation of the poet's art. It is far otherwise. It is an acknowledgment of the beauty of the universe,[8] an acknowledgment the more sincere, because not formal, but indirect; it is a task light and easy to him who looks at the world in the spirit of love: further, it is a homage paid to the native and naked dignity of man, to the grand elementary principle of pleasure, by which he knows, and feels, and lives, and moves. We have no sympathy but what is propagated by pleasure: I would not be misunderstood; but wherever we sympathise with pain, it will be found that the sympathy is produced and carried on by subtle combinations with pleasure. We have no knowledge, that is, no general principles drawn from the contemplation of particular facts, but what has been built up by pleasure, and exists in us by pleasure alone. The man of science, the chemist and mathematician, whatever difficulties and disgusts they may have had to struggle with, know and feel this. However painful may be the objects with which the anatomist's knowledge is connected, he feels that his knowledge is pleasure; and where he has no pleasure he has no knowledge. What then does the poet? He considers man and the objects that surround him as acting and re-acting upon each other, so as to produce an infinite complexity of pain and pleasure; he considers man in his own nature and in his ordinary life as contemplating this with a certain quantity of immediate knowledge, with certain convictions, intuitions, and deductions, which from habit acquire the quality of intuitions; he considers him as looking upon this complex scene of ideas and sensations, and finding everywhere objects that immediately excite in him sympathies which, from the necessities of his nature, are accompanied by an overbalance of enjoyment.

[7] **philosophic:** more philosophic than history (*Poetics*, IX).

[8] **universe:** this pleasure of poetry is, therefore, the pleasure of the poet himself. Compare the noble treatments of this theme in Wordsworth's poetry, especially in *The Prelude*. In writing his poem, the poet may have no conscious purpose like that of the didactic poet or the mere entertainer, but his *effect* upon the reader will be to give "immediate pleasure," because the reader will share the pleasure of the poet sympathetically, and his "affections" will be "strengthened and purified."

To this knowledge which all men carry about with them, and to these sympathies in which, without any other discipline than that of our daily life, we are fitted to take delight, the poet principally directs his attention. He considers man and nature as essentially adapted to each other, and the mind of man as naturally the mirror of the fairest and most interesting properties of nature. And thus the poet, prompted by this feeling of pleasure, which accompanies him through the whole course of his studies, converses with general nature, with affections akin to those which, through labour and length of time, the man of science has raised up in himself, by conversing with those particular parts of nature which are the objects of his studies. The knowledge both of the poet and the man of science is pleasure; but the knowledge of the one cleaves to us as a necessary part of our existence, our natural and unalienable inheritance; the other is a personal and individual acquisition, slow to come to us, and by no habitual and direct sympathy connecting us with our fellow-beings. The man of science seeks truth as a remote and unknown benefactor; he cherishes and loves it in his solitude: the poet, singing a song in which all human beings join with him, rejoices in the presence of truth as our visible friend and hourly companion. Poetry is the breath and finer spirit of all knowledge; it is the impassioned expression which is in the countenance of all science. Emphatically may it be said of the poet, as Shakespeare[9] hath said of man, "that he looks before and after." He is the rock of defence for human nature; an upholder and preserver, carrying everywhere with him relationship and love. In spite of difference of soil and climate, of language and manners, of laws and customs: in spite of things silently gone out of mind, and things violently destroyed, the poet binds together by passion and knowledge the vast empire of human society, as it is spread over the whole earth and over all time. The objects of the poet's thoughts are everywhere; though the eyes and senses of man are, it is true, his favourite guides, yet he will follow wheresoever he can find an atmosphere of sensation in which to move his wings. Poetry is the first and last of all knowledge—it is as immortal as the heart of man. If the labours of men of science should ever create any material revolution, direct or indirect, in our condition, and in the impressions which we habitually receive, the poet will sleep then no more than at present; he will be ready to follow the steps of the man of science, not only in those general indirect effects, but he will be at his side, carrying sensation into the midst of the objects of the science itself. The remotest discoveries of the chemist, the botanist, or mineralogist, will be as proper objects of the poet's art as any upon which it can be employed, if the time should ever come when these things shall be familiar to us, and the relations under which they are contemplated by the followers of these respective sciences shall be manifestly and palpably material to us as enjoying and suffering beings. If the time should ever come when what is now called science, thus familiarised to men, shall be ready to put on, as it were, a form of flesh and blood, the poet will lend his divine spirit to aid the transfiguration, and will welcome the being thus produced as a dear and genuine inmate of the household of man.—It is not, then, to be supposed that any one who holds that sublime notion of poetry which I have attempted to convey, will break in upon the sanctity and truth of his pictures by transitory and accidental ornaments, and endeavour to excite admiration

[9] **Shakespeare:** cf. *Hamlet*, IV, iv, 37.

of himself by arts, the necessity of which must manifestly depend upon the assumed meanness of his subject.

What has been thus far said applies to poetry in general, but especially to those parts of composition where the poet speaks through the mouths of his characters; and upon this point it appears to authorise the conclusion that there are few persons of good sense who would not allow that the dramatic parts of composition are defective, in proportion as they deviate from the real language of nature, and are coloured by a diction of the poet's own, either peculiar to him as an individual poet or belonging simply to poets in general; to a body of men who, from the circumstance of their compositions being in metre, it is expected will employ a particular language.

It is not, then, in the dramatic parts of composition that we look for this distinction of language; but still it may be proper and necessary where the poet speaks to us in his own person and character. To this I answer by referring the reader to the description before given of a poet. Among the qualities there enumerated as principally conducing to form a poet, is implied nothing differing in kind from other men, but only in degree. The sum of what was said is, that the poet is chiefly distinguished from other men by a greater promptness to think and feel without immediate external excitement, and a greater power in expressing such thoughts and feelings as are produced in him in that manner. But these passions and thoughts and feelings are the general passions and thoughts and feelings of men. And with what are they connected? Undoubtedly with our moral sentiments and animal sensations, and with the causes which excite these; with the operations of the elements, and the appearances of the visible universe; with storm and sunshine, with the revolutions of the seasons, with cold and heat, with loss of friends and kindred, with injuries and resentments, gratitude and hope, with fear and sorrow. These, and the like, are the sensations and objects which the poet describes, as they are the sensations of other men, and the objects which interest them. The poet thinks and feels in the spirit of human passions. How, then, can his language differ in any material degree from that of all other men who feel vividly and see clearly? It might be *proved* that it is impossible. But supposing that this were not the case, the poet might then be allowed to use a peculiar language when expressing his feelings for his own gratification, or that of men like himself. But poets do not write for poets alone, but for men. Unless, therefore, we are advocates for that admiration which subsists upon ignorance, and that pleasure which arises from hearing what we do not understand, the poet must descend from this supposed height; and, in order to excite rational sympathy, he must express himself as other men express themselves. To this it may be added, that while he is only selecting from the real language of men, or, which amounts to the same thing, composing accurately in the spirit of such selection, he is treading upon safe ground, and we know what we are to expect from him. Our feelings are the same with respect to metre; for, as it may be proper to remind the reader,[10] the distinction of metre is regular and uniform, and not, like that which is produced by what is usually called *poetic diction*, arbitrary, and subject to infinite caprices, upon which no calculation whatever can be made. In the one case, the reader is utterly at the mercy of the

[10] **reader:** last word of the long passage added in 1802.

poet, respecting what imagery or diction he may choose to connect with the passion; whereas, in the other, the metre obeys certain laws, to which the poet and reader both willingly submit because they are certain, and because no interference is made by them with the passion but such as the concurring testimony of ages has shown to heighten and improve the pleasure which co-exists with it.

It will now be proper to answer an obvious question, namely, Why, professing these opinions, have I written in verse? To this, in addition to such answer as is included in what has been already said, I reply, in the first place, because, however I may have restricted myself, there is still left open to me what confessedly constitutes the most valuable object of all writing, whether in prose or verse; the great and universal passions of men, the most general and interesting of their occupations, and the entire world of nature before me—to supply endless combinations of forms and imagery. Now, supposing for a moment that whatever is interesting in these objects may be as vividly described in prose, why should I be condemned for attempting to superadd to such description the charm which, by the consent of all nations, is acknowledged to exist in metrical language? To this, by such as are yet unconvinced, it may be answered that a very small part of the pleasure given by poetry depends upon the metre, and that it is injudicious to write in metre, unless it be accompanied with the other artificial distinctions of style with which metre is usually accompanied, and that, by such deviation, more will be lost from the shock which will thereby be given to the reader's associations than will be counterbalanced by any pleasure which he can derive from the general power of numbers.* In answer to those who still contend for the necessity of accompanying metre with certain appropriate colours of style in order to the accomplishment of its appropriate end, and who also, in my opinion, greatly underrate the power of metre in itself, it might, perhaps, as far as relates to these volumes, have been almost sufficient to observe, that poems are extant, written upon more humble subjects, and in a still more naked and simple style, which have continued to give pleasure from generation to generation. Now, if nakedness and simplicity be a defect, the fact here mentioned affords a strong presumption that poems somewhat less naked and simple are capable of affording pleasure at the present day; and what I wished *chiefly* to attempt, at present, was to justify myself for having written under the impression of this belief.

But various causes might be pointed out why, when the style is manly, and the subject of some importance, words metrically arranged will long continue to impart such a pleasure to mankind as he who proves the extent of that pleasure will be desirous to impart. The end of poetry is to produce excitement in co-existence with an overbalance of pleasure; but, by the supposition, excitement is an unusual and irregular state of the mind; ideas and feelings do not, in that state, succeed each other in accustomed order. If the words, however, by which this excitement is produced be in themselves powerful, or the images and feelings have an undue proportion of pain connected with them, there is some danger that the excitement may be carried beyond its proper bounds. Now the co-presence of something regular, something to which the mind has been accustomed in various moods and in a less excited state, cannot but have great efficacy in

* **numbers:** see Glossary.

tempering and restraining the passion by an intertexture of ordinary feeling, and of feeling not strictly and necessarily connected with the passion. This is unquestionably true; and hence, though the opinion will at first appear paradoxical, from the tendency of metre to divest language, in a certain degree, of its reality, and thus to throw a sort of half-consciousness of unsubstantial existence over the whole composition, there can be little doubt but that more pathetic situations and sentiments, that is, those which have a greater proportion of pain connected with them, may be endured in metrical composition, especially in rhyme, than in prose. The metre of the old ballads is very artless; yet they contain many passages which would illustrate this opinion; and, I hope, if the following poems be attentively perused, similar instances will be found in them. This opinion may be further illustrated by appealing to the reader's own experience of the reluctance with which he comes to the re-perusal of the distressful parts of *Clarissa Harlowe*, or the *Gamester*,[11] while Shakespeare's writings, in the most pathetic scenes, never act upon us as pathetic beyond the bounds of pleasure—an effect which, in a much greater degree than might at first be imagined, is to be ascribed to small, but continual and regular impulses of pleasurable surprise from the metrical arrangement.—On the other hand (what it must be allowed will much more frequently happen), if the poet's words should be incommensurate with the passion, and inadequate to raise the reader to a height of desirable excitement, then (unless the poet's choice of his metre has been grossly injudicious) in the feelings of pleasure which the reader has been accustomed to connect with metre in general, and in the feeling, whether cheerful or melancholy, which he has been accustomed to connect with that particular movement of metre, there will be found something which will greatly contribute to impart passion to the words, and to effect the complex end which the poet proposes to himself.

If I had undertaken a *systematic* defence of the theory here maintained, it would have been my duty to develop the various causes upon which the pleasure received from metrical language depends. Among the chief of these causes is to be reckoned a principle which must be well known to those who have made any of the arts the object of accurate reflection; namely, the pleasure which the mind derives from the perception of similitude in dissimilitude. This principle is the great spring of the activity of our minds, and their chief feeder. From this principle the direction of the sexual appetite, and all the passions connected with it, take their origin; it is the life of our ordinary conversation; and upon the accuracy with which similitude in dissimilitude, and dissimilitude in similitude, are perceived, depend our taste and our moral feelings. It would not be a useless employment to apply this principle to the consideration of metre, and to show that metre is hence enabled to afford much pleasure, and to point out in what manner that pleasure is produced. But my limits will not permit me to enter upon this subject, and I must content myself with a general summary.

I have said that poetry is the spontaneous overflow of powerful feelings: it takes its origin from emotion recollected in tranquillity; the emotion is contemplated till, by a species of re-action, the tranquillity gradually disappears, and an emotion, kindred to that which was before the subject of contemplation, is gradually produced, and does itself

[11] **Gamester:** a domestic tragedy by Edward Moore, pub. 1753.

actually exist in the mind. In this mood successful composition generally begins, and in a mood similar to this it is carried on; but the emotion, of whatever kind, and in whatever degree, from various causes, is qualified by various pleasures, so that in describing any passions whatsoever, which are voluntarily described, the mind will, upon the whole, be in a state of enjoyment. If nature be thus cautious to preserve in a state of enjoyment a being so employed, the poet ought to profit by the lesson held forth to him, and ought especially to take care that, whatever passions he communicates to his reader, those passions, if his reader's mind be sound and vigorous, should always be accompanied with an overbalance of pleasure. Now the music of harmonious metrical language, the sense of difficulty overcome, and the blind association of pleasure which has been previously received from works of rhyme or metre of the same or similar construction, an indistinct perception perpetually renewed of language closely resembling that of real life, and yet, in the circumstance of metre, differing from it so widely—all these imperceptibly make up a complex feeling of delight, which is of the most important use in tempering the painful feeling always found intermingled with powerful descriptions of the deeper passions. This effect is always produced in pathetic and impassioned poetry; while in lighter compositions, the ease and gracefulness with which the poet manages his numbers are themselves confessedly a principal source of the gratification of the reader. All that it is *necessary* to say, however, upon this subject, may be effected by affirming, what few persons will deny, that of two descriptions, either of passions, manners, or characters, each of them equally well executed, the one in prose and the other in verse, the verse will be read a hundred times where the prose is read once.

Having thus explained a few of my reasons for writing in verse, and why I have chosen subjects from common life, and endeavoured to bring my language near to the real language of men, if I have been too minute in pleading my own cause, I have at the same time been treating a subject of general interest; and for this reason a few words shall be added with reference solely to these particular poems, and to some defects which will probably be found in them. I am sensible that my associations must have sometimes been particular instead of general, and that, consequently, giving to things a false importance, I may have sometimes written upon unworthy subjects; but I am less apprehensive on this account, then that my language may frequently have suffered from those arbitrary connections of feelings and ideas with particular words and phrases from which no man can altogether protect himself. Hence I have no doubt that, in some instances, feelings, even of the ludicrous, may be given to my readers by expressions which appeared to me tender and pathetic. Such faulty expressions, were I convinced they were faulty at present, and that they must necessarily continue to be so, I would willingly take all reasonable pains to correct. But it is dangerous to make these alterations on the simple authority of a few individuals, or even of certain classes of men; for where the understanding of an author is not convinced, or his feelings altered, this cannot be done without great injury to himself: for his own feelings are his stay and support; and, if he set them aside in one instance, he may be induced to repeat this act till his mind shall lose all confidence in itself, and become utterly debilitated. To this it may be added, that the critic ought never to forget that he is himself exposed to the same errors as the poet, and, perhaps, in a much greater degree: for there can be no presumption in saying of most readers, that it is not probable they will be so well acquainted with the various stages of meaning through which words have passed, or with the fickleness or stability of the relations of particular ideas to each other; and, above all, since they are so much less interested in the subject, they may decide lightly and carelessly.

Long as the reader has been detained, I hope he will permit me to caution him against a mode of false criticism which has been applied to poetry in which the language closely resembles that of life and nature. Such verses have been triumphed over in parodies, of which Dr. Johnson's stanza is a fair specimen:—

> I put my hat upon my head
> And walked into the Strand,
> And there I met another man
> Whose hat was in his hand.[12]

Immediately under these lines let us place one of the most justly-admired stanzas of the *Babes in the Wood.*

> These pretty babes with hand in hand
> Went wandering up and down;
> But never more they saw the man
> Approaching from the town.

In both these stanzas the words, and the order of the words, in no respect differ from the most unimpassioned conversation. There are words in both, for example, "the Strand," and "the town," connected with none but the most familiar ideas; yet the one stanza we admit as admirable, and the other as a fair example of the superlatively contemptible. Whence arises this difference? Not from the metre, not from the language, not from the order of the words; but the *matter* expressed in Dr. Johnson's stanza is contemptible. The proper method of treating trivial and simple verses, to which Dr. Johnson's stanza would be a fair parallelism, is not to say, this is a bad kind of poetry, or, this is not poetry; but, this wants sense; it is neither interesting in itself, nor can *lead* to anything interesting; the images neither originate in that same state of feeling which arises out of thought, nor can excite thought or feeling in the reader. This is the only sensible manner of dealing with such verses. Why trouble yourself about the species till you have previously decided upon the genus? Why take pains to prove that an ape is not a Newton, when it is self-evident that he is not a man?[13]

One request I must make of my reader, which is, that in judging these poems he would decide by his own feelings genuinely, and not by reflection upon what will probably be the judgment of others. How common is it to hear a person say, I myself do not object to this style of composition, or this or that expression, but to such and such classes of people it will appear mean or ludicrous! This mode of criticism, so destructive of all sound unadulterated judgment, is almost universal: let the reader then abide, independently, by his own feelings, and, if he finds himself affected, let him not suffer such conjectures to interfere with his pleasure.

[12] **hand:** *Poems* (Oxford, 1941), pp. 156–158. A parody of a ballad by Bishop Percy.
[13] **man:** a reference to Pope's *Essay on Man*, II, 34.

If an author, by any single composition, has impressed us with respect for his talents, it is useful to consider this as affording a presumption that on other occasions where we have been displeased he, nevertheless, may not have written ill or absurdly; and further, to give him so much credit for this one composition as may induce us to review what has displeased us with more care than we should otherwise have bestowed upon it. This is not only an act of justice, but, in our decisions upon poetry especially, may conduce, in a high degree, to the improvement of our own taste; for an *accurate* taste in poetry, and in all the other arts, as Sir Joshua Reynolds[14] has observed, is an *acquired* talent, which can only be produced by thought and a long-continued intercourse with the best models of composition. This is mentioned, not with so ridiculous a purpose as to prevent the most inexperienced reader from judging for himself (I have already said that I wish him to judge for himself), but merely to temper the rashness of decision, and to suggest that, if poetry be a subject on which much time has not been bestowed, the judgment may be erroneous; and that, in many cases, it necessarily will be so.

Nothing would, I know, have so effectually contributed to further the end which I have in view, as to have shown of what kind the pleasure is, and how that pleasure is produced, which is confessedly produced by metrical composition essentially different from that which I have here endeavoured to recommend: for the reader will say that he has been pleased by such composition; and what more can be done for him? The power of any art is limited; and he will suspect that, if it be proposed to furnish him with new friends, that can be only upon condition of his abandoning his old friends. Besides, as I have said, the reader is himself conscious of the pleasure which he has received from such composition, composition to which he has peculiarly attached the endearing name of poetry; and all men feel an habitual gratitude, and something of an honourable bigotry, for the objects which have long continued to please them: we not only wish to be pleased, but to be pleased in that particular way in which we have been accustomed to be pleased. There is in these feelings enough to resist a host of arguments; and I should be the less able to combat them successfully, as I am willing to allow that, in order entirely to enjoy the poetry which I am recommending, it would be necessary to give up much of what is ordinarily enjoyed. But would my limits have permitted me to point out how this pleasure is produced, many obstacles might have been removed, and the reader assisted in perceiving that the powers of language are not so limited as he may suppose; and that it is possible for poetry to give other enjoyments, of a purer, more lasting, and more exquisite nature. This part of the subject has not been altogether neglected, but it has not been so much my present aim to prove that the interest excited by some other kinds of poetry is less vivid, and less worthy of the nobler powers of the mind, as to offer reasons for presuming that if my purpose were fulfilled, a species of poetry would be produced which is genuine poetry; in its nature well adapted to interest mankind permanently, and likewise important in the multiplicity and quality of its moral relations.

From what has been said, and from a perusal of the poems, the reader will be able clearly to perceive the object which I had in view: he will determine how far it has been

[14] **Reynolds:** *Discourses*, II, VI, VIII.

attained; and, what is a much more important question, whether it be worth attaining: and upon the decision of these two questions will rest my claim to the approbation of the public.

Appendix[15]

Perhaps, as I have no right to expect that attentive perusal, without which, confined, as I have been, to the narrow limits of a preface, my meaning cannot be thoroughly understood, I am anxious to give an exact notion of the sense in which the phrase *poetic diction* has been used; and for this purpose, a few words shall here be added, concerning the origin and characteristics of the phraseology which I have condemned under that name.

The earliest poets of all nations generally wrote from passion excited by real events; they wrote naturally, and as men: feeling powerfully as they did, their language was daring, and figurative. In succeeding times, poets, and men ambitious of the fame of poets, perceiving the influence of such language, and desirous of producing the same effect without being animated by the same passion, set themselves to a mechanical adoption of these figures of speech, and made use of them, sometimes with propriety, but much more frequently applied them to feelings and thoughts with which they had no natural connection whatsoever. A language was thus insensibly produced, differing materially from the real language of men in *any situation*. The reader or hearer of this distorted language found himself in a perturbed and unusual state of mind: when affected by the genuine language of passion he had been in a perturbed and unusual state of mind also: in both cases he was willing that his common judgment and understanding should be laid asleep, and he had no instinctive and infallible perception of the true to make him reject the false; the one served as a passport for the other. The emotion was in both cases delightful, and no wonder if he confounded the one with the other, and believed them both to be produced by the same or similar causes. Besides, the poet spake to him in the character of a man to be looked up to, a man of genius and authority. Thus, and from a variety of other causes, this distorted language was received with admiration; and poets, it is probable, who had before contented themselves for the most part with misapplying only expressions which at first had been dictated by real passion, carried the abuse still further, and introduced phrases composed apparently in the spirit of the original figurative language of passion, yet altogether of their own invention, and characterised by various degrees of wanton deviation from good sense and nature.

It is indeed true that the language of the earliest poets was felt to differ materially from ordinary language, because it was the language of extraordinary occasions; but it was really spoken by men, language which the poet himself had uttered when he had been affected by the events which he described, or which he had heard uttered by those around him. To this language it is probable that metre of some sort or other was early superadded. This separated the genuine language of poetry still further from common life, so that whoever read or heard the poems of these earliest poets felt himself moved in

[15] **Appendix:** See p. 32, "by what is usually called *poetic diction*." (W.'s introductory note. This is the second great addition in 1802 to the Preface, and is included here, because W. makes clear his conception of "poetic diction.")

a way in which he had not been accustomed to be moved in real life, and by causes manifestly different from those which acted upon him in real life. This was the great temptation to all the corruptions which have followed: under the protection of this feeling succeeding poets constructed a phraseology which had one thing, it is true, in common with the genuine language of poetry, namely, that it was not heard in ordinary conversation; that it was unusual. But the first poets, as I have said, spake a language which, though unusual, was still the language of men. This circumstance, however, was disregarded by their successors; they found that they could please by easier means: they became proud of modes of expression which they themselves had invented, and which were uttered only by themselves. In process of time metre became a symbol or promise of this unusual language, and whoever took upon him to write in metre, according as he possessed more or less of true poetic genius, introduced less or more of this adulterated phraseology into his compositions, and the true and the false were inseparably interwoven until, the taste of men becoming gradually perverted, this language was received as a natural language, and at length, by the influence of books upon men, did to a certain degree really become so. Abuses of this kind were imported from one nation to another, and with the progress of refinement this diction became daily more and more corrupt, thrusting out of sight the plain humanities of nature by a motley masquerade of tricks, quaintnesses, hieroglyphics, and enigmas.[16]

Examples of Wordsworth's Diction

ANECDOTE FOR FATHERS

I have a boy of five years old;
His face is fair and fresh to see;
His limbs are cast in beauty's mould,
And dearly he loves me.

One morn we strolled on our dry walk,
Our quiet home all full in view,
And held such intermitted talk
As we are wont to do.

My thoughts on former pleasures ran;
I thought of Kilve's delightful shore,
Our pleasant home when spring began,
A long, long year before.

A day it was when I could bear
Some fond regrets to entertain;
With so much happiness to spare,
I could not feel a pain.

[16] **enigmas:** the remaining half of the Appendix consists chiefly of illustrations of poetic diction in Dr. Johnson and Cowper.

The green earth echoed to the feet
Of lambs that bounded through the glade,
From shade to sunshine, and as fleet
From sunshine back to shade.

Birds warbled round me—and each trace
Of inward sadness had its charm;
Kilve, thought I, was a favoured place,
And so is Liswyn farm.

My boy beside me tripped, so slim
And graceful in his rustic dress!
And, as we talked, I questioned him,
In very idleness.

"Now tell me, had you rather be,"
I said, and took him by the arm,
"On Kilve's smooth shore, by the green sea,
Or here at Liswyn farm?"

In careless mood he looked at me,
While still I held him by the arm,
And said, "At Kilve I'd rather be
Than here at Liswyn farm."

"Now, little Edward, say why so:
My little Edward, tell me why."—
"I cannot tell, I do not know."—
"Why, this is strange," said I;

"For here are woods, hills smooth and warm:
There surely must some reason be
Why you would change sweet Liswyn farm
For Kilve by the green sea."

At this my boy hung down his head,
He blushed with shame, nor made reply;
And three times to the child I said,
"Why, Edward, tell me why?"

His head he raised—there was in sight,
It caught his eye, he saw it plain—
Upon the house-top, glittering bright,
A broad and gilded vane.

Then did the boy his tongue unlock,
And eased his mind with this reply:
"At Kilve there was no weather-cock;
And that's the reason why."

Oh dearest, dearest boy! my heart
For better lore would seldom yearn,
Could I but teach the hundredth part
Of what from thee I learn.

1798 WILLIAM WORDSWORTH (1770–1850)

SHE DWELT AMONG THE UNTRODDEN WAYS

She dwelt among the untrodden ways
  Beside the springs of Dove,
A maid whom there were none to praise
  And very few to love:

A violet by a mossy stone
  Half hidden from the eye!
—Fair as a star, when only one
  Is shining in the sky.

She lived unknown, and few could know
  When Lucy ceased to be;
But she is in her grave, and, oh,
  The difference to me!

1799 WILLIAM WORDSWORTH (1770–1850)

THE REVERIE OF POOR SUSAN

At the corner of Wood Street, when daylight appears,
Hangs a thrush that sings loud, it has sung for three years:
Poor Susan has passed by the spot, and has heard
In the silence of morning the song of the bird.

'Tis a note of enchantment; what ails her? She sees
A mountain ascending, a vision of trees;
Bright volumes of vapour through Lothbury glide,
And a river flows on through the vale of Cheapside.

Green pastures she views in the midst of the dale,
Down which she so often has tripped with her pail;
And a single small cottage, a nest like a dove's,
The one only dwelling on earth that she loves.

She looks, and her heart is in heaven: but they fade,
The mist and the river, the hill and the shade:
The stream will not flow, and the hill will not rise,
And the colours have all passed away from her eyes!

1797 WILLIAM WORDSWORTH (1770–1850)

THE HERITAGE OF WORDSWORTH AND OF POPE

The revolution in diction and subject matter announced by the Preface to *Lyrical Ballads* reached maturity in conjunction with FREE VERSE about the beginning of World War I, with the publication in Boston, in 1915, of a small volume of verse called *Some Imagist Poets.* In order to understand the precise aims of the six poets, three British and three American,* represented in this volume, the main portion of their Preface is included here:

> The poets in this volume do not represent a clique. Several of them are personally unknown to the others, but they are united by certain common principles, arrived at independently. These principles are not new; they have fallen into desuetude. They are the essentials of all great poetry, indeed of all great literature, and they are simply these:
>
> 1. To use the language of common speech, but to employ always the *exact* word, not the nearly-exact, nor the merely decorative word.
> 2. To create new rhythms—as the expression of new moods—and not to copy old rhythms, which merely echo old moods. We do not insist upon "free-verse" as the only method of writing poetry. We fight for it as for a principle of liberty. We believe that the individuality of a poet may often be better expressed in free-verse than in conventional forms. In poetry, a new cadence means a new idea.
> 3. To allow absolute freedom in the choice of subject. It is not good art to write badly about aeroplanes and automobiles; nor is it necessarily bad art to write well about the past. We believe passionately in the artistic value of modern life, but we wish to point out that there is nothing so uninspiring nor so old-fashioned as an aeroplane of the year 1911.
> 4. To present an image (hence the name: "Imagist"). We are not a school of painters, but we believe that poetry should render particulars exactly and not deal in vague generalities, however magnificent or sonorous. It is for this reason that we oppose the cosmic poet, who seems to us to shirk the real difficulties of his art.
> 5. To produce poetry that is hard and clear, never blurred nor indefinite.
> 6. Finally, most of us believe that concentration is of the very essence of poetry.

Ezra Pound, a temporary member of the Imagist group, wrote the following poem representative of the statements of the Preface:

* Richard Aldington (1892–1962), F. S. Flint (1885–1960), D. H. Lawrence (1885–1930), H. D. (Hilda Doolittle) (1886–1961), John Gould Fletcher (1886–1950), Amy Lowell (1874–1925).

IN A STATION OF THE METRO

The apparition of these faces in the crowd;
Petals on a wet, black bough.

EZRA POUND (1885–)

H. D. (Hilda Doolittle), who has been called "the perfect imagist," wrote consistently in this style:

HEAT

O wind, rend open the heat,
cut apart the heat,
rend it to tatters.

Fruit cannot drop
through this thick air—
fruit cannot fall into heat
that presses up and blunts
the points of pears
and rounds the grapes.

Cut through the heat—
plow through it,
turning it on either side
of your path.

H. D. (1886–1961)

Of the original group of Imagist poets, only H. D. consistently wrote in the manner described in the Preface throughout her long career as a poet. The others, including Amy Lowell, apparently found the demands of paragraphs 4, 5, and 6 too difficult to meet. Indeed, Miss Lowell's most successful poems (*Lilacs, Patterns*) deal in emotions rather than images and evade the requirement of "concentration." Like Wordsworth, these poets found a novel emphasis in the theory of poetry easier to describe than to practice. The six poets, however, believed in their theory and published two further anthologies together, in 1916 and 1917, and continued to write in free verse with application of imagism in diction and subject matter.* Ezra Pound discarded both the theory and the practice: "Imagism was a point on the curve of my development. Some people remained at that point. I moved on."

Modern critics have recognized in the poems of Robert Frost a development of the use of rural subject matter and colloquial speech, as in *The Death of the Hired Man, After Apple Picking*, and many others. A brief example is *The Pasture*, the first poem in Frost's first volume, *A Boy's Will*, published in 1913:

* For additional examples of Imagist poetry, see pp. 294–96.

THE PASTURE

I'm going out to clean the pasture spring;
I'll only stop to rake the leaves away
(And wait to watch the water clear, I may):
I shan't be gone long.—You come too.

I'm going out to fetch the little calf
That's standing by the mother. It's so young
It totters when she licks it with her tongue.
I shan't be gone long.—You come too.

ROBERT FROST (1874–1963)

The revolution in subject matter and in the use of the common vocabulary heralded in 1798 continues today in topics and language Wordsworth could hardly have anticipated. The following twentieth-century poems are good examples:

BUICK

As a sloop with a sweep of immaculate wing on her delicate spine
And a keel as steel as a root that holds in the sea as she leans,
Leaning and laughing, my warm-hearted beauty, you ride, you ride,
You tack on the curves with parabola speed and a kiss of goodbye,
Like a thoroughbred sloop, my new high-spirited spirit, my kiss.

As my foot suggests that you leap in the air with your hips of a girl,
My finger that praises your wheel and announces your voices of song,
Flouncing your skirts, you blueness of joy, you flirt of politeness,
You leap, you intelligence, essence of wheelness with silvery nose,
And your platinum clocks of excitement stir like the hairs of a fern.

But how alien you are from the booming belts of your birth and the smoke
Where you turned on the stinging lathes of Detroit and Lansing at night
And shrieked at the torch in your secret parts and the amorous tests,
But now with your eyes that enter the future of roads you forget;
You are all instinct with your phosphorous glow and your streaking hair.

And now when we stop it is not as the bird from the shell that I leave
Or the leathery pilot who steps from his bird with a sneer of delight,
And not as the ignorant beast do you squat and watch me depart,
But with exquisite breathing you smile, with satisfaction of love,
And I touch you again as you tick in the silence and settle in sleep.

KARL SHAPIRO (1913–   )

THE DEATH OF THE BALL TURRET GUNNER

From my mother's sleep I fell into the State,
And I hunched in its belly till my wet fur froze.
Six miles from earth, loosed from its dream of life,
I woke to black flak and the nightmare fighters.
When I died they washed me out of the turret with a hose.

RANDALL JARRELL (1914–1965)

Although the most famous names in English literature representing poetic diction vs. "the language really used by men in a state of vivid sensation" are Pope and Wordsworth, it is probably accurate to say that one of these two views has governed every poet, every critic, every reader in our literary history. Some students asked to write a poem seek out the "poetic" subject, to be clothed in "poetic" diction; others deliberately seek the nonpoetic or the antipoetic, to be expressed in the language of the street, or even the gutter. In evaluating the poems we read, we should be aware of our preconceptions: Are we, actually, twentieth-century critics from the school of Pope, or twentieth-century successors to the school of Wordsworth?

EXERCISE 5

Choose what you consider to be an appropriate subject for poetry in the manner of Pope. (If in doubt, consult an edition of his complete poems.) Using poetic diction, try to develop the subject in prose of a style you consider similar to that of Pope. If you attempt "elegant variation," provide your reader with a glossary.

EXERCISE 6

Choose a subject which Wordsworth might have chosen for a short poem. Using a "selection of the language really used by men in a state of vivid sensation," develop the subject in a prose description, written in the manner of Wordsworth.

EXERCISE 7

Consider the possibility of a *subject* on which both Pope and Wordsworth might have written. List some subjects which you think both poets might have chosen. In a paper, one or two pages in length, discuss the diction and poetic diction in which this subject would probably be described by the two poets. Which treatment do you prefer? Why?

EXERCISE 8

A study of the manuscript revisions appearing in the handwritten drafts of the poet frequently gives us insight into the poetic process, particularly in the choice of words. Examine carefully the draft of the stanza given below from Keats' *The Eve of St. Agnes.** Porphyro, who has secretly entered Madeline's bedroom, is preparing a feast for St. Agnes' Eve for his beloved. Take each change in diction separately: What is the difference between "sweets," "fruits," "apple," "Quince," in sound, in meaning? Compare the draft with the final copy which Keats published (see p. 234).

~~But~~
~~And still she slept:~~
And still she slept an azure-lidded sleep
In blanched linen smooth and lavender'd;
While he from forth the closet brought a heap
~~fruits~~
Of candied ~~sweets~~ ~~sweets with~~ and plumb and gourd
apple Quince
creamed
With jellies soother than the ~~dairy~~ curd
tinct
And lucent syrups ~~smooth~~ with crannamon
~~And sugar'd dates from that o'er Euphrates fard~~
~~in Brigantine transferred~~
~~transferred~~
Manna and daites in Bragine ~~wild transferrd~~
~~and Manna~~
~~And Manna wild and~~ ~~Bragantine~~
~~sugar'd~~ dates transferrd
argosy
~~In Brigantine from Fez~~
From fez—and spiced danties every one
~~glutted~~
From ~~wealthy~~ Sakmarchand to cedard lebanon
silken

EXERCISE 9

A. E. Housman's third volume of poems, *More Poems*, was published after his death. His instructions directed his brother Laurence to select and publish "any poems which appear to him to be completed and to be not inferior to the average of my published poems." Of the two poems given below Laurence Housman writes: "there existed two complete variants, with no indication as

* The transcription is based on that of Wright Thomas and S. G. Brown in *Reading Poems* (New York: Oxford University Press, 1941), p. 623.

to which of the two the author preferred; and though I have a slight preference myself, I am not so confident of my judgment being right as to deny to others the interest and pleasure of making their own choice."* Consider the two versions given below. Which do you prefer? Why?

THE WEEPING PLEIADS WESTER

The weeping Pleiads wester,
  And the moon is under seas;
From bourn to bourn of midnight
  Far sighs the rainy breeze:

It sighs from a lost country
  To a land I have not known;
The weeping Pleiads wester,
  And I lie down alone.

A. E. HOUSMAN (1859–1936)

THE RAINY PLEIADS WESTER

The rainy Pleiads wester,
  Orion plunges prone,
And midnight strikes and hastens,
  And I lie down alone.

The rainy Pleiads wester
  And seek beyond the sea
The head that I shall dream of
  That will not dream of me.

A. E. HOUSMAN (1859–1936)

* A. E. Housman, *More Poems*, Preface by Laurence Housman (New York: Alfred A. Knopf, 1936).

III

Metaphorical Language: The Image and the Figure

The "strangeness," the seeming difficulty of poetry, lies not only in the use of formal metrical patterns and the devices of rhyme, but also in the different use of language. This difficulty may seem even more difficult on turning for guidance to a series of definitions, with examples, of FIGURES OF SPEECH. Students who are required to learn these definitions and to seek other examples in poems often conclude from this orderly and disciplined training in the "means" of poetic expression that the language of poetry is vague, ornamental, or, in their usual term, "flowery." This response is linked, not unnaturally, with the idea that the construction of poetry is a sort of intellectual game, in which the contestants are required to find the most obscure and unusual ways of describing common observations and experiences. The reader begins to think of himself as a decoding expert, required to solve complex intellectual puzzles in order to understand the poem.

Actually, this attempt to study poetry from an examination of the finished product, in order to deduce the manner in which it was composed, and to classify the types of METAPHORICAL LANGUAGE which have been used, is probably much less illuminating than the reverse process, an effort to understand the poetic process by duplicating its initial techniques. To describe exactly in one's own words an object experienced by one of the senses may seem, at first, a simple, childish assignment. The key to the problem is, however, that the process is not *childish* (with its dubious connotations), but *childlike*, and it is, therefore, an assignment which requires the student to forget ways of experiencing an object that he has acquired through education and through the experiences of other people. This assignment requires him to forget, also, ways of describing in the language of others which he remembers. It requires an alertness of the senses which most of us have allowed to become dull, and sharp awareness of the variations of language which most of us have allowed to rub smooth, just as a newly minted coin becomes smooth in the process of rubbing through many hands as a means of approximate exchange between the metal and some other object. Thus, the person who remarks that he is as cold as ice and intends to convey his physical sensation has, of course, borrowed a comparison so often used that it no longer has the sharpness of any experience, except "very cold." It has so long ago lost the original experience that when he is reminded that it is literally inexact, since no living person can be as cold as ice, he must grope back to the original experience to realize that the Anonymous who first reported his experience in this way was not in search of scientific but of emotional accuracy. He must remember and re-experience his first contact with a piece of ice—its coldness, its texture, its hardness, its resistance to alteration from coldness, even when surrounded by warmth—and then remember a recent experience with his own cold hands in bed, late at night, hard, cold, stiff, smooth, and apparently impervious to surrounding blankets and friction.

We have been examining in detail a piece of metaphorical language so overused that it is now no longer usable as the metaphorical language of poetry. Even in ordinary speech, it would be labeled "cliché" or "trite," but it still serves as the coin, the legal tender, of communication. The process of poetic communication, however, requires the writer to experience an object with his senses and to participate fully in the experience with as many of his senses as he can bring into vivid contact with the object; then he must report this experience in language which he has not borrowed. The report which he then makes will be the most accurate answer he can find to such a question as "Exactly how cold were my hands last night?" One example of a student's poetic answer to this question is the poem that appears below:

DISILLUSION

My hands, too big for pockets from the cold,
Are curled, finger-tip deep, leaving the thumb
Of each snuggled for shelter in a fold
Of sweater, now that washing's made them numb.

The plunge into a frozen moonlit spring
Has iced them into hands no longer quick
At dipping pails, or nailing anything,
Or whittling a door-stop from a stick.

I should not want to have myself tonight
For bedfellow—such hands would frost the sheet
And pillow case, put out the candle light
Before we'd finished tucking up our feet.

1935 FLORENCE FRENCH DUNBAR (1915–)

The origin of metaphorical language (for most of us) lies in the IMAGE: the sensory experience of an object and the description of that object. Any report of an experience of the physical senses is probably made in the form of an image: My hands were cold—picture: hands; temperature: cold. How cold? The wish to communicate wretched physical discomfort, inability to get warm in order to go to sleep, the attempt to answer "How cold?" leads straight to the most accurate, original report we can conceive. When we examine the answer we have made to that question, we shall probably discover that we have been able to achieve it only in metaphorical language—by comparison with something which we believe our readers will have experienced in some way and which they will understand.

First attempts to report an answer to "How cold?" may be "As cold as a blizzard in Alaska." This description will not do very well, since blizzards come down in small flakes, quite different from the hands under the blankets. "As cold as the wind from the North Pole." This will not do, either, since the hands are substantial and the wind is not. "Cold as two stone bottles buried under a glacier"—not perfect, but more like the *truth*. And we stop here, because the critic, looking at the last expression, might say that the comparison is farfetched, that the writer is seeking the bizarre, the unusual, and who would have buried the bottles under the glacier? But no fair-minded critic could describe the comparison as "flowery" or "ornamental." A thoughtful critic would realize that it is not inexact. How cold would two stone bottles buried under a glacier be? (No, sheets and blankets are not glaciers, but sheets are generally white, and neither they nor blankets are warm in themselves.)*

The basic problem, then, of the language of poetry is, first, accuracy and immediacy of experience and, next, accuracy of expression in order to communicate that experience. Neither kind of accuracy is easily achieved. Fundamental to the poet's experience is a way of experiencing, a way that is distinct from the ways of experiencing in the sciences, which aim also at accuracy. In the ancient argument between the scientists and the poets the resolution lies in the idea that there may be more than one kind of accuracy. To the scientist, as to Adam, was given the privilege of the naming of objects. He names them by

* To the archaeologist and the anthropologist there may be problems about the age of glaciers and the date of the man who made and buried the bottles. To the poet, it does not matter how the bottles came to be under the glaciers: he knows, as we do, that they will be very cold.

a process of classification based on minute observation of their parts, of the relationships between the parts and between one object and another. This careful study of relationships by intellectual means is one kind of experience. But there are others. The poet, knowing nothing of the scientific relationships of the forsythia (not even its scientific name), looks at the bush, suddenly flowering yellow on an April morning, and reports, "Forsythia, full of wings." To him the relationship is to all sudden, flying things: flowers, butterflies, birds, angels. It is not scientifically true that any flower is sudden, but it is emotionally true: yesterday there was nothing to be seen, except the bush, from the vantage point of the poet's observation. Today, it is a wonder that the yellow wings do not suddenly ascend the sky. There is, actually, no quarrel between the scientific and the poetic ways of experience; they have much to offer each other, but it must be recognized that they are different. Neither is wrong, neither is right. They do not contradict each other; they complement each other.

THE IMAGE

The basis of metaphorical language in sensory experience is the image. The image in itself is not, however, metaphorical language, nor is metaphorical language an essential in the writing of every poem. It is possible to write descriptive poetry that consists of a series of images reporting the experiences of the various physical senses. From the image to metaphorical language the step is from a single image to two linked images. In the SIMILE the linking is explicit, as in Burns' "O my luve is like a red, red rose": on one side the young woman, "my luve," on the other the "red, red rose." In the METAPHOR the relationship is experienced more immediately, almost as an identity: "my love *is* a red, red rose," or Keats' urn *is* "Thou still unravished bride of quietness." In PERSONIFICATION the inanimate is identified with a living being, as in Collins' *Ode to Evening*, in which evening becomes a young woman. The various types of metaphorical language, to the poet, are, in a sense, all one. As he uses them, he chooses the most exact, immediate, vivid expression of his experience. It is, moreover, difficult for the student, analyzing the result, always to classify exactly. Keats' Grecian urn may be personified as a bride, or it may be metaphorically "identified with" a bride. Nor is the response of all poets to a similar experience by any means the same. Collins reports a pleasant evening; Eliot reports an evening "spread out against the sky / Like a patient etherised upon a table." Burns' girl is not the beloved of Nims' "My clumsiest dear," where the language used is descriptive:

My clumsiest dear, whose hands shipwreck vases,
At whose quick touch all glasses chip and ring,
Whose palms are bulls in china, burs in linen,
And have no cunning with any soft thing

Except all ill-at-ease fidgeting people:
The refugee uncertain at the door
You make at home; deftly you steady
The drunk clambering on his undulant floor.

From JOHN FREDERICK NIMS, *Love Poem*, 1947

Language which evokes an image is language which evokes a response from one of the physical senses. Such responses may be classified as the following types of image:

	Image	*Sense*
1.	Visual	Sight
2.	Auditory	Sound
3.	Olfactory	Smell
4.	Gustatory	Taste
5.	Tactile	Touch
6.	Kinesthetic	Muscular tension
7.	Thermal	Temperature

It is important to note that imagery is not limited to *visual* experience only, although this kind of image predominates, and that a single word may evoke the response of more than one sense: "violet," for example, is primarily visual, but it is also olfactory, tactile, and thermal. In identifying images, the student should differentiate between an auditory image, such as the word "music," and ONOMATOPOEIA, such as "crash," a word whose sound imitates the noise heard. In the list given above, "touch" is used, instead of "feeling," with its emotional overtones. Images report responses of the physical senses and are not primarily concerned with emotions.

EXERCISE 10

TO AUTUMN

Season of mists and mellow fruitfulness,
  Close bosom-friend of the maturing sun;
Conspiring with him how to load and bless
  With fruit the vines that round the thatch-eaves run;
To bend with apples the moss'd cottage-trees,

And fill all fruit with ripeness to the core;
To swell the gourd, and plump the hazel shells
With a sweet kernel; to set budding more,
And still more, later flowers for the bees,
Until they think warm days will never cease,
For Summer has o'er-brimm'd their clammy cells.

Who hath not seen thee oft amid thy store?
Sometimes whoever seeks abroad may find
Thee sitting careless on a granary floor,
Thy hair soft-lifted by the winnowing wind;
Or on a half-reap'd furrow sound asleep,
Drows'd with the fume of poppies, while thy hook
Spares the next swath and all its twined flowers;
And sometimes like a gleaner thou dost keep
Steady thy laden head across a brook;
Or by a cider-press, with patient look,
Thou watchest the last oozings hours by hours.

Where are the songs of Spring? Ay, where are they?
Think not of them, thou hast thy music too,—
While barred clouds bloom the soft-dying day,
And touch the stubble-plains with rosy hue;
Then in a wailful choir the small gnats mourn
Among the river sallows, borne aloft
Or sinking as the light wind lives or dies;
And full-grown lambs loud bleat from hilly bourn;
Hedge-crickets sing; and now with treble soft
The red-breast whistles from a garden-croft;
And gathering swallows twitter in the skies.

JOHN KEATS (1795–1821)

In the poem given above, list under the seven types of image each image-evoking word. Remember that a single word may appear in more than one column. Try to experience the poem with as many of your senses as possible.

THE FIGURE

Like *To Autumn*, a poem may be purely descriptive, and rely chiefly on images to achieve its effects. More commonly, some of the images used are the basis for metaphor. A good example of descriptive poetry in which both image and metaphor are used is Karl Shapiro's *The Fly*:

THE FLY

O hideous little bat, the size of snot,
With polyhedral eye and shabby clothes,
To populate the stinking cat you walk
The promontory of the dead man's nose,
Climb with the fine leg of a Duncan-Phyfe
  The smoking mountains of my food
    And in a comic mood
  In mid-air take to bed a wife.

Riding and riding with your filth of hair
On gluey foot or wing, forever coy,
Hot from the compost and green sweet decay,
Sounding your buzzer like an urchin toy—
You dot all whiteness with diminutive stool,
  In the tight belly of the dead
    Burrow with hungry head
  And inlay maggots like a jewel.

At your approach the great horse stomps and paws
Bringing the hurricane of his heavy tail;
Shod in disease you dare to kiss my hand
Which sweeps against you like an angry flail;
Still you return, return, trusting your wing
  To draw you from the hunter's reach
    That learns to kill to teach
  Disorder to the tinier thing.

My peace is your disaster. For your death
Children like spiders cup their pretty hands
And wives resort to chemistry of war.
In fens of sticky paper and quicksands
You glue yourself to death. Where you are stuck
  You struggle hideously and beg,
    You amputate your leg
  Imbedded in the amber muck.

But I, a man, must swat you with my hate,
Slap you across the air and crush your flight,
Must mangle with my shoe and smear your blood,
Expose your little guts pasty and white,
Knock your head sidewise like a drunkard's hat,
  Pin your wings under like a crow's,
    Tear off your flimsy clothes
  And beat you as one beats a rat.

Then like Gargantua I stride among
The corpses strewn like raisins in the dust,
The broken bodies of the narrow dead
That catch the throat with fingers of disgust.
I sweep. One gyrates like a top and falls
And stunned, stone blind, and deaf
Buzzes its frightful F
And dies between three cannibals.

KARL SHAPIRO (1913–)

EXERCISE 11

In poems in this book, find examples of the following figures of speech:

1. simile
2. metaphor
3. SYNECDOCHE
4. personification
5. metaphysical CONCEIT
6. SYMBOL

In what way do they contribute to, or detract from, the passages in which they appear?

In poems in this book, find examples of the following devices:

1. IRONY
2. ALLUSION
    a. direct
    b. indirect
3. INVERSION
4. onomatopoeia
5. APOSTROPHE

In what way do these devices contribute to the passages in which they appear?

EXERCISE 12

To the student wishing to understand the poet's experience and the language used to express and communicate it, a most significant comment is also one of the oldest: "But the greatest thing by far is to be a master of metaphor. It is the one thing that cannot be learned from others; and it is also a sign of genius, since a good metaphor implies an intuitive perception of the similarity in dissimilars" (Aristotle, *Poetics*, XXII).

The longer one considers this comment, whether in trying to report one's own experiences accurately or in trying to understand the poetic reports of the experiences of others, the more profound this comment seems to become. Metaphorical language is not a poetic ornament; it is one of the basic means of poetic communication.

Construct good original examples of the figures and devices listed in Exercise 11. Try to avoid sentimentality, clichés, and trite diction.

EXERCISE 13.1

From your experiences in the natural sciences, or from direct outdoor observation, choose an object, process, or experiment to describe, *e.g.*, bringing water to a boil or a single small flower. The object or process should be limited in size or scope and directly observable. You should have the means to repeat your observations. *Do not attempt to work from memory*. In your description, write accurately and clearly, including only what can be apprehended by the physical senses. Your description should be simple enough to be understood by a literate layman: necessary technical terms should be explained. The result should be a competent essay, not an article for a technical journal or an explanation for a textbook.

*EXERCISE 13.2**

Take the same object, process, or experiment which you used for Exercise 13.1. Write another description of it. In your first essay, you probably recorded the experience of a single physical sense (visual and tactile observations are apt to be most common). In this second essay, observe again, using *as many senses* as you can profitably and safely use: taste, hearing, smell, etc. Try to experience the object or process as fully as possible and to share your experiences, through your essay, with your reader.

*EXERCISE 13.3**

THE FLEA

Mark but this flea, and mark in this,
How little that which thou deny'st me is;
It suck'd me first, and now sucks thee,
And in this flea, our two bloods mingled be;
Thou know'st that this cannot be said
A sin, nor shame, nor loss of maidenhead,
   Yet this enjoys before it woo,
   And pamper'd swells with one blood made of two,
   And this, alas, is more than we would do.

Oh stay, three lives in one flea spare,
Where we almost, yea more than married are.

* Exercise 13.2 should not be tackled until the instructor has returned Exercise 13.1, and Exercise 13.3 should wait until the correction of Exercise 13.2.

This flea is you and I, and this
Our marriage bed, and marriage temple is;
Though parents grudge, and you, we're met,
And cloistered in these living walls of jet.
  Though use make you apt to kill me,
  Let not to that, self-murder added be,
  And sacrilege, three sins in killing three.

Cruel and sudden, hast thou since
Purpled thy nail, in blood of innocence?
Wherein could this flea guilty be,
Except in that drop which it suck'd from thee?
Yet thou triumph'st, and say'st that thou
Find'st not thyself, nor me the weaker now;
  'Tis true, then learn how false fears be:
  Just so much honour, when thou yield'st to me,
  Will waste, as this flea's death took life from thee.

JOHN DONNE (1572–1631)

THE PULLEY

When God at first made man,
Having a glass of blessings standing by,
"Let us," said He, "pour on him all we can;
Let the world's riches, which dispersèd lie,
Contract into a span."

So strength first made a way,
Then beauty flow'd, then wisdom, honour, pleasure;
When almost all was out, God made a stay,
Perceiving that, alone of all his treasure,
Rest in the bottom lay.

"For if I should," said He,
"Bestow this jewel also on my creature,
He would adore my gifts instead of me,
And rest in Nature, not the God of Nature:
So both should losers be.

"Yet let him keep the rest,
But keep them with repining restlessness;
Let him be rich and weary, that at least,
If goodness lead him not, yet weariness
May toss him to my breast."

GEORGE HERBERT (1593–1633)

Take the object, process, or experiment which you have used for the descriptive essays of Exercises 13.1 and 13.2. Consider thoughtfully what it might represent, either as metaphor or as symbol. As examples of the use of figurative devices, study Donne's poem *The Flea* or Herbert's *The Pulley*. In a brief statement, indicate how you would use your material in a poem. Try to avoid the cliché and the trite; for example, do not use a tree flowering in the spring to represent faith, hope, or the benevolence of God.

IV

The Development of Blank Verse

A study of the development of iambic verse is essential to an understanding of English prosody—the formal pattern of verse—for the iamb (◡ ´) has been the basic foot in use in most metrical poems in English since the fourteenth century.

Chaucer made the iambic foot the basic unit of the five-foot line (pentameter) he adopted in *Troilus and Criseyde* (*c.* 1385) and in most of *The Canterbury Tales* (*c.* 1387 ff.), the long works which he wrote at the end of his career. Both these works, however, are written in rhymed verse. The use of rhyme represents a borrowing from French or Italian forms; it was not a device used in classical prosody. It remained, therefore, for the poets of the English Renaissance in the sixteenth century to adapt classical meter without rhyme for their poems—to develop the unrhymed iambic pentameter known as BLANK VERSE.

The first example given the student for analysis is a selection from the Earl of Surrey's translation of the *Aeneid*, dated about 1540. Since this work is translation, it is well to remember that the translator has less freedom with the *content* of his material than the original poet. And because this poem is probably the first extended use of unrhymed iambic pentameter in English, it is well to remember also that Surrey had no English models to follow. The first major poet (and dramatist) to use the form in original work was Christopher Marlowe, about 1593; his example was followed by Shakespeare and the many playwrights of the Elizabethan and Jacobean period.

DIRECTIONS FOR THE ANALYSIS OF BLANK VERSE

In order to understand the structure of patterned verse, the student should read it aloud, as meaningfully as possible. When he does not understand the meaning and tone of the passage, he cannot read it effectively. After reading it aloud several times, he should put stress marks (′) on the syllables he actually stresses in reading, as he did in the prose passages of Exercises 1 and 2. No provision is made in conventional English prosody for secondary stress as indicated in standard dictionaries.* Syllables should be marked as either stressed (′) or unstressed (◡). Since all stressed syllables are presumed to be lengthened by the stress, the conventional mark is ⊥. There are, however, in English verse, some long syllables (determined by the amount of time required to pronounce them) which will not be stressed. These should be marked simply: —.

After thoughtful reading and marking of syllables, the student should attempt to determine the feet. He should start, usually, at the end of the line and work backward until he reaches a difficult place. Then he should start at the beginning of the line, but remember that the first foot in many iambic passages is often a TROCHEE. Since a piece of scansion is simply a picture of the aural pattern the reader perceives, he should try to draw a true picture. Ordinarily the verse given in this book will not include DACTYLS, amphibrachs (see CLASSICAL PROSODY), amphimacers (this foot is not even in the Glossary), or monosyllabic feet, although FEMININE ENDINGS are often used. After the scansion is done, the student can *see* what he has heard and try to understand the reasons for the SUBSTITUTIONS of non-iambic feet. Scansion is not simply a mechanical exercise: the student must remain aware that a good poet substitutes for the standard or "normal" iambic foot with the intent (conscious or subconscious) of matching the sound of his verse to the emotional or intellectual content of the word or line in which the substitution is made; and in evaluating the purpose of the significant substitutions, the critic, whether student or expert, should not be content with the comment, "to avoid monotony."

The following passage from Shakespeare's *The Merchant of Venice* (IV, i) illustrates the procedure to be used in analysis:

* This comment must be modified for minor-accent rhyme (see under RHYME).

<table>
<tr><th colspan="5">Substitutions by feet</th><th></th><th></th></tr>
<tr><th>1</th><th>2</th><th>3</th><th>4</th><th>5</th><th></th><th></th></tr>
<tr><td></td><td>P</td><td></td><td>P</td><td>S</td><td></td><td>The qual|ity | of mer|cy is | not strain'd.|</td></tr>
<tr><td></td><td>P</td><td></td><td></td><td></td><td>F</td><td>It drop|peth as | the gen|tle rain | from heav|en</td></tr>
<tr><td>P</td><td></td><td></td><td>P</td><td>S</td><td></td><td>Upon | the place | beneath.| It is | twice blest:|</td></tr>
<tr><td></td><td></td><td></td><td></td><td></td><td></td><td>It bless|eth him | that gives,| and him | that takes.|</td></tr>
<tr><td></td><td>P</td><td>A</td><td>P</td><td>A</td><td></td><td>'Tis might|iest | in the might|iest.| It becomes|</td></tr>
<tr><td></td><td></td><td></td><td>P</td><td></td><td></td><td>The thron|ed mon|arch bet|ter than | his crown;|</td></tr>
<tr><td></td><td></td><td></td><td></td><td>A</td><td>F</td><td>His scep|tre shows | the force | of tem|poral pow|er,</td></tr>
<tr><td></td><td></td><td></td><td></td><td>P</td><td></td><td>The at|tribute | to awe | and maj|esty,|</td></tr>
<tr><td></td><td></td><td></td><td></td><td></td><td></td><td>Wherein | doth sit | the dread | and fear | of kings;|</td></tr>
<tr><td></td><td>P</td><td></td><td></td><td></td><td></td><td>But mer|cy is | above | this scep|tred sway;|</td></tr>
</table>

ABBREVIATIONS: **1**, **2**, etc.: first, second, etc., foot in line. P: pyrrhic; S: spondee; A: anapest; F: feminine ending.

The normal or basic metrical pattern of this passage is iambic pentameter, and if the verse were perfectly regular, the ten lines would add up to 50 iambic feet. The percentage of substitutions is obtained by dividing 50 into 15—the total number of substitutions as indicated by the chart to the left of the passage. The percentage of substitutions of individual feet can be obtained in the same way.

Total substitutions	30%	Trochaic substitutions	0
Pyrrhic substitutions	20%	Dactylic substitutions	0
Anapestic substitutions	6%	Feminine endings: 2 out of 10, or 20%	
Spondaic substitutions	4%		

Of the ten endings, two are feminine. A feminine ending is not counted as an additional foot, or half foot, but its presence has a noticeable effect on the line or passage.

A table like the above will show the precise amount and type of substitution. By itself the detection of substitutions is not valuable. The substitutions must be interpreted to show the effect the changes make on the content (intellectual or emotional) of the passage. Some substitutions are notable and noticeable. Others are not. For example, a pyrrhic combined with a spondee, as in line 186, cancels the effect, so that the reader *hears* nothing unusual. The most interesting line in the passage is line 188, which combines pyrrhic and

189. In texts printed before about 1850, *-ed*, when spelled out, should be read as a light syllable, especially if a light syllable is needed for the meter.

anapestic substitutions, with the result that there is an unusually large number of light syllables. It would be our judgment that Shakespeare, in this line which declares the immense power of the quality of mercy—the word "mightiest" is repeated twice—suggests the gentleness and subtlety of that power by use of the light syllables, while by the diction he indicates the greatness of the power. To the student who would protest that this analysis attributes too much thoughtful technique to the poet, we would answer that few poets (perhaps none) undertake this process consciously. The techniques once learned and mastered, a good poet almost instantly and unconsciously selects those which will most effectively express his intention, both in diction and prosody.

HISTORIC EXAMPLES OF BLANK VERSE

The passages included in Exercises 14–20, beginning with Surrey and ending with Eliot and Wallace Stevens, show the development of English blank verse. For purposes of comparison, each passage on which an exercise is based is ten lines long. In preparation for the critical examination of each passage, the student should (1) copy the passage and scan it, indicating foot endings; (2) mark substitutions and feminine endings to the left of the passage, as in the example above; (3) make a table of percentages of substitutions and feminine endings, as shown. Since correct scansion depends on correct pronunciation, the student should look up any words or names about whose pronunciation he is uncertain; some frequently mispronounced words are *italicized* in the passages below.

EXERCISE 14

Forthwith Fame flieth through the great Libyan towns,
A mischief Fame, there is none else so swift;
That moving grows, and flitting, gathers force:
First small for dread, soon after climbs the skies,
Stayeth on earth, and hides her head in clouds.
Whom our Mother the Earth, tempted by wrath
Of gods, begat: the last sister, they write,
To *Coeus*, and to Enceladus eke;
Speedy of foot, of wing likewise as swift,
A monster huge, and dreadful to describe.

From Henry Howard, Earl of Surrey, *Aeneid*, *c.* 1540, Bk. IV

223. Fame is what we now call Rumor.
230. Enceladus: We do not know how Surrey pronounced Latin, but the pronunciation "Éncĕládŭs" produces more accurate verse than the modern pronunciation "Ĕncélădŭs."

Was this the face that launch'd a thousand ships,
And burnt the topless towers of Ilium?
Sweet Helen, make me immortal with a kiss.
Her lips suck forth my soul; see where it flies!
Come, Helen, come, give me my soul again.
Here will I dwell, for Heaven is in these lips,
And all is dross that is not Helena.
I will be Paris, and for love of thee,
Instead of Troy, shall Wittenberg be sack'd:
And I will *combat* with weak *Menelaus*.

From CHRISTOPHER MARLOWE, *Doctor Faustus*, *c.* 1593, Sc. XIII

∧ Nów | hāst thóu | bŭt óne | bāre hōur | tŏ líve,|
And then thou must be damn'd perpetually!
Stand still, you ever-moving spheres of Heaven,
That time may cease, and midnight never come;
Fair Nature's eye, rise, rise again, and make
Perpetual day; or let this hour be but
A year, a month, a week, a natural day,
That Faustus may repent and save his soul!
. . .
The stars move still, time runs, the clock will strike,
The Devil will come, and Faustus must be damn'd.

Ibid., Sc. XIV

After scanning the three passages and tabulating the substitutions, comment in separate paragraphs on the relationships (if any) between substitutions made and the content of each of the passages.

The Effect of Cadence on the Pattern of Blank Verse

In the development of blank verse, the earliest verse is characterized by end-stopping (see END-STOPPED LINE). It is apparently easier for the writer who is inexperienced in handling the pentameter line to think and express himself in units of five feet. A "normal" pattern of terminal pauses for blank verse might be considered to be a pause at the end of each line. But just as, with practice, writers learn freer and more effective use of metrical substitution, with the development of skill and ease in writing blank verse they begin to omit the end-stopping and to replace the more "normal" light medial pause with a heavy one (see CESURA). Light or brief pauses in the reading of a line of verse should be indicated by a slanting mark drawn through the line: /. Heavy or long

58. This line is an example of INITIAL TRUNCATION. The light syllable of the first iambic foot has been omitted.

pauses should be indicated by a double slanting mark: //. In the passage from *The Merchant of Venice* (p. 61), pauses might be marked in this way:

> The quality of mercy is not strain'd.//
> It droppeth as the gentle rain from heaven
> Upon the place beneath.// It is twice blest://

It should be noted that the placement of pauses is the significant factor in the sound of the verse, rather than the foot marks, which are not heard as such and are used as a convenient mark of measurement (like the bar mark in a musical score). Because line 185, in the passage given, is a run-on line, it is *heard* as a unit of eight feet followed (the second part of line 186) by a unit of two feet. In this way, the expected "normal" CADENCES—two passages of five iambic feet—become one of eight and another of two. Variety in the length of cadences is another way in which the poet may achieve special effects. Variety may also be achieved by the use of brief or light pauses at the end of the line instead of heavy end-stopping, as in lines 191 and 192:

> The attribute to awe and majesty,/
> Wherein doth sit the dread and fear of kings;//

In the examples from *The Merchant of Venice*, pauses occur at the ends of metrical feet only. It is possible, however, for a poet to alter or even reverse his "normal" metrical pattern, as the ear hears it, by the placement of pauses *within* a foot:

> The barge she sat in, like a burnish'd throne,/
> Búrn'd ŏn | thĕ wá|tĕr.// Thĕ póop | wăs béat|ĕn góld;|//
> Purple the sails,/ and so perfumed that
> The winds were lovesick with them;// the oars were silver,/
> Which to the tune of flutes kept stroke / and made
> The water which they beat to follow faster,/
> As amorous of their strokes.// For her own person,/
> Ĭt bég|găr'd áll | dĕscríp|tĭon.// Shé | dĭd líe|
> Ĭn hér | păvíl|iŏn,/ clóth-|ŏf-góld | ŏf tís|sŭe,/
> O'er-picturing that Venus where we see
> . . .

From WILLIAM SHAKESPEARE, *Antony and Cleopatra*, *c.* 1606, II, ii

In line 197 an anapest is substituted in the third foot, but the substitution is heard rather as a feminine ending followed by a heavy pause and succeeded by an iambic foot. In line 203 a similar effect is obtained by the use of a heavy pause in the middle of the fourth iambic foot. Again, in line 204 a light pause divides the third foot.

The following passage also illustrates how the placement of the pauses can alter the effect of the meter:

> There would have been a time for such a word.//
> Tomor|row,/ and | tomor|row,/ and | tomor|row,
> Creeps in this petty pace from day to day
> To the last syllable of recorded time;//
> And all our yesterdays have lighted fools
> The way to dusty death.// Out,/ out,/ brief candle!//
> Life's but a walking shadow,/ a poor player,/
> That struts and frets his hour upon the stage
> And then is heard no more.// It is a tale
> Told by | an id|iot,/ full | of sound | and fu|ry,/
> . . .

From William Shakespeare, *Macbeth*, *c.* 1606, V, v

In line 19, scansion shows the substitution of pyrrhics in the second and fourth foot and a feminine ending. The placement of the pauses turns the line, as actually heard, into one composed of an amphibrach (◡ ⊥ ◡) and two anapests, each followed by a feminine ending:

> Tomorrow,/ and tomorrow,/ and tomorrow,

This technique (as well as the verbal repetition with which it is combined) emphasizes the everlasting and monotonous return of "tomorrow." In line 23 the use of several cesuras breaks the spondaic

> Out, out

to lengthen the spondee even more and to emphasize the rhetorical command, while the image of a candle flickering out is reinforced by the feminine ending followed by a heavy pause. In line 27 the initial trochaic substitution and the use of the pause in the middle of the third foot convert the basic iambic line into one that *sounds* entirely trochaic, to complement the emphasis of the sound and fury.

In determining the pauses, students reading aloud should, of course, note the pauses indicated by punctuation. Light pauses, however, may occur where no punctuation is indicated. The pauses made in reading aloud will reflect the interpretation of the meaning of the passage.

In Exercise 15 and all future exercises, pauses should be indicated and additions be made to the table of metrical substitutions as follows:

Antony and Cleopatra

No. of pauses	13
End-stop: heavy	1
End-stop: light	5
Medial pauses	7
Heavy	4
Light	3
Midfoot	3

Macbeth

No. of pauses	13
End-stop: heavy	3
End-stop: light	2
Medial pauses	8
Heavy	2
Light	6
Midfoot	5

EXERCISE 15

The endeavour of this present breath may buy
That honour which shall bate his scythe's keen edge,
And make us heirs of all eternity.
Therefore, brave conquerors,—for so you are,
That war against your own affections*
And the huge army of the world's desires,—
Our late edict shall strongly stand in force:
Navarre shall be the wonder of the world;
Our court shall be a little *Academe*,
Still and *contemplative* in living art.

From WILLIAM SHAKESPEARE, *Love's Labour's Lost*, *c.* 1590, I, i

He jests at scars that never felt a wound.
But soft! What light through yonder window breaks?
It is the East, and Juliet is the sun!
Arise, fair sun, and kill the envious moon,
Who is already sick and pale with grief
That thou, her maid, art far more fair than she.
Be not her maid, since she is envious.
Her vestal livery is but sick and green,
And none but fools do wear it. Cast it off.
It is my lady; O, it is my love!

From WILLIAM SHAKESPEARE, *Romeo and Juliet*, *c.* 1595, II, ii

To be, or not to be: that is the question:
Whether 'tis nobler in the mind to suffer
The slings and arrows of outrageous fortune,

* **affections:** In the sixteenth–seventeenth century this word was pronounced as though it had four syllables: "af-féc-ti-ons." Other words ending in "-tion" probably had similar pronunciation.

Or to take arms against a sea of troubles,
And by opposing end them. To die: to sleep;
No more; and by a sleep to say we end
The heart-ache, and the thousand natural shocks
That flesh is heir to, 'tis a consummation
Devoutly to be wish'd. To die, to sleep;
To sleep: perchance to dream: ay, there's the rub;

From WILLIAM SHAKESPEARE, *Hamlet*, *c.* 1602, III, i

Our revels now are ended. These our actors,
As I foretold you, were all spirits, and
Are melted into air, into thin air;
And, like the baseless fabric of this vision,
The cloud-capp'd towers, the gorgeous palaces,
The solemn temples, the great globe itself—
Yea, all which it inherit—shall dissolve,
And, like this insubstantial pageant faded,
Leave not a rack behind. We are such stuff
As dreams are made on, and our little life
[Is rounded with a sleep.]*

From WILLIAM SHAKESPEARE, *The Tempest*, *c.* 1610, IV, i

Scan the four passages from Shakespeare and make up tables for substitutions and pauses (see pp. 61 and 66). Bear in mind here and in subsequent exercises that pronunciation may be affected by the nationality of the author (British or American), and that a correct pronunciation at the date of writing may differ from modern pronunciation. Look up italicized words.

Comment on the relevance of significant metrical substitutions to the intended effect of the passage. Do you note any development in the metrical techniques employed in the successive passages?

After all the technical work in this exercise has been completed, use the tables of scansion and those of pauses, together with the passages themselves, to study the development of the techniques of blank verse in Shakespeare. (Note that the passages are marked with approximate dates of composition.) In a brief essay, discuss the development you observe, relating the use of various techniques to the content of the passage. In writing this essay, great care should be taken to avoid simple restatement in words of the statistics exhibited in the tables of analysis.

EXERCISE 16

Take the two passages from Marlowe in Exercise 14, and carefully read them aloud, marking the pauses. Set up tables of pauses for these passages like

* Omit in scansion exercise.

those on p. 66. On the basis of your tables for Exercises 14–16 and your interpretation of the development of Shakespeare's blank verse, write an essay comparing the blank verse of Marlowe with that of Shakespeare. Note that Marlowe's play was written at approximately the same time as the two early passages from Shakespeare and much earlier than *Hamlet* or *The Tempest*. The work of Shakespeare, therefore, cannot be simply evaluated as a whole, but must be considered with reference to the suggested dates.

EXERCISE 17

On alternate lines of wide-spaced theme paper, put down the pattern of normal iambic pentameter:

◡ ´ | ◡ ´ | ◡ ´ | ◡ ´ | ◡ ´ |

Underneath the normal pattern, write ten original lines of blank verse. Limit your substitutions to approximately the number you have found in general use in the works of the sixteenth-century poets you have analyzed. Try to develop an idea in appropriate modern diction and word order. Before handing in your work, copy it out and mark it with the actual scansion you hear in it. Tabulate the substitutions and feminine endings for your own work, as in the model on p. 61. Be prepared to comment in class on the problems you encountered in doing this exercise and to evaluate your verse in comparison with the passages you have analyzed.

EXERCISE 18

At the beginning of *Paradise Lost*, Milton wrote:

THE VERSE

The measure is English heroic verse without rhyme, as that of Homer in Greek, and of Virgil in Latin; rhyme being no necessary adjunct or true ornament of poem or good verse, in longer works especially, but the invention of a barbarous age, to set off wretched matter and lame metre; graced indeed since by the use of some famous modern poets, carried away by custom, but much to their own vexation, hindrance, and constraint to express many things otherwise, and for the most part worse than else they would have expressed them. Not without cause therefore some both Italian and Spanish poets of prime note have rejected rhyme both in longer and shorter works, as have also long since our best English tragedies, as a thing of itself, to all judicious ears, trivial and of no true musical delight; which consists only in apt numbers,* fit quantity* of syllables, and the sense variously drawn out from one verse into another, not in the jingling sound of like endings,

* See Glossary for definitions.

a fault avoided by the learned ancients both in poetry and all good oratory. This neglect then of rhyme so little is to be taken for a defect, though it may seem so perhaps to vulgar readers, that it rather is to be esteemed an example set, the first in English, of ancient liberty recovered to heroic poem from the troublesome and modern bondage of rhyming.

In a letter to his friend J. H. Reynolds, Keats wrote in 1819:

I have given up Hyperion—there were too many Miltonic inversions in it—Miltonic verse cannot be written but in an artful or rather artist's humour. I wish to give myself up to other sensations. English ought to be kept up. It may be interesting to you to pick out some lines from Hyperion and put a mark × to the false beauty proceeding from art, and one || to the true voice of feeling. Upon my soul 'twas imagination I cannot make the distinction— Every now and then there is a Miltonic intonation— But I cannot make the division properly.

To George and Georgiana Keats, the poet later in the same year (September, 1819) wrote:

I shall never become attach'd to a foreign idiom so as to put it into my writings. The Paradise Lost though so fine in itself is a corruption of our language—it should be kept as it is unique—a curiosity, a beautiful and grand curiosity. The most remarkable production of the world—a northern dialect accommodating itself to Greek and Latin inversions and intonations. The purest English I think—or what ought to be the purest—is Chatterton's. The language had existed long enough to be entirely uncorrupted of Chaucer's gallicisms and still the old words are used. Chatterton's language is entirely northern. I prefer the native music of it to Milton's cut by feet. I have but lately stood on my guard against Milton. Life to him would be death to me. Miltonic verse cannot be written but in the vein of art—I wish to devote myself to another sensation.

The following excerpts illustrate the two poets' practice:

. . .
Weighs his spread wings, at leisure to behold
Far off th'empyreal Heav'n extended wide
In circuit, undetermin'd square or round,
With opal tow'rs and battlements adorn'd
Of living sapphire, once his native seat;
And fast by, hanging in a golden chain,
This pendent world, in bigness as a star
Of smallest magnitude close by the moon.
Thither full fraught with mischievous revenge,
Accurst, and in a cursed hour he hies.

From JOHN MILTON, *Paradise Lost*, *c.* 1660, Bk. II

Deep in the shady sadness of a vale
Far sunken from the healthy breath of morn,
Far from the fiery noon, and eve's one star,
Sat gray-hair'd Saturn, quiet as a stone,
Still as the silence round about his lair;
Forest on forest hung about his head
Like cloud on cloud. No stir of air was there,
Not so much life as on a summer's day
Robs not one light seed from the feather'd grass,
But where the dead leaf fell, there did it rest.

From JOHN KEATS, *Hyperion*, *c.* 1820, I

Analyze the passages from Milton's *Paradise Lost* and Keats' *Hyperion* for meter and pauses. Consider the diction used in relation to the content of the passages. In *Paradise Lost*, Milton is describing Satan who has come from Hell to investigate a "world" he has heard about and the possibility of taking revenge against God through injury to the new creature of this world: man. In *Hyperion*, Keats is describing the deposed Saturn, an ancient Greco-Roman god, a Titan whom Jupiter succeeded. *Paradise Lost* is a complete epic poem in twelve books. *Hyperion* was projected as an epic, but the two drafts were broken off after a few pages; the poem was never completed.

After careful analysis of the two passages, write a short essay in answer to the question: Is *Hyperion* Miltonic? Consider what Keats may have meant by the term "Miltonic." Evaluate the number, kind, and appropriateness of the INVERSIONS in both passages. Before concluding your essay, express a considered opinion about Keats' decision to "give up" *Hyperion*. Do you believe that the poem in complete form would have been a successful original epic, or an imitation of Milton's epic? Why?

EXERCISE 19

The old order changeth, yielding place to new,
And God fulfils himself in many ways,
Lest one good custom should corrupt the world.
Comfort thyself; what comfort is in me?
I have lived my life, and that which I have done
May He within himself make pure! but thou,
If thou shouldst never see my face again,
Pray for my soul. More things are wrought by prayer
Than this world dreams of. Wherefore, let thy voice
Rise like a fountain for me night and day.

From ALFRED, LORD TENNYSON, *Idylls of the King: The Passing of Arthur*, 1869

. . .
To let a truth slip. Don't object, "His works
Are here already; nature is complete:
Suppose you reproduce her (which you can't)
There's no advantage! you must beat her, then."
For, don't you mark? we're made so that we love
First when we see them painted, things we have passed
Perhaps a hundred times nor cared to see;
And so they are better, painted—better to us,
Which is the same thing. Art was given for that;
God uses us to help each other so.

From ROBERT BROWNING, *Fra Lippo Lippi*, 1855

But swinging doesn't bend them down to stay.
Ice-storms do that. Often you must have seen them
Loaded with ice a sunny winter morning
After a rain. They click upon themselves
As the breeze rises, and turn many-colored
As the stir cracks and crazes their enamel.
Soon the sun's warmth makes them shed crystal shells
Shattering and avalanching on the snow-crust—
Such heaps of broken glass to sweep away
You'd think the inner dome of heaven had fallen.

From ROBERT FROST, *Birches*, 1916

. . .
Again; and he rode on, under the stars,
Out of the world, into he knew not what,
Until a vision chilled him and he saw,
Now as in Camelot, long ago in the garden,
The face of Galahad who had seen and died,
And was alive, now in a mist of gold.
He rode on into the dark, under the stars,
And there were no more faces. There was nothing.
But always in the darkness he rode on,
Alone; and in the darkness came the Light.

From EDWIN ARLINGTON ROBINSON, *Lancelot*, 1920, IX

Analyze and compare the blank-verse passages of Tennyson and Robinson. Both passages are excerpts from long poems: in Tennyson, King Arthur, dying, speaks to his faithful knight Sir Bedivere; in Robinson, Lancelot, denied the achievement of the Holy Grail because of his adulterous relationship with Arthur's queen, Guinevere, rides off into the darkness.

After reading *Fra Lippo Lippi* and *Birches* in their entirety in an anthology or the collected works of Browning and Frost, analyze and compare the two excerpts from these poems. Special attention should be given to the use of conversational or colloquial DICTION. What effect does the diction have on the passages?

TWENTIETH-CENTURY EXAMPLES OF BLANK VERSE

A number of twentieth-century poets express discomfort in using blank verse, characterizing it as an outworn tradition; they complain that its relative looseness makes it easy to write but difficult to write well. After a careful examination of the variety achieved in this meter in earlier centuries, it is easy to understand the frustration of the modern poet who feels that everything possible has already been done with this meter. Major poets of the twentieth century have, however, put blank verse to significant use. Seeking "the old way to be new," Robert Frost, who more often rhymes, wrote *The Gift Outright* in unrhymed iambic pentameter, though his iambics are almost as irregular as Spender's in *The Express* (see Exercise 4); Frost's poem includes only three wholly iambic lines (6, 13, 15).

THE GIFT OUTRIGHT

The land | was ours | before | we were | the land's.|
She was | our land | more than | a hun|dred years|
Before | we were | her peo|ple. She | was ours|
In Massachusetts, in Virginia,
But we were England's, still colonials,
Possess|ing what | we still | were un|possessed | by,
Possessed by what we now no more possessed.
Something we were withholding made us weak
Until we found out that it was ourselves
We were | withhold|ing from | our land | of liv|ing,
And forth|with found | salva|tion in | surren|der.
Such as we were we gave ourselves outright
(The deed | of gift | was man|y deeds | of war)|
To the land vaguely realizing westward,
But still | unsto|ried, art|less, un|enhanced,|
Such as she was, such as she would become.

ROBERT FROST (1874–1963)

Trochees help to underscore the syntax of contrast in lines 1–3. Probably the idea of the whole—the vagueness of the early American's allegiance, the formlessness of the country—is reinforced by the irregular meter and the feminine endings of lines 6, 10, 11.

We have chosen *The Gift Outright* to discuss because it is short enough to be reprinted in its entirety. Two longer and more famous poems by Frost—*The Death of the Hired Man* and *"Out, Out—,"* in which a boy using a buzz saw loses his hand, and, shortly after, his life, in an accident—illustrate still other important aspects of Frost's modern use of blank verse: its adaptability to the rhythms of ordinary conversation in the first poem, and to machine-age subject matter in the second. Although the conversational method was surely used by Shakespeare and, more recently, by Browning, Frost speaks in the idiom of our own century.

A number of other contemporary poets have adopted and extended these potentials of blank verse: indeed, this antique and once rather "grand" verse form has become, in the hands of many twentieth-century poets, a vehicle for commenting upon modern society's most jejune aspects. T. S. Eliot and Hart Crane are among those who illustrate this kind of blank verse. Printed below, for comparison, are the first two strophes of a poem of Crane's and one of Eliot's:

The mind | has shown | itself | at times|
Too much | the baked | and la|beled dough|
Divided by accepted multitudes.
Across the stacked partitions of the day—
Across the memoranda, baseball scores,
The stenographic smiles and stock quotations
∧ Smut|ty wings | flash out | equiv|oca|tions.

The mind is brushed by sparrow wings;
Numbers, rebuffed by asphalt, crowd
The margins of the day, accent the curbs,
Convoy|ing di|vers dawns | on ev|ery cor|ner
To druggist, barber and tobacconist,
Until the graduate opacities of evening
Take them | away | as sud|denly | to some|where
Virginal | perhaps,| less frag|mentar|y, cool.|

From HART CRANE (1899–1932), *For the Marriage of Faustus and Helen*

MORNING AT THE WINDOW

They are rat|tling break|fast plates | in base|ment kitch|ens,
And along the trampled edges of the street
I am | aware | of the | damp souls | of house|maids
Sprouting despondently at area gates.

The brown | ∧ waves | of fog | toss up | to me|
Twisted | faces | from the bot|tom of | the street,|
And tear | from a pas|ser-by | with mud|dy skirts|
An aimless smile that hovers in the air
And van|ishes | along | the lev|el of | the roofs.|

T. S. ELIOT (1888–1965)

The similarity between these two pieces of blank verse makes very evident the influence of Eliot upon Crane. Both poems contain numerous metrical irregularities—feminine endings that give an inconclusiveness to the whole; very conspicuous substituted feet, such as spondees and anapests, in places, such as the third or fourth foot, that make them even more so (see Crane's lines 7, 15; Eliot's lines 3, 5, 6, 7); occasional variations in line length (the first two lines in both of Crane's strophes have four feet; Eliot's last line has six feet). Even before noticing the specific metrical similarities, of course, the reader is struck by the similarity in diction. Both poets juxtapose commonplace concrete items ("memoranda," "baseball scores," "barber and tobacconist," "basement kitchens," "housemaids") with semi-abstractions that create mood ("stacked partitions of the day," "opacities of evening," "damp souls . . . sprouting despondently"). Both poems seem to evoke city streets haunted by rather bedraggled bourgeois ghosts.

It is perhaps germane to our discussion of prosody to observe that, despite such a noteworthy point of contact between the two poets as these poems demonstrate, Crane and Eliot later veered off in different prosodic directions. Crane tended to remain within the iambic framework, generally pentameter and generally rhymed, throughout his career. Some critics consider him at his best and most "natural" when using iambic pentameter in the grand manner of Elizabethans like Marlowe and Jonson. Eliot tended more and more to invent his own forms, though drawing upon the conventions of meter and rhyme in doing so.

Wallace Stevens, too often regarded only as a poet of remarkable sound effects, is termed by Harvey Gross* "the superlative master" of blank verse.

* Harvey Gross, *Sound and Form in Modern Poetry* (Ann Arbor: University of Michigan Press, 1964), p. 18.

Other critics, including Yvor Winters, have acclaimed Stevens' use of the form "Shakespearean." One suspects that the latter critics are linking Stevens with Shakespeare by way of compliment rather than objective comparison, for Wallace Stevens' blank verse is like that of no one else. It is true that he shares with Shakespeare and many other poets the conviction that blank verse is a natural idiom for some of his most personal utterances.

A rising to climactic abandon is characteristic of much of Stevens' blank verse. The following poem, for example, starts as a philosophical argument and ends in a blast of rowdy music:

A HIGH-TONED OLD CHRISTIAN WOMAN

Poetry | is the | supreme | fiction,| madame.|
∧ Take | the mor|al law | and make | a nave | of it | *or:* Take the mor
And from the nave build haunted heaven. Thus,
The conscience is converted into palms,
Like windy citherns hankering for hymns.
We agree | in prin|ciple.| That's clear.| But take|
The oppos|ing law | and make | a per|istyle,|
And from the peristyle project a masque
Beyond | the plan|ets. Thus,| our bawd|iness,|
Unpurged by epitaph, indulged at last,
Is equally converted into palms,
Squiggling like saxophones. And palm for palm,
Madame, we are where we began. Allow,
Therefore, that in the planetary scene
Your disaffected flagellants, well-stuffed,
Smacking their muzzy bellies in parade,
Proud of such novelties of the sublime,
Such tink | and tank | and tunk-|a-tunk-|tunk,|
May, mere|ly may,| madame,| whip from | themselves|
A jovial hullabaloo among the spheres.
This will make widows wince. But fictive things
Wink as | they will.| Wink most | when wid|ows wince.|

WALLACE STEVENS (1879–1955)

Scansion of this poem is difficult, for there are several lines (2, 6, 7) in which initial anapests (◡ ◡ ⊥) might also be read: stress, light syllable, stress (⊥ ◡ ⊥). Also, there are many spondees and trochees in the third or fourth feet, where they are particularly conspicuous (see lines 1, 6, 19, and 22). The last foot of line 18 contains only one syllable: "tunk." As we have seen, such irregularities in themselves could not produce the "jovial hullabaloo" of this poem, for Crane and other very different poets use them too. The effect comes from the metrical irregularities *plus* many other factors: the smuggling of "squiggling saxophones" into the dignified company of "heaven" and "moral law"; the comic yet surrealistic scene of flagellants whacking their fat complacent bellies instead of each other's lean backs; most of all, the totally undignified "tink and tank and tunk-a-tunk-tunk," whose merry music the last two lines carry out with a burst of alliteration (eight *w*'s) and assonance (eleven short *i*'s). The speaker in the poem laughs at "moral law," at organized religion, by making the "music of the spheres" a most unseemly tune; it is fitting that the poet makes dignified blank verse dance to it, winking at the wincing widow all the while.

EXERCISE 20

Assemble the passages of blank verse you have analyzed thus far, beginning with Surrey's *Aeneid.* Using the analyses and essays you have already prepared, write a paper tracing the development of blank verse from Surrey's initial experiment to the twentieth century, terminating with the work of Stevens. What do you consider to be the "future" of blank verse?

V

The Development of Pentameter Couplet

In the verse of the Old English period, terminal rhyme is virtually unknown, but in the twelfth and thirteenth centuries, with the emergence of verse in Middle English, examples of the use of rhyme appear in lyrics by anonymous poets, in Layamon's *Brut*, and in other works as well. The first major poet who uses rhyme consistently in both long and short poems is Chaucer, whose early poetry (*e.g.*, *The Legend of Good Women*, *c.* 1385) shows the strong influence of his French predecessors. In *The Canterbury Tales*, however, he not only explores the versatility of the pentameter line but also makes use of the COUPLET rhyme for most of the tales.

The materials of the *Tales*, as the excerpts on p. 78 may suggest, vary—descriptive, expository, argumentative, narrative—and, as one would expect, the techniques of versification vary also. But Chaucer was not a theorist; we have no essays in which he explains his consciousness of his metrical experiments. An examination of the *Tales* shows that, while he uses the couplet rhyme (both masculine and feminine; see under RHYME), he never fixed upon a set pattern for the placement of medial or terminal pauses, and makes frequent use of feminine endings. The type of couplet he favored, characterized by ENJAMBEMENT, or the run-on line, is called *open couplet* (see under COUPLET). Since the time of Chaucer, it has had a long history, as the examples below will demonstrate.

HISTORIC EXAMPLES OF PENTAMETER COUPLET: OPEN COUPLET

Whan that Aprill with his shoures soote
The droghte of March hath perced to the roote, — *feminine rhyme*
And bathed every veyne in swich licour
Of which vertu engendred is the flour;
Whan Zephirus eek with his sweete breeth
Inspired hath in every holt and heeth
The tendre croppes, and the yonge sonne
Hath in the Ram his halve cours yronne, — *feminine rhyme*
And smale foweles maken melodye,
That slepen al the nyght with open ye — *feminine rhyme*
. . .

From Geoffrey Chaucer, *The Canterbury Tales: General Prologue*, c. 1387

And up they stirte, al dronken in this rage,
And forth they goon towardes that village
Of which the taverner hadde spoke biforn.
And many a grisly ooth thanne han they sworn,
And Cristes blessed body al torente—
Deeth shal be deed, if that they may hym hente!
Whan they han goon nat fully half a mile,
Right as they wolde han troden over a stile,
An oold man and a povre with hem mette.
This olde man ful mekely hem grette,
. . .

From Geoffrey Chaucer, *The Pardoner's Tale*, c. 1393

Tho to the greene wood they speeden hem all,
To fetchen home May with their musicall;
And home they bringen in a royall throne,
Crowned as king; and his queene attone
Was Lady Flora, on whom did attend
A fayre flocke of faeries, and a fresh bend
Of lovely nymphs. (O that I were there,
To helpen the ladyes their Maybush beare!)
Ah Piers, bene not thy teeth on edge, to thinke,
How great sport they gaynen with little swinck?

1. soote: sweet. **6. holt:** woodland.
710. hente: catch.
27. Tho: then. **30. attone:** together. **35. bene:** are. **36. swinck:** toil.

PIERS

Perdie so farre am I from envie,
That their fondnesse inly I pitie.

From EDMUND SPENSER, *The Shepherd's Calendar: May*, 1579

This gallant pins the wenches on his sleeve.
Had he been Adam, he had tempted Eve.
He can carve too, and lisp: why, this is he
That kiss'd his hand away in courtesy;
This is the ape of form, monsieur the nice,
That, when he plays at tables, chides the dice
In honourable terms: nay, he can sing
A mean most meanly, and, in ushering,
Mend him who can: the ladies call him, sweet;
The stairs, as he treads on them, kiss his feet.

minor-accent rhyme* (he / courtesy)

minor-accent rhyme (sing / ushering)

From WILLIAM SHAKESPEARE, *Love's Labour's Lost*, *c.* 1590, V, ii

Let man's soul be a sphere, and then, in this,
The intelligence that moves, devotion is;
And as the other spheres, by being grown
Subject to foreign motions, lose their own,
And being by others hurried every day,
Scarce in a year their natural form obey:
Pleasure or business, so, our souls admit
For their first mover, and are whirl'd by it.
Hence is't, that I am carried towards the west
This day, when my soul's form bends toward the east.

assonantal rhyme* (this / is)

consonantal rhyme* (west / east)

From JOHN DONNE, *Good Friday, 1613. Riding Westward*

Could all this be forgotten? Yes, a schism
Nurtured by foppery and barbarism,
Made great Apollo blush for this his land.
Men were thought wise who could not understand
His glories: with a puling infant's force
They sway'd about upon a rocking horse,
And thought it Pegasus. Ah dismal soul'd!
The winds of heaven blew, the ocean roll'd
Its gathering waves—ye felt it not. The blue
Bared its eternal bosom, and the dew

* See under RHYME. Rhymes other than accurate masculine should be noted, and their effect on the poem or passage studied.

Of summer nights collected still to make
The morning precious: beauty was awake!
Why were ye not awake? But ye were dead
To things ye knew not of,—were closely wed
To musty laws lined out with wretched rule
And compass vile: so that ye taught a school
Of dolts to smooth, inlay, and clip, and fit,
Till, like the certain wands of Jacob's wit,
Their verses tallied. Easy was the task:
A thousand handicraftsmen wore the mask
Of Poesy. Ill-fated, impious race!
That blasphemed the bright Lyrist to his face,
And did not know it,—no, they went about,
Holding a poor, decrepid [*sic*] standard out
Mark'd with most flimsy mottos, and in large
The name of one Boileau!

From JOHN KEATS, *Sleep and Poetry*, 1817

The student may be interested in comparing the passage from *Sleep and Poetry*, both in form and content, with Pope's "rules" for the closed or HEROIC COUPLET as formulated in a letter (p. 93) and in *An Essay on Criticism* (pp. 17ff., 93f.), as well as with some other examples of his practice (pp. 14ff., 94).

The history of the open pentameter couplet breaks off temporarily in the practice of major poets early in the seventeenth century, when Jonson and Dryden began to work with the closed or heroic couplet, which will be treated in the second part of this chapter. Toward the end of the eighteenth century, the Preface to the *Lyrical Ballads* (1798) heralded a revolt not only against the subject matter and diction of Pope (see Chapter II) but also against the end-stopped form. The excerpt from Keats' *Sleep and Poetry* (1817) documents this revolt; Keats' first long poem, *Endymion* (1818), was written in open couplet. In this form, the individual line and the couplet rhyme are not emphasized, and the effect of the enjambement is to create a kind of VERSE PARAGRAPH, similar to the paragraphing achieved in the blank verse of the mature Shakespeare and of Milton, but with the addition of rhyme. The handling of pauses in the open couplet is similar, also, to the pauses of blank verse. Comparable, perhaps, to the freedom of cadence in the excerpt given on p. 67 from *The Tempest* are the passages below:

There was a Being whom my spirit oft
Met on its visioned wanderings, far aloft,
In the clear golden prime of my youth's dawn,
Upon the fairy isles of sunny lawn,
Amid the enchanted mountains, and the caves

Of divine sleep, and on the air-like waves
Of wonder-level dream, whose tremulous floor
Paved her light steps;—on an imagined shore,
Under the gray beak of some promontory
She met me, robed in such exceeding glory,
[That I beheld her not.]*

From PERCY BYSSHE SHELLEY, *Epipsychidion*, 1821

The woods were long austere with snow: at last
Pink leaflets budded on the beach, and fast
Larches, scattered through pine-tree solitudes,
Brightened, "as in the slumbrous heart o' the woods
Our buried year, a witch, grew young again
To placid incantations, and that stain
About were from her cauldron, green smoke blent
With those black pines!"—so Eglamor gave vent
To a chance fancy. Whence a just rebuke
From his companion; brother Naddo shook
. . .

From ROBERT BROWNING, *Sordello*, 1840, Bk. II

The following passage is included here as an illustration of the way rhymed verse should be marked.

a A thing of beauty is a joy for ever:
a Its loveliness increases; it will never — feminine rhyme
b Pass into nothingness; but still will keep
b A bower quiet for us, and a sleep
c Full of sweet dreams, and health, and quiet breathing.
c Therefore, on every morrow, are we wreathing — feminine rhyme
d A flowery band to bind us to the earth,
d Spite of despondence, of the inhuman dearth
e Of noble natures, of the gloomy days,
e Of all the unhealthy and o'erdarkened ways
. . .

From JOHN KEATS, *Endymion*, 1818, I

In the exercise that follows and in all future exercises where rhyme is part of the pattern of the verse, rhymes should be indicated, and the type of rhyme, when it is not accurate masculine, should be shown: feminine rhyme, minor-accent rhyme, approximate (consonantal or assonantal) rhyme. Because rhyme is determined by sound, not by spelling, and by stress, all work done with rhymed verse should be read aloud. The relationship of the rhyme to end-stopping or enjambement is also significant. In the passage from Keats only

* Omit this line in scansion exercise.

lines 1 and 5 have full stops. Throughout the passage the use of run-on lines, together with the two pairs of feminine rhymes, contributes to the paragraphing of the verse, the free development of an idea. When the technical work on passages to be studied has been completed, the tables of scansion, pauses, and rhymes should be carefully examined in the light of the *content* of the passage to determine whether these techniques work toward the intended effect or against it. Technical analysis in and for itself is of no value. The devices of prosody are not external to what the poet wishes to convey; they are essential to its communication. Were he to use different devices, what he would convey would be different too.

EXERCISE 21

Using all the techniques of analysis for blank verse, scan the passages from Shakespeare, Donne, Shelley, and Browning, and set up tables similar to those used in the preparation of analysis of blank verse. In addition, note the number and use of terminal rhymes other than those of the accurate masculine type. Consider carefully the relationship of these rhymes to the content and intended effect of the passage in which they appear: Shakespeare is describing an Elizabethan gallant in a play; Donne is meditating on the significance of Good Friday as he rides in the direction of the setting sun (Son); while Shelly is contemplating a personified ideal Beauty, and Browning is chiefly concerned with the description of scenery. The differences in effect between a rhyme followed by a pause and one which is part of a run-on line should be observed, since a rhyme followed by a pause tends to be more heavily stressed and therefore more noticeable to the reader. What similarities in technique do you notice between open-couplet pentameter and the blank verse you have studied? What differences? What effects do you think can be achieved with the rhymed forms that are not available to blank verse?

EXERCISE 22

Put down the pattern of normal iambic pentameter with couplet rhyme, leaving wide spaces between the lines:

a ∪ ⊥ | ∪ ⊥ | ∪ ⊥ | ∪ ⊥ | ∪ ⊥ |

a ∪ ⊥ | ∪ ⊥ | ∪ ⊥ | ∪ ⊥ | ∪ ⊥ |

Underneath the normal pattern, write at least ten original lines of open pentameter couplet. Limit your substitutions approximately to the number you have found in general use in the passages you have analyzed, and try to follow the general average of run-on lines and accurate masculine rhyming. Try to develop your idea in appropriate modern diction and word order. Before handing in your work, copy it out and mark it with the actual scansion and rhymes you hear in it. Add the statistical tables for your own work as you did in the passages in Exercise 21. Be prepared to comment in class on the problems you encountered in doing this exercise and to evaluate your verse in comparison with the passages you have analyzed.

TWENTIETH-CENTURY EXAMPLES OF PENTAMETER COUPLET: OPEN COUPLET

An early modern experiment with the open couplet is Robinson's *The Man Against the Sky*, 1916. In this work by a meticulous craftsman, the line length varies from pentameter to tetrameter to dimeter, while a basic pentameter is maintained to indicate the stumbling, groping progress, both spiritual and physical, of the man. In the same way, and probably for the same reason, the basic couplet structure of the rhymes begins to break in line 13, with the minor-accent "imaginings," and the *c* rhyme of line 14, which is not picked up again until lines 20 and 22, trimeter lines that express the restlessness and loneliness of the seeker. Line 15 does not find its rhyming partner until line 18, where the four-line passage ends with a definitive statement, an accurate masculine rhyme, and a long pause, marked by a semicolon. But even within this four-line group, the spiritual uncertainty is indicated by the rhyming of a tetrameter line, line 16, with the pentameter, line 17. In lines 19 and 21, accurate pentameter rhyming is used, but these lines alternate with two trimeter *c* rhymes, and there the passage closes—its prosody as deliberately uncertain as the spiritual progress of the man against the sky.

a^5 Dark, marvelous, and inscrutable he moved on
a^5 Till down the fiery distance he was gone,
b^5 Like one of those eternal, remote things
b^5 That range across a man's imaginings
c^5 When a sure music fills him and he knows
d^5 What he may say thereafter to few men,—
e^4 The touch of ages having wrought
e^5 An echo and a glimpse of what he thought
d^5 A phantom or a legend until then;
f^5 For whether lighted over ways that save,
c^3 Or lured from all repose,
f^5 If he go on too far to find a grave,
c^3 Mostly alone he goes.

From EDWIN ARLINGTON ROBINSON, *The Man Against the Sky*, 1916

Frost, in 1936, in the brief poem *Moon Compasses*, shows that he can handle the conventional open couplet, but in 1942, in *A Considerable Speck*, he carries on the experiments of Robinson for his own purposes.* The whole poem is in regular iambic pentameter, and the first six lines are in the traditional open couplet with accurate masculine rhymes. Line 8, however, ends in a word, "mite" (marked *e*), which has no rhyme to couple with it in the entire poem of thirty-three lines: it signals the poet's realization that what he has before him is a living particle, not a dust speck; the surprise of the rhymeless line conveys, in part, the surprise of the poet. From this point onward, the rhymes alternate and vary, as the "considerable speck" moves, halts, races, across the manuscript page on which the poet is writing. But with the resolution of his ideas on the observed action of the thoughtful speck—because he recognizes this creature as a being with a mind—the rhymes become accurate open couplets once more.

MOON COMPASSES

I stole forth dimly in the dripping pause — approximate rhyme?
Between two downpours to see what there was.
And a masked moon had spread down compass rays
To a cone mountain in the midnight haze,
As if the final estimate were hers, — minor-accent rhyme
And as it measured in her calipers,
The mountain stood exalted in its place.
So love will take between the hands a face. . . .†

1936 — ROBERT FROST (1874–1963)

A CONSIDERABLE SPECK (MICROSCOPIC)

a A speck that would have been beneath my sight
a On any but a paper sheet so white
b Set off across what I had written there.
b And I had idly poised my pen in air
c To stop it with a period of ink
c When something strange about it made me think.
d This was no dust speck by my breathing blown,
e But unmistakably a living mite
d With inclinations it could call its own.
f It paused as with suspicion of my pen,
f And then came racing wildly on again
g To where my manuscript was not yet dry;
h Then paused again and either drank or smelt—

* Another interesting modern use of open pentameter couplet can be seen in Robert Lowell's *The Mills of the Kavanaughs*, 1946 (see p. 238).

† The punctuation is Frost's; the poem is printed complete.

g With loathing, for again it turned to fly.
h Plainly with an intelligence I dealt.
i It seemed too tiny to have room for feet,
i Yet must have had a set of them complete
g To express how much it didn't want to die.
j It ran with terror and with cunning crept.
k It faltered: I could see it hesitate;
i Then in the middle of the open sheet
j Cower down in desperation to accept
k Whatever I accorded it of fate.
l I have none of the tenderer-than-thou
m Collectivistic regimenting love
j With which the modern world is being swept.
l But this poor microscopic item now!
m Since it was nothing I knew evil of
j I let it lie there till I hope it slept.
n I have a mind myself and recognize
n Mind when I meet with it in any guise.
o No one can know how glad I am to find
o On any sheet the least display of mind.

1942 ROBERT FROST (1874–1963)

The work of Robert Lowell offers an interesting glimpse of a poet in the process of prosodic growth. In his first major publication, *Lord Weary's Castle*, 1944, Lowell's metrics—as well as his diction, in general—are characterized by thorough traditionalism. For example, in "Katherine's Dream," given below, the speaker writhes in a nightmare, but her voice is heard in exact masculine rhymed couplets of fairly regular iambic pentameter:

It must have been a Friday. I could hear
The top-floor typist's thunder and the beer
That you had brought in cases hurt my head;
I'd sent the pillows flying from my bed,
I hugged my knees together and I gasped.
The dangling telephone receiver rasped
Like someone in a dream who cannot stop
For breath or logic till his victim drop
To darkness and the sheets. I must have slept,
But still could hear my father who had kept
Your guilty presents but cut off my hair.
He whispers that he really doesn't care
If I am your kept woman all my life,
Or ruin your two children and your wife;
But my dishonor makes him drink. Of course

I'll tell the court the truth for his divorce.
I walk through snow into St. Patrick's yard.
Black nuns with glasses smile and stand on guard
Before a bulkhead in a bank of snow,
Whose charred doors open, as good people go
Inside by twos to the confessor. One
Must have a friend to enter there, but none
Is friendless in this crowd, and the nuns smile.
I stand aside and marvel; for a while
The winter sun is pleasant and it warms
My heart with love for others, but the swarms
Of penitents have dwindled. I begin
To cry and ask God's pardon of our sin.
. . .

From ROBERT LOWELL, *Between the Porch and the Altar* (1944), III, "Katherine's Dream"

Critics have wondered whether regular iambic pentameter couplets, even open ones, as most of them are in this poem, are the accurate form for nightmare. In a review, the poet William Carlos Williams wrote that Lowell's lines seem to be trying to escape from the rhyme. Critics have also suggested that certain words and phrases—"really" in line 12, "of course" in line 15, "on guard" in line 18, for example—appear simply because of the need for five feet. (Lowell has attracted a considerable amount of perhaps carping criticism because he, like Theodore Roethke, seems to be emerging as a major poet of the twentieth century.) Lowell's collection *For the Union Dead*, published in 1964, twenty years after *Lord Weary's Castle*, seems to mark the poet's escape both from regular rhyme scheme and from a total commitment to iambic pentameter. *The Public Garden* is a particularly interesting example, for it is a reworking of a much earlier, much longer, poem.

THE PUBLIC GARDEN

a^{5} Burnished, burned-out, still burning as the year
b^{4} you lead me to our stamping ground.
b^{5} The city and its cruising cars surround
c^{4} the Public Garden. All's alive—
c^{5} the children crowding home from school at five,
$a?\ d?^{5}$ punting a football in the bricky air,
e^{5} the sailors and their pick-ups under trees

f^5 with Latin labels. And the jaded flock
f^4 of swanboats paddles to its dock.
g^2 The park is drying.
h^4 Dead leaves thicken to a ball
d^5 inside the basin of a fountain, where
d^4 the heads of four stone lions stare
i^4 and suck on empty fawcets. Night
j^4 deepens. From the arched bridge, we see
k^5 the shedding park-bound mallards, how they keep
i^5 circling and diving in the lanternlight,
l^5 searching for something hidden in the muck.
m^5 And now the moon, earth's friend, that cared so much
n^5 for us, and cared so little, comes again—
o^4 always a stranger! As we walk,
o^2 it lies like chalk
b^5 over the waters. Everything's aground.
p^4 Remember summer? Bubbles filled
b^4 the fountain, and we splashed. We drowned
q^5 in Eden, while Jehovah's grass-green lyre
r^5 was rustling all about us in the leaves
$b?^5$ that gurgled by us, turning upside down . . .
b^5 The fountain's failing waters flash around
q^4 the garden. Nothing catches fire.

1964 ROBERT LOWELL (1917–)

The rhyme scheme is complicated, involving neither couplets nor real interlocking rhyme, yet giving the appearance of both: *abbcc(d)effghddij*, and so on. The lines, still basically iambic, contain numerous spondaic substitutions and vary in length from five to two feet, a flexibility which allows the poet to break in on a rather idyllic fall scene in the park with a frightening reassessment of autumn and its meaning: "The park is drying." The abruptness of this line, or of line 22, "it lies like chalk," when one would have expected the moon to have a more lyrical, more fluid effect on the scene, is an important phase in the shifting attitudes that constitute the poem. Yet Lowell is still what we are calling a "traditionalist." He has developed, from the forms of the past and within them, a form to suit his present subject.

Archibald MacLeish also introduces a flexible rhyme scheme and varying line lengths into rhymed iambic verse in *The Silent Slain.*

THE SILENT SLAIN

a^5 We too, we too, descending once again
b^5 The hills | of our | own land,| we too | have heard|
a^5 Far off—Ah, que ce cor a longue haleine— (approximate rhyme)
a^6 The horn of Roland in the passages of Spain,
b^5 The first, the second blast, the failing third,
c^5 And with the third turned back and climbed once more
d^5 The steep road southward, and heard faint the sound
c^5 Of swords, of horses, the disastrous war,
d^5 And crossed the dark defile at last, and found
a^5 At Roncevaux upon the darkening plain
d^6 The dead against the dead and on the silent ground
a^2 The silent slain—

ARCHIBALD MACLEISH (1892–)

Though the poem is distinctly iambic, there are numerous spondaic substitutions (in the first two lines alone there are four striking spondees and there is another in line 3), and the line, though basically pentameter, sometimes attains a length of six feet (lines 4 and 11) and sometimes dwindles to two (line 12). Justification for both irregularities can easily be made: the spondees convey the ghostly marching surely going on in the poem; the long line 4 illustrates the "longue haleine"—the long breath—of Roland's distant horn; the long line 11 points up the abruptness, the deathly silence, of the last line. But it is probably the irregularity of the rhyme scheme that causes the reader to mistake the poem for blank verse at first glance. Yet the rhyme scheme is far from being a loose one, since it employs only four rhyme sounds, but these appear at irregular intervals (*abaabcdcdada*) in run-on lines.

HISTORIC EXAMPLES OF PENTAMETER COUPLET: CLOSED OR HEROIC COUPLET

The pentameter couplet followed another major line of development, that of the *closed couplet* (see under COUPLET), of which the first illustrious example occurs in Spenser's satirical work of 1591, *Mother Hubberd's Tale.*

3. "Ah, what a long sound that horn has." Phonetic transcription: [ɑ kɔ sɔ kɔ:ʀ a lɔ̃:g alɛn].

Although Spenser is not regarded primarily as a satirist, he appears to have been the first poet to use the end-stopped couplet with a preponderance of accurate masculine rhymes for satiric purposes. An illustration of his work is given below, as is later work in the same pattern by Ben Jonson. Although the satiric use of the end-stopped "heroic" couplet is usually credited to Pope, who developed this form to its greatest excellence, the skill of his predecessors, Spenser, Jonson, Waller, and, notably, Dryden, should not be overlooked.

Whilome (said she) before the world was civill,
The Foxe and th'Ape, disliking of their evill
And hard estate, determined to seeke
Their fortunes farre abroad, lyeke with his lyeke:
For both were craftie and unhappie witted;
Two fellowes might no where be better fitted.
The Foxe, that first this cause of griefe did finde,
Gan first thus plaine his case with words unkinde.
Neighbour Ape, and my gossip eke beside,
(Both two sure bands in friendship to be tide),
To whom may I more trustely complaine
The evill plight that doth me sore constraine,
And hope thereof to finde due remedie?
Heare then my paine and inward agonie.
Thus manie yeares I now have spent and worne,
In meane regard, and basest fortunes scorne,
Dooing my countrey service as I might,
No lesse I dare saie than the prowdest wight;
And still I hoped to be up advaunced,
For my good parts; but still it hath mischaunced.

From Edmund Spenser, *Mother Hubberd's Tale,* 1591

ON SOMETHING THAT WALKS SOMEWHERE

At court I met it, in clothes brave enough,
To be a courtier; and looks grave enough,
To seem a statesman: as I near it came,
It made me a great face; I ask'd the name.
A lord, it cried, buried in flesh and blood,
And such from whom let no man hope least good,
For I will do none: and as little ill,
For I will dare none. Good Lord, walk dead still.

c. 1612 Ben Jonson (1572–1637)

48. lyeke: like with his like, each one with one of his own kind. **52. plaine:** complain. **53. gossip:** friend.

TO JOHN DONNE

Donne, the delight of Phoebus and each Muse,
Who, to thy one, all other brains refuse;
Whose every work, of thy most early wit,
Came forth example, and remains so, yet:
Longer a knowing, than most wits do live;
And which no affection praise enough can give!
To it, thy language, letters, arts, best life,
Which might with half mankind maintain a strife;
All which I meant to praise, and, yet, I would;
But leave, because I cannot as I should!

BEN JONSON (1572–1637)

And they who write to Lords, rewards to get,
Are they not like singers at doors for meat?
And they who write, because all write, have still
That excuse for writing, and for writing ill;
But he is worst, who (beggarly) doth chaw
Others' wits' fruits, and in his ravenous maw
Rankly digested, doth those things out-spew,
As his own things; and they are his own, 'tis true,
For if one eat my meat, though it be known
The meat was mine, th'excrement is his own.

From JOHN DONNE, *Satire II, c.* 1593

Dryden believed that only Edmund Waller (1606–1687) had surpassed Spenser in the harmony of his verse. Pope later expressed a similar view in *An Essay on Criticism* (II, 360–361):

And praise the easy vigour of a line,
Where Denham's* strength and Waller's sweetness join.†

In the preface to Waller's posthumous poems, 1690, we find this account of his work:

He was indeed the parent of English verse, and the first that showed us our tongue had beauty and numbers‡ in it. . . . The tongue came into his hands like a rough diamond; he polished it first, and to that degree, that all artists since him have admired the workmanship without pretending to mend it. . . . He undoubtedly stands first in the list of refiners, and for aught I know, last, too. . . . We are no

1. The English metaphysical poet, 1572–1631, is apostrophized here.
* Denham was a seventeenth-century poet, best known for a descriptive poem, *Cooper's Hill*, 1642.
† Students of the eighteenth century believe that in the correct pronunciation of the period "join" was "jine."
‡ In the critical vocabulary of the eighteenth century, "numbers" refers to what we now call "meter" or "scansion."

less beholden to him for the new turn of verse which he brought in, and the improvement he made in our numbers. Before his time men rhymed, indeed, and that was all: as for the harmony of measure, and that dance of words which good ears are so much pleased with, they knew nothing of it. Their poetry then was made up almost entirely of monosyllables, which, when they come together in any cluster, are certainly the most harsh, untunable things in the world. . . . There was no distinction of parts, no regular stops, nothing for the ear to rest upon. But as soon as the copy began, down it went like a larum, incessantly; and the reader was sure to be out of breath before he got to the end of it: so that really verse in those days was but downright prose, tagged with rhymes. Mr. Waller removed all these faults, brought in more polysyllables and smoother measures, bound up his thoughts better and in a cadence more agreeable to the nature of the verse he wrote in: so that wherever the natural stops of that were, he contrived the little breakings of his sense so as to fall in with them. And for that reason, since the stress of our verse lies commonly upon the last syllable, you will hardly ever find him using a word of no force there.

Here is a sampling of Waller's closed couplets:

So earnest with thy God, can no new care,
No sense of danger interrupt thy pray'r?
The sacred Wrestler, till a blessing giv'n,
Quits not his hold, but halting conquers Heav'n:
Nor was the stream of thy devotion stopp'd,
When from the body such a limb was lopp'd,
As to thy present state was no less maim,
Though thy wise choice has since repair'd the same.
Bold Homer durst not so great virtue feign
In his best pattern: of Patroclus slain,
. . .

From EDMUND WALLER, *Of His Majesty's Receiving the News of the Duke of Buckingham's Death*, c. 1645

Saintsbury, in his life of Dryden, describes Dryden's use of the couplet in this way:

In versification the great achievement of Dryden was the alteration of what may be called the balance of the line, causing it to run more quickly, and to strike its rhymes with a sharper and less prolonged sound. One obvious means of obtaining this end was, as a matter of course, the isolation of the couplet, and the avoidance of overlapping the different lines one upon the other. . . . [Open couplets] are less well suited for satire, for argument, and for the moral reflections which the age of Dryden loved. He, therefore, set himself to elaborate the couplet with its sharp point, its quick delivery, and the pistol-like detonation of its rhyme. But there is

10. Achilles was, to Homer, "his best pattern."

> an obvious objection, or rather there are several obvious objections which present themselves to the couplet. It was natural that to one accustomed to the more varied range of the older rhythm and metre, there might seem to be a danger of the snip-snap monotony into which, as we know, it did actually fall when it passed out of the hands of its first great practitioners. There might also be a fear that it would not always be possible to compress the sense of a complete clause within the narrow limits of twenty syllables. To meet these difficulties Dryden resorted to three mechanical devices—the hemistich, the alexandrine, and the triplet;* all three of which could be used indifferently to eke out the space or to give variety of sound. . . . In poetry proper the hemistich is anything but pleasing, and Dryden, becoming convinced of the fact, almost discarded it. The alexandrine and the triplet he always continued to use.

For a time, Dryden attempted to use the heroic couplet in his plays, and in his *Essay on Heroic Plays*, 1672, he wrote, "Whether Heroic Verse ought to be admitted into serious plays, is not now to be disputed; 'tis already in possession of the stage; and I dare confidently affirm, that very few tragedies, in this age, shall be received without it." He wrote perhaps five plays using couplets, but by 1678, in *All for Love*, he returned to blank verse. His most important use of the couplet in nondramatic verse was in satire:

Of these the false Achitophel was first,
A name to all succeeding ages curst.
For close designs and crooked counsels fit,
Sagacious, bold, and turbulent of wit,
Restless, unfixt in principles and place,
In pow'r unpleased, impatient of disgrace;
A fiery soul, which, working out its way,
Fretted the pigmy body to decay:
And o'er-informed the tenement of clay.
A daring pilot in extremity;
Pleased with the danger, when the waves went high
He sought the storms; but, for a calm unfit,
Would steer too nigh the sands to boast his wit.

From JOHN DRYDEN, *Absalom and Achitophel*, 1681, I

Pope's "Rules" for the Heroic Couplet

Pope aspired to be a "correct" poet, and he believed that all the GENRES of English poetry could be rendered in the heroic couplet, without the use of

* See ALEXANDRINE and *triplet* (under STANZA) in the Glossary. *Hemistich* here means a fragmentary line.

other forms. He was, however, aware that lack of skill in handling this form resulted in awkwardnesses.

In a letter to Cromwell,* in 1710, Pope enunciated certain rules:

> 1. As to the hiatus,† it is certainly to be avoided as often as possible; but on the other hand, since the reason of it is only for the sake of the numbers, so if, to avoid it, we incur another fault against their smoothness, methinks the very end of that nicety is destroyed. . . .
>
> 2. I would except against all expletives in verse, as *do* before verbs plural, or even the frequent use of *did* and *does* to change the termination of the rhyme. . . .
>
> 3. Monosyllable lines, unless very artfully managed, are stiff, languishing, and hard.
>
> 4. The repeating of the same rhymes within four or six lines of each other, which tire the ear with too much of the like sound, [is objectionable].
>
> 5. [Also to be avoided is] the too frequent use of alexandrines which are never graceful but‡ when there is some majesty added to the verse by them, or when there cannot be found a word in them but what is absolutely needful.
>
> 6. Every nice ear must, I believe, have observed that in any smooth English verse of ten syllables, there is naturally a pause either at the fourth, fifth, or sixth syllable. . . . Now I fancy that, to preserve an exact harmony and variety, none of these pauses should be continued above three lines together, without the interposition of another: else it will be apt to weary the ear with one continued tone.

Although the heroic couplet is usually attributed to Pope, it is clear that a development toward this form preceded him by several centuries. The most obvious characteristic of the heroic couplet (as distinguished from the open couplet found in Chaucer's *Canterbury Tales*) is the end-stopping of both lines, with heavy end-stopping at the close of the couplet. It is notable that Pope's "rules" make no mention of enjambement or end-stopping. The following excerpts show the use of the heroic couplet by Pope himself and by Byron:

These equal syllables alone require,
Though oft the ear the open vowels tire;
While expletives their feeble aid do join;
And ten low words oft creep in one dull line:
While they ring round the same unvaried chimes,
With sure returns of still expected rhymes;
Where'er you find "the cooling western breeze,"
In the next line, it "whispers through the trees":
If crystal streams "with pleasing murmurs creep,"
The reader's threaten'd (not in vain) with "sleep":

* Henry Cromwell, an elderly friend of Pope's who frequented the coffee houses.

† See Glossary for definition.

‡ *but* here means "except."

Then, at the last and only couplet fraught
With some unmeaning thing they call a thought,
A needless alexandrine ends the song,
That, like a wounded snake, drags its slow length along.

From ALEXANDER POPE, *An Essay on Criticism*, 1711, II

And now, unveil'd, the toilet stands display'd,
Each silver vase in mystic order laid.
First, robed in white, the nymph intent adores,
With head uncover'd, the cosmetic powers.
A heav'nly image in the glass appears,
To that she bends, to that her eyes she rears;
Th'inferior priestess, at her altar's side,
Trembling begins the sacred rites of Pride.
Unnumber'd treasures ope at once, and here
The various off'rings of the world appear.

From ALEXANDER POPE, *The Rape of the Lock*, 1712 (rev. 1714), Canto I

Come, Abelard! for what hast thou to dread?
The torch of Venus burns not for the dead.
Nature stands check'd; Religion disapproves;
Ev'n thou art cold—yet Eloisa loves.
Ah hopeless, lasting flames! like those that burn
To light the dead and warm th'unfruitful urn.
What scenes appear where'er I turn my view?
The dear Ideas, where I fly, pursue,
Rise in the grove, before the altar rise,
Stain all my soul, and wanton in my eyes.

From ALEXANDER POPE, *Eloisa to Abelard*, 1717

Behold! in various throngs the scribbling crew,
For notice eager, pass in long review:
Each spurs his jaded Pegasus apace,
And rhyme and blank maintain an equal race;
Sonnets on sonnets crowd, and ode on ode;
And tales of terror jostle on the road;
Immeasurable measures move along;
For simpering folly loves a varied song,
To strange mysterious dulness still the friend,
Admires the strain she cannot comprehend.

From George Gordon, LORD BYRON, *English Bards and Scotch Reviewers*, 1809

EXERCISE 23

Scan the passages from Dryden, Pope, and Byron, and indicate both medial and terminal pauses. Set up tables for these as you have done for the passages in blank verse, and indicate types of rhyme. Use only the first ten lines from Pope's *Essay on Criticism* and from Dryden's *Absalom and Achitophel*, so that your statistical tables will be comparable. Examine the rhymes used. Are they always masculine and accurate? Are they all in couplet? What effect do the rhymes have on the passages selected?

The three passages from Pope are excerpts from three different kinds of work: an essay in verse, a mock-heroic epic satire, and a romantic verse-letter purporting to have been written by one of the most famous ladies of history to her beloved after he left her. Dryden, using a Biblical story for symbolic purposes, is engaged in contemporary satire of a political figure. Byron, a century later than Pope, comments on the popular literature of his time, including the "tales of terror," or Gothic novels.

To what extent and with what effect do the three poets, Dryden, Pope, and Byron, follow the theory of end-stopping within and at the end of each couplet? In completing this exercise, take the rules from Pope's letter and apply them to the three passages of his work. To what extent does he follow or violate his own prescriptions? What effect does this conformity or lack of conformity have on the passages? Byron learned the technique of the heroic couplet from Pope. Examine the passage from Byron in the light of Pope's rules. To what extent does he observe the conventions of end-stopping in the heroic couplet? What effects does Byron achieve through the use of these devices?

EXERCISE 24

With the help of the examples given in this chapter, write one heroic couplet, according to Pope's rules and epigrammatic style. Although Pope, following French usage, speaks of the decasyllabic couplet, the meter he used, in keeping with a general trend in English verse, was basically iambic pentameter. In attempting to find a suitable "subject" for your couplet, consider proverbs, platitudes and familiar moral statements not expressed in couplet form, *e.g.*, "A rolling stone gathers no moss," or "Honesty is the best policy." Mark your couplet for its meter, pauses, and rhyme. Be prepared to discuss in class the difficulties that you encountered in writing your couplet. To what extent do you think you succeeded in solving the problems presented by this form?

TWENTIETH-CENTURY EXAMPLES OF PENTAMETER COUPLET: CLOSED OR HEROIC COUPLET

The significant poets of the nineteenth century preferred to work in open couplet, and it is difficult to find examples of the closed or heroic couplet in the twentieth century. Karl Shapiro's *Essay on Rime* (1945) is a kind of modern *Essay on Criticism*, but the form used is open couplet. W. H. Auden, however, in the two poems given below has made interesting adaptations of the couplet, in the tradition of Dryden:

ADOLESCENCE

a˘ By landscape reminded / once of / his mother's figure*/
a˘ The mountain heights / he remembers get bigger and bigger://
b˘ With the finest of mapping pens / he fondly traces
b˘ All the | family | names / on | the famil|iar plac|es.//

c˘ Among | green pas|tures stray|ing he walks | by still wat|ers;
c˘ Surely | a swan | he seems |/ to earth's | unwise daugh|ters,/
d˘ Bending | a beau|tiful head,|/ worshipping |/ not ly|ing,/
d˘ "Dear" / the | dear beak |/ in the dear | concha | crying.|//

e˘ Under the trees the summer bands were playing;//
e˘ "Dear boy,|/ be brave | as these roots," |/ he heard | them say|ing://
f˘ Carries the good news gladly / to a world in danger,/
f˘ Is ready to argue,/ he smiles,/ with any stranger.//

g˘ And yet this prophet,/ homing the day is ended,/
g˘6 Receives | odd wel|come / from | the coun|try he so | defend|ed://
h˘6 The band | roars / "Cow|ard,/ Cow|ard,"/ in | his hu|man fe|ver,/
h˘ The gi|antess shuf|fles near|er,/ cries |/ "Deceiv|er."//

W. H. AUDEN (1907–)

Although this poem is spaced in four stanzas, analysis shows it to be organized in pentameter closed couplets, with feminine rhymes throughout. The effect of these feminine rhymes is to emphasize the adolescent's uncertainty. There are also a number of unusual substitutions, especially in lines 5–9, which sound almost like alexandrines; but the two real alexandrines are lines 14 and 15. While these substitutions, a marked departure from the technique used by

* In American pronunciation the rhyme of "figure" and "bigger" is approximate, but in British pronunciation it is an accurate feminine rhyme. The mark for an unstressed syllable after a rhyme notation (as in *a*˘) signifies a feminine rhyme.

Dryden, accord with the tone of doubt and confusion of the poem, the end-stopped couplets signify that, even as the adolescent's doubts are part of the normal process of maturation, the irregularities of the verse are contained in a well-known and common framework.

PETITION

a	Sir,/ no man's enemy,/ forgiving all	
a	But will its negative inversion,/ be prodigal://	minor-accent rhyme
b	Send to us power and light,/ a sovereign touch/	
b	Curing the intolerable neural itch,/	consonance
c[4]	The exhaus|tion of wean|ing,/ the li|ar's quin|sy,/	
c	And the | distor|tions of in|grown virgin|ity.|//	feminine, related sound
d	Prohibit sharply the rehearsed response/	
d	And gradually correct the coward's stance;//	consonance
e	Cover in time with beams those in retreat/	
e	That, spot|ted,/ they turn |/ though the | reverse | were great;|//	consonance
f	Publish each healer that in city lives/	
f	Or country houses / at the end of drives;//	consonance
g	Harrow | the house | of the dead;|// look shin|ing at|	
g	New styles | of ar|chitec|ture,/ a change | of heart.|//	minor-accent, related sound

W. H. AUDEN (1907–)

In this poem, one possible reading has been indicated above. All lines except 1 and 13 have some pause at the end, but there is no full stop between line 2 and the end of line 6. The technique suggests that the poem is a petition, as the title says, and that the petitioner expects, but does not entirely trust, an affirmative answer. His doubts are further indicated by the variety of rhymes. There is not a single pair of accurate masculine rhymes in the poem, and in two places the end words—"quinsy" and "virginity" and, notably, at the end, "at" and "heart"—can only be described as having related sound patterns. Nearly all lines are some sort of pentameter, but the substitutions are unusual, especially in the lines marked with scansion; indeed some lines sound like tetrameter, though only line 5 actually is. Internal pauses (cesuras) are notably few, so that the full line length is heard. The end pauses, however, are usually maintained, as the petitioner keeps his petition within limits, although asking for what he believes he needs. The final couplet ends the poem with the definiteness of the final *t*, but with the indefiniteness of the minor accent and of the coupling of "at" with the *rt* of "heart." The prosody, like the diction, expresses hope and doubt, conveys petition not yet answered.

VI

The Ballad and the Quatrain

To define the term "ballad" is notoriously difficult. One reason for the difficulty may be that most English-speaking people, as a result of listening to folk music and to contemporary hit-parade sagas of violence and unrequited passion on radio and television, and of being exposed in school to some of the ballads, have a sort of feeling for what a ballad is. They know one when they hear one, and no definition can be made to cover all the vaguely felt ways by which this recognition is achieved. In this book, the Glossary attempts to define the ballad in terms of its traditional subject matter and its basic stanza forms, $a^4 b^3 c^4 b^3$ or $a^4 b^4 a^4 b^4$.

THE POPULAR BALLAD AND THE LITERARY BALLAD

Scholars have long been fascinated by the body of half-oral and half-written, half-literary and half-musical, material that constitutes the *popular ballad* (see under BALLAD). The mere existence, over a period of many centuries and over a wide geographical spread, of compositions which, despite being anonymous, have specific types of subject matter and a very definite formal pattern arouses speculation. The popular ballad comes to us by way of a long oral tradition. We do not know the names of the authors of these works, but the likelihood is that, composed long ago, they were sung for centuries before they were first written down. During that period they were probably not regarded seriously as literature—a possible reason for the lack of written recording. Most of the ballads we now have were first recorded about two hundred years ago, when a combination of circumstances produced a sudden interest in popular culture.

Two aspects of the rise of romanticism in the late eighteenth century were a romanticizing of medieval works and a romanticizing of the interests of the common people. Collecting and recording of popular ballads from people who knew and sang them from memory and from old manuscripts became a respectable literary and scholarly occupation. The antiquary Bishop Thomas Percy collected three volumes, *Reliques of Ancient English Poetry* (1765), the most famous and influential of the eighteenth-century collections. Another important stimulus to interest in ballad lore was the publication in 1802–03 of a collection of ballads—some of them authentic popular ballads, some "retouched," and perhaps some original—by Sir Walter Scott, called *Minstrelsy of the Scottish Border*.

Ballad scholarship falls into two main categories: that which seeks to know origins of the tradition, and that which is devoted to compiling versions of the extant ballads. The outstanding scholar of the ballad, Francis James Child, worked in the latter category. In five volumes entitled *English and Scottish Popular Ballads* (1882–98), Child attempted to include every existing version of every ballad. In his compilation there are, for example, eighteen differing versions of *Sir Patrick Spence*, drawn from manuscripts of which the earliest is dated 1765; Child suggests in an introductory note that the historical event which may have stimulated this song occurred in the latter part of the thirteenth century. But the most significant aspect of Child's work does not consist in such theorizing about the origin of the song as a song, but in the concrete task of assembling actual manuscripts. Of these, the oldest—*Judas*—dates from the thirteenth century; the next oldest is from the mid-fifteenth. Some texts of the Robin Hood ballads and a few others are from the sixteenth century, but, in all, only eleven manuscripts antedate the 1650 Folio, which was used by Bishop Percy and which Child considered the most important. Most of the ballad collections from which Child drew were compiled in the eighteenth and nineteenth centuries.

Apparently Child believed that he had succeeded in including in his book all known ballads, as well as a few songs which he felt might not, strictly speaking, fall into that category. More recent scholars point out that the ballad tradition—far from being closed in the late nineteenth century—is still continuing prolifically, hence that "Child's Ballads" cannot be regarded as a complete canon; his compilation remains, however, the most thorough and exhaustive in the field.

A recently published companion piece to Child's great work, Bertrand Harrison Bronson's *The Traditional Tunes of the Child Ballads*, vigorously reminds students of the ballad that they are dealing with an oral and musical, as well as a written, tradition. In his insistence on the ballad as a sung form, Bronson touches upon the other side of scholarly interest in the popular ballad, the ballad's beginnings. The tune of the ballad, he maintains, with its pattern most typically one of four, three, four, and three beats, must have predated (and thus controlled) the words. For evidence he points to the frequency with which the recognizable end of a musical phrase substitutes for exact rhyme:

> "O dinna ye mind, young man," said she,
> "When ye was in the tavern a-drinking,
> That ye made the healths gae round and round,
> And slighted Barbara Allan?"

He also cites the obvious melodic and rhythmic, rather than story-telling, function of many ballad REFRAINS:

> Seven lang years he served the King,
> *With a hey lillelu and a how lo lan;*
> And it's a' for the sake of his dochter Jean,
> *And the birk and the brume blooms bonnie.*

It might further be pointed out in support of the music-first theory that the arrangement of beats found in the ballad is also found in many nonballads, *e.g.*, the common hymn and some traditional blues melodies, even those without words.

Numerous scholars concur that the subject and tone of the ballad, as well as its form, result at least partly from its belonging to an oral tradition, no matter whether the words or the music came first. For a work to be remembered and repeated, its subject must be universal; hence the ballad's recurrent themes of painful love, violence in man and nature, family discord, and the trials and achievements of work; hence, too, much rough sexual humor and the preoccupation with supernatural objects of fascination and fear. On the other hand, memories are imperfect and tastes differ; hence the additions, omissions, and other changes leading to the existence of multiple versions of the same ballad. But if the song is to be remembered as a song and not merely as a story, it must also have a simple, catchy form; hence the frequent use of refrains, which can be sung even when the rest of the words are forgotten, and the convenient restriction to only two basic ballad patterns, which allows a considerable number of ballads to be sung to the same tunes.

Other scholars have explored, less fruitfully, the question of precisely what was responsible for the springing up of the ballad tradition and have tried to determine when the first ballads appeared. Several theories are significant:

1. The idea that balladry developed in the Middle Ages, possibly as early as 1000 A.D., as an outgrowth or poor man's version of the medieval romance. This theory relies for support primarily on the similarity in subject matter between certain ballads and certain romances. Objectors to the theory point out that, although the oral ballad is certain to have preceded the written ballad by a long time, there is no concrete evidence for supposing it to have been *that* long a time—most recorded ballads, as was previously noted, dating from the eighteenth and nineteenth centuries, with only a few belonging clearly to the seventeenth or an earlier period. Furthermore, this theory in no way explains the development of the ballad *form*.

2. The "communal theory": the idea that villagers extemporized the earliest ballads as they danced on the village green. The repetitive structure of a number of the ballads is sometimes cited as evidence for this theory. The limited number of compositions of lasting merit that have been spontaneously generated by large groups engaged in dancing may be cited as evidence against it.

3. A conjecture, in direct opposition to the communal theory, that a ballad was composed as an entity by a single author, just as other poems are composed, and that this author then receded into obscurity as the poem was taken over and adapted by the public.

To develop this last idea further, let us suppose that there was *an* original author-composer of each popular ballad that has come down to us marked simply "Anonymous." The original author differed from modern poets only in that his composition was oral and that the method of "publication" was oral transmission. If we call the original author Anonymous A and his ballad the A-form, we may call the first person who heard and learned the ballad, by oral transmission, Anonymous B. Anonymous B may have forgotten part of the ballad he heard in the A-form; he may have learned it incorrectly; he may (in a tradition which had little regard for the sanctity of the work of the original author) have tried to improve the ballad he had heard by additions, substitutions, deletions, or rearrangement. Anonymous B's rendering of the ballad thus becomes the B-form. If we suppose that Anonymous A composed his ballad in the year 1000 and Bishop Percy collected it in 1765, with a whole alphabet of Anonymous poets, singers, and forgetful people altering the A-form, we must conclude that the popular ballad we now have probably has almost no resemblance to Anonymous A's ballad, even though we have available a number of versions.

As Whiting* states, the theory of the single original author eliminates much of the mystery concerning the origin of the ballad, but raises a number of

* B. J. Whiting, ed., *Traditional British Ballads* (New York: Appleton-Century-Crofts, 1955), pp. xi–xii.

other questions, such as: Why did these anonymous poets apparently write only for the lower classes, never for the moneyed gentry? Why did no one, not even their contemporaries, record any of their names?

So far, we have been speaking of the popular ballad, as opposed to the imitation ballad, or *literary ballad* (see under BALLAD). In one respect it is very easy to distinguish between the two types: for the popular ballad no author is known, and thus no certain time or place of origin, whereas for the literary ballad author, date, and locale are known. The literary ballad presents to the scholar none of the popular ballad's mysteries concerning its birth and growth. It does, however, present interesting problems in verse craftsmanship.

The writing of the literary ballad became an acceptable literary or poetic art in the late eighteenth and the nineteenth century, when poets like Scott, Coleridge, Keats, and Rossetti, under the influence of the romantic movement, wanted to imitate the folk art of the popular ballad. Careful poets tried to imitate the subject matter, the approximate rhymes, the inaccuracies of meter of the old ballads. Often these literary ballads are interesting poems, but it is unwise to compare them too rigorously with the popular ballads, which most critics regard as superior. The most significant difference between the two forms is the subjectivity of the literary ballad as compared with the objectivity of the popular ballad. The popular ballad usually begins *in medias res* and ends in catastrophe, without analysis of motivation or meaning. The poets of the literary ballad, by contrast, are artful and subjective: characters are motivated; their actions are explained; the meaning of the catastrophe is explained, moralized upon, or at least strongly suggested.*

One who has studied carefully both types of ballad can usually distinguish between them *without* looking to see whether the signature at the bottom is "Anon." or "Ezra Pound." The processes of their production are evidently quite different: a writer like Scott, despite careful study of both types of ballad, never achieved a convincing equivalent of a popular ballad. Perhaps we are thrown back to the intangible, "felt" distinctions which make defining the ballad a hard task. One purpose of the exercises on both kinds of ballad is to help make these distinctions more specific and concrete.

The student should also notice, in viewing the results of these exercises in the context of analyses done previously, that many techniques used in the popular ballads—approximate rather than accurate rhyme, indeterminate numbers of syllables per line, WRENCHED ACCENTS, and the like—are to be found in serious works by major poets. Once considered signs of ineptitude, rather

* An excellent illustration of this difference is the popular ballad *Edward*, in either its American or its British forms, and the book-length expanded poem by Robinson Jeffers, *Such Counsels You Gave to Me* (see p. 236).

than techniques, these means of achieving variety and subtlety (when skillfully handled) derive some of the respectability which they now enjoy from having been consciously borrowed from the popular ballad by literary imitators.

It is impossible in a text of this scope to include all relevant, or even genuinely representative, ballads. The student is referred to the following books for a more thorough treatment of the popular and literary ballad:

1. British texts

F. J. Child, *English and Scottish Popular Ballads.* 5 vols.; Boston: Houghton, 1882–98.

Thomas Percy, *Reliques of Ancient English Poetry, etc.* 3 vols.; London, 1765. Many subsequent editions, *e.g.,* London: J. M. Dent, 1906, 2 vols.

Walter Scott, *Minstrelsy of the Scottish Border, etc.*, ed. T. F. Henderson. 3 vols.; Kelso, Scotland, 1802–03. Many subsequent editions, *e.g.,* London: William Blackwood, 1902, 4 vols.

2. American texts

Louise Pound, *American Ballads and Songs.* New York: Scribner's, 1922.

3. Combined British and American texts, popular and literary, with some music scores and extensive bibliographies

MacEdward Leach, *The Ballad Book.* New York: Harper, 1955.

Evelyn Kendrick Wells, *The Ballad Tree.* New York: Ronald, 1950.

4. Music texts and recordings

Bertrand Harrison Bronson, *The Traditional Tunes of the Child Ballads.* 3 vols.; Princeton: Princeton University Press, 1959–66.

A List of American Folksongs Currently Available on Records, compiled by the Archive of American Folksong of the Library of Congress. Washington, D.C.: Library of Congress, 1953.

Check-List of Recorded Songs in the English Language in the Archive of American Folk Song, to July, 1940. 3 parts; Washington, D.C.: Library of Congress, Music Division, 1942.

EXAMPLES OF BALLAD TYPES

The ballads on the following pages have been grouped according to theme—each theme a characteristic one for ballad writers—and the various groups have been carefully selected to include both British and American examples of the popular ballad, and recent as well as older examples of British and American literary ballads.

Ballads of the Sea

The anonymous ballad *Sir Patrick Spence*, which does not have an American counterpart in popular balladry, is here grouped with Coleridge's *The Rime of the Ancient Mariner*, which is, among other things, the record of a voyage struck by disaster. Two other literary ballads which unfold dramas of the sea, Longfellow's *The Wreck of the Hesperus* and Dylan Thomas' *Ballad of the Long-Legged Bait*, are presented for comparison.

SIR PATRICK SPENCE

1 The king sits in Dumferling toune,
Drinking the blude-reid wine:
"O whar will I get guid sailor,
To sail this schip of mine?"

2 Up and spak an eldern knicht,
Sat at the kings richt kne:
"Sir Patrick Spence is the best sailor
That sails upon the se."

3 The king has written a braid letter,
And sign'd it wi his hand,
And sent it to Sir Patrick Spence,
Was walking on the sand.

4 The first line that Sir Patrick red,
A loud lauch lauched he;
The next line that Sir Patrick red,
The teir blinded his ee.

5 "O wha is this has don this deid,
This ill deid don to me,
To send me out this time o' the yeir,
To sail upon the se!

6 "Mak hast, mak haste, my mirry men all,
Our guid schip sails the morne."
"O say na sae, my master deir,
For I feir a deadlie storme.

7 "Late late yestreen I saw the new moone,
Wi the auld moone in hir arme,

1. Consult a map of Scotland for the location of Dunfermline, an ancient capital of Scotland. **9. braid:** broad. **14. lauch:** laugh. **16. ee:** eye.

And I feir, I feir, my deir master,
That we will cum to harme."

8 O our Scots nobles wer richt laith
To weet their cork-heild schoone;
But lang owre a' the play wer playd,
Thair hats they swam aboone.

9 O lang, lang may their ladies sit,
Wi thair fans into their hand,
Or eir they se Sir Patrick Spence
Cum sailing to the land.

10 O lang, lang may the ladies stand,
Wi thair gold kems in their hair,
Waiting for thair ain deir lords,
For they'll se thame na mair.

11 Haf owre, haf owre to Aberdour,
It's fiftie fadom deip,
And thair lies guid Sir Patrick Spence,
Wi the Scots lords at his feit.

Anonymous

THE RIME OF THE ANCIENT MARINER*

Part I

An ancient Mariner meeteth three Gallants bidden to a wedding-feast, and detaineth one.

It is an ancient Mariner,
And he stoppeth one of three.
"By thy long grey beard and glittering eye,
Now wherefore stopp'st thou me?

The Bridegroom's doors are opened wide,
And I am next of kin;
The guests are met, the feast is set:
May'st hear the merry din."

He holds him with his skinny hand,
"There was a ship," quoth he.
"Hold off! unhand me, grey-beard loon!"
Eftsoons his hand dropt he.

29. laith: loath. **30. cork-heild schoone:** cork-heeled shoes. **35. or eir:** before.

* Coleridge supplied the marginal glosses. The notes are from R. C. Bald, ed., *Selected Poems of Samuel Taylor Coleridge* (New York: Appleton-Century-Crofts, 1956).

12. Eftsoons: at once.

The Wedding-Guest is spell-bound by the eye of the old seafaring man, and constrained to hear his tale.

He holds him with his glittering eye—
The Wedding-Guest stood still,
And listens like a three years' child:
The Mariner hath his will.

The Wedding-Guest sat on a stone:
He cannot choose but hear;
And thus spake on that ancient man,
The bright-eyed Mariner.

"The ship was cheered, the harbour cleared,
Merrily did we drop
Below the kirk, below the hill,
Below the lighthouse top.

The Mariner tells how the ship sailed southward with a good wind and fair weather, till it reached the Line.

The Sun came up upon the left,
Out of the sea came he!
And he shone bright, and on the right
Went down into the sea.

Higher and higher every day,
Till over the mast at noon——"
The Wedding-Guest here beat his breast,
For he heard the loud bassoon.

The Wedding-Guest heareth the bridal music; but the Mariner continueth his tale.

The bride hath paced into the hall,
Red as a rose is she;
Nodding their heads before her goes
The merry minstrelsy.

The Wedding-Guest he beat his breast,
Yet he cannot choose but hear;
And thus spake on that ancient man,
The bright-eyed Mariner.

The ship driven by a storm toward the South Pole.

"And now the Storm-blast came, and he
Was tyrannous and strong:
He struck with his o'ertaking wings,
And chased us south along.

With sloping masts and dipping prow,
As who pursued with yell and blow
Still treads the shadow of his foe,
And forward bends his head,
The ship drove fast, loud roared the blast,
And southward aye we fled.

And now there came both mist and snow,
And it grew wondrous cold:
And ice, mast-high, came floating by,
As green as emerald.

The land of ice, and of fearful sounds where no living thing was to be seen.

And through the drifts the snowy clifts
Did send a dismal sheen:
Nor shapes of men nor beasts we ken—
The ice was all between.

The ice was here, the ice was there,
The ice was all around:
It cracked and growled, and roared and howled,
Like noises in a swound!

Till a great sea-bird, called the Albatross, came through the snow-fog, and was received with great joy and hospitality.

At length did cross an Albatross,
Thorough the fog it came;
As if it had been a Christian soul,
We hailed it in God's name.

It ate the food it ne'er had eat,
And round and round it flew.
The ice did split with a thunder-fit;
The helmsman steered us through!

And lo! the Albatross proveth a bird of good omen, and followeth the ship as it returned northward through fog and floating ice.

And a good south wind sprung up behind;
The Albatross did follow,
And every day, for food or play,
Came to the mariners' hollo!

In mist or cloud, on mast or shroud,
It perched for vespers nine;
Whiles all the night, through fog-smoke white,
Glimmered the white Moon-shine."

"God save thee, ancient Mariner!
From the fiends, that plague thee thus!—
Why look'st thou so?"—"With my cross-bow
I shot the Albatross.

The ancient Mariner inhospitably killeth the pious bird of good omen.

Part II

The Sun now rose upon the right:
Out of the sea came he,
Still hid in mist, and on the left
Went down into the sea.

55. clifts: cliffs. **62. swound:** swoon.

And the good south wind still blew behind,
But no sweet bird did follow,
Nor any day for food or play
Came to the mariners' hollo!

His shipmates cry out against the ancient Mariner, for killing the bird of good luck.

And I had done a hellish thing,
And it would work 'em woe:
For all averred, I had killed the bird
That made the breeze to blow.
Ah wretch! said they, the bird to slay,
That made the breeze to blow!

But when the fog cleared off, they justify the same, and thus make themselves accomplices in the crime.

Nor dim nor red, like God's own head,
The glorious Sun uprist:
Then all averred, I had killed the bird
That brought the fog and mist.
'Twas right, said they, such birds to slay,
That bring the fog and mist.

The fair breeze continues; the ship enters the Pacific Ocean, and sails northward, even till it reaches the Line.

The fair breeze blew, the white foam flew,
The furrow followed free;
We were the first that ever burst
Into that silent sea.

The ship hath been suddenly becalmed.

Down dropt the breeze, the sails dropt down,
'Twas sad as sad could be;
And we did speak only to break
The silence of the sea!

All in a hot and copper sky,
The bloody Sun, at noon,
Right up above the mast did stand,
No bigger than the Moon.

Day after day, day after day,
We stuck, nor breath nor motion;
As idle as a painted ship
Upon a painted ocean.

And the Albatross begins to be avenged.

Water, water, every where,
And all the boards did shrink;
Water, water, every where,
Nor any drop to drink.

The very deep did rot: O Christ!
That ever this should be!
Yea, slimy things did crawl with legs
Upon the slimy sea.

About, about, in reel and rout
The death-fires danced at night;
The water, like a witch's oils,
Burnt green, and blue and white.

A Spirit had followed them; one of the invisible inhabitants of this planet, neither departed souls nor angels; concerning whom the learned Jew, Josephus, and the Platonic Constantinopolitan, Michael Psellus, may be consulted. They are very numerous, and there is no climate or element without one or more.

And some in dreams assurèd were
Of the Spirit that plagued us so;
Nine fathom deep he had followed us
From the land of mist and snow.

And every tongue, through utter drought,
Was withered at the root;
We could not speak, no more than if
We had been choked with soot.

The shipmates, in their sore distress, would fain throw the whole guilt on the ancient Mariner: in sign whereof they hang the dead sea-bird round his neck.

Ah! well a-day! what evil looks
Had I from old and young!
Instead of the cross, the Albatross
About my neck was hung.

Part III

There passed a weary time. Each throat
Was parched, and glazed each eye.
A weary time! a weary time!
How glazed each weary eye,
When looking westward, I beheld
A something in the sky.

The ancient Mariner beholdeth a sign in the element afar off.

At first it seemed a little speck,
And then it seemed a mist;
It moved and moved, and took at last
A certain shape, I wist.

A speck, a mist, a shape, I wist!
And still it neared and neared:
As if it dodged a water-sprite,
It plunged and tacked and veered.

With throats unslaked, with black lips baked,
We could nor laugh nor wail;
Through utter drought all dumb we stood!
I bit my arm, I sucked the blood,
And cried, A sail! a sail!

At its nearer approach, it seemeth him to be a ship; and at a dear ransom he freeth his speech from the bonds of thirst.

With throats unslaked, with black lips baked,
Agape they heard me call:
Gramercy! they for joy did grin,

A flash of joy;

And all at once their breath drew in,
As they were drinking all.

And horror follows. For can it be a ship that comes onward without wind or tide?

See! see! (I cried) she tacks no more!
Hither to work us weal;
Without a breeze, without a tide,
She steadies with upright keel!

The western wave was all a-flame.
The day was well nigh done!
Almost upon the western wave
Rested the broad bright Sun;
When that strange shape drove suddenly
Betwixt us and the Sun.

It seemeth him but the skeleton of a ship.

And straight the Sun was flecked with bars,
(Heaven's Mother send us grace!)
As if through a dungeon-grate he peered
With broad and burning face.

Alas! (thought I, and my heart beat loud)
How fast she nears and nears!
Are those her sails that glance in the Sun,
Like restless gossameres?

And its ribs are seen as bars on the face of the setting Sun. The Spectre-Woman and her Death-mate, and no other on board the skeleton ship. Like vessel, like crew!

Are those her ribs through which the Sun
Did peer, as through a grate?
And is that Woman all her crew?
Is that a Death? and are there two?
Is Death that Woman's mate?

Her lips were red, her looks were free,
Her locks were yellow as gold:
Her skin was as white as leprosy,
The Night-mare Life-in-Death was she,
Who thicks man's blood with cold.

Death and Life-in-Death have diced for the ship's crew, and she (the latter) winneth the ancient Mariner.

The naked hulk alongside came,
And the twain were casting dice;
'The game is done! I've won! I've won!'
Quoth she, and whistles thrice.

No twilight within the courts of the Sun.

The Sun's rim dips; the stars rush out:
At one stride comes the dark;
With far-heard whisper, o'er the sea,
Off shot the spectre-bark.

188. a Death: a skeleton.

We listened and looked sideways up!
Fear at my heart, as at a cup,
My life-blood seemed to sip!
The stars were dim, and thick the night,
The steerman's face by his lamp gleamed white;
From the sails the dew did drip—
Till clomb above the eastern bar
The hornèd Moon, with one bright star
Within the nether tip.

At the rising of the Moon,

One after another,

One after one, by the star-dogged Moon,
Too quick for groan or sigh,
Each turned his face with a ghastly pang,
And cursed me with his eye.

His shipmates drop down dead.

Four times fifty living men
(And I heard nor sign nor groan),
With heavy thump, a lifeless lump,
They dropped down one by one.

But Life-in-Death begins her work on the ancient Mariner.

The souls did from their bodies fly,—
They fled to bliss or woe!
And every soul, it passed me by,
Like the whizz of my cross-bow!"

Part IV

The Wedding-Guest feareth that a Spirit is talking to him;

"I fear thee, ancient Mariner!
I fear thy skinny hand!
And thou art long, and lank, and brown,
As is the ribbed sea-sand.

I fear thee and thy glittering eye,
And thy skinny hand, so brown."—
"Fear not, fear not, thou Wedding-Guest!
This body dropt not down.

But the ancient Mariner assureth him of his bodily life, and proceedeth to relate his horrible penance.

Alone, alone, all, all alone,
Alone on a wide wide sea!
And never a saint took pity on
My soul in agony.

He despiseth the creatures of the calm,

The many men, so beautiful!
And they all dead did lie:
And a thousand thousand slimy things
Lived on; and so did I.

226–27. These two lines were contributed by Worsdworth.

And envieth that *they* should live, and so many lie dead.

I looked upon the rotting sea,
And drew my eyes away;
I looked upon the rotting deck,
And there the dead men lay.

I looked to Heaven, and tried to pray;
But or ever a prayer had gusht,
A wicked whisper came, and made
My heart as dry as dust.

I closed my lids, and kept them close,
And the balls like pulses beat;
For the sky and the sea, and the sea and the sky
Lay like a load on my weary eye,
And the dead were at my feet.

But the curse liveth for him in the eye of the dead men.

The cold sweat melted from their limbs,
Nor rot nor reek did they:
The look with which they looked on me
Had never passed away.

An orphan's curse would drag to hell
A spirit from on high;
But oh! more horrible than that
Is the curse in a dead man's eye!
Seven days, seven nights, I saw that curse,
And yet I could not die.

In his loneliness and fixedness he yearneth towards the journeying Moon, and the stars that still sojourn, yet still move onward; and every where the blue sky belongs to them, and is their appointed rest, and their native country and their own natural homes, which they enter unannounced, as lords that are certainly expected and yet there is a silent joy at their arrival.

The moving Moon went up the sky,
And no where did abide:
Softly she was going up,
And a star or two beside—

Her beams bemocked the sultry main,
Like April hoar-frost spread;
But where the ship's huge shadow lay,
The charmèd water burnt alway
A still and awful red.

By the light of the Moon he beholdeth God's creatures of the great calm.

Beyond the shadow of the ship,
I watched the water-snakes:
They moved in tracks of shining white,
And when they reared, the elfish light
Fell off in hoary flakes.

Within the shadow of the ship
I watched their rich attire:
Blue, glossy green, and velvet black,

They coiled and swam; and every track
Was a flash of golden fire.

Their beauty and their happiness.

O happy living things! no tongue
Their beauty might declare:
A spring of love gushed from my heart,
And I blessed them unaware:
Sure my kind saint took pity on me,
And I blessed them unaware.

He blesseth them in his heart.

The spell begins to break.

The self-same moment I could pray;
And from my neck so free
The Albatross fell off, and sank
Like lead into the sea.

Part V

Oh sleep! it is a gentle thing,
Beloved from pole to pole!
To Mary Queen the praise be given!
She sent the gentle sleep from Heaven,
That slid into my soul.

By grace of the holy Mother, the ancient Mariner is refreshed with rain.

The silly buckets on the deck,
That had so long remained,
I dreamt that they were filled with dew;
And when I awoke, it rained.

My lips were wet, my throat was cold,
My garments were all dank;
Sure I had drunken in my dreams,
And still my body drank.

I moved, and could not feel my limbs:
I was so light—almost
I thought that I had died in sleep,
And was a blessèd ghost.

He heareth sounds and seeth strange sights and commotions in the sky and the element.

And soon I heard a roaring wind:
It did not come anear;
But with its sound it shook the sails,
That were so thin and sere.

The upper air burst into life!
And a hundred fire-flags sheen,
To and fro they were hurried about!
And to and fro, and in and out,
The wan stars danced between.

297. silly: simple, lowly. **312. sere:** dry. **314. sheen:** shining.

And the coming wind did roar more loud,
And the sails did sigh like sedge;
And the rain poured down from one black cloud;
The Moon was at its edge.

The thick black cloud was cleft, and still
The Moon was at its side:
Like waters shot from some high crag,
The lightning fell with never a jag,
A river steep and wide.

The bodies of the ship's crew are inspired and the ship moves on;

The loud wind never reached the ship,
Yet now the ship moved on!
Beneath the lightning and the Moon
The dead men gave a groan.

They groaned, they stirred, they all uprose,
Nor spake, nor moved their eyes;
It had been strange, even in a dream,
To have seen those dead men rise.

The helmsman steered, the ship moved on;
Yet never a breeze up-blew;
The mariners all 'gan work the ropes,
Where they were wont to do;
They raised their limbs like lifeless tools—
We were a ghastly crew.

The body of my brother's son
Stood by me, knee to knee:
The body and I pulled at one rope,
But he said nought to me."

"I fear thee, ancient Mariner!"
"Be calm, thou Wedding-Guest!
'Twas not those souls that fled in pain,
Which to their corses came again,
But a troop of spirits blest:

But not by the souls of the men, nor by daemons of earth or middle air, but by a blessed troop of angelic spirits, sent down by the invocation of the guardian saint.

For when it dawned—they dropped their arms,
And clustered round the mast;
Sweet sounds rose slowly through their mouths,
And from their bodies passed.

Around, around, flew each sweet sound,
Then darted to the Sun;
Slowly the sounds came back again,
Now mixed, now one by one.

Sometimes a-dropping from the sky
I heard the sky-lark sing;
Sometimes all little birds that are,
How they seemed to fill the sea and air
With their sweet jargoning!

And now 'twas like all instruments,
Now like a lonely flute;
And now it is an angel's song,
That makes the Heavens be mute.

It ceased; yet still the sails made on
A pleasant noise till noon,
A noise like of a hidden brook
In the leafy month of June,
That to the sleeping woods all night
Singeth a quiet tune.

Till noon we quietly sailed on,
Yet never a breeze did breathe:
Slowly and smoothly went the ship,
Moved onward from beneath.

The lonesome Spirit from the South Pole carries on the ship as far as the Line, in obedience to the angelic troop, but still requireth vengeance.

Under the keel nine fathom deep,
From the land of mist and snow,
The Spirit slid: and it was he
That made the ship to go.
The sails at noon left off their tune,
And the ship stood still also.

The Sun, right up above the mast,
Had fixed her to the ocean:
But in a minute she 'gan stir,
With a short uneasy motion—
Backwards and forwards half her length
With a short uneasy motion.

Then like a pawing horse let go,
She made a sudden bound:
It flung the blood into my head,
And I fell down in a swound.

The Polar Spirit's fellow-daemons, the invisible inhabitants of the element, take part in his wrong; and two of them relate, one to the other,

How long in that same fit I lay,
I have not to declare;
But ere my living life returned,
I heard and in my soul discerned
Two voices in the air.

that penance long and heavy for the ancient Mariner hath been accorded to the Polar Spirit, who returneth southward.

'Is it he?' quoth one, 'is this the man?
By Him who died on cross,
With his cruel bow he laid full low
The harmless Albatross.

The Spirit who bideth by himself
In the land of mist and snow,
He loved the bird that loved the man
Who shot him with his bow.'

The other was a softer voice,
As soft as honey-dew:
Quoth he, 'The man hath penance done,
And penance more will do.'

Part VI

FIRST VOICE

'But tell me, tell me! speak again,
Thy soft response renewing—
What makes that ship drive on so fast?
What is the Ocean doing?'

SECOND VOICE

'Still as a slave before his lord,
The Ocean hath no blast;
His great bright eye most silently
Up to the Moon is cast—

If he may know which way to go;
For she guides him smooth or grim.
See, brother, see! how graciously
She looketh down on him.'

FIRST VOICE

The Mariner hath been cast into a trance; for the angelic power causeth the vessel to drive northward faster than human life could endure.

'But why drives on that ship so fast,
Without or wave or wind?'

SECOND VOICE

'The air is cut away before,
And closes from behind.

Fly, brother, fly! more high, more high!
Or we shall be belated:
For slow and slow that ship will go,
When the Mariner's trance is abated.'

The supernatural motion is retarded; the Mariner awakes, and his penance begins anew.

I woke, and we were sailing on
As in a gentle weather:
'Twas night, calm night, the Moon was high;
The dead men stood together.

All stood together on the deck,
For a charnel-dungeon fitter:
All fixed on me their stony eyes,
That in the Moon did glitter.

The pang, the curse, with which they died,
Had never passed away:
I could not draw my eyes from theirs,
Nor turn them up to pray.

The curse is finally expiated.

And now this spell was snapt: once more
I viewed the ocean green,
And looked far forth, yet little saw
Of what had else been seen—

Like one, that on a lonesome road
Doth walk in fear and dread,
And having once turned round walks on,
And turns no more his head;
Because he knows, a frightful fiend
Doth close behind him tread.

But soon there breathed a wind on me,
Nor sound nor motion made:
Its path was not upon the sea,
In ripple or in shade.

It raised my hair, it fanned my cheek
Like a meadow-gale of spring—
It mingled strangely with my fears,
Yet it felt like a welcoming.

Swiftly, swiftly flew the ship,
Yet she sailed softly too:
Sweetly, sweetly blew the breeze—
On me alone it blew.

And the ancient Mariner beholdeth his native country.

Oh! dream of joy! is this indeed
The light-house top I see?
Is this the hill? is this the kirk?
Is this mine own countree?

We drifted o'er the harbour-bar,
And I with sobs did pray—
O let me be awake, my God!
Or let me sleep alway.

The harbour-bay was clear as glass,
So smoothly it was strewn!
And on the bay the moonlight lay,
And the shadow of the Moon.

The rock shone bright, the kirk no less,
That stands above the rock:
The moonlight steeped in silentness
The steady weathercock.

And the bay was white with silent light,
Till rising from the same,
Full many shapes, that shadows were,
In crimson colours came.

The angelic spirits leave the dead bodies,

A little distance from the prow
Those crimson shadows were:
I turned my eyes upon the deck—
Oh, Christ! what saw I there!

And appear in their own forms of light.

Each corse lay flat, lifeless and flat,
And, by the holy rood!
A man all light, a seraph-man,
On every corse there stood.

This seraph-band, each waved his hand:
It was a heavenly sight!
They stood as signals to the land,
Each one a lovely light;

This seraph-band, each waved his hand,
No voice did they impart—
No voice; but oh! the silence sank
Like music on my heart.

But soon I heard the dash of oars,
I heard the Pilot's cheer;
My head was turned perforce away
And I saw a boat appear.

The Pilot and the Pilot's boy,
I heard them coming fast:
Dear Lord in Heaven! it was a joy
The dead men could not blast.

I saw a third—I heard his voice:
It is the Hermit good!
He singeth loud his godly hymns
That he makes in the wood.
He'll shrieve my soul, he'll wash away
The Albatross's blood.

Part VII

The Hermit of the Wood,

This Hermit good lives in that wood
Which slopes down to the sea.
How loudly his sweet voice he rears!
He loves to talk with marineres
That come from a far countree.

He kneels at morn, and noon, and eve—
He hath a cushion plump:
It is the moss that wholly hides
The rotted old oak-stump.

The skiff-boat neared: I heard them talk,
'Why, this is strange, I trow!
Where are those lights so many and fair,
That signal made but now?'

Approacheth the ship with wonder.

'Strange, by my faith!' the Hermit said—
'And they answered not our cheer!
The planks looked warped! and see those sails,
How thin they are and sere!
I never saw aught like to them,
Unless perchance it were

Brown skeletons of leaves that lag
My forest-brook along;
When the ivy-tod is heavy with snow,
And the owlet whoops to the wolf below,
That eats the she-wolf's young.'

'Dear Lord! it hath a fiendish look—
(The Pilot made reply)
I am a-feared'—'Push on, push on!'
Said the Hermit cheerily.

The boat came closer to the ship,
But I nor spake nor stirred;
The boat came close beneath the ship,
And straight a sound was heard.

512. shrieve: shrive, absolve. **535. ivy-tod:** tuft or cluster of ivy.

Under the water it rumbled on,
Still louder and more dread:
It reached the ship, it split the bay;
The ship went down like lead.

The ship suddenly sinketh.

Stunned by that loud and dreadful sound,
Which sky and ocean smote,
Like one that hath been seven days drowned
My body lay afloat;
But swift as dreams, myself I found
Within the Pilot's boat.

The ancient Mariner is saved in the Pilot's boat.

Upon the whirl, where sank the ship,
The boat spun round and round;
And all was still, save that the hill
Was telling of the sound.

I moved my lips—the Pilot shrieked
And fell down in a fit;
The holy Hermit raised his eyes,
And prayed where he did sit.

I took the oars: the Pilot's boy,
Who now doth crazy go,
Laughed loud and long, and all the while
His eyes went to and fro.
'Ha! ha!' quoth he, 'full plain I see,
The Devil knows how to row.'

And now, all in my own countree,
I stood on the firm land!
The Hermit stepped forth from the boat,
And scarcely he could stand.

The ancient Mariner earnestly entreateth the Hermit to shrieve him; and the penance of life falls on him.

'O shrieve me, shrieve me, holy man!'
The Hermit crossed his brow.
'Say quick,' quoth he, 'I bid thee say—
What manner of man art thou?'

Forthwith this frame of mine was wrenched
With a woful agony,
Which forced me to begin my tale;
And then it left me free.

And ever and anon throughout his future life an agony constraineth him to travel from land to land;

Since then, at an uncertain hour,
That agony returns:
And till my ghastly tale is told,
This heart within me burns.

I pass, like night, from land to land;
I have strange power of speech;
That moment that his face I see,
I know the man that must hear me:
To him my tale I teach.

What loud uproar bursts from that door!
The wedding-guests are there:
But in the garden-bower the bride
And bride-maids singing are:
And hark the little vesper bell,
Which biddeth me to prayer!

O Wedding-Guest! this soul hath been
Alone on a wide wide sea:
So lonely 'twas, that God himself
Scarce seemèd there to be.

O sweeter than the marriage-feast,
'Tis sweeter far to me,
To walk together to the kirk
With a goodly company!—

To walk together to the kirk,
And all together pray,
While each to his great Father bends,
Old men, and babes, and loving friends
And youths and maidens gay!

Farewell, farewell! but this I tell
To thee, thou Wedding-Guest!
He prayeth well, who loveth well
Both man and bird and beast.

And to teach, by his own example, love and reverence to all things that God made and loveth.

He prayeth best, who loveth best
All things both great and small;
For the dear God who loveth us,
He made and loveth all."

The Mariner, whose eye is bright,
Whose beard with age is hoar,
Is gone: and now the Wedding-Guest
Turned from the bridegroom's door.

He went like one that hath been stunned,
And is of sense forlorn:
A sadder and a wiser man,
He rose the morrow morn.

1797–98, rev.

Samuel Taylor Coleridge (1772–1834)

EXERCISE 25

Read *Sir Patrick Spence* and *The Rime of the Ancient Mariner*. Analyze the metrical substitutions, the rhyme, and the development of the narrative closely in the first four stanzas of each poem. Taking each poem as a whole, consider the following topics:

1. The use of repetition.
2. The use of adjectives: standard, cliché, or "literary."
3. Variations on the stanza form of the ballad.
4. Variations on the rhyme scheme of the ballad.
5. Approximate rhyming and its effect on the ballad in the place where it appears.
6. Narrative technique: the use of description, exposition, dialogue, characterization.
7. Possible symbolism.

On the basis of your study of these questions, write an essay describing the results of your analysis. What effects do the various devices enumerated in 1–7 have on each poem? Give specific examples of significant devices used. In the conclusion of your essay, try to distinguish between the qualities characteristic of the popular ballad and those of the literary ballad. Do not attempt to determine which poem or form is the more effective.

Another example, this time the work of an American poet, of a ballad based on an experience at sea is Longfellow's *The Wreck of the Hesperus*:

THE WRECK OF THE HESPERUS

It was the schooner Hesperus,
  That sailed the wintry sea;
And the skipper had taken his little daughter,
  To bear him company.

Blue were her eyes as the fairy-flax,
  Her cheeks like the dawn of day,
And her bosom white as the hawthorn buds,
  That ope in the month of May.

The skipper he stood beside the helm,
  His pipe was in his mouth,
And he watched how the veering flaw did blow
  The smoke now West, now South.

Then up and spake an old Sailor,
  Had sailed the Spanish Main,
"I pray thee, put into yonder port,
  For I fear a hurricane.

"Last night the moon had a golden ring,
  And to-night no moon we see!"
The skipper he blew a whiff from his pipe,
  And a scornful laugh laughed he.

Colder and louder blew the wind,
  A gale from the Northeast;
The snow fell hissing in the brine,
  And the billows frothed like yeast.

Down came the storm, and smote amain
  The vessel in its strength;
She shuddered and paused, like a frightened steed,
  Then leaped her cable's length.

"Come hither! come hither! my little daughter,
  And do not tremble so;
For I can weather the roughest gale,
  That ever wind did blow."

He wrapped her warm in his seaman's coat
  Against the stinging blast;
He cut a rope from a broken spar,
  And bound her to the mast.

"O father! I hear the church-bells ring,
  O say, what may it be?"
"'Tis a fog-bell on a rock-bound coast!"
  And he steered for the open sea.

"O father! I hear the sound of guns,
  O say, what may it be?"
"Some ship in distress, that cannot live,
  In such an angry sea!"

"O father! I see a gleaming light,
  O say, what may it be?"
But the father answered never a word,
  A frozen corpse was he.

Lashed to the helm, all stiff and stark,
  With his face turned to the skies,
The lantern gleamed through the gleaming snow
  On his fixed and glassy eyes.

Then the maiden clasped her hands and prayed
  That saved she might be;
And she thought of Christ, who stilled the wave,
  On the Lake of Galilee.

And fast through the midnight dark and drear,
  Through the whistling sleet and snow,
Like a sheeted ghost, the vessel swept
  Tow'rds the reef of Norman's Woe.

And ever the fitful gusts between
  A sound came from the land;
It was the sound of the trampling surf,
  On the rocks and the hard sea-sand.

The breakers were right beneath her bows,
  She drifted a dreary wreck,
And a whooping billow swept the crew
  Like icicles from her deck.

She struck where the white and fleecy waves
  Looked soft as carded wool,
But the cruel rocks, they gored her side
  Like the horns of an angry bull.

Her rattling shrouds, all sheathed in ice,
  With the masts went by the board;
Like a vessel of glass, she stove and sank,
  Ho! Ho! the breakers roared!

At daybreak, on the bleak sea-beach,
  A fisherman stood aghast,
To see the form of a maiden fair,
  Lashed close to a drifting mast.

The salt sea was frozen on her breast,
  The salt tears in her eyes;
And he saw her hair, like the brown sea-weed
  On the billows fall and rise.

Such was the wreck of the Hesperus
  In the midnight and the snow!
Christ save us all from a death like this,
  On the reef of Norman's Woe!

1842 Henry Wadsworth Longfellow (1807–1882)

Like *The Rime of the Ancient Mariner*, the *Ballad of the Long-Legged Bait* is clearly a literary derivative of ballad form in which the tale or story is deeply symbolic. Symbolic of what? For Coleridge's much older poem, many commentators have written their interpretations of the meaning, although they have never reached agreement. For Thomas' poem there appear to be two major interpretations: that of Elder Olson,* who regards the voyage as a search for salvation to be achieved by mortification of the flesh (represented by the girl: "Sin who had a woman's shape"); and that of William York Tindall, who says: "One afternoon at Cavanagh's on West 23rd Street, sitting at the bar, Dylan told me what this poem is about."† To Professor Tindall the many-layered poem—filled with paradox, plays on words, allusions to the Bible, to many literary works, and to scientific works as well—is the story of every man, and also the story of Thomas; the voyage is, as so often, the voyage of life, but, more specifically, the fisherman's adventures represent sexual experiences leading to the settled responsibilities of marriage. Thomas' one hundred and fifty work sheets for the poem, deposited in the Library of the University of Buffalo, permit study of his revisions and notes.

BALLAD OF THE LONG-LEGGED BAIT

The bows glided down, and the coast
Blackened with birds took a last look
At his thrashing hair and whale-blue eye;
The trodden town rang its cobbles for luck.

Then good-bye to the fishermanned
Boat with its anchor free and fast
As a bird hooking over the sea,
High and dry by the top of the mast,

Whispered the affectionate sand
And the bulwarks of the dazzled quay.
For my sake sail, and never look back,
Said the looking land.

Sails drank the wind, and white as milk
He sped into the drinking dark;
The sun shipwrecked west on a pearl
And the moon swam out of its hulk.

* Elder Olson, *The Poetry of Dylan Thomas* (Chicago: The University of Chicago Press, Phoenix Edition, 1961), pp. 24–25, 50–52.
† William York Tindall, *A Reader's Guide to Dylan Thomas* (New York: Farrar, Straus, 1962), p. 248.

Funnels and masts went by in a whirl.
Good-bye to the man on the sea-legged deck
To the gold gut that sings on his reel
To the bait that stalked out of the sack,

For we saw him throw to the swift flood
A girl alive with his hooks through her lips;
All the fishes were rayed in blood,
Said the dwindling ships.

Good-bye to chimneys and funnels,
Old wives that spin in the smoke,
He was blind to the eyes of candles
In the praying windows of waves

But heard his bait buck in the wake
And tussle in a shoal of loves.
Now cast down your rod, for the whole
Of the sea is hilly with whales,

She longs among horses and angels,
The rainbow-fish bend in her joys,
Floated the lost cathedral
Chimes of the rocked buoys.

Where the anchor rode like a gull
Miles over the moonstruck boat
A squall of birds bellowed and fell,
A cloud blew the rain from its throat;

He saw the storm smoke out to kill
With fuming bows and ram of ice,
Fire on starlight, rake Jesu's stream;
And nothing shone on the water's face

But the oil and bubble of the moon,
Plunging and piercing in his course
The lured fish under the foam
Witnessed with a kiss.

Whales in the wake like capes and Alps
Quaked the sick sea and snouted deep,
Deep the great bushed bait with raining lips
Slipped the fins of those humpbacked tons

And fled their love in a weaving dip.
Oh, Jericho was falling in their lungs!
She nipped and dived in the nick of love,
Spun on a spout like a long-legged ball

Till every beast blared down in a swerve
Till every turtle crushed from his shell
Till every bone in the rushing grave
Rose and crowed and fell!

Good luck to the hand on the rod,
There is thunder under its thumbs;
Gold gut is a lightning thread,
His fiery reel sings off its flames,

The whirled boat in the burn of his blood
Is crying from nets to knives,
Oh the shearwater birds and their boatsized brood
Oh the bulls of Biscay and their calves

Are making under the green, laid veil
The long-legged beautiful bait their wives.
Break the black news and paint on a sail
Huge weddings in the waves,

Over the wakeward-flashing spray
Over the gardens of the floor
Clash out the mounting dolphin's day,
My mast is a bell-spire,

Strike and smoothe, for my decks are drums,
Sing through the water-spoken prow
The octopus walking into her limbs
The polar eagle with his tread of snow.

From salt-lipped beak to the kick of the stern
Sing how the seal has kissed her dead!
The long, laid minute's bride drifts on
Old in her cruel bed.

Over the graveyard in the water
Mountains and galleries beneath
Nightingale and hyena
Rejoicing for that drifting death

Sing and howl through sand and anemone
Valley and sahara in a shell,
Oh all the wanting flesh his enemy
Thrown to the sea in the shell of a girl

Is old as water and plain as an eel;
Always good-bye to the long-legged bread
Scattered in the paths of his heels
For the salty birds fluttered and fed

And the tall grains foamed in their bills;
Always good-bye to the fires of the face,
For the crab-backed dead on the sea-bed rose
And scuttled over her eyes,

The blind, clawed stare is cold as sleet.
The tempter under the eyelid
Who shows to the selves asleep
Mast-high moon-white women naked

Walking in wishes and lovely for shame
Is dumb and gone with his flame of brides.
Sussanah's drowned in the bearded stream
And no-one stirs at Sheba's side

But the hungry kings of the tides;
Sin who had a woman's shape
Sleeps till Silence blows on a cloud
And all the lifted waters walk and leap.

Lucifer that bird's dropping
Out of the sides of the north
Has melted away and is lost
Is always lost in her vaulted breath,

Venus lies star-struck in her wound
And the sensual ruins make
Seasons over the liquid world,
White springs in the dark.

Always good-bye, cried the voices through the shell,
Good-bye always for the flesh is cast
And the fisherman winds his reel
With no more desire than a ghost.

Always good luck, praised the finned in the feather
Bird after dark and the laughing fish
As the sails drank up the hail of thunder
And the long-tailed lightning lit his catch.

The boat swims into the six-year weather,
A wind throws a shadow and it freezes fast.
See what the gold gut drags from under
Mountains and galleries to the crest!

See what clings to hair and skull
As the boat skims on with drinking wings!
The statues of great rain stand still,
And the flakes fall like hills.

Sing and strike his heavy haul
Toppling up the boatside in a snow of light!
His decks are drenched with miracles.
Oh miracle of fishes! The long dead bite!

Out of the urn the size of a man
Out of the room the weight of his trouble
Out of the house that holds a town
In the continent of a fossil

One by one in dust and shawl,
Dry as echoes and insect-faced,
His fathers cling to the hand of the girl
And the dead hand leads the past,

Leads them as children and as air
On to the blindly tossing tops;
The centuries throw back their hair
And the old men sing from newborn lips:

Time is bearing another son.
Kill Time! She turns in her pain!
The oak is felled in the acorn
And the hawk in the egg kills the wren.

He who blew the great fire in
And died on a hiss of flames
Or walked on the earth in the evening
Counting the denials of the grains

Clings to her drifting hair, and climbs;
And he who taught their lips to sing
Weeps like the risen sun among
The liquid choirs of his tribes.

The rod bends low, divining land,
And through the sundered water crawls
A garden holding to her hand
With birds and animals

With men and women and waterfalls
Trees cool and dry in the whirlpool of ships
And stunned and still on the green, laid veil
Sand with legends in its virgin laps

And prophets loud on the burned dunes;
Insects and valleys hold her thighs hard,
Time and places grip her breast bone,
She is breaking with seasons and clouds;

Round her trailed wrist fresh water weaves,
With moving fish and rounded stones
Up and down the greater waves
A separate river breathes and runs;

Strike and sing his catch of fields
For the surge is sown with barley,
The cattle graze on the covered foam,
The hills have footed the waves away,

With wild sea fillies and soaking bridles
With salty colts and gales in their limbs
All the horses of his haul of miracles
Gallop through the arched, green farms,

Trot and gallop with gulls upon them
And thunderbolts in their manes.
O Rome and Sodom To-morrow and London
The country tide is cobbled with towns,

And steeples pierce the cloud on her shoulder
And the streets that the fisherman combed
When his long-legged flesh was a wind on fire
And his loin was a hunting flame

Coil from the thoroughfares of her hair
And terribly lead him home alive
Lead her prodigal home to his terror,
The furious ox-killing house of love.

Down, down, down, under the ground,
Under the floating villages,
Turns the moon-chained and water-wound
Metropolis of fishes,

There is nothing left of the sea but its sound,
Under the earth the loud sea walks,
In deathbeds of orchards the boat dies down
And the bait is drowned among hayricks,

Land, land, land, nothing remains
Of the pacing, famous sea but its speech,
And into its talkative seven tombs
The anchor dives through the floors of a church.

Good-bye, good luck, struck the sun and the moon,
To the fisherman lost on the land.
He stands alone at the door of his home,
With his long-legged heart in his hand.

1941 DYLAN THOMAS (1914–1953)

Ballads of Enchantment

Enchanting ladies and knights who are enthralled by them are common subjects for ballads, and the siren lady has by no means disappeared from contemporary and presumably sophisticated society, which is scornful of the supernatural. *Thomas Rymer* represents the popular ballad of this tradition, and Keats' *La Belle Dame* the literary. A contemporary literary example could not be found, but perhaps a student examining these poems might try, as an additional exercise, to write about the neighborhood enchantress and her innocently beguiled victim.

THOMAS RYMER

1 True Thomas lay oer yond grassy bank,
And he beheld a ladie gay,
A ladie that was brisk and bold,
Come riding oer the fernie brae.

2 Her skirt was of the grass-green silk,
Her mantel of the velvet fine,
At ilka tett of her horse's mane
Hung fifty silver bells and nine.

3 True Thomas he took off his hat,
And bowed him low down till his knee:
"All hail, thou mighty Queen of Heaven!
For your peer on earth I never did see."

4 "O no, O no, True Thomas," she says,
"That name does not belong to me;
I am but the queen of fair Elfland,
And I'm come here for to visit thee.*

* * *

4. brae: bank. **7. ilka tett:** each lock.
* The asterisks indicate a gap in this version of the ballad.

5 "But ye maun go wi me now, Thomas,
True Thomas, ye maun go wi me,
For ye maun serve me seven years,
Thro weel or wae as may chance to be."

6 She turned about her milk-white steed,
And took True Thomas up behind,
And aye wheneer her bridle rang,
The steed flew swifter than the wind.

7 For forty days and forty nights
He wade thro red blude to the knee,
And he saw neither sun nor moon,
But heard the roaring of the sea.

8 O they rade on, and further on,
Until they came to a garden green:
"Light down, light down, ye ladie free,
Some of that fruit let me pull to thee."

9 "O no, O no, True Thomas," she says,
"That fruit maun not be touched by thee,
For a' the plagues that are in hell
Light on the fruit of this countrie.

10 "But I have a loaf here in my lap,
Likewise a bottle of claret wine,
And now ere we go farther on,
We'll rest a while, and ye may dine."

11 When he had eaten and drunk his fill,
"Lay down your head upon my knee,"
The lady sayd, "ere we climb yon hill,
And I will show you fairlies three.

12 "O see not ye yon narrow road,
So thick beset wi thorns and briers?
That is the path of righteousness,
Tho after it but few enquires.

13 "And see not ye that braid braid road,
That lies across yon lillie leven?
That is the path of wickedness,
Tho some call it the road to heaven.

14 "And see not ye that bonny road,
Which winds about the fernie brae?

44. fairlies: wonders. **50. lillie leven:** lovely glade.

That is the road to fair Elfland,
  Where you and I this night maun gae.

15 "But Thomas, ye maun hold your tongue,
  Whatever you may hear or see,
For gin ae word you should chance to speak,
  You will neer get back to your ain countrie."

16 He has gotten a coat of the even cloth,
  And a pair of shoes of velvet green,
And till seven years were past and gone
  True Thomas on earth was never seen.

Anonymous

Both Sir Walter Scott, in his *Imitations of the Ancient Ballad*, and Rudyard Kipling, in *The Seven Seas*, made literary ballads of the explicit materials of *Thomas Rymer*. Both are very long; for the purposes of comparison, we have chosen, instead, a similar tale of the enthrallment of a young man by a beautiful lady from the "other world," the celebrated literary ballad of John Keats:

LA BELLE DAME SANS MERCI

Ah, what can ail thee, wretched wight,
  Alone and palely loitering;
The sedge is wither'd from the lake,
  And no birds sing.

Ah, what can ail thee, wretched wight,
  So haggard and so woe-begone?
The squirrel's granary is full,
  And the harvest's done.

I see a lilly on thy brow,
  With anguish moist and fever dew;
And on thy cheek a fading rose
  Fast withereth too.

I met a lady in the meads
  Full beautiful, a faery's child;
Her hair was long, her foot was light,
  And her eyes were wild.

I set her on my pacing steed,
  And nothing else saw all day long;
For sideways would she lean, and sing
  A faery's song.

59. gin: if.

I made a garland for her head,
  And bracelets too, and fragrant zone;
She look'd at me as she did love,
  And made sweet moan.

She found me roots of relish sweet,
  And honey wild, and manna dew;
And sure in language strange she said,
  I love thee true.

She took me to her elfin grot,
  And there she gaz'd and sighed deep,
And there I shut her wild sad eyes—
  So kiss'd to sleep.

And there we slumber'd on the moss,
  And there I dream'd, ah woe betide,
The latest dream I ever dream'd
  On the cold hill side.

I saw pale kings, and princes too,
  Pale warriors, death-pale were they all;
Who cry'd—"La belle Dame sans merci
  Hath thee in thrall!"

I saw their starv'd lips in the gloam
  With horrid warning gaped wide,
And I awoke, and found me here
  On the cold hill side.

And this is why I sojourn here
  Alone and palely loitering,
Though the sedge is wither'd from the lake,
  And no birds sing.

1819 John Keats (1795–1821)

EXERCISE 26

Read the popular ballad *Thomas Rymer* and Keats' literary ballad, *La Belle Dame sans Merci.* Consider carefully the following possibilities:

1. The original form of *Thomas Rymer*, as it was produced by its first composer and before any changes were made through oral transmission or scribal error. Do you think the poem would have been longer or shorter in its original form? Examine the topics suggested in Exercise 25, and try to imagine how these devices might have differed in the

original poem from those in the text you are now reading. Can you suggest probable reasons for the changes?

2. The probable changes in *La Belle Dame* if it had undergone oral transmission for several centuries. Would this poem be lengthened or shortened in oral transmission? Taking the topics suggested in Exercise 25, try to imagine the changes which might occur in a later version of this poem. As you imagine the new form of the poem, would it be more or less effective? Why?

On the basis of your study of these questions in relation to *Thomas Rymer* and *La Belle Dame*, write an essay discussing the significant differences in the technique of the popular ballad and the literary ballad. Can you decide which form is of greater merit?

Ballads of Domestic Tragedy

Just as some ballads, both popular and literary, appear to take their origin from a distortion of historical events (*Sir Patrick Spence, Mary Hamilton, The Ballad of Medgar Evers*), or from romanticized events of public record (*The Ancient Mariner, Casey Jones*), other ballads seem to have originated in what might be called "domestic tragedy." *Lord Randal*, given here in one British and two American popular forms, is an example of the type. Although the practice of poisoning one's once-beloved is by no means outmoded—as a glance at the tabloid newspapers will show—we were unable to find the exact counterpart of *Lord Randal* in the literary ballad. We have accordingly substituted two dark narratives of marital infidelity: Sir Walter Scott's *The Eve of St. John* and Yeats' *Colonel Martin.*

Lord Randal shows one of the characteristics of the popular ballad, sometimes imitated in the literary ballad: a dialogue of question and answer kept up throughout the poem, often with the use of INCREMENTAL REPETITION in the form of the question (as in *Lord Randal* and in both the British and the American forms of *Edward*), the answers to which build up mounting tension in the reader or listener. Regular REPETITION may be used also, as in the final lines of the stanzas of *Lord Randal.*

A REFRAIN, as distinct from repetition, is frequently used in the ballad, apparently as part of the musical accompaniment. Literary imitations of the practice are seen in Dante Gabriel Rossetti's *Sister Helen* and Yeats' *The Three Bushes* (1936–39), where the refrain is maintained in traditional identical form throughout.

LORD RANDAL

1 "O where ha you been, Lord Randal, my son?
And where ha you been, my handsome young man?"
"I ha been at the greenwood; mother, mak my bed soon,
For I'm wearied wi hunting, and fain wad lie down."

2 "An wha met ye there, Lord Randal, my son?
An wha met you there, my handsome young man?"
"O I met wi my true-love; mother, mak my bed soon,
For I'm wearied wi hunting, and fain wad lie down."

3 "And what did she give you, Lord Randal, my son?
And what did she give you, my handsome young man?"
"Eels fried in a pan; mother, mak my bed soon,
For I'm wearied wi huntin, and fain wad lie down."

4 "An wha gat your leavins, Lord Randal, my son?
And wha gat your leavins, my handsome young man?"
"My hawks and my hounds; mother, mak my bed soon,
For I'm wearied wi huntin, and fain wad lie down."

5 "And what becam of them, Lord Randal, my son?
And what becam of them, my handsome young man?"
"They stretched their legs out and died; mother, mak my bed soon,
For I'm wearied wi huntin, and fain wad lie down."

6 "O I fear you are poisoned, Lord Randal, my son!
I fear you are poisoned, my handsome young man!"
"O yes, I am poisoned; mother, mak my bed soon,
For I'm sick at the heart, and I fain wad lie down."

7 "What d'ye leave to your mother, Lord Randal, my son?
What d'ye leave to your mother, my handsome young man?"
"Four and twenty milk kye; mother, mak my bed soon,
For I'm sick at the heart, and I fain wad lie down."

8 "What d'ye leave to your sister, Lord Randal, my son?
What d'ye leave to your sister, my handsome young man?"
"My gold and my silver; mother, mak my bed soon,
For I'm sick at the heart, an I fain wad lie down."

9 "What d'ye leave to your brother, Lord Randal, my son?
What d'ye leave to your brother, my handsome young man?"
"My houses and my lands; mother, mak my bed soon,
For I'm sick at the heart, and I fain wad lie down."

10 "What d'ye leave to your true-love, Lord Randal, my son?
What d'ye leave to your true-love, my handsome young man?"

"I leave her hell and fire; mother, mak my bed soon,
For I'm sick at the heart, and I fain wad lie down."

Anonymous

American Version (A)

JOHNNY RANDALL

1 "Where was you last night, Johnny Randall, my son?
Where was you last night, my heart's loving one?"
"A-fishing, a-fowling; mother, make my bed soon,
For I'm sick at my heart, and I fain would lie down."

2 "What had you for breakfast, my own pretty boy?
What had you for breakfast, my heart's loving joy?"
"Fresh trout and slow poison; mother, make my bed soon,
For I'm sick at my heart, and I fain would lie down."

3 "What will you will your brother, my own pretty boy?
What will you will your brother, my heart's loving joy?"
"My horse and my saddle; mother, make my bed soon,
For I'm sick at my heart, and I fain would lie down."

4 "What will you will your sister, my own pretty boy?
What will you will your sister, my heart's loving joy?"
"My watch and my fiddle; mother, make my bed soon,
For I'm sick at my heart, and I fain would lie down."

5 "What will you will your mother, my own pretty boy,
What will you will your mother, my heart's loving joy?"
"A twisted hemp rope, for to hang her up high;
Mother, make my bed easy till I lie down and die."

Anonymous

American Version (B)

JIMMY RANDOLPH

1 "What you will to your father, Jimmy Randolph my son?
What you will to your father, my oldest dearest one?"
"My horses, my buggies, mother make my bed soon,
For I am sick-hearted, and I want to lie down."

2 "What you will to your brothers, Jimmy Randolph my son?
What you will to your brothers, my oldest dearest one?"
"My mules and my waggons, mother make my bed soon,
For I am sick-hearted, and I want to lie down."

3 "What you will to your sisters, Jimmy Randolph my son?
What you will to your sisters, my oldest dearest one?"
"My gold and my silver, mother make my bed soon,
For I am sick-hearted, and I want to lie down."

Anonymous

THE EVE OF ST. JOHN*

The Baron of Smaylho'me rose with day,
He spurr'd his courser on,
Without stop or stay, down the rocky way,
That leads to Brotherstone.

He went not with the bold Buccleuch,
His banner broad to rear;
He went not 'gainst the English yew,
To lift the Scottish spear.

Yet his plate-jack was braced, and his helmet was laced,
And his vaunt-brace of proof he wore;
At his saddle-gerthe was a good steel sperthe,
Full ten pound weight and more.

The Baron return'd in three days' space,
And his looks were sad and sour;
And weary was his courser's pace,
As he reach'd his rocky tower.

He came not from where Ancram Moor
Ran red with English blood;
Where the Douglas true, and the bold Buccleuch,
'Gainst keen Lord Evers stood.

Yet was his helmet hack'd and hew'd,
His acton pierced and tore,
His axe and his dagger with blood imbrued,—
But it was not English gore.

He lighted at the Chapellage,
He held him close and still;
And he whistled thrice for his little foot-page,
His name was English Will.

* The Feast of St. John the Baptist is June 24; immediately preceding it is Midsummer's Eve, June 23. **11. sperthe:** battle-ax. **17. Ancram Moor:** Here, in 1545, the Scots, under Archibald Douglas, Earl of Angus, and Sir Walter Scott of Buccleuch, defeated the English under Lord Evers, who was killed. **22. acton:** stuffed jacket worn under armor.

"Come thou hither, my little foot-page,
  Come hither to my knee;
Though thou art young, and tender of age,
  I think thou art true to me.

"Come, tell me all that thou hast seen,
  And look thou tell me true!
Since I from Smaylho'me tower have been,
  What did thy lady do?"

"My lady, each night, sought the lonely light,
  That burns on the wild Watchfold;
For, from height to height, the beacons bright
  Of the English foemen told.

"The bittern clamour'd from the moss,
  The wind blew loud and shrill;
Yet the craggy pathway she did cross
  To the eiry Beacon Hill.

"I watch'd her steps, and silent came
  Where she sat her on a stone;—
No watchman stood by the dreary flame,
  It burnèd all alone.

"The second night I kept her in sight,
  Till to the fire she came,
And, by Mary's might! an Armed Knight
  Stood by the lonely flame.

"And many a word that warlike lord
  Did speak to my lady there;
But the rain fell fast, and loud blew the blast,
  And I heard not what they were.

"The third night there the sky was fair,
  And the mountain-blast was still,
As again I watch'd the secret pair,
  On the lonesome Beacon Hill.

"And I heard her name the midnight hour,
  And name this holy eve;
And say, 'Come this night to thy lady's bower;
  Ask no bold Baron's leave.

"'He lifts his spear with the bold Buccleuch;
  His lady is all alone;
The door she'll undo, to her knight so true,
  On the eve of good St. John.'—

"'I cannot come; I must not come;
  I dare not come to thee;
On the eve of St. John I must wander alone:
  In thy bower I may not be.'—

"'Now, out on thee, fainthearted knight!
  Thou shouldst not say me nay;
For the eve is sweet, and when lovers meet,
  Is worth the whole summer's day.

"'And I'll chain the blood-hound, and the warder shall not sound,
  And rushes shall be strewed on the stair;
So, by the black rood-stone, and by holy St. John,
  I conjure thee, my love, to be there!'—

"'Though the blood-hound be mute, and the rush beneath my foot,
  And the warder his bugle should not blow,
Yet there sleepeth a priest in the chamber to the east,
  And my footstep he would know.'—

"'O fear not the priest, who sleepeth to the east!
  For to Dryburgh the way he has ta'en;
And there to say mass, till three days do pass,
  For the soul of a knight that is slayne.'—

"He turn'd him around, and grimly he frown'd;
  Then he laughed right scornfully—
'He who says the mass-rite for the soul of that knight,
  May as well say mass for me:

"'At the lone midnight hour, when bad spirits have power,
  In thy chamber will I be.'—
With that he was gone, and my lady left alone,
  And no more did I see."

Then changed, I trow, was that bold Baron's brow,
  From the dark to the blood-red high—
"Now, tell me the mien of the knight thou hast seen,
  For, by Mary, he shall die!"—

"His arms shone full bright, in the beacon's red light:
  His plume it was scarlet and blue;
On his shield was a hound, in a silver leash bound,
  And his crest was a branch of the yew."—

"Thou liest, thou liest, thou little foot-page,
  Loud dost thou lie to me!
For that knight is cold, and now laid in the mould,
  All under the Eildon-tree."—

"Yet hear but my word, my noble lord!
  For I heard her name his name;
And that lady bright, she called the knight
  Sir Richard of Coldinghame."—

The bold Baron's brow then changed, I trow,
  From high blood-red to pale—
"The grave is deep and dark—and the corpse is stiff and stark—
  So I may not trust thy tale.

"Where fair Tweed flows round holy Melrose,
  And Eildon slopes to the plain,
Full three nights ago, by some secret foe,
  That gay gallant was slain.

"The varying light deceived thy sight,
  And the wild winds drown'd the name;
For the Dryburgh bells ring, and the white monks do sing,
  For Sir Richard of Coldinghame!"

He pass'd the court-gate, and he oped the tower-gate,
  And he mounted the narrow stair,
To the bartizan-seat, where, with maids that on her wait,
  He found his lady fair.

That lady sat in mournful mood;
  Look'd over hill and vale;
Over Tweed's fair flood, and Mertoun's wood,
  And all down Teviotdale.

"Now hail, now hail, thou lady bright!"—
  "Now hail, thou Baron true!
What news, what news, from Ancram fight?
  What news from the bold Buccleuch?"—

"The Ancram Moor is red with gore,
  For many a southron fell;
And Buccleuch has charged us, evermore,
  To watch our beacons well."—

The lady blush'd red, but nothing she said:
  Nor added the Baron a word:
Then she stepp'd down the stair to her chamber fair,
  And so did her moody lord.

In sleep the lady mourn'd, and the Baron toss'd and turn'd,
  And oft to himself he said,—
"The worms around him creep, and his bloody grave is deep . . .
  It cannot give up the dead!"—

It was near the ringing of matin-bell,
  The night was wellnigh done,
When a heavy sleep on that Baron fell,
  On the eve of good St. John.

The lady look'd through the chamber fair,
  By the light of a dying flame;
And she was aware of a knight stood there—
  Sir Richard of Coldinghame!

"Alas! away, away!" she cried,
  "For the holy Virgin's sake!"—
"Lady, I know who sleeps by thy side;
  But, lady, he will not awake.

"By Eildon-tree, for long nights three,
  In bloody grave have I lain;
The mass and the death-prayer are said for me,
  But, lady, they are said in vain.

"By the Baron's brand, near Tweed's fair strand,
  Most foully slain, I fell;
And my restless sprite on the beacon's height,
  For a space is doom'd to dwell.

"At our trysting-place, for a certain space,
  I must wander to and fro;
But I had not had power to come to thy bower
  Had'st thou not conjured me so."—

Love master'd fear—her brow she cross'd;
  "How, Richard, hast thou sped?
And art thou saved, or art thou lost?"—
  The vision shook his head!

"Who spilleth life, shall forfeit life;
  So bid thy lord believe:
That lawless love is guilt above,
  This awful sign receive."

He laid his left palm on an oaken beam;
His right upon her hand;
The lady shrunk, and fainting sunk,
For it scorch'd like a fiery brand.

The sable score, of fingers four,
Remains on that board impress'd;
And for evermore that lady wore
A covering on her wrist.

There is a nun in Dryburgh bower,
Ne'er looks upon the sun;
There is a monk in Melrose tower,
He speaketh word to none.

That nun, who ne'er beholds the day,
That monk, who speaks to none—
That nun was Smaylho'me's Lady gay,
That monk the bold Baron.

1803 SIR WALTER SCOTT (1771–1832)

COLONEL MARTIN

I

The Colonel went out sailing,
He spoke with Turk and Jew,
With Christian and with Infidel,
For all tongues he knew.
"O what's a wifeless man?" said he,
And he came sailing home.
He rose the latch and went upstairs
And found an empty room.
The Colonel went out sailing.

II

"I kept her much in the country
And she was much alone,
And though she may be there," he said,
"She may be in the town.
She may be all alone there,
For who can say?" he said.
"I think that I shall find her
In a young man's bed."
The Colonel went out sailing.

III

The Colonel met a pedlar,
Agreed their clothes to swop,
And bought the grandest jewelry
In a Galway shop,
Instead of thread and needle
Put jewelry in the pack,
Bound a thong about his hand,
Hitched it on his back.
The Colonel went out sailing.

IV

The Colonel knocked on the rich man's door,
"I am sorry," said the maid,
"My mistress cannot see these things,
But she is still abed,
And never have I looked upon
Jewelry so grand."
"Take all to your mistress,"
And he laid them on her hand.
The Colonel went out sailing.

V

And he went in and she went on
And both climbed up the stair,
And O he was a clever man,
For he his slippers wore.
And when they came to the top stair
He ran on ahead,
His wife he found and the rich man
In the comfort of a bed.
The Colonel went out sailing.

VI

The Judge at the Assize Court,
When he heard that story told,
Awarded him for damages
Three kegs of gold.
The Colonel said to Tom his man,
"Harness an ass and cart,
Carry the gold about the town,
Throw it in every part."
The Colonel went out sailing.

VII

And there at all street-corners
A man with a pistol stood,
And the rich man had paid them well
To shoot the Colonel dead;
But they threw down their pistols
And all men heard them swear
That they could never shoot a man
Did all that for the poor.
The Colonel went out sailing.

VIII

"And did you keep no gold, Tom?
You had three kegs," said he.
"I never thought of that, Sir."
"Then want before you die."
And want he did; for my own grand-dad
Saw the story's end,
And Tom make out a living
From the seaweed on the strand.
The Colonel went out sailing.

c. 1936–39 WILLIAM BUTLER YEATS (1865–1939)

EXERCISE 27

Read carefully the three versions of *Lord Randal*, Scott's *The Eve of St. John*, and Yeats' *Colonel Martin*. Scan representative stanzas and note all variants from the $a^4 b^3 c^4 b^3$ ballad stanza which are consistently used, in meter and/or rhyme, including the internal rhyme (see under RHYME) used by Scott. What effect do these variants have upon the poem in which they appear? Does the refrain in *Colonel Martin* have the same effect in each stanza? Would "correction" to make these poems consistent with the traditional form improve them? Use specific lines and rhymes to illustrate your points.

All these poems use dialogue and repetition or refrain. *Lord Randal* (all versions) was composed to be sung or recited; Scott and Yeats wrote to be read, silently. The difference in intention and in the audience or readers should be considered in evaluating the effects of the devices in each of the poems. Consider each poem separately, and then compare the effectiveness of the variants of *Lord Randal* in its British and American forms. Decide which version of *Lord Randal* you prefer and explain your reasons. Do not attempt to compare *Lord Randal* with the literary ballads.

Ballads of Unrequited Love

The two English ballads that follow—*Barbara Allan*, the most persistent and ubiquitous of the popular ballads, and David Mallet's *David and Margaret*, 1724, one of the earliest literary ballads—deal with the death of the lover owing to unrequited love. The absence of a more modern literary treatment of this ancient theme suggests that the idea is now rather generally regarded as romantic nonsense, although it was widely popular in various types of literature for nearly a thousand years. *Barbara Allan*, of which there are also many American versions, is probably a popular descendant of the medieval aristocratic code of courtly love, according to which the lady could and did reject her beloved for the least slight, or rumor of slight, and the beloved died of his loss.

BARBARA ALLAN

1 It was in and about the Martinmas time,
When the green leaves were a-falling,
That Sir John Graeme, in the West Country,
Fell in love with Barbara Allan.

2 He sent his man down through the town,
To the place where she was dwelling:
"O haste and come to my master dear,
Gin ye be Barbara Allan."

3 O hooly, hooly rose she up
To the place where he was lying,
And when she drew the curtain by—
"Young man, I think you're dying."

4 "O it's I'm sick, and very, very sick,
And 'tis a' for Barbara Allan."
"O the better for me ye's never be,
Tho your heart's blood were a-spilling.

5 "O dinna ye mind, young man," said she,
"When ye was in the tavern a-drinking,
That ye made the healths gae round and round,
And slighted Barbara Allan?"

6 He turnd his face unto the wall,
And death was with him dealing:
"Adieu, adieu, my dear friends all,
And be kind to Barbara Allan."

9. hooly: slowly, softly.

7 And slowly, slowly raise she up,
And slowly, slowly left him,
And sighing said, she could not stay,
Since death of life had reft him.

8 She had not gane a mile but twa,
When she heard the dead-bell ringing,
And every jow that the dead-bell geid,
It cry'd, "Woe to Barbara Allan!"

9 "O mother, mother, make my bed!
O make it saft and narrow!
Since my love died for me to-day,
I'll die for him to-morrow."

Anonymous

WILLIAM AND MARGARET

'Twas at the silent, solemn hour,
When night and morning meet;
In glided Margaret's grimly ghost,
And stood at William's feet.

Her face was like an April morn,
Clad in a wintry cloud:
And clay-cold was her lilly hand,
That held her sable shroud.

So shall the fairest face appear,
When youth and years are flown;
Such is the robe that kings must wear,
When death has reft their crown.

Her bloom was like the springing flower,
That sips the silver dew;
The rose was budded in her cheek,
Just opening to the view.

But love had, like the canker-worm,
Consum'd her early prime:
The rose grew pale, and left her cheek;
She dy'd before her time.

Awake! she cry'd, thy True Love calls,
Come from her midnight grave;
Now let thy Pity hear the maid,
Thy Love refus'd to save.

31. jow: stroke.

This is the dumb and dreary hour,
  When injur'd ghosts complain;
When yauning graves give up their dead
  To haunt the faithless swain.

Bethink thee, William, of thy fault,
  Thy pledge, and broken oath:
And give me back my maiden vow,
  And give me back my troth.

Why did you promise love to me,
  And not that promise keep?
Why did you swear my eyes were bright,
  Yet leave those eyes to weep?

How could you say my face was fair,
  And yet that face forsake?
How could you win my virgin heart,
  Yet leave that heart to break?

Why did you say, my lip was sweet,
  And made the scarlet pale?
And why did I, young witless maid!
  Believe the flattering tale?

That face, alas! no more is fair;
  Those lips no longer red:
Dark are my eyes, now clos'd in death,
  And every charm is fled.

The hungry worm my sister is;
  This winding-sheet I wear:
And cold and weary lasts our night,
  Till that last morn appear.

But hark!—the cock has warn'd me hence;
  A long and late adieu!
Come, see, false man, how low she lies,
  Who dy'd for love of you.

The lark sung loud; the morning smil'd,
  With beams of rosy red:
Pale William quak'd in every limb,
  And raving left his bed.

He hy'd him to the fatal place
Where Margaret's body lay:
And stretch'd him on the grass-green turf,
That wrap'd her breathless clay.

And thrice he call'd on Margaret's name,
And thrice he wept full sore:
Then laid his cheek to her cold grave,
And word spake never more!

1724 DAVID MALLET (1705–1765)

Ballads of the Supernatural

Some of the ballads already quoted indicate the concern of ballad composers, both popular and literary, with the supernatural. One popular ballad, in its Scots form, *The Wife of Usher's Well,* is included here, because its focus is almost entirely on the theme of revenants—those who come back to this world after death—here, three brothers who must return to the other world, like the ghost of Hamlet's father, at cockcrow.

THE WIFE OF USHER'S WELL

1 There lived a wife at Usher's Well,
And a wealthy wife was she;
She had three stout and stalwart sons,
And sent them oer the sea.

2 They hadna been a week from her,
A week but barely ane,
Whan word came to the carline wife
That her three sons were gane.

3 They hadna been a week from her,
A week but barely three,
Whan word came to the carlin wife
That her sons she'd never see.

4 "I wish the wind may never cease,
Nor fashes in the flood,
Till my three sons come hame to me,
In earthly flesh and blood."

7. carline wife: old woman. **14. fashes:** troubles, storms.

5 It fell about the Martinmass,
When nights are lang and mirk,
The carlin wife's three sons came hame,
And their hats were o the birk.

6 It neither grew in syke nor ditch,
Nor yet in ony sheugh;
But at the gates o Paradise,
That birk grew fair eneugh.*

* * *

7 "Blow up the fire, my maidens,
Bring water from the well;
For a' my house shall feast this night,
Since my three sons are well."

8 And she has made to them a bed,
She's made it large and wide,
And she's taen her mantle her about,
Sat down at the bed-side.

* * *

9 Up then crew the red, red cock,
And up and crew the gray;
The eldest to the youngest said,
"'Tis time we were away."

10 The cock he hadna crawd but once,
And clappd his wings at a',
When the youngest to the eldest said,
"Brother, we must awa.

11 "The cock doth craw, the day doth daw,
The channerin worm doth chide;
Gin we be mist out o our place,
A sair pain we maun bide.

12 "Fare ye weel, my mother dear!
Fareweel to barn and byre!
And fare ye weel, the bonny lass
That kindles my mother's fire!"

Anonymous

21. syke: rivulet. **22. sheugh:** trench. **42. channerin:** fretting, gnawing. **43. gin:** if.
* As B. J. Whiting points out in *Traditional British Ballads* (New York: Appleton–Century–Crofts, 1955, p. 155), since "Martinmas is November 11, the very fact that the sons' hats are of unseasonal birch is enough to indicate that they are revenants even without the explicit statement that this is not earthly birch." The asterisks here and below indicate that the text in this version is incomplete.

As a modern variant of the revenant theme, we have included Ezra Pound's *Ballad of the Goodly Fere*. This, too, is a revenant story, concerning the Jesus who appeared to the disciples on the road to Emmaus, after his death, and who revealed himself to them in the breaking of bread, before his ascension to the other world. In form the poem resembles the old English ballads, and the language is a dialect chosen to evoke a speaker of humble origins who might have lived in medieval England. This may seem a strange way to present the story of the crucifixion of Christ, who was a Jew from the Near East, a thousand years before this dialect was spoken. But through the use of this dialect, by a speaker who is obviously a common man, perhaps a sailor, or a carpenter, like Jesus himself, Pound makes the familiar story personal, real, and universal. The carpenter of Nazareth is a real person to this workman of the Middle English period, for he speaks of Jesus as a good companion. He tells the story of the last days with admiration. Not a capon priest, but a man of men was he, a strong man who could take action. Simon says:

> I ha' seen him drive a hundred men
> Wi' a bundle o' cords swung free,
> That they took the high and holy house
> For their pawn and treasury.

He is impressed by the miracles, the healing of the lame and the blind, the raising of the dead, but he is impressed most of all by the brave way in which this man met his death on the cross. And, as almost anyone would, he boasts about his friend. They may think they have killed him, but "They are fools eternally./ I ha' seen him eat o' the honey-comb / Sin' they nailed him to the tree." This happening seems to the speaker to be a village miracle: he has seen this with his own eyes, and he believes what he has seen. As we read the poem in its imitation of Middle English dialect and form, we feel, almost without thinking about it, the universality of this story, which happened in Palestine almost two thousand years ago. By reminding us of the reality the story had to a common workman living in England a thousand years ago, the poem endows it with a special immediacy for us living today.

BALLAD OF THE GOODLY FERE

Simon Zelotes speaketh it somewhile after the Crucifixion

Ha' we lost the goodliest fere o' all
For the priests and the gallows tree?
Aye lover he was of brawny men,
O' ships and the open sea.

1. fere: companion; pronounced like "fear."

When they came wi' a host to take Our Man
His smile was good to see,
"First let these go!" quo' our Goodly Fere,
"Or I'll see ye damned," says he.

Aye he sent us out through the crossed high spears
And the scorn of his laugh rang free,
"Why took ye not me when I walked about
Alone in the town?" says he.

Oh we drank his "Hale" in the good red wine
When we last made company,
No capon priest was the Goodly Fere
But a man o' men was he.

I ha' seen him drive a hundred men
Wi' a bundle o' cords swung free,
That they took the high and holy house
For their pawn and treasury.

They'll no' get him a' in a book I think
Though they write it cunningly;
No mouse of the scrolls was the Goodly Fere
But aye loved the open sea.

If they think they ha' snared our Goodly Fere
They are fools to the last degree.
"I'll go to the feast," quo' our Goodly Fere,
"Though I go to the gallows tree."

"Ye ha' seen me heal the lame and blind,
And wake the dead," says he,
"Ye shall see one thing to master all:
'Tis how a brave man dies on the tree."

A son of God was the Goodly Fere
That bade us his brothers be.
I ha' seen him cow a thousand men.
I have seen him upon the tree.

He cried no cry when they drave the nails
And the blood gushed hot and free,
The hounds of the crimson sky gave tongue
But never a cry cried he.

I ha' seen him cow a thousand men
On the hills o' Galilee,
They whined as he walked out calm between,
Wi' his eyes like the grey o' the sea,

Like the sea that brooks no voyaging
With the winds unleashed and free,
Like the sea that he cowed at Genseret
Wi' twey words spoke' suddenly.

A master of men was the Goodly Fere,
A mate of the wind and sea,
If they think they ha' slain our Goodly Fere
They are fools eternally.

I ha' seen him eat o' the honey-comb
Sin' they nailed him to the tree.

1909 EZRA POUND (1885–)

EXERCISE 28

Read *The Wife of Usher's Well* and Pound's *Ballad of the Goodly Fere* carefully. Scan them both and try to account for the numerous substitutions in the meter of Pound's work. Note that his entire poem uses variants of the same *b* rhyme. In what way does this device affect the poem? How do the repetitions of phrases in sequential stanzas affect *The Wife of Usher's Well*?

Pound's ballad is intentionally and frankly an attempt to write what might have been a genuine popular ballad of medieval times. Does this technique seem to you to be in any way false or "insincere"? Explain. How does the poem compare with other literary ballads you have studied in the effectiveness of its imitation of the popular form?

The Wife of Usher's Well reflects a commonly accepted view of the activities of real people in relation to revenants. Versions of it have had wide popularity in both Britain and America. Is belief in revenants essential to an understanding of the poem? Do you see any relationship between the attitude toward supernatural events expressed in the two poems and your own attitude toward phenomena which you have not personally examined (whether these are explained by science or not yet accounted for scientifically)?

Ballads of American Working Life

This final pair of ballads makes use of a typically American popular theme. In *John Henry* a railroad man chooses to die rather than give in to the steam drill. The literary counterpart to this narrative is Stephen Vincent Benét's *The Ballad of William Sycamore*, in which a man dies because of the fencing-in of the open prairie.

JOHN HENRY

1 John Henry was a railroad man,
He worked from six 'till five,
"Raise 'em up bullies and let 'em drop down,
I'll beat you to the bottom or die."

2 John Henry said to his captain:
"You are nothing but a common man,
Before that steam drill shall beat me down,
I'll die with my hammer in my hand."

3 John Henry said to the Shakers:
"You must listen to my call,
Before that steam drill shall beat me down,
I'll jar these mountains till they fall."

4 John Henry's captain said to him:
"I believe these mountains are caving in."
John Henry said to his captain: "Oh Lord!
That's my hammer you hear in the wind."

5 John Henry he said to his captain:
"Your money is getting mighty slim,
When I hammer through this old mountain,
Oh Captain will you walk in?"

6 John Henry's captain came to him
With fifty dollars in his hand,
He laid his hand on his shoulder and said:
"This belongs to a steel driving man."

7 John Henry was hammering on the right side,
The big steam drill on the left,
Before that steam drill could beat him down,
He hammered his fool self to death.

8 They carried John Henry to the mountains,
From his shoulder his hammer would ring,
She caught on fire by a little blue blaze,
I believe these old mountains are caving in.

9 John Henry was lying on his death bed,
He turned over on his side,
And these were the last words John Henry said:
"Bring me a cool drink of water before I die."

10 John Henry had a little woman,
Her name was Pollie Ann,
He hugged and kissed her just before he died,
Saying, "Pollie, do the very best you can."

11 John Henry's woman heard he was dead,
  She could not rest on her bed,
She got up at midnight, caught that No. 4 train,
  "I am going where John Henry fell dead."

12 They carried John Henry to that new burying ground,
  His wife all dressed in blue,
She laid her hand on John Henry's cold face,
  "John Henry, I've been true to you."

Anonymous

THE BALLAD OF WILLIAM SYCAMORE
(1790-1871)

My father, he was a mountaineer,
His fist was a knotty hammer;
He was quick on his feet as a running deer,
And he spoke with a Yankee stammer.

My mother, she was merry and brave,
And so she came to her labor,
With a tall green fir for her doctor grave
And a stream for her comforting neighbor.

And some are wrapped in the linen fine,
And some like a godling's scion;
But I was cradled on twigs of pine
In the skin of a mountain lion.

And some remember a white, starched lap
And a ewer with silver handles;
But I remember a coonskin cap
And the smell of bayberry candles.

The cabin logs, with the bark still rough,
And my mother who laughed at trifles,
And the tall, lank visitors, brown as snuff,
With their long, straight squirrel-rifles.

I can hear them dance, like a foggy song,
Through the deepest one of my slumbers,
The fiddle squeaking the boots along
And my father calling the numbers.

The quick feet shaking the puncheon-floor,
And the fiddle squealing and squealing,
Till the dried herbs rattled above the door
And the dust went up to the ceiling.

There are children lucky from dawn till dusk,
But never a child so lucky!
For I cut my teeth on "Money Musk"
In the Bloody Ground of Kentucky!

When I grew tall as the Indian corn,
My father had little to lend me,
But he gave me his great, old powder-horn
And his woodsman's skill to befriend me.

With a leather shirt to cover my back,
And a redskin nose to unravel
Each forest sign, I carried my pack
As far as a scout could travel.

Till I lost my boyhood and found my wife,
A girl like a Salem clipper!
A woman straight as a hunting-knife
With eyes as bright as the Dipper!

We cleared our camp where the buffalo feed,
Unheard-of streams were our flagons;
And I sowed my sons like the apple-seed
On the trail of the Western wagons.

They were right, tight boys, never sulky or slow,
A fruitful, a goodly muster.
The eldest died at the Alamo.
The youngest fell with Custer.

The letter that told it burned my hand.
Yet we smiled and said, "So be it!"
But I could not live when they fenced the land,
For it broke my heart to see it.

I saddled a red, unbroken colt
And rode him into the day there;
And he threw me down like a thunderbolt
And rolled on me as I lay there.

The hunter's whistle hummed in my ear
As the city-men tried to move me,
And I died in my boots like a pioneer
With the whole wide sky above me.

Now I lie in the heart of the fat, black soil,
Like the seed of the prairie-thistle;
It has washed my bones with honey and oil
And picked them clean as a whistle.

And my youth returns, like the rains of Spring,
And my sons, like the wild-geese flying;
And I lie and hear the meadow-lark sing
And have much content in my dying.

Go play with the towns you have built of blocks,
The towns where you would have bound me!
I sleep in my earth like a tired fox,
And my buffalo have found me.

1922 STEPHEN VINCENT BENÉT (1898–1943)

EXERCISE 29

The traditional ballad, whether popular or literary, is a narrative. Consider the ballads *John Henry* and *The Ballad of William Sycamore* as stories. Who or what is the hero in each poem? (How would you define "hero"?) What is the difference between William Sycamore's wife and John Henry's woman, Pollie Ann?

Note the differences especially in the rhyming of the two poems. What effect do the rhymes have on the poems in which they appear?

Comment on the difference between the dialogue used in *John Henry* and the first-person (from beyond the grave) narrative of *The Ballad of William Sycamore*. Where *John Henry* uses quoted speech, Benét uses descriptive diction with images and metaphors. To what effect?

From your study of popular and literary ballads, especially the two examined in this exercise, try to make some critical generalizations about the differences between the two types. Do not undertake a decision about which type has greater artistic or literary merit.

EXERCISE 30

Choose a sensational story current in the news: murder, suicide, crimes of violence, supernatural events, or other materials which the original writers of ballads might have chosen. Using the techniques and form of the popular ballad so far as possible, write a ballad. Do not attempt humor. Remember that some of the apparent crudities of the old ballads, inexpertly handled, may produce ridiculous rather than awesome effects. To what extent do you think you have succeeded in solving the problems presented by ballad materials and techniques?

QUATRAIN FORMS

The differing kinds of subject matter, as well as the sheer number of ballads that exist, attest to the flexibility of the two basic ballad stanzas. Thus it is not surprising that poets have adapted ballad form, sometimes intact and sometimes with major variations, to other types of subject matter.

Hymns come to mind immediately as the second largest body of verse utilizing ballad stanzas, which emerge, slightly polished in rhythm and rhyme, as COMMON MEASURE ($a^4 b^3 c^4 b^3$ or $a^4 b^3 a^4 b^3$), LONG MEASURE ($a^4 b^4 a^4 b^4$), or SHORT MEASURE ($a^3 b^3 a^3 b^3$). Almost any familiar hymn fits one of these three ballad variants, though often, as in the well-known song quoted below, the tune changes with the second QUATRAIN, so that a stanza seems to be a unit of eight lines. Each stanza, however, begins $a^4 b^3 a^4 b^3$:

O beautiful for spacious skies,*
For amber waves of grain,
For purple mountain majesties
Above the fruited plain!
America! America!
God shed his grace on thee,
And crown thy good with brotherhood
From sea to shining sea.

From KATHARINE LEE BATES, *America the Beautiful*, 1893

Emily Dickinson made the ballad or hymn stanza a vehicle for serious poetry, using these stanzas or a variant of them in almost all her poems. In the poem given below, the middle two stanzas follow the commonest ballad stanza ($a^4 b^3 c^4 b^3$) exactly. In stanza 1, the *b* rhyme is "approximate" or "related sound"; in stanza 4, the third line has three instead of four stresses:

I TASTE A LIQUOR NEVER BREWED

I taste a liquor never brewed—
b From Tankards scooped in Pearl—
Not all the Vats upon the Rhine
b? Yield such an Alcohol!

Inebriate of Air—am I—
And Debauchee of Dew—
Reeling—thro endless summer days—
From inns of Molten Blue—

* The symbol ` indicates secondary or minor stress (see ACCENT).

When "Landlords" turn the drunken Bee
Out of the Foxglove's door—
When Butterflies—renounce their "dreams"—
I shall but drink the more!

Till Seraphs swing their snowy Hats—
And Saints—to windows run—
To see the little Tippler
Leaning against the—Sun—

EMILY DICKINSON (1830–1886)

Robert Graves, a twentieth-century poet, writes a literary ballad using both common measure (*e.g.*, stanza 2) and short measure (*e.g.*, stanzas 1 and 3). In this poem, the student will notice that the subject matter, absence of extensive motivation or explanation, and dialogue form typical of the popular ballad have been imitated:

A FROSTY NIGHT

"Alice, dear, what ails you,
Dazed and lost and shaken?
Has the chill night numbed you?
Is it fright you have taken?"

"Mother, I am very well,
I was never better.
Mother, do not hold me so,
Let me write my letter."

"Sweet, my dear, what ails you?"
"No, but I am well.
The night was cold and frosty—
There's no more to tell."

"Ay, the night was frosty,
Coldly gaped the moon,
Yet the birds seemed twittering
Through green boughs of June.

"Soft and thick the snow lay,
Stars danced in the sky—
Not all the lambs of May-day
Skip so bold and high.

"Your feet were dancing, Alice,
Seemed to dance on air,
You looked a ghost or angel
In the star-light there.

"Your eyes were frosted star-light;
Your heart, fire and snow.
Who was it said, 'I love you'?"
"Mother, let me go!"

1920, rev. ROBERT GRAVES (1895–)

Numerous examples of short measure can also be found in Emily Dickinson's work.

When A. E. Housman uses long measure in *"On Wenlock Edge,"* the result is neither ballad nor hymn:

ON WENLOCK EDGE

a^4 On Wenlock Edge the wood's in trouble;
b^4 His forest fleece the Wrekin heaves;
a^4 The gale, it plies the saplings double,
b^4 And thick on Severn snow the leaves.

'Twould blow like this through holt and hangar
When Uricon the city stood:
'Tis the old wind in the old anger,
But then it threshed another wood.

Then, 'twas before my time, the Roman
At yonder heaving hill would stare:
The blood that warms an English yeoman,
The thoughts that hurt him, they were there.

There, like the wind through woods in riot,
Through him the gale of life blew high;
The tree of man was never quiet:
Then 'twas the Roman, now 'tis I.

The gale, it plies the saplings double,
It blows so hard, 'twill soon be gone:
To-day the Roman and his trouble
Are ashes under Uricon.

A. E. HOUSMAN (1859–1936)

Since Housman here deals with violence of several kinds and ordinary man's reaction to it, always the same despite time's intervention, the ballad stanza, venerable and popular in the strictest sense of the word, seems highly appropriate. Perhaps because Housman returns frequently to this general theme of time—especially the paradox of time as the killer of all things and yet the continuator of the cycle of regeneration—he uses the ballad or hymn stanza, particularly long measure, frequently. In long measure, we find *Reveille, "When I Watch the Living Meet," "When the Lad for Longing Sighs,"* and many others.

A number of Housman's most famous works, notably *"With Rue My Heart Is Laden"* and *"Is My Team Ploughing"* (p. 363), are in short measure; and exactly the same slight variation on common measure which we saw in *America the Beautiful* on p. 158 (pairs of quatrains grouped to form an eight-line unit) is used in *"When I Was One-and-Twenty."*

So far, we have been looking at samples of genuine ballad or hymn stanzas, differing primarily from their metric models in subject matter or degree of refinement. When we consider some of Emily Dickinson's rhymes, however, or Graves' willingness to vary short measure with common measure in the same poem, we realize that the "requirements" of ballad meter—loose and undemanding though they seem—can be loosened still further. There are, in fact, numerous quatrain types that appear to be variations on ballad or hymn meter.

Not all these types are "looser" than the typical ballad stanza; in the lines given immediately below, for example, a single rhyme sound is used throughout the quatrain.

a God, temper with tranquillity
a My manifold activity
a That I may do my work for Thee
a With very great simplicity.

Anonymous

Seldom used, perhaps because of the fairly demanding rhyme scheme, the *aaaa* variant nevertheless appears in *The Ballad of Davy Crockett*, a song that enjoyed many weeks on the Hit Parade in the 1950's:

Born on a mountain top in Tennessee,
Greenest state in the land of the Free;
Raised in the woods so he knew every tree;
Killed him a b'ar when he was only three.

A variation on long measure (which uses four stresses in each line) is exemplified by a poem whose subject matter is far removed from balladry, Shelley's *The Sensitive Plant*, and by a popular work song of our century, *Sixteen Tons*, in which subject matter and tone closely resemble ballad materials. In looking at the single stanzas given below of these two pieces of verse, the student will notice that the only difference between this type of quatrain and long measure is a slight variation in the rhyme scheme—couplets instead of alternating rhymes:

a A Sensitive Plant in a garden grew,
a And the young winds fed it with silver dew,
b And it opened its fan-like leaves to the light,
b And closed them beneath the kisses of night.

From PERCY BYSSHE SHELLEY, *The Sensitive Plant*, 1820

SIXTEEN TONS

a You load sixteen tons and what do you get—
a Another day older and deeper in debt.
b Saint Peter, don't you call me 'cause I can't go—
b I owe my soul to the company sto'.

Anonymous, mid-20th cent.

There are several other variant quatrains which differ from the ballad stanzas not in the rhyme scheme, like the ones treated previously, but in meter. In one type, a variation on common meter, the second and fourth lines contain two stresses instead of the typical three:

a^4 Weep with me all you that read
b^2 This little story;
a^4 And know, for whom a tear you shed,
b^2 Death's self is sorry.

From BEN JONSON, *Epitaph on Salathiel Pavy*, 1616

The so-called "heroic quatrain" is a metrical variation on long measure; each line has five feet instead of four:

a^5 The boast of heraldry, the pomp of power,
b^5 And all that beauty, all that wealth e'er gave,
a^5 Await alike th'inevitable hour.
b^5 The paths of glory lead but to the grave.

From THOMAS GRAY, *Elegy Written in a Country Churchyard*, 1750

a^5 But these are flowers that fly and all but sing:
b^5 And now from having ridden out desire
a^5 They lie closed over in the wind and cling
b^5 Where wheels have freshly sliced the April mire.

From ROBERT FROST, *Blue-Butterfly Day*, 1923

Poets have also experimented with a six-foot quatrain. D. H. Lawrence and William Henley both make use of six-foot, couplet-rhymed stanzas:

We'll go no more a-roving by the light of the moon.
November glooms are barren beside the dusk of June.
The summer flowers are faded, the summer thoughts are sere.
We'll go no more a-roving, lest worse befall, my dear.

From WILLIAM ERNEST HENLEY, *"We'll Go No More a-Roving,"* 1888

Softly, in the dusk, a woman is singing to me;
Taking me back down the vista of years, till I see
A child sitting under the piano, in the boom of the tingling strings
And pressing the small, poised feet of a mother who smiles as she sings.

From D. H. LAWRENCE, *Piano*, 1929

Lawrence alters the couplet-rhymed long-measure variant still further in a poem consisting of a single quatrain of seven-foot lines:

A WHITE BLOSSOM

A tiny moon as small and white as a single jasmine flower
Leans all alone above my window, on night's wintry bower,
Liquid as lime-tree blossom, soft as brilliant water or rain
She shines, the first white love of my youth, passionless and in vain.

D. H. LAWRENCE (1885–1930)

This seven-foot quatrain is of special interest because it is the basis of one of the theories concerning the development of the most common ballad stanza, $a^4 b^3 c^4 b^3$: that this four-line stanza was originally a rhyming seven-foot couplet. Arranged as follows on the page, Lawrence's *A White Blossom* falls neatly into common measure quatrains, $a^4 b^3 c^4 b^3$:

A tiny moon as small and white
  As a single jasmine flower
Leans all alone above my window,
  On night's wintry bower,
. . .

Certain quatrains, though probably offshoots of ballad and hymn stanzas, have attained separate identity because of the fame of the poems in which they first received wide notice. Most notable among such quatrains is the so-called *In Memoriam* stanza (see under STANZA), which, like some of the variant quatrains we have looked at earlier, such as Shelley's *The Sensitive Plant*, differs from a traditional ballad stanza in the arrangement of its rhymes: here, *abba* instead of the typical *abab*.

A number of poets have used this *abba* quatrain in distinctly different ways. The samples given below differ in their line lengths as well as their content:

a^4 Strong Son of God, immortal Love,
b^4 Whom we, that have not seen Thy face,
b^4 By faith, and faith alone, embrace,
a^4 Believing where we cannot prove;

From ALFRED, LORD TENNYSON, *In Memoriam*, 1850, St. 1

a^6 Still, citizen sparrow, this vulture which you call
b^5 Unnatural, let him but lumber again to air
b^5 Over the rotten office, let him bear
a^5 The carrion ballast up, and at the tall

a^5 Tip of the sky lie cruising. Then you'll see
b^6 That no more beautiful bird is in heaven's height,
b^6 No wider more placid wings, no watchfuller flight;
a^5 He shoulders nature there, the frightfully free,

a^5 The naked-headed one. Pardon him, you
b^5 Who dart in the orchard aisles, for it is he
b^5 Devours death, mocks mutability,
a^5 Has heart to make an end, keeps nature new.

From RICHARD WILBUR, *"Still, Citizen Sparrow,"* 1947

a^2 I sang as one
b^4 Who on | a tilt|ing deck | ∧ sings|
b^5 To keep men's courage up, though the wave hangs
$a^3(a^2)$ That shall | cut off | their sun.| (*or* ⏑ ⏑ ∠ | ⏑ ⏑ ∠)

a^2 As storm-cocks sing,
b^6 Flinging | their nat|ural an|swer in | the wind's | ∧ teeth,|
b^4 And care not if it is waste of breath
a^3 Or birth-carol of spring.

a^3 As ocean-flyer clings
b^6 To height, to the last drop of spirit driving on
b^4 While yet ahead is land to be won
a^2 And work for wings.

From C. DAY LEWIS, *The Conflict*, 1933

In *The Conflict*, the student should notice that all the *b* rhymes are the type of approximate rhyme known as consonance (see RHYME, CONSONANTAL), but that accurate masculine *a* rhymes enclose and unify each quatrain. This unifying effect of the full *a* rhymes is particularly necessitated by the lack of uniformity in the lengths of the lines. (Because the lines are hard to divide into feet with any degree of assurance, scansion is open to question. For one outstandingly difficult line alternative scansions are provided.)

The type of quatrain which Edward Fitzgerald made famous by using it throughout his adaptation of *The Rubáiyát* differs from its ancestor, long measure, both in rhyme scheme and in meter. Each line has five feet, and the *a* rhyme appears three times; the third line of each stanza, which for uniformity's sake we have labeled *b*, does not rhyme with anything.

a^5 A Book of Verses underneath the Bough,
a^5 A Jug of Wine, a Loaf of Bread—and Thou
b^5 Beside me singing in the Wilderness—
a^5 Ah, Wilderness were Paradise enow!

From EDWARD FITZGERALD, *The Rubáiyát of Omar Khayyám*, 1859, St. 12

So numerous and so widely varied are the quatrain types in English and American verse that it would be impossible to give even a fully representative sampling, much less an exhaustive compilation. Many examples, by a wide range of poets, could be cited for almost every one of the quatrain variants that we have discussed here, and there are certainly many which we have not discussed: among them, the stanza of Keats' literary ballad *La Belle Dame* (p. 133), which uses the stanza pattern $a^4 b^4 c^4 b^2$, an unusual variation on long measure; or some of Emily Dickinson's quatrains, which play tricks on ears that she leads to expect an ordinary hymn stanza.

Several of Emily Dickinson's tricks-on-the-ear are worth looking at individually here, for they represent extremes in variation on the ballad or hymn quatrain. One of the most striking is this well-known poem:

I'M NOBODY

I'm Nobody! Who are you?
Are you—Nobody—too?
Then there's a pair of us!
Don't tell! they'd banish us—you know!

How dreary—to be—Somebody!
How public—like a Frog—
To tell your name—the livelong day—
To an admiring Bog!

EMILY DICKINSON (1830–1886)

Because of the second stanza, one tends to hear this poem as either common measure ($a^4 b^3 a^4 b^3$) or short measure ($a^3 b^3 a^3 b^3$). Then one begins to scan—and discovers that it is neither, and both, depending on individual reading (the student might find it instructive to scan this poem himself); and one is almost always startled to discover that the last line in stanza 1 rhymes accurately with nothing whatever, although it is related to the terminal sound of lines 1 and 2.

In another poem, sometimes titled *Mysteries*, Miss Dickinson leads the reader to expect quatrains—a variation on short meter, $a^3 a^3 b^3 b^3$; then she shocks the ear with a fifth line at the end of every four-line unit. The poem gains unity as well as surprise from this device, since the first fifth line uses a terminal *l* sound, which is repeated in the same place in the next two stanzas. All three terminal fifth lines are of the same length:

MYSTERIES

a^3 The Murmur of a Bee
a^3 A Witchcraft—yieldeth me—
b^3 If any ask me why—
b^3 'Twere easier to die—
c^1 Than tell—

a^3 The Red upon the Hill
a^3 Taketh away my will—
b^3 If anybody sneer—
b^3 Take care—for God is here—
a^1 That's all. approximate rhyme

a^3 The Breaking of the Day approximate rhyme
a^3 Addeth to my Degree—
b^3 If any ask me how— approximate rhyme
b^3 Artist—who drew me so—
c^1 Must tell!

EMILY DICKINSON (1830–1886)

Such experimentation with the quatrain paves the way for what might appear to be the most extreme variation on this stanza form, the completely unrhymed quatrain. It is interesting to notice that this "extreme" was practiced as far back as the eighteenth century:

5 How air is hush'd, save where the weak-ey'd bat,
5 With short shrill shriek, flits by on leathern wing,
3 Or where the beetle winds
3 His small but sullen horn,

From WILLIAM COLLINS, *Ode to Evening*, 1746

TWENTIETH-CENTURY EXAMPLES OF QUATRAIN FORMS

Experimentation with the quatrain, particularly with the loosely rhymed or entirely unrhymed kind, continues currently. One of the best places to listen for the quatrain, especially the ballad stanza, is, as has already been suggested, the radio or television. It is perhaps no accident that in the 1940's the term "ballad" was used for almost every popular song, even those seemingly least like the ballad in subject and tone: such nonnarrative songs as *Smoke Gets in Your Eyes* ($a^3a^3b^3b^3$) and *Too Young* (essentially $a^4a^4b^4b^4$). Many serious contemporary poets also continue to use the ballad stanzas and their variants. Two examples appear below; many more could be given.

A GIFT OF GREAT VALUE

Oh that horse I see so high
when the world shrinks into its
relationships, my mother
sees as well as I.

She was born, but I bore with her.
This horse was a mighty occasion!
The intensity of its feet! The height
of its immense body!

Now then in wonder at evening, at
the last small entrance of the night,
my mother calls it, and I
call it *my father*.

With angry face, with no
rights, with impetuosity and
sterile vision—and a great
wind we ride.

1956–58 ROBERT CREELEY (1926–)

RECAPITULATIONS

I

a^4 I was born downtown on a wintry day
b^4 And under the roof where Poe expired;
a^4 Tended by nuns my mother lay
b^4 Dark-haired and beautiful and tired.

Doctors and cousins paid their call,
The rabbi and my father helped.
A crucifix burned on the wall
Of the bright room where I was whelped.

At one week all my family prayed,
Stuffed wine and cotton in my craw;
The rabbi blessed me with a blade
According to the Mosaic Law.

The white steps blazed in Baltimore
And cannas and white statuary.
I went home voluble and sore
Influenced by Abraham and Mary.

II

$a^{\smile 4}$ At one the Apocalypse had spoken,
$a^{\smile 4}$ Von Moltke fell, I was housebroken.

At two how could I understand
The murder of Archduke Ferdinand?

France was involved with history,
I with my thumbs when I was three.

A sister came, we neared a war,
Paris was shelled when I was four.

I joined in our peach-kernel drive
For poison gas when I was five.

At six I cheered the big parade,
Burned sparklers and drank lemonade.

At seven I passed at school though I
Was far too young to say *Versailles*.

At eight the boom began to tire,
I tried to set our house on fire.

The Bolsheviks had drawn the line,
Lenin was stricken, I was nine.

—What evils do not retrograde
To my first odious decade?

III

a^4 Saints by whose pages I would swear,
$b(a?)^4$ My Zarathustra, Edward Lear,
a^4 Ulysses, Werther, fierce Flaubert,
$b(a?)^4$ Where are my books of yesteryear?

Sixteen and sixty are a pair;
We twice live by philosophies;
My marginalia of the hair,
Are you at one with Socrates?

Thirty subsides yet does not dare,
Sixteen and sixty bang their fists.
How is it that I no longer care
For Kant and the Transcendentalists?

17, 18. For an explanation of the rhyme notation, see RHYME, FEMININE.

Public libraries lead to prayer,
  EN APXH ἦν ὁ λόγος—still
Eliot and John are always there
  To tempt our admirari nil.

IV

a^3 I lived in a house of panels,
b^3   Victorian, darkly made;
c^3 A virgin in bronze and marble
b^3   Leered from the balustrade.

The street was a tomb of virtues,
  Autumnal for dreams and haunts;
I gazed from the polished windows
  Toward a neighborhood of aunts.

Mornings I practiced piano,
  Wrote elegies and sighed;
The evenings were conversations
  Of poetry and suicide.

Weltschmerz and mysticism,
  What tortures we undergo!
I loved with the love of Heinrich
  And the poison of Edgar Poe.

V

a^5 My first small book was nourished in the dark,
b^5 Secretly written, published, and inscribed.
a^5 Bound in wine-red, it made no brilliant mark.
b^5 Rather impossible relatives subscribed.

The best review was one I wrote myself
Under the name of a then-dearest friend.
Two hundred volumes stood upon my shelf
Saying my golden name from end to end.

I was not proud but seriously stirred;
Sorrow was song and money poetry's maid!
Sorrow I had in many a ponderous word,
But were the piper and the printer paid?

50. Transliterated, the Greek reads "En archē ēn ho logos," *i.e.,* "In the beginning was the Word" (John 1:1). **52. admirari nil:** wondering at, or being moved by, nothing. **65. Weltschmerz:** sorrow for the state of the world. **67. Heinrich:** Heinrich Heine, German poet, 1797–1856.

VI

a^5 The third-floor thoughts of discontented youth
a^5 Once saw the city, hardened against truth,
b^5 Get set for war. He coupled a last rime
b^5 And waited for the summons to end time.

It came. The box-like porch where he had sat,
The four bright boxes of a medium flat,
Chair he had sat in, glider where he lay
Reading the poets and prophets of his day,

He assigned abstractly to his dearest friend,
Glanced at the little street hooked at the end,
The line of poplars lately touched with spring,
Lovely as Laura, breathless, beckoning.

Mother was calm, until he left the door;
The trolley passed his sweetheart's house before
She was awake. The Armory was cold,
But naked, shivering, shocked he was enrolled.

It was the death he never quite forgot
Through the four years of death, and like as not
The true death of the best of all of us
Whose present life is largely posthumous.

VII

a^4 We waged a war within a war,
b^3 A cause within a cause;
c^4 The glory of it was withheld
b^3 In keeping with the laws
d^4 Whereby the public need not know
d^4 The pitfalls of the status quo.

Love was the reason for the blood:
The black men of our land
Were seen to walk with pure white girls
Laughing and hand in hand.
This most unreasonable state
No feeling White would tolerate.

We threw each other from the trams,
We carried knives and pipes,
We sacrificed in self-defense
Some of the baser types,
But though a certain number died
You would not call it fratricide.

The women with indignant tears
Professed to love the Blacks,
And dark and wooly heads still met
With heads of English flax.
Only the Cockney could conceive
Of any marriage so naïve.

Yet scarcely fifty years before
Their fathers rode to shoot
The undressed aborigines,
Though not to persecute.
A fine distinction lies in that
They have no others to combat.

By order of the high command
The black men were removed
To the interior and north;
The crisis thus improved,
Even the women could detect
Their awful fall from intellect.

VIII

a^3 I plucked the bougainvillaea
b^3 In Queensland in time of war;
c^3 The train stopped at the station
b^3 And I reached it from my door.

I have never kept a flower
And this one I never shall
I thought as I laid the blossom
In the leaves of *Les Fleurs du Mal.*

I read my book in the desert
In the time of death and fear,
The flower slipped from the pages
And fell to my lap, my dear.

I sent it inside my letter,
The purplest kiss I knew,
And thus you abused my passion
With "A most Victorian Jew."

1943 KARL SHAPIRO (1913–)

144. Les Fleurs du Mal: collection of poems by Charles Baudelaire.

VII

The Development of Tetrameter and Four-Stress Verse

There are two major kinds of verse in English that employ four stresses to the line. One, four-stress verse proper, takes no account of the number of syllables in a line; it is the oldest type of verse employed in English. The other, tetrameter, differs from the first in being a metrical verse, in which the line is organized into four feet and usually consists of eight syllables (hence the name "octosyllabic verse," also given to this type of verse). The origins of the two types are quite different. We shall consider tetrameter first.

TETRAMETER

English tetrameter probably derives from French octosyllabic verse, a syllable-counting verse (see SYLLABIC VERSE) which was commonly written with couplet rhyme. The French octosyllabic couplet was the usual meter of the medieval romances, written by such authors as Wace and Chrétien de Troyes. Although the meter (or adaptations of it) appears in both Old and Middle English verse, Biblical paraphrases, romances, etc., the first major poet to use the form was Chaucer in his early poems *The Book of the Duchess*, *c.* 1369, and *The House of Fame*, *c.* 1380. These works reflect the strong influence of thirteenth-century French poets such as Machaut, who used the octosyllabic couplet; but even a cursory examination of lines in Chaucer will show that the syllable counting is far from exact: the lines vary from seven to nine syllables (or even more, according to some readings). To Chaucer's ear, the French octosyllabic became in English an iambic tetrameter (see under METER), with various substitutions. He apparently recognized also the dangers of this form in English: when the couplets are regularly end-stopped and a precisely medial CESURA is used, the form quickly becomes monotonous. Chaucer undertook variations through the use of ENJAMBEMENT, flexible placement of the cesura, double or feminine rhymes (see under RHYME), etc. Although both *The Book of the Duchess* and *The House of Fame* are poems of distinction, it is worth noting that Chaucer's major poems, the works of his maturity, *The Canterbury Tales* and *Troilus and Criseyde*, are written for the most part in iambic pentameter. By way of contrast with Chaucer's use of the octosyllabic or tetrameter couplet, the student should glance at what R. M. Alden calls "the interminable narrative" of the *Confessio Amantis*, written by Chaucer's contemporary John Gower, who was widely admired in the fourteenth century for his moral seriousness, to which Chaucer himself alludes.

Since the fourteenth century, the octosyllabic couplet has been used for narrative poems by such authors as Scott, Burns, Wordsworth, Byron, and Whittier, and for satire by Samuel Butler, Swift, and others. It is not, however, a meter favored by the major poets for their longer, serious works. Marvell, in *To His Coy Mistress*, and Milton, in his "twin poems" *L'Allegro* and *Il Penseroso*, use the meter for meditative, descriptive verse with notable success. Scholars and critics have despaired of accounting for Milton's technique in these poems, but students who undertake Exercise 32 will have an opportunity to test some of the techniques used.

HISTORIC EXAMPLES OF TETRAMETER COUPLET

This was the tale: There was a king
That highte Seys, and had a wif,
The beste that mighte bere lyf,
And this quene highte Alcyone.
So it befil, thereafter soone,
This king wol wenden over see.
To tellen shortly, whan that he
Was in the see, thus in this wise,
Such a tempest gan to rise
That brak her mast and made it falle,
And clefte her ship, and dreinte hem alle,
That never was founden, as it telles,

63. highte: called. **64. bere lyf:** be alive. **72. dreinte:** drowned.

Bord ne man, ne nothing elles.
Right thus this king Seys loste his lif.
Now for to speken of his wif:—
This lady, that was left at hom,
Hath wonder that the king ne com
Hom, for it was a longe terme.
Anon her herte began to erme;
. . .

From Geoffrey Chaucer, *The Book of the Duchess*, *c.* 1369

This finde I write in Poesie:
Ceïx the king of Trocinie
Hadde Alceone to his wif,
Which as hire oghne hertes lif
Him loveth; and he hadde also
A brother, which was cleped tho
Dedalion, and he per cas
Fro kinde of man forschape was
Into a goshauk of liknesse;
Whereof the king gret hevynesse
Hath take, and thoghte in his corage
To gon upon a pelrinage
Into a strange regioun
Wher he hath his devocioun
To don his sacrifice and preie,
If that he mihte in eny weie
Toward the goddes finde grace
His brother hele to pourchace,
So that he mihte be reformed
Of that he hadde be transformed.
To this pourpos and to this ende
This king is redy forto wende,
As he which wolde go be schipe;
And forto don him felaschipe
His wif unto the see him broghte,
With al hire herte and him besoghte,
That he the time hire wolde sein
Whan that he thoghte come ayein:
"Withinne," he seith, "two monthe day."

From John Gower, *Confessio Amantis*, *c.* 1395, IV

74. ne . . . ne: neither . . . nor. **80. erme:** grieve, be sad. **2930. oghne:** own. **2932. cleped:** named. **2934. kinde:** nature; **forschape:** transformed. **2935. goshauk:** a kind of hawk. **2938. pelrinage:** pilgrimage. **2944. hele:** health, well-being. **2954. ayein:** again.

EXERCISE 31

Although modern readers would unquestionably designate Chaucer as the major English poet of the fourteenth century, his contemporaries preferred "moral Gower" for his didactic qualities. The two excerpts given above are both the beginning of a narrative of the tragic tale of King Ceyx and his wife Alcyone. Chaucer uses the tale in *The Book of the Duchess* as part of the dream structure of his poem: the narrator says he fell asleep after reading the story in Ovid. Gower, in the *Confessio Amantis*, uses this story (and many others) as an illustration, offered by the Priest of Venus to the confessing, unsuccessful lover, of the deadly sin of sloth against secular love. The tale is, therefore, part of a framework which enables Gower to tell a number of famous stories, just as the pilgrimage serves as a framework for *The Canterbury Tales*. Examine the two excerpts, which are of the same length, for narrative technique, especially characterization and motivation. Although Professor Alden is unquestionably correct about the tedious length of Gower's poem, careful examination of selected passages will reveal a skillful narrative poet.

In the following examples tetrameter is adapted to a variety of purposes besides narrative:

But let my due feet never fail
To walk the studious cloister's pale,
And love the high embowed roof,
With antique pillars massy proof,
And storied windows richly dight,
Casting a dim religious light.
There let the pealing organ blow,
To the full-voic'd quire below,
In service high and anthems clear,
As may with sweetness, through mine ear,
Dissolve me into ecstasies,
And bring all heav'n before mine eyes.
And may at last my weary age
Find out the peaceful hermitage,
The hairy gown and mossy cell,
Where I may sit and rightly spell
Of every star that heav'n doth shew,
And every herb that sips the dew;
Till old experience do attain
To something like prophetic strain.
These pleasures, Melancholy, give,
And I with thee will choose to live.

From JOHN MILTON, *Il Penseroso*, c. 1634

A sect, whose chief devotion lies
In odd, perverse antipathies;
In falling out with that or this,
And finding something still amiss;
More peevish, cross, and splenetic
Than dog distract, or monkey sick.
That with more care keep holy-day
The wrong, than others the right way:
Compound for sins they are inclin'd to
By damning those they have no mind to;

From SAMUEL BUTLER, *Hudibras*,* 1663, Canto I

But at my back I always hear
Time's winged chariot hurrying near;
And yonder all before us lie
Deserts of vast eternity.
Thy beauty shall no more be found,
Nor, in thy marble vault, shall sound
My echoing song; then worms shall try
That long preserv'd virginity,
And your quaint honour turn to dust,
And into ashes all my lust.
The grave's a fine and private place,
But none I think do there embrace.

From ANDREW MARVELL, *To His Coy Mistress*, *c.* 1660

When chapman billies leave the street,
And drouthy neebors neebors meet;
As market-days are wearing late,
An' folk begin to tak the gate;
While we sit bousing at the nappy,
An' getting fou and unco happy,
We think na on the lang Scots miles,
The mosses, waters, slaps, and stiles,
That lie between us and our hame,
Whare sits our sulky, sullen dame,
Gathering her brows like gathering storm,
Nursing her wrath to keep it warm.

From ROBERT BURNS, *Tam O'Shanter*, 1790

Breathes there the man, with soul so dead,
Who never to himself hath said,
This is my own, my native land!

* A modern work comparable to *Hudibras* is W. H. Auden's *The Double Man* (see p. 237).
1. chapman billies: peddlers. **5. bousing at the nappy:** drinking ale. **6. fou:** full; **unco:** uncommonly. **8. mosses:** bogs; **slaps:** gaps, passes.

Whose heart hath ne'er within him burn'd,
As home his footsteps he hath turn'd,
From wandering on a foreign strand!
If such there breathe, go, mark him well;
For him no Minstrel raptures swell;
High though his titles, proud his name,
Boundless his wealth as wish can claim;
Despite those titles, power, and pelf,
The wretch, concentred all in self,
Living, shall forfeit fair renown,
And, doubly dying, shall go down
To the vile dust, from whence he sprung,
Unwept, unhonour'd, and unsung.

O Caledonia! stern and wild,
Meet nurse for a poetic child!
Land of brown heath and shaggy wood,
Land of the mountain and the flood,
Land of my sires! what mortal hand
Can e'er untie the filial band,
. . .

From SIR WALTER SCOTT, *The Lay of the Last Minstrel*, *c.* 1800, Canto VI, Sts. 1–2

They chain'd us each to a column stone,
And we were three—yet, each alone;
We could not move a single pace,
We could not see each other's face,
But with that pale and livid light
That made us strangers in our sight:
And thus together—yet apart,
Fetter'd in hand, but joined in heart,
'Twas still some solace, in the dearth
Of the pure elements of earth,
[To hearken to each other's speech,]*

From George Gordon, LORD BYRON, *The Prisoner of Chillon*, 1816

The sun that brief December day
Rose cheerless over hills of gray,
And, darkly circled, gave at noon
A sadder light than waning moon.
Slow tracing down the thickening sky
Its mute and ominous prophecy,
A portent seeming less than threat,

* Omit in scansion exercise.

It sank from sight before it set.
A chill no coat, however stout,
Of homespun stuff could quite shut out,
A hard, dull bitterness of cold,
That checked, mid-vein, the circling race
Of life-blood in the sharpened face,
The coming of the snow-storm told.
The wind blew east; we heard the roar
Of Ocean on his wintry shore
And felt the strong pulse throbbing there
Beat with low rhythm our inland air.

Meanwhile we did our nightly chores,
Brought in the wood from out of doors,
Littered the stalls, and from the mows
Raked down the herd's-grass for the cows:
. . .

From John Greenleaf Whittier, *Snow-Bound*, 1866

EXERCISE 32

Count the number of *syllables* in each line of the passages from Milton, Scott, and Whittier. Write the number of syllables at the end of each line, thus:

1 2 3 4 5 6 7 8
Alas for him who never sees 8

Scan the passages, indicating pauses and rhyme. Make up a statistical table of the substitutions as you did for the passages in iambic pentameter. You will discover that, although the 22 lines in each passage are usually octosyllabic, they are more accurately to be described as iambic tetrameter; to arrive at the percentages, therefore, 22×4 (88) must be divided into the number of substitutions.

Although the subject matter of the three poems is quite different—Milton is discussing some of the pleasures of the thoughtful or scholarly man; Scott is writing in praise of patriotism, especially of devotion to Scotland; Whittier is beginning a long poem with a description of a snowstorm—it should be possible to compare the skill with which each poet manages the available poetic devices. The chief difficulty with so-called "octosyllabic" or iambic tetrameter couplet in English is its tendency to monotony in long passages. The monotony may be avoided, at least to some extent, by altering the number of syllables, the type of feet, and the placement of cesuras and terminal pauses, by variation in the accuracy and types of rhyme, and by the use of appropriately striking diction. It might be noted that tetrameter has been used in English, for the most part, by minor poets (often for narrative) and by major poets in OCCASIONAL POETRY or short poems. After making your technical analysis of these three passages, consider diction and imagery. Then write a short essay in which you try to account for the effects achieved in each passage. Which poet uses the form most successfully in view of the content of his work? Why?

TWENTIETH-CENTURY EXAMPLES OF TETRAMETER COUPLET

Two modern examples of iambic tetrameter, as used in complete poems by Walter de la Mare and Robert Frost, follow. One of the poems is essentially description, the other wry commentary. Both are brief. The student may be interested in using the techniques applied in the exercise on Milton, Scott, and Whittier to evaluate these poems. No major contemporary poet has used tetrameter couplet for extended (book-length) narrative, though poems of several pages may be found in Frost. The poems in this section may help the reader decide how effectively tetrameter couplet, or some variant of it, can be used in this century.

SILVER

Slowly, silently, now the moon
Walks the night in her silver shoon;
This way, and that, she peers, and sees
Silver fruit upon silver trees;
One by one the casements catch
Her beams beneath the silvery thatch;
Couched in his kennel, like a log,
With paws of silver sleeps the dog;
From their shadowy cote the white breasts peep
Of doves in a silver-feathered sleep;
A harvest mouse goes scampering by,
With silver claws and a silver eye;
And moveless fish in the water gleam,
By silver reeds in a silver stream.

WALTER DE LA MARE (1873–1956)

THE NIGHT LIGHT

She always had to burn a light
Beside her attic bed at night.
It gave bad dreams and broken sleep,
But helped the Lord her soul to keep.
Good gloom on her was thrown away.
It is on me by night or day,
Who have, as I suppose, ahead
The darkest of it still to dread.

1947 ROBERT FROST (1874–1963)

EXERCISE 33

Write a poem in "octosyllabic couplet," really iambic tetrameter couplet. You may introduce variations, but the approximate number and kinds of variations should not exceed those you found in the poems in this form which you have studied. Note the types of material, satire, narrative, description, used by earlier poets in this meter. For your own poem, do the scansion and make up the statistical tables as you did in Exercise 32. Consider carefully your use of diction and figures. Do you think that you have managed to avoid monotony in the poem you have written? If not, where and why did you fail?

In the following examples of modern tetrameter verse, the first presents a nearly conventional handling of tetrameter couplet, which contrasts with the intermittent and often much modified use of tetrameter in the others.

SOLO FOR EAR-TRUMPET

a^4 The carriage brushes through the bright
a^4 Leaves (vi|olent jets | from life | to light).|
b^5 Strong polished speed is plunging, heaves
b^4 Between the showers of bright hot leaves.
c^4 The window-glasses glaze our faces
c^4 And jar them to the very basis,—
d^4 But they could never put a polish
d^4 Upon my manners, or abolish
e^4 My most distinct disinclination
e^4 For calling on a rich relation!
f^4 In her house,—bulwark built between
f^4 The life man lives and visions seen,—
g^4 The sunlight hiccups white as chalk,
g^4 Grown drunk with emptiness of talk,
h^4 And silence hisses like a snake,
h^4 Invertebrate and rattling ache. . . .*

c–e: feminine rhymes

i^4 Till suddenly, Eternity
i^4 Drowns all the houses like a sea,
j^4 And down the street the Trump of Doom
j^5 Blares,—barely shakes this drawing-room

minor-accent rhyme

* The dots are the author's. The poem has been printed complete.

k^4 Where raw-edged shadows sting forlorn
k^4 As dank dark nettles. Down the horn
l^4 Of her ear-trumpet I convey
l^4 The news that: "It is Judgment Day!"
m^4 "Speak louder; I don't catch, my dear."
m^4 I roared: *"It is the Trump we hear!"*
n^4 "The *What*?"—"The TRUMP!" . . . "I shall complain—
n^4 The boy-scouts practising again!"

1919 EDITH SITWELL (1887–1964)

A more experimental use of tetrameter is seen in Karl Shapiro's *Recapitulations* (p. 167), in which each of the eight sections is in a different form. The poem can be considered a kind of survey of variants on open pentameter couplet, ballad meter, and tetrameter couplet.

MacLeish's *Ars Poetica*, a highly experimental poem in couplet, is not only a statement on the art of poetry (the title is borrowed from the classical work by Horace), but a compendium of nearly every kind of image and, in the final section, of metaphor and symbol. Although the basic meter appears to be tetrameter, there is great variety in line length and types of rhyme.

ARS POETICA

a^5 A poem should be palpable and mute
a^2 As a globed fruit,

b^1 Dumb
b^4 As old medallions to the thumb,

c^4 Silent as the sleeve-worn stone
c^5 Of casement ledges where the moss has grown—

d^3 A poem should be wordless — omit unstressed syllable
$d?^3$ As the flight of birds. — omit final *s*

*

e^5 A poem should be motionless in time
$e?^2$ As the moon climbs, — omit final *s*

f^4 Leaving, as the moon releases
f^5 Twig by twig the night-entangled trees, — *f*: assonantal rhyme

f^6 Leaving, as the moon behind the winter leaves,
$e?^5$ Memory by memory the mind— — related to *e* rhyme

e^5 A poem should be motionless in time
$e?^2$ As the moon climbs. — omit final *s*

*

g^4 A poem should be equal to:
g^1 Not true.

h^4 For all the history of grief
h^5 An empty doorway and a maple leaf.

$h?^1$ For love — related sound*
i^6 The leaning grasses and two lights above the sea—

i^3 A poem should not mean — assonantal rhyme
i^1 But be.

1926 ARCHIBALD MACLEISH (1892–)

Yeats' poem *A Crazed Girl* appears to be a tetrameter variant on the SONNET form, especially in the OCTAVE, which clearly adheres to the tetrameter of tradition (except in lines 1 and 5) and uses interlocking rhymes, as the girl dances crazily to her improvised music. The SESTET picks up the *e* rhyme from the octave twice, in "wound" and "sound," but other lines are unrhymed, or have only related sounds. Line 13, though it has four stresses, does not have four feet, and cannot be scanned as tetrameter. The function of the prosody in the sestet is to hold a pattern, still related, however distantly, to recognizable conventions, while emphasizing the incomprehensible madness of the girl and her singing.

A CRAZED GIRL

a^5 That crazed girl improvising her music,
b^4 Her poetry, dancing upon the shore,
c^4 Her soul in division from itself
b^4 Climbing, falling she knew not where, — consonantal rhyme
d^5 Hiding amid the cargo of a steamship,
b^4 Her knee-cap broken, that girl I declare
d^4 A beautiful lofty thing, or a thing — assonantal rhyme
e^4 Heroically lost, heroically found.

f^4 No matter what disaster occurred
e^4 She stood in desperate music wound,
h^4 Wound, wound, and she made in her triumph
i^4 Where the bales and the baskets lay
e^4 No common intelligible sound
i^4 But sang, "O sea-starved, hungry sea." — related sound

1936–39 WILLIAM BUTLER YEATS (1865–1939)

* The *v* of "love" is the voiced sound corresponding to the unvoiced *f* in "grief" and "leaf," a distant but still perceptible relationship.

FOUR-STRESS VERSE

The second type of verse in English employing four stresses to a line—the type to which the term "four-stress verse" properly applies—is actually the oldest type of English verse known to us, and, in its original form, without rhyme, perhaps the only verse we practice which has Germanic rather than Romance or classical origins. This verse should not be called "tetrameter," since "meter" suggests measurement by feet, and Anglo-Saxon verse, the earliest example of it, was measured only by stresses, four to each line (see STRESS PROSODY). Four-stress verse as defined here* is exactly the opposite of syllable-counting, octosyllabic verse, since the number of syllables to a line has no significance; syllables, as such, seem not to have been heard—most of this verse is of oral composition, for recitation. In theory, at least, the number of syllables could have ranged from four (all stressed) to twelve or more, as Coleridge suggests in his Preface to *Christabel*. Virtually all Anglo-Saxon poetry that has come down to us is composed of four-stress verse, without terminal rhyme, but characterized by regularly patterned alliteration in each line. The "rules" for ANGLO-SAXON PROSODY were derived by James Wilson Bright, in the nineteenth century, from a close study of the long Anglo-Saxon poem *Beowulf*; the major points from these rules appear below. We have no statement of poetic theory written by critics or poets of the Old and Middle English periods.

Literary remains in Old English from the period following the Norman Conquest in 1066 are few. Poetry written in England was composed in Latin, French, or Anglo-Norman. When English poetry of merit begins to reappear in the thirteenth century and in the works of Chaucer and Gower in the fourteenth century, much of it shows the strong influence of the Romance languages (derived from Latin) and the techniques of Romance versification. In the fourteenth century, there were, however, two major poets who wrote in the Middle English language in an adaptation of the old Anglo-Saxon alliterative line. One of these was William Langland, in the long poem *Piers Plowman*, which has come down to us in three forms, probably representing major revisions, the A-, B-, and C-text, in more than fifty manuscripts—a number suggesting the wide popularity of the work in its own time. Like *Beowulf*, *Piers Plowman* makes use of a regular pattern of alliteration which binds the lines together in a fashion similar to that of terminal rhyme in Romance versification. This type of alliteration should properly be called *structural alliteration* (see

* The term TUMBLING VERSE, sometimes applied to four-stress verse, usually designates *rhyming* four-stress verse. It may also designate rhyming stress verse employing more or fewer than four stresses to a line, *e.g.*, SKELTONIC VERSE.

under ALLITERATION), because the alliteration is directly related to the structure of the line. In the other tradition of English verse, which dominates English poetry from Chaucer to modern times, alliteration is used for ornament, and the structure is governed by meter and terminal rhyme. The alliteration of *Piers Plowman* differs in use, to some extent, from that of *Beowulf*, but the basic pattern is still present. The second major poet who used a type of the alliterative four-stress line in the fourteenth century is the anonymous author of *The Pearl* and *Sir Gawain and the Green Knight*. The versification of these two poems is extremely complex (see p. 186), but both use the basic four-stress line in combination with an elaborate scheme of terminal rhymes. The so-called "Alliterative Revival" of the fourteenth century was abortive, however, and the form was not employed again in any major poem before the twentieth century.

Both knowledge of the two older forms of our language and critical theory about Anglo-Saxon and Middle English verse were virtually nonexistent until the middle of the nineteenth century. In the early nineteenth century, Coleridge began to compose *Christabel* (which he never finished) in what he describes in his Preface to the poem as a "new principle." The poem is actually based on the old Anglo-Saxon principle of four stresses to each line, but no use is made of structural alliteration. Instead, the poem is written in four-stress rhyming couplets of widely varying numbers of syllables, and represents—unknown to Coleridge—a combination of the Anglo-Saxon tradition with the dominant European or Continental (especially French and Italian) tradition characterized by the use of terminal rhyme. After Coleridge, some poets familiar with earlier verse forms, notably Gerard Manley Hopkins and W. H. Auden, wrote verse based on stress, in which structural alliteration was frequently used as well. Auden's long poem *The Age of Anxiety* and Pound's imitation or translation of the Anglo-Saxon *The Sea Farer*, as well as Cummings' "*All in Green Went My Love Riding*," are contemporary adaptations of the versification of *Beowulf*.

*Professor Bright's Rules for Anglo-Saxon Versification**

Anglo-Saxon poetry is composed in a kind of blank-verse, in long unrimed (but alliterative) . . . lines.

General Principles

1. Every *line* consists of two parts, the first half-line and the second half-line; these half-lines are separated by a caesura [pause] and united by alliteration (*i.e.* initial rime; end-rime occurs occasionally, but merely as an incidental ornament).

* James W. Bright, *An Anglo-Saxon Reader* (New York: Henry Holt, 1891).

2. Every *half-line* has two rhythmical stresses, or accents, and consequently two rhythmical measures . . .; it is a structural unit and has a scansion of its own, independent of that of its complementary half-line. . . .

6. *Alliteration, i.e.* the riming of the initial sounds of words, or syllables, is employed to unite the two half-lines into the larger rhythmical unit of the complete line. Alliteration is confined to rhythmically accented syllables; any alliteration of unaccented syllables is to be regarded as accidental, and therefore without significance in the structure of the line. Alliterating syllables have the same initial consonant (*st*, *sp*, and *sc* alliterate each with itself only), or they have an initial vowel sound, any vowel or diphthong whatever alliterating with itself or with any other vowel sound. [An alliterative sound used in a given line is not repeated in the next six lines.]

7. The *rhythmical accentuation* coincides in general with the accentuation required by the sense. The four chief stresses of a complete line therefore fall upon the four most significant words or syllables of that line. . . .

8. *Alliteration* and *rhythmical accentuation*, therefore, conjointly give prominence to the logically significant elements of the line, but alliteration does not attend every rhythmical stress: in the second half-line alliteration marks the first stress; in the first half-line it marks either the first stress, or the first and the second, or, less frequently, the second only.

HISTORIC EXAMPLES OF FOUR-STRESS VERSE

The language of *Beowulf* is Anglo-Saxon, the ancient precursor of modern English. Although the sense of the passage will probably remain obscure, the sound of it can be approximated by noting the stressed alliteration:

Hwaet, we Gar-Dena   in geardagum
Theodcyninga   thrym gefrunon,
Hu tha aethelingas   ellen fremedon!
Oft Scyld Scefing   sceathena threatum
Monegum maegthum   meodosetla ofteah;
Egsode eorlas,   syththan aerest wearth
Feasceaft funden;   he thaes frofre gebad,
Weox under wolcnum,   weorthmyndum thah,
Oth thaet him aeghwylc   thara ymbsittendra
Ofer hronrade   hyran scolde,
. . .

From *Beowulf*, 7th cent.

3, 6, 9. Occasional lines use stressed vowels.

The language of *Piers Plowman*, of which the opening lines are cited below, is Middle English, the English heavily influenced by French which emerged after the Norman Conquest (1066) to become the literary language of the fourteenth century.

In a somer seson . whan soft was the sonne,
I shope me in shroudes . as I a shepe were,
In habite as an heremite . unholy of workes,
Went wyde in this world . wondres to here.
Ac on a May mornynge . on Malverne hulles,
Me byfel a ferly . of fairy, me thoughte;
I was wery forwandred . and went me to reste
Under a brode banke . bi a bornes side,
And as I lay and lened . and loked in the wateres,
I slombred in a slepyng . it sweyved so merye.

From William Langland, *Piers Plowman*, B-text, *c.* 1377

Only the stresses marked by alliteration have been indicated in both the above passages. There are four stresses in each line, but only line 1 of *Piers Plowman* stresses the *s* four times. The dot in the middle of Langland's lines indicates the medial pause, or cesura. This same cesura is frequently marked in modern texts of *Beowulf* by an open space in the middle of the line, as here. Old and Middle English letters for *th* and *gh* have been silently corrected.

The anonymous author of *Sir Gawain and the Green Knight* wrote his poem in four-stress alliterative verse in STROPHES, of varying length, each followed by five lines in metrical verse with terminal rhyme, $a^1 b^3 a^3 b^3 a^3$. This appendage is called the bob (a^1) and wheel (the three-foot remainder of the rhyming stanza); it is not a refrain, because the material in the bob and wheel continues and completes the ideas of the alliterative strophe. As in Anglo-Saxon verse, there is a cesura in each line of the strophe. The alliteration is set by the initial stressed sound of the word bearing the third stress; this sound also appears at the beginning of at least one stressed syllable (sometimes two) before the cesura.

The combination of stress verse and metrical verse in *Sir Gawain* is an interesting one. The same author probably used a variant combination in *The Pearl*, where the four-stress alliterative verse is combined with terminal rhyme in twelve-line stanzas with a consistent rhyme pattern of *abab, abab, bcbc*; the

2. shope: clothed; **shroudes:** clothes; **shepe:** shepherd. **6. ferly:** marvel; **fairy:** fairy-land. **7. forwandred:** tired with wandering. **8. bornes:** brook. **10. sweyved:** sounded.

terminal *c* line (or a variant) is used for five stanzas and serves as a link to the first line of the sixth, throughout a poem of one hundred stanzas.

The illustration given below is a description of the Green Knight as he rides into King Arthur's castle during the Christmas feast to present his challenge. Although the dialect is more difficult than that of Chaucer, the student may be able to visualize the overwhelming greenness of this apparition on horseback in the great hall.

Two Middle English letters not now used have been silently corrected.

Ande al graythed in grene this gome and his wedes:
A strayte cote ful streght, that stek on his sides,
A meré mantile abof, mensked withinne
With pelure pured apert, the pane ful clene
With blythe blaunner ful bryght, and his hod bothe,
That watz laght fro his lokkez and layde on his schulderes;
Heme wel-haled hose of that same grene,
That spenet on his sparlyr, and clene spures under
Of bryght golde, upon silk bordes barred ful ryche,
And scholes under schankes there the schalk rides;
And alle his vesture verayly watz clene verdure,
Bothe the barres of his belt and other blythe stones,
That were richely rayled in his aray clene
Aboutte hymself and his sadel, upon silk werkez.
That were to tor for to telle of tryfles the halve
That were enbrauded abof, wyth bryddes and flyghes,
With gay gaudi of grene, the golde ay inmyddes.
The pendauntes of his payttrure, the proude cropure,
His molaynes, and alle the metail anamayld was thenne,
The steropes that he stod on stayned of the same,
And his arsounz al after and his athel sturtes,
That ever glemered and glent al of grene stones;
The fole that he ferkkes on fyn of that ilke,

151. gome: man; **wedes:** garments. **152. stek:** clung. **153. mensked:** trimmed. **154. pelure pured apert:** fur closely cut; **pane:** outside. **155. blaunner:** ermine (?). **156. laght:** caught back. **157. haled:** neat. Alliteration lacking after cesura. **158. spenet:** clung; **sparlyr:** calves. **160. scholes:** guards; **schalk:** leather. **163. rayled:** arranged. **165. tor:** hard. **166. bryddes and flyghes:** birds and butterflies. **168. payttrure:** bit, studs; **cropure:** crupper. **169. molaynes:** breast-trappings. **171. arsounz:** saddle-bows; **athel sturtes:** studded nails. **173. fole:** horse; **ferkkes:** bestrode.

sertayn,
A grene | hors gret | and thikke,|
A stede | ful stif | to strayne,|
In brawd|en bry|del quik—|
To the gome | he watz | ful gayn.|

From *Sir Gawain and the Green Knight, c.* 1375

EXERCISE 34

Following the rules for Anglo-Saxon alliterative verse, write a poem in this form. Mark the alliterative stressed syllables, and indicate the major alliterative sound to the left of your finished work. The alliteration should mark from two to four of the four syllables you would accent naturally in a meaningful reading:

S With scented assassins, salad-eaters
V And value our vanities, provide our souls

From W. H. Auden, *The Age of Anxiety*, 1947

Make sure that the alliterative consonant is the initial consonant sound in the *stressed* syllable, which is not necessarily the first syllable of the word. In writing alliteration, remember that the letter *c* has the sound of either *k* or *s*; *s* may be *s* or *z* in sound; *th* may be voiced, as in "thine," or unvoiced, as in "thin"; *wh* correctly pronounced does not alliterate with *w*.

To what extent do you think that the techniques of Anglo-Saxon verse can be poetically successful in modern English verse? Can you suggest variations on these techniques which might improve the form in contemporary use?

Following the "Alliterative Revival" of the fourteenth century, with Langland and the nameless author of *Gawain* and *The Pearl*, no major poet used the four-stress line until 1797, when Coleridge did in his unfinished poem *Christabel*. Because of the absence of linguistic and prosodic studies of Middle English at that date, Coleridge was probably unaware of the principles governing Anglo-Saxon and Middle English stress verse. He presents an account of the principles governing *Christabel* in his Preface, of which an excerpt here precedes some passages from the poem:

> I have only to add that the metre of Christabel is not, properly speaking, irregular, though it may seem so from its being founded on a new principle: namely, that of counting in each line the accents, not the syllables. Though the latter may vary from seven to twelve, yet in each line the accents will be found to be only four. Nevertheless, this occasional variation in number of syllables is not introduced

176. strayne: hard to curb. **177. brawden:** broidered. **178. gayn:** necessary.

wantonly, or for the mere ends of convenience, but in correspondence with some transition in the nature of the imagery or passion.

'Tis the middle of the night by the castle clock,
And the owls have awakened the crowing cock;
Tu—whit!——Tu—whoooo!
And hark, again! the crowing cock,
How drowsily it crew.
. . .

There is not wind enough to twirl
The one red leaf, the last of its clan,
That dances as often as dance it can,
Hanging so light, and hanging so high,
On the topmost twig that looks up at the sky.
. . .

They passed the hall, that echoes still,
Pass as lightly as you will!
The brands were flat, the brands were dying,
Amid their own white ashes lying;
But when the lady passed there came
A tongue of light, a fit of flame;
And Christabel saw the lady's eye,
And nothing else saw she thereby,
Save the boss of the shield of Sir Leoline tall,
Which hung in a murky old niche in the wall.
. . .

"Bard Bracy! bard Bracy! your horses are fleet,
Ye must ride up the hall, your music so sweet,
More loud than your horses' echoing feet!
And loud and loud to Lord Roland call,
Thy daughter is safe in Langdale hall!
Thy beautiful daughter is safe and free—
Sir Leoline greets thee thus through me!"

From SAMUEL TAYLOR COLERIDGE, *Christabel,* 1797–1800

EXERCISE 35

After reading the complete text of *Christabel,* in an anthology or in an edition of Coleridge's works, consider the excerpt from his Preface and carefully examine the passages cited. Count the number of syllables in each line. Is the poet accurate in commenting that the number of syllables in these lines varies from seven to twelve? In determining the number of accents, remember that the poet has given directions for meaningful reading. Wherever possible, four stresses should be given to each line. Comment on those lines in which you find it difficult or impossible to read the lines with four stresses. For each line in which the number of syllables varies from the "normal" eight, try to find justification for Coleridge's comment that these variations occur "in correspondence with some transition in the nature of the imagery or passion." Are there lines in which you feel that the variation in syllables is "introduced wantonly, or for the mere ends of convenience"?

TWENTIETH-CENTURY EXAMPLES OF FOUR-STRESS VERSE

An example of the revival of the four-stress alliterative line in a long poem is W. H. Auden's *The Age of Anxiety*, which won the Pulitzer Prize in 1948. As the title suggests, the poem deals with the problems of a century very remote from those of the heroic epic. The lines quoted below are spoken by the PERSONA to his mirror image in a Third Avenue bar:

My deuce, my double, my dear image,
Is it lively there, that land of glass
Where song is a grimace, sound logic
A suite of gestures? You seem amused.
How well and witty when you wake up,
How glad and good when you go to bed,
Do you feel, my friend? What flavor has
That liquor you lift with your left hand;
Is it cold by contrast, cool as this
To a soiled soul; does your self like mine
Taste of untruth? . . .

From W. H. AUDEN, *The Age of Anxiety*, 1947, Part I

Cummings' poem *"All in Green Went My Love Riding"* is included here as an example of twentieth-century experimentation: the materials are derived from courtly love and from the ballad tradition; the prosody is based on stress verse. Alternating stanzas of 4, 3, and 3, and 4 and 3, stresses are used—there are some variants. Alliteration and repetition occur, though not in the strict patterns of medieval and Renaissance verse, and there are variant types of terminal rhyme. The images of the poem are provocative. A trained reader suspects Freudian symbolism and symbolism, not clearly identifiable, related to the Elizabethan puns on "deer"/"dear" and "hart"/"heart."

ALL IN GREEN WENT MY LOVE RIDING

All in green went my love riding
on a great horse of gold
into the silver dawn.

four lean hounds crouched low and smiling
the merry deer ran before.

Fleeter be they than dappled dreams
the swift sweet deer
the red rare deer.

Four red roebuck at a white water
the cruel bugle sang before.

Horn at hip went my love riding
riding the echo down
into the silver dawn.

four lean hounds crouched low and smiling
the level meadows ran before.

Softer be they than slippered sleep
the lean lithe deer
the fleet flown deer.

Four fleet does at a gold valley
the famished arrow sang before.

Bow at belt went my love riding
riding the mountain down
into the silver dawn.

four lean hounds crouched low and smiling
the sheer peaks ran before.

Paler be they than daunting death
the sleek slim deer
the tall tense deer.

Four tall stags at a green mountain
the lucky hunter sang before.

All in green went my love riding
on a great horse of gold
into the silver dawn.

four lean hounds crouched low and smiling
my heart fell dead before.

1923 E. E. CUMMINGS (1894–1962)

EXERCISE 36

Mark the stressed syllables in Cummings' poem, and compare its pattern of alliteration with that in the selection from *Sir Gawain* (p. 187).

For the Middle English poem mark the cesura in each line, and in the margin note the recurrences of the stressed consonant sound before and after the cesura, thus:

2+1 S Til hit watz sóne sésoun / that the súnne ryses

For purposes of clarity in your analysis of Cummings' poem, choose at random a different colored pencil for each of his *major* alliterative sounds (see under ALLITERATION), *e.g.*, red for *g*, blue for *h*. Mark each major alliterative sound with the color you have chosen, in order to visualize the sound pattern. Be sure to attach a brief chart of the colors and sounds to your exercise, *e.g.*, red=*g*, blue=*h*, etc. Comment on the effectiveness of the stress verse and the structural alliteration in each poem.

Examine the descriptive diction in each poem. To what end does it seem to be used? In Cummings' poem, try to identify the images and repetitions with coherent symbolism. (To do this with the mysterious Green Knight and his unusual challenge, you would need to read the whole poem—but he, too, is clearly a symbolic figure, as are the events of the poem.) What effect, beyond mere variety, is added by the use of the bob and wheel in *Sir Gawain*? By the variant rhyming in Cummings? Both poets are experimenting (six centuries apart) with the basic four-stress alliterative line in symbolic narrative. Comment on possible future experiments in this form.

ORNAMENTAL ALLITERATION IN METRICAL VERSE

As already indicated, English verse from the time of Chaucer to the present has employed alliteration chiefly as a decorative or ornamental device (see ALLITERATION, ORNAMENTAL). By contrast with the structural alliteration of Anglo-Saxon verse, which required from two to four repetitions of the alliterative sound in each line and did not employ the same alliterative sound within the next six lines, ornamental alliteration has no "rules," but the most successful poets are careful not to repeat the same sounds too frequently in a single line, because the result tends to be ludicrous. Some skilled poets also extend the use of similar consonantal sounds through a number of lines to gain certain auditory and emotional effects.

A particularly sensitive user of ornamental alliteration in the English tradition is Spenser, "the poet's poet," examples from whose *Faerie Queene* are given below; the two stanzas are rich in both major and minor ornamental alliteration. For contrast (overuse), the student may examine typical poems by Swinburne in the nineteenth century, where the effect tends to be hypnotic.

> Therewith she spewd out of her filthy maw
> A floud of poyson horrible and blacke,
> Full of great lumpes of flesh and gobbets raw,
> Which stunck so vildly,* that it forst him slacke
> His grasping hold, and from her turne him backe:
> Her vomit full of bookes and papers was,
> With loathly frogs and toades, which eyes did lacke,
> And creeping sought way in the weedy gras:
> Her filthy parbreake† all the place defiled has.

From EDMUND SPENSER, *The Faerie Queene*, Bk. I (*c.* 1590), Canto I, St. 20

> And more, to lulle him in his slumber soft,
> A trickling streame from high rocke tumbling downe,
> And ever-drizling raine upon the loft,
> Mixt with a murmuring winde, much like the sowne
> Of swarming bees, did cast him in a swowne:
> No other noyse, nor peoples troublous cryes,
> As still are wont t'annoy the walled towne,
> Might there be heard: but carelesse Quiet lyes,
> Wrapt in eternall silence farre from enemyes.

Ibid., St. 41

> When the hounds of spring are on winter's traces,
> The mother of months in meadow or plain
> Fills the shadows and windy places
> With lisp of leaves and ripple of rain;
> And the brown bright nightingale amorous
> Is half assuaged for Itylus,
> For the Thracian ships and the foreign faces,
> The tongueless vigil, and all the pain.

From ALGERNON CHARLES SWINBURNE, Chorus from *Atalanta in Calydon*, 1865

> And death shall have no dominion.
> Dead men naked they shall be one
> With the man in the wind and the west moon;
> When their bones are picked clean and the clean bones gone,
> They shall have stars at elbow and foot;
> Though they go mad they shall be sane,

* **vildly:** vilely. † **parbreake:** vomit.

Though they sink through the sea they shall rise again;
Though lovers be lost love shall not;
And death shall have no dominion.

From DYLAN THOMAS, *"And Death Shall Have No Dominion,"* 1939

End in the mud-flat detritus of death.
My heart, beat faster, faster. In Black Mud
Hungarian workmen give their blood
For the martyre Stephen, who was stoned to death.

From ROBERT LOWELL, *Colloquy in Black Rock*, 1944

EXERCISE 37

For one of the two stanzas of Spenser's *The Faerie Queene* cited above, select the alliterative sounds, both major and minor (see under ALLITERATION), which seem to you most important to the impression the lines produce. As in Exercise 36, use colors to show the alliterative pattern (making sure to provide a key relating each color to a sound). In a brief paragraph, comment on the effect intended in the passage, and indicate how the use of ornamental alliteration contributes to, or detracts from, that effect.

NOTE: In all subsequent exercises, examine and mark the verse passage for alliteration, and add your evaluation of this technique to your other analyses and criticisms.

VIII

The Sonnet

ADAPTATION AND DEVELOPMENT OF THE SONNET IN ENGLISH

The sonnet in English owes its origins and its initial popularity among Elizabethan poets to the profound influence of the Italian Renaissance on the literary and artistic life of sixteenth-century England. The Italian sonnet, of which Francis Petrarch was one of the most gifted practitioners (see SONNET, PETRARCHAN), was probably introduced into England in the form of translation, or near-translation, by two of the great innovators in verse technique in English, Henry Howard, Earl of Surrey, and Sir Thomas Wyatt. Both these Englishmen conceived of the sonnet, as did Petrarch, as a formal poem using the subject matter of real or imagined courtly love, with all its conventions. The Italian sonnet by Petrarch given below is a typical example of his form and materials. It is followed by a near-translation of the same poem by Wyatt.

AMOR, CHE NEL PENSER MIO VIVE E REGNA

a Amor, che nel penser mio vive e regna,
b E'l suo seggio maggior nel mio cor tene,
b Talor armato ne la fronte vene:
a Ivi si loca, ed ivi pon sua insegna.
a Quella ch'amare e sofferir ne'nsegna,
b E vol che'l gran desio, l'accesa spene,
b Ragion, vergogna e reverenza affrene,
a Di nostro ardir fra sè stessa si sdegna.

c Onde Amor paventoso fugge al core,
d Lasciando ogni sua impresa, e piange e trema:
c Ivi s'asconde, e non appar più fore.
c Che poss'io far, temendo il mio signore,
d Se non star seco infin a l'ora estrema?
c Ché bel fin fa chi ben amando more.

FRANCIS PETRARCH (1304–1374), *Rime*, Sonnet 109

THE LONG LOVE THAT IN MY THOUGHT DOTH HARBOR

a	The long love that in my thought doth harbor,	feminine rhyme
b	And in mine heart doth keep his residence,	minor-accent
b	Into my face presseth with bold pretence,	
a	And therein campeth, spreading his banner.	feminine approximate
a	She that me learneth to love and suffer,	feminine approximate
b	And wills that my trust and lust's negligence	minor-accent
b	Be reined by reason, shame, and reverence,	minor-accent
a	With his hardiness taketh displeasure.	feminine approximate
c	Wherewithal, unto the heart's forest he fleith,	feminine ending, sound related to *d*
d	Leaving his enterprise with pain and cry;	
e	And there him hideth and not appeareth.	feminine rhymes
e	What may I do when my master feareth,	
d	But in the field with him to live and die?	
d	For good is the life ending faithfully.	minor-accent, approximate

SIR THOMAS WYATT (1503?–1542)

It is useful to note that while Petrarch uses the standard Italian OCTAVE (*abba, abba*), Wyatt uses approximate feminine *a* rhymes (which can also be considered minor-accent rhymes) and minor-accent *b* rhymes in which the rhyme occurs on the secondary stress of words like "residence."* In the SESTET, Petrarch uses *cdc cdc*, while Wyatt uses *cd ee dd*. Two of the *d* rhymes, "cry" and "die," are conventionally accurate masculine rhymes, while in the final line "faithfully" is both minor-accent and approximate. This arrangement *may* be the result of the most obvious difference between the sonnet in Italian and the sonnet in English: the difficulty, in the latter, of maintaining a sequence of accurate rhymes on the same major or stressed syllable. It may, however, be attributed to the subtlety of Wyatt's poetic craftsmanship, by which the assertion of the final line that the life of the faithful lover is good is deliberately undermined by a rhyme trailing off uncertainly in a minor accent.

* Under RHYME, see *approximate rhyme*; *feminine rhyme*; *minor-accent rhyme*.

Wyatt was among the first poets, but by no means the last writing in English, to discover and to struggle with the tightly interwoven rhyme pattern of the Italian sonnet. Detailed study of the numerous poems of Wyatt in the sonnet as well as other forms suggests that, like the experimental poets of the twentieth century, he was deliberately manipulating a variety of rhymes to help convey an uncertain and dissatisfied state of mind. His arrangement of the *c* and *d* rhymes indicates that it is inaccurate to describe even the earliest English examples of the Italian sonnet as terminating in either *cde cde* or *cd cd cd* and never in a couplet. The constant practice of many of the Elizabethan writers in this form involved the use of a final couplet, and this practice can be illustrated from so-called Petrarchan sonnets written in Italian.

An interesting comparison in the translation or imitation of Petrarch's sonnet is offered by Surrey's *Complaint of a Lover Rebuked.* Surrey must be ranked as one of the major innovators in the technique of English verse—for his translation of the Latin hexameter into English blank verse, and especially for his use of the form and materials of the Italian sonnet to produce the first sonnets in what is now described as the Shakespearean or English form (see SONNET, SHAKESPEAREAN). But his achievement in poetic technique becomes obscured when his work is compared with that of more skillful versifiers, many of whom were introduced to the forms by his works. The critical student should remember that these forms might not have been developed so beautifully by later and greater poets without the pioneer work of Surrey.

COMPLAINT OF A LOVER REBUKED

a Love that doth reign and live within my thought,
b And build his seat within my captive breast,
a Clad in the arms wherein with me he fought,
b Oft in my face he doth his banner rest.
c But she that taught me love and suffer pain,
d My doubtful hope and eke my hot desire
c With shamefast look to shadow and refrain,
d Her smiling grace converteth straight to ire.
e And coward Love then to the heart apace
c Taketh his flight, where he doth lurk and plain
e His purpose lost, and dare not show his face.
c For my lord's guilt thus faultless bide I pain;
f Yet from my lord shall not my foot remove. approximate
f Sweet is the death that taketh end by love. rhyme

HENRY HOWARD, EARL OF SURREY (*c.* 1517–1547)

Prosodic theorists writing on the form of the Petrarchan sonnet and its English adaptation, the Shakespearean sonnet, tend to be dogmatic about the "rules" for the organization of the rhyme patterns and the sharp differentiation between octave and sestet in the Italian sonnet by contrast with the "turns" in idea in the three quatrains of the Shakespearean sonnet. An inductive study of the practice of the major sonneteers in English, of which important examples are included here, will show that the poets adapt the forms of the sonnet to the materials, emotional and intellectual, as poets have adapted forms to material in all types of verse. It is true that what we now call a sonnet has fourteen lines of iambic pentameter (although the Elizabethan poet Sidney wrote one of his most famous sonnets in alexandrines, "'Fool,' said my Muse to me, 'look in thy heart and write,'" and Auden has included a twenty-one-line poem, *The Cross-Roads*, in his sonnet sequence). The Petrarchan and Shakespearean forms are used in about the same number of important sonnets written in English, and rhyme schemes and "turns" of idea, in practice, show a large number of variations. In analyzing and evaluating the use of a particular rhyme scheme, the student should be aware that an interlocking pattern (*abba abba*) inevitably develops an idea in a different way and with a different effect from an alternating pattern (*abab cdcd*). It is also true that an enclosed octave, based on only two rhymes, as in the typical Petrarchan sonnet, is quite different in treatment from the three quatrains of the typical Shakespearean sonnet. And a concluding couplet, often used to summarize preceding ideas or to make a comment upon them, is to be distinguished from the Petrarchan alternating sestet (*cd cd cd* or *cde cde*), which tends to rise to a memorable and climactic final line (*e.g.*, Milton's "They also serve who only stand and wait").

Although the sonnet in English probably found its most numerous practitioners in the Elizabethan period, it has tempted and tested nearly all the major poets from the sixteenth century to the present. The difficulty of its tight formal pattern and its compactness can result in poetry of great and concentrated beauty, but "great" sonnets are few in proportion to the number attempted. Of Wordsworth's hundreds, half a dozen, at most, are memorable; of Milton's eighteen in English, the proportion is higher, two or three. Robert Frost, who wrote about twenty-seven (including all the variants), remarked that most sonnets are actually twelve-line poems expanded to fill a fourteen-line unit, or sixteen-line poems compressed. Any novice attempting the sonnet in whatever form will discover for himself the truth of most of the comments made by poets and critics on the problems the form presents; he will learn, moreover, that it is probably as difficult to write a bad sonnet as a good one, although ease in the management of the form *does* come with practice. All verse writers can testify to the essential truth of the statement written on an examination paper: "There are three types of sonnet: the Shakespearean, the Spenserian, and the Pedestrian." Although the last surely constitutes the largest group, we have tried to omit it from the examples.

EXERCISE 38

Both Wyatt and Surrey wrote in Petrarchan style, accepting the conventions of courtly love, a relationship in which the young man is afflicted by a storm of emotions until he fears that he will die, while the lady remains impervious and becomes the "lord" of the lover. Analyze the two sonnets by Wyatt and Surrey separately. Notice especially the use of rhyme, the diction, and the development of figures. Since both poems are written in the same courtly convention and both are limited in expression by being near-translations of a sonnet by Petrarch, consider the effect of the difference in rhyme and structure on the ideas of the two sonnets. What effects seem to be achieved by Wyatt's adaptation of the conventional Italian rhyme scheme? What other effects seem to be achieved by Surrey's use of quatrains, the future Shakespearean form? Can you suggest another poetic form for either or both of these poems which might be more suitable?

HISTORIC EXAMPLES OF THE SHAKESPEAREAN OR ENGLISH SONNET

SONNET 116

Let me not to the marriage of true minds
Admit impediments. Love is not love
Which alters when it alteration finds,
Or bends with the remover to remove.
O, no! It is an ever-fixed mark,
That looks on tempests and is never shaken;
It is the star to every wandering bark,
Whose worth's unknown, although his height be taken.
Love's not Time's fool, though rosy lips and cheeks
Within his bending sickle's compass come;
Love alters not with his brief hours and weeks,
But bears it out even to the edge of doom.
If this be error, and upon me proved,
I never writ, nor no man ever loved.

c. 1590 WILLIAM SHAKESPEARE (1564–1616)

EXERCISE 39

The Shakespearean or English sonnet is an adaptation (and simplification) of the rhyme scheme and structure of the Petrarchan or Italian sonnet form. A common technique for the development of the theme in the Shakespearean form is to state the theme in the first quatrain; restate it or vary it by the use of another type of diction or figure in the second quatrain; restate or vary the theme, perhaps with some development, in the third quatrain; conclude with a summary in the final couplet.

Analyze meter, cadences, and the use of rhyme in Shakespeare's *Sonnet 116.* To what extent are the statements made in the paragraph above accurate for this sonnet? What kind of diction is employed in the first quatrain? What constitutes an "impediment" to marriage, in the legal sense?

Analyze the metaphor in the second quatrain. (Note that "his" in line 8 is the common Elizabethan equivalent of "its.") Picture vividly the personification of the third quatrain. If possible, attempt to draw the persons according to the directions Shakespeare gives. What is the effect of the personification on Shakespeare's explication of the nature of love?

Using the materials derived from your analysis, write a brief essay evaluating the sonnet.

Like *Sonnet 116*, *Sonnet 18* belongs to the large group of Shakespeare's sonnets (126 of 154) believed to be addressed to a young male friend.

SONNET 18

Shall I compare thee to a summer's day?
Thou art more lovely and more temperate.
Rough winds do shake the darling buds of May,
And summer's lease hath all too short a date;
Sometimes too hot the eye of heaven shines,
And often is his gold complexion dimm'd;
And every fair from fair sometime declines,
By chance or nature's changing course untrimm'd.
But thy eternal summer shall not fade,
Nor lose possession of that fair thou ow'st;
Nor shall Death brag thou wander'st in his shade,
When in eternal lines to time thou grow'st.
So long as men can breathe, or eyes can see,
So long lives this, and this gives life to thee.

c. 1590 WILLIAM SHAKESPEARE (1564–1616)

EXERCISE 40

Analyze meter, cadences, and the use of rhyme in Shakespeare's *Sonnet 18.* What kind of rhyme is "temperate" and "date"? What kinds of diction and figures are used? What effect do they achieve?

Comment on the "turn" of idea in the three quatrains.

What is the effect of the third quatrain? Of the final couplet?

In comparison with *Sonnet 116*, how would you evaluate *Sonnet 18*?

Love's Farewell, the poem by which Drayton is generally remembered, belongs to a SONNET SEQUENCE of 54 poems called *Idea.* Scholars have not been able to determine to whom the sequence was addressed, or even whether the beloved was a real woman, or only an idea.

LOVE'S FAREWELL

Since there's no help, come, let us kiss and part.
Nay, I have done; you get no more of me,
And I am glad, yea, glad with all my heart,
That thus so cleanly I myself can free.
Shake hands for ever, cancel all our vows,
And when we meet at any time again,
Be it not seen in either of our brows
That we one jot of former love retain.
Now at the last gasp of Love's latest breath,
When, his pulse failing, Passion speechless lies,
When Faith is kneeling by his bed of death,
And Innocence is closing up his eyes,—
Now, if thou would'st, when all have given him over,
From death to life thou might'st him yet recover.

1594 MICHAEL DRAYTON (1563–1631)

EXERCISE 41

Analyze Drayton's sonnet *Love's Farewell.* Note the development in psychology of the lover's quarrel through the three quatrains.

Do you see any special significance to the word "when" in line 6? How would the poem differ had the word "if" been substituted?

What is the major figure of the third quatrain? Could you draw this scene? What is the poet trying to tell us about the death of Love?

Comment on the final couplet. Can you account for the use of feminine and approximate rhyme in the conclusion of the poem? Can you *justify* the rhyme?

It is also possible to interpret Drayton's sonnet not as spoken by the lover, alone, but as a dialogue.* Line 1, enclosed in quotation marks, may be spoken by the lady (who, in courtly convention, as in modern times, enjoys the right to reject) *or* by the lover. Lines 2 through 4 may be a second speaker, rejecting the offered kiss of line 1. The second quatrain returns (in this inter-

* This interpretation of Drayton's sonnet, by John S. Phillipson, University of Akron, appeared in a brief article published in *The CEA Critic,* April, 1963.

pretation) to the speaker of line 1, who may be the lover, offering here the masculine handshake. According to both readings, the *appearance* of love (lines 7–8) is to be denied. Ambiguous phrasing suggests that the speaker may wish, by appearing uninterested, to deceive a still-beloved. If the speaker of the first line is the lady, she may well be the speaker of the whole sestet, who has changed her mind and does not wish the affair to end. The reader should decide for himself whether the change of TONE in the poem is due to the presence of two persons or to the shifting mood of just one; and whether, if the poem is to be read as a dialogue, the lines should be assigned in one of the ways suggested above, or whether a different distribution would fit the form and content of the poem better. Another poem (not in sonnet form) presenting this type of dialogue—if it is a dialogue—is Muriel Rukeyser's *Effort at Speech Between Two People* (1935), which a reader may find incomprehensible at first because no quotation marks are used.

The seventeenth century employed innumerable complicated rhyming stanzas but, perhaps in revolt against the "sugar'd sonnets" in the long sequences of the Elizabethan age, made little use of the Shakespearean form. A notable exception is the work of George Herbert, whose devotional sonnets continue a tradition of religious meditation begun by the Elizabethan sonneteers, who explored some themes other than secular love. The example given below also represents a practice, followed in the twentieth century by E. A. Robinson, of using the sonnet for narrative-parable.

REDEMPTION

Having been tenant long to a rich Lord,
Not thriving, I resolved to be bold,
And make a suit unto Him, to afford
A new small-rented lease, and cancel th'old.
In heaven at his manor I Him sought:
They told me there, that He was lately gone
About some land, which He had dearly bought
Long since on earth, to take possession.
I straight return'd, and knowing his great birth,
Sought Him accordingly in great resorts—
In cities, theatres, gardens, parks, and courts:
At length I heard a ragged noise and mirth
Of thieves and murderers; there I Him espied,
Who straight, "Your suit is granted," said, and died.

1633 GEORGE HERBERT (1593–1633)

Because of the predominant interest of major eighteenth-century Augustan poets in developing and perfecting the heroic couplet, examples of the sonnet from this period are omitted here. The great sonnets of Wordsworth are written in Petrarchan form. Thus, the next illustration of the Shakespearean form is an untitled sonnet by John Keats, usually known by its first line:

WHEN I HAVE FEARS

When I have fears that I may cease to be
Before my pen has glean'd my teeming brain,
Before high-piled books, in charactery,
Hold like rich garners the full ripen'd grain;
When I behold, upon the night's starr'd face,
Huge cloudy symbols of a high romance,
And think that I may never live to trace
Their shadows, with the magic hand of chance;
And when I feel, fair creature of an hour,
That I shall never look upon thee more,
Never have relish in the faery power
Of unreflecting love;—then on the shore
Of the wide world I stand alone, and think
Till love and fame to nothingness do sink.

1817 John Keats (1795–1821)

EXERCISE 42

Scan the sonnet, indicating pauses and noting the rhyme scheme. What is the figure in the first quatrain? The second quatrain refers to the "symbols of a high romance." In order to understand the quatrain precisely: How are stars and constellations named? To what body of literature do their names refer? Because of the early death of Keats, this sonnet has sometimes been interpreted (in the words of the title bestowed on it in one major anthology) as "The Fear of Death." Compare the octave of this sonnet with the concluding lines of Shakespeare's *Sonnet 18* (p. 200), to determine the actual topic.

In the third quatrain, it is probably safe to interpret the "fair creature" as Fanny Brawne, the young woman whom Keats loved deeply, but who did not return his love. In the last two and a half lines Keats undertakes a resolution of the questions raised by the three "when" clauses of the three quatrains. How do you interpret the concluding lines? How does the sonnet compare in technique and emotion with Shakespeare's *Sonnet 18*?

TWENTIETH-CENTURY EXAMPLES OF THE SHAKESPEAREAN OR ENGLISH SONNET*

THE MASTER SPEED

No speed of wind or water rushing by
But you have speed far greater. You can climb
Back up a stream of radiance to the sky,
And back through history up the stream of time.
And you were given this swiftness, not for haste
Nor chiefly that you may go where you will,
But in the rush of everything to waste,
That you may have the power of standing still—
Off any still or moving thing you say.
Two such as you with such a master speed
Cannot be parted nor be swept away
From one another once you are agreed
That life is only life forevermore
Together wing to wing and oar to oar.

1936 ROBERT FROST (1874–1963)

CONCEIVE A MAN

conceive a man,should he have anything
would give a little more than it away

(his autumn's winter being summer's spring
who moved by standing in november's may)
from whose(if loud most howish time derange

the silent whys of such a deathlessness)
remembrance might no patient mind unstrange
learn(nor could all earth's rotting scholars guess
that life shall not for living find the rule)

and dark beginnings are his luminous ends
who far less lonely than a fire is cool
took bedfellows for moons mountains for friends

—open your thighs to fate and(if you can
withholding nothing)World,conceive a man

1935 E. E. CUMMINGS (1894–1962)

* See also pp. 215, 217, 219.

EXERCISE 43

Traditional themes for the sonnet are love and religion, although a number of others have been used. A sonnet is usually a serious meditation on the theme chosen. Write a Shakespearean sonnet. Do not attempt unusual variations in the form, but try to stay within the average number of variations in the sonnets you have studied. Write out an analysis for your sonnet as you did for Shakespeare's *Sonnet 116*. What particular problems in idea, expression, or form confronted you in writing the sonnet? Are you satisfied with your solutions to the problems?

HISTORIC EXAMPLES OF THE PETRARCHAN SONNET

WITH HOW SAD STEPS, O MOON

With how sad steps, O Moon, thou climb'st the skies!
How silently, and with how wan a face!
What! may it be that even in heavenly place
That busy archer his sharp arrows tries?
Sure, if that long-with-love-acquainted eyes
Can judge of love, thou feel'st a lover's case;
I read it in thy looks,—thy languished grace
To me, that feel the like, thy state descries.
Then, ev'n of fellowship, O Moon, tell me,
Is constant love deemed there but want of wit?
Are beauties there as proud as here they be?
Do they above love to be loved, and yet
Those lovers scorn whom that love doth possess?
Do they call virtue there ungratefulness?

Sir Philip Sidney (1554–1586), *Astrophel and Stella*, *c.* 1580–81, XXI

DEATH, BE NOT PROUD

Death, be not proud, though some have called thee
Mighty and dreadful, for thou art not so;
For those whom thou think'st thou dost overthrow
Die not, poor Death, nor yet canst thou kill me.
From rest and sleep, which but thy pictures be,
Much pleasure: then from thee much more must flow;
And soonest our best men with thee do go—
Rest of their bones, and souls' delivery.

Thou art slave to Fate, Chance, kings, and desperate men,
And dost with poison, war, and sickness dwell;
And poppy or charms can make us sleep as well,
And better than thy stroke. Why swell'st thou then?
One short sleep past, we wake eternally,
And death shall be no more: Death, thou shalt die.

JOHN DONNE (1572–1631), *Holy Sonnets*, 1633, X

ON HIS BLINDNESS

When I consider how my light is spent,
Ere half my days, in this dark world and wide,
And that one talent which is death to hide
Lodg'd with me useless, though my soul more bent
To serve therewith my Maker, and present
My true account, lest He returning chide,—
"Doth God exact day-labour, light deny'd?"
I fondly* ask. But Patience, to prevent
That murmur, soon replies: "God doth not need
Either man's work, or His own gifts. Who best
Bear His mild yoke, they serve Him best. His state
Is kingly: thousands at His bidding speed,
And post o'er land and ocean without rest;
They also serve who only stand and wait."

c. 1655 JOHN MILTON (1608–1674)

LONDON, 1802

Milton! thou shouldst be living at this hour:
England hath need of thee: she is a fen
Of stagnant waters: altar, sword, and pen,
Fireside, the heroic wealth of hall and bower,
Have forfeited their ancient English dower
Of inward happiness. We are selfish men;
Oh! raise us up, return to us again;
And give us manners, virtue, freedom, power.
Thy soul was like a Star, and dwelt apart;
Thou hadst a voice whose sound was like the sea:
Pure as the naked heavens, majestic, free,
So didst thou travel on life's common way,
In cheerful godliness; and yet thy heart
The lowliest duties on herself did lay.

WILLIAM WORDSWORTH (1770–1850)

* **fondly:** foolishly.

EXERCISE 44

The two sonnets by Milton and Wordsworth assume knowledge of biographical and historical fact. Milton's long-projected plan to write a literary epic (which, as *Paradise Lost,* was published in 1667) was delayed by the English Civil War and by Milton's public service to the Puritan government of Oliver Cromwell as Latin Secretary, the equivalent of foreign minister, from 1649 to 1660. By 1654, he had become totally blind, and the sonnet quoted here reflects his contemplation of the almost insuperable difficulty of composing his epic in these circumstances. The reference in line 3 to Matthew 25:14ff. is an allusion fundamental to an understanding of the poem. The final line is frequently misinterpreted as consolatory advice to those who are unable to do anything effective. This reading is an oversimplification which distorts the "high seriousness" of Milton's poem. What do you think he really meant?

Wordsworth had hoped in vain that the French Revolution, which began in 1789, would spread to England and there improve the lot of the lower and middle classes. In 1802, a disillusioned radical, he wrote the sonnet addressed to Milton, which appeals to the spirit of the Puritan radical of the 1640's to rouse a stagnant England.

Taking into account the difference in subject matter, analyze the sonnets for technique, with special attention to diction, figure, and allusion. Wordsworth is attempting not only an appeal to the spirit of Milton but, in his use of a variant of Milton's form, a "poetic compliment" as well. To what extent is his technique effective? Why?

For those of us who cannot read Greek easily, knowledge of Homer must come from the available English translations. Readers of the early nineteenth century, like young John Keats, knew Homer usually as Pope presented him in his famous eighteenth-century translations of *The Iliad* and *The Odyssey*. For Pope, as we know, there was only one suitable English meter, the HEROIC COUPLET, and he was by common consent the greatest writer in this form in the period of its perfection. The passage reproduced here from Pope's translation of *The Odyssey* is a sampling from the Homer Keats believed to be *the* Homer. His astonishment, as a young man who had recently completed his formal schooling, at the Elizabethan translation of Homer by the playwright George Chapman in the dramatic open pentameter COUPLET of the seventeenth century is exhibited for us in the famous sonnet *On First Looking into Chapman's Homer.* That Keats read Chapman's *Homer* all night and returned the book to its owner, accompanied by the sonnet, early the next morning is one of the celebrated stories of literary composition. Too few readers of the sonnet, however, have an opportunity to examine the reasons for the young poet's profound excitement, although most readers can empathize with the excitement of discovery, whether literary, geographical, or planetary.

There stands a rock, high eminent and steep,
Whose shaggy brow o'erhangs the shady deep,
And views Gortyna on the western side;
On this rough Auster drove th'impetuous tide:
With broken force the billows roll'd away,
And heav'd the fleet into the neighb'ring bay;
Thus saved from death, they gain'd the Phaestan shores,
With shatter'd vessels and disabled oars:
But five tall barks the winds and waters toss'd,
Far from their fellows on th'Egyptian coast.
There wander'd Menelaus through foreign shores,
Amassing gold, and gath'ring naval stores;
While curs'd Aegisthus the detested deed
By fraud fulfill'd, and his great brother bled.
Sev'n years the traitor rich Mycenae sway'd,
And his stern rule the groaning land obey'd;
The eighth, from Athens to his realm restor'd,
Orestes brandish'd the revenging sword,
Slew the dire pair, and gave to funeral flame
The vile assassin and adult'rous dame.

From HOMER, *The Odyssey*, Bk. III, trans. Alexander Pope, *c.* 1715

There is a rock, on which the sea doth drive,
Bare, and all broken, on the confines set
Of Gortys, that the dark seas likewise fret;
And hither sent the South a horrid drift
Of waves against the top, that was the left
Of that torn cliff as far as Phaestus' strand.
A little stone the great sea's rage did stand.
The men here driven 'scap'd hard the ships' sore shocks,
The ships themselves being wracked against the rocks,
Save only five that blue fore-castles bore,
Which wind and water cast on Egypt's shore.
When he (there victling well, and store of gold
Aboard his ships brought) his wild way did hold,
And t'other languag'd men was forced to roam,
Mean space Aegisthus made sad work at home,
And slew his brother, forcing to his sway
Atrides' subjects, and did seven years lay
His yoke upon the rich Mycenian state.
But in the eighth, to his affrighting fate,

Divine Orestes home from Athens came,
And what his royal father felt, the same
He made the false Aegisthus groan beneath.
Death evermore is the reward of death.

From HOMER, *The Odyssey*, Bk. III, trans. George Chapman, *c.* 1614–16

ON FIRST LOOKING INTO CHAPMAN'S HOMER

Much have I travell'd in the realms of gold,
And many goodly states and kingdoms seen;
Round many western islands have I been
Which bards in fealty to Apollo hold.
Oft of one wide expanse had I been told
That deep-brow'd Homer ruled as his demesne;
Yet did I never breathe its pure serene
Till I heard Chapman speak out loud and bold:
Then felt I like some watcher of the skies
When a new planet swims into his ken;
Or like stout Cortez when with eagle eyes
He star'd at the Pacific—and all his men
Look'd at each other with a wild surmise—
Silent, upon a peak in Darien.

1816 JOHN KEATS (1795–1821)

EXERCISE 45

The Petrarchan or Italian sonnet, with its interlocked rhyme scheme, tends to develop a single theme through the first eight lines, or octave. In the sestet, the idea is usually given a new turn and rises to a climactic last line. (In actuality, a number of famous sonnets which use the Italian rhyme scheme in the octave conclude the sestet with a couplet, *e.g.*, Sidney's *"With How Sad Steps, O Moon"* and Donne's *"Batter My Heart."*)

Analyze Keats' sonnet *On First Looking into Chapman's Homer*. In the sestet, as innumerable commentators have pointed out, the *fact* is that Balboa discovered the Pacific, first viewed from the isthmus of Darien. What effect would the correction of the error have on the poem?

In revising the poem, Keats altered line 7 from a first draft that read "Yet could I never judge what men could mean" to its present form, which may be indebted to Dante: "That holier joy/Brooded the deep serene" (*Paradiso*, Canto XXXII, ll. 87–88, trans. Henry Francis Cary). What, in the context of the sonnet, is the meaning of "pure serene"? Which line is preferable? Why?

Does the sonnet divide the octave into two quatrains? How is the octave developed? Does the sestet, especially in the final line, achieve a climactic effect?

On the basis of your analysis and your answers to all the questions, write a brief essay evaluating the sonnet.

The following two sonnets belong to nineteenth-century sonnet sequences. Elizabeth Barrett Browning's sequence is the well-known *Sonnets from the Portuguese*; Rossetti's is called *The House of Life*.

HOW DO I LOVE THEE

How do I love thee? Let me count the ways.
I love thee to the depth and breadth and height
My soul can reach, when feeling out of sight
For the ends of Being and ideal Grace.
I love thee to the level of every day's
Most quiet need, by sun and candlelight.
I love thee freely, as men strive for Right;
I love thee purely, as they turn from Praise.
I love thee with the passion put to use
In my old griefs, and with my childhood's faith.
I love thee with a love I seemed to lose
With my lost saints,—I love thee with the breath,
Smiles, tears, of all my life!—and, if God choose,
I shall but love thee better after death.

c. 1850 ELIZABETH BARRETT BROWNING (1806–1861)

LOVESIGHT

When do I see thee most, beloved one?
When in the light the spirits of mine eyes
Before thy face, their altar, solemnize
The worship of that Love through thee made known?
Or when in the dusk hours (we two alone),
Close-kissed and eloquent of still replies,
Thy twilight-hidden glimmering visage lies,
And my soul only sees thy soul its own?
O love, my love! if I no more should see
Thyself, nor on the earth the shadow of thee,
Nor image of thine eyes in any spring,—
How then should sound upon Life's darkening slope
The ground-whirl of the perished leaves of Hope,
The wind of Death's imperishable wing?

1870 DANTE GABRIEL ROSSETTI (1828–1882)

EXERCISE 46

Write an essay comparing Mrs. Browning's *"How Do I Love Thee"* with Rossetti's *Lovesight*. Examine each quatrain for its precise meaning. If necessary, paraphrase each one. Consider the use of abstract nouns and the use of figures. What effects are created by the various types of rhyming? In your conclusion, try to determine which poem is more successful in the expression of love. Give reasons to support your point of view.

TWENTIETH-CENTURY EXAMPLES OF THE PETRARCHAN SONNET

REUBEN BRIGHT

Because he was a butcher and thereby
Did earn an honest living (and did right),
I would not have you think that Reuben Bright
Was any more a brute than you or I;
For when they told him that his wife must die,
He stared at them, and shook with grief and fright,
And cried like a great baby half that night,
And made the women cry to see him cry.
And after she was dead, and he had paid
The singers and the sexton and the rest,
He packed a lot of things that she had made
Most mournfully away in an old chest
Of hers, and put some chopped-up cedar boughs
In with them, and tore down the slaughter-house.

1890–97 EDWIN ARLINGTON ROBINSON (1869–1935)

AUGUST

Why should this Negro insolently stride
Down the red noonday on such noiseless feet?
Piled in his barrow, tawnier than wheat,
Lie heaps of smouldering daisies, sombre-eyed,
Their copper petals shrivelled up with pride,
Hot with a superfluity of heat,
Like a great brazier borne along the street
By captive leopards, black and burning pied.
Are there no water-lilies, smooth as cream,
With long stems dripping crystal? Are there none
Like those white lilies, luminous and cool,
Plucked from some hemlock-darkened northern stream
By fair-haired swimmers, diving where the sun
Scarce warms the surface of the deepest pool?

1921 ELINOR WYLIE (1885–1928)

WHAT LIPS MY LIPS HAVE KISSED

What lips my lips have kissed, and where, and why,
I have forgotten, and what arms have lain
Under my head till morning; but the rain
Is full of ghosts tonight, that tap and sigh
Upon the glass and listen for reply,
And in my heart there stirs a quiet pain
For unremembered lads that not again
Will turn to me at midnight with a cry.
Thus in the winter stands the lonely tree,
Nor knows what birds have vanished one by one,
Yet knows its boughs more silent than before:
I cannot say what loves have come and gone,
I only know that summer sang in me
A little while, that in me sings no more.

1931 EDNA ST. VINCENT MILLAY (1892–1950)

ANY SIZE WE PLEASE

No one was looking at his lonely case,
So like a half-mad outpost sentinel,
Indulging an absurd dramatic spell,
Albeit not without some shame of face,
He stretched his arms out to the dark of space
And held them absolutely parallel
In infinite appeal. Then saying, "Hell,"
He drew them in for warmth of self-embrace.
He thought if he could have his space all curved,
Wrapped in around itself and self-befriended,
His science needn't get him so unnerved.
He had been too all out, too much extended.
He slapped his breast to verify his purse
And hugged himself for all his universe.

1947 ROBERT FROST (1874–1963)

EXERCISE 47

Write a Petrarchan sonnet. Analyze your sonnet according to the directions and questions for writing the Shakespearean sonnet. Is the Petrarchan form more or less difficult to write than the Shakespearean? Can you give reasons for your answer? Do you think the material you chose for this sonnet would have been more or less effective in Shakespeare's form? Why?

VARIETY OF THEMES AND FORMS OF THE SONNET

Although the sonnet is commonly regarded as the strictest form in regular use in English, experimentation began with the first practitioners, Wyatt and Surrey, and it is difficult to find an "exact" Petrarchan sonnet. Shakespeare's own variants on what is defined as the Shakespearean form should be noted, especially *Sonnet 145*, "Those lips that love's own hand did make," which is written throughout in tetrameter. To the reader (even in the Elizabethan period) satiated with the courtly convention of the beautiful, blond, starry-eyed, coral-lipped, rosy-cheeked mistress, *Sonnet 130*—which begins "My mistress' eyes are nothing like the sun" and proceeds inexorably to point out that the traditional objects of comparison, coral, snow, roses, perfume, and melody (for her voice), are far superior to her physical attributes—comes as an amusing parody. When, in the final couplet, Shakespeare says:

> And yet, by heaven, I think my love as rare
> As any she belied with false compare

we realize that this atypical mistress is loved as much as the modern beloved of Nims' "My clumsiest dear" (see p. 52).

These two sonnets are not the sum of Shakespeare's variants: *Sonnet 87* with its legal phrasing approaches the metaphysical language of Donne and, with only two exceptions—both polysyllabic minor-accent rhymes—uses feminine rhyme, usually approximate, in harmony with the theme of "Farewell" and "Please come back again" that we have seen in Drayton's more regular "Since there's no help." Approximate and feminine rhymes are used in *Sonnet 29* ("When in disgrace with fortune and men's eyes") and *30* ("When to the sessions of sweet silent thought"), and minor accents and feminine and approximate rhymes appear throughout *66* ("Tir'd with all these, for restful death I cry")—in keeping with the dissatisfaction, grief, and disappointment expressed in the diction and turns of the quatrains of these sonnets. Shakespeare's sonnets show a close correspondence of treatment with the poems of Donne, probably written at about the same time (1590–1600). Compare the puns on the author's name—Shakespeare's "Will" in *135* and *136* and Donne's "When thou hast done, thou hast not done" (*Hymn to God the Father*)—and the diction, alliteration, and assonance, and the bitter emotion, in *Sonnet 129* ("The expense of spirit in a waste of shame / Is lust in action; and till action, lust . . .") and Donne's *The Apparition*:

THE APPARITION

When by thy scorn, O murd'ress, I am dead,
And that thou think'st thee free
From all solicitation from me,
Then shall my ghost come to thy bed,
And thee, feign'd vestal, in worse arms shall see;
Then thy sick taper will begin to wink,
And he, whose thou art then, being tired before,
Will, if thou stir, or pinch to wake him, think
Thou call'st for more,
And in false sleep will from thee shrink,
And then poor aspen wretch, neglected, thou
Bath'd in a cold quicksilver sweat wilt lie
A verier ghost than I;
What I will say, I will not tell thee now,
Lest that preserve thee; and since my love is spent,
I'd rather thou shouldst painfully repent,
Than by my threat'nings rest still innocent.

JOHN DONNE (1572–1631)

Shakespeare's *Sonnet 71* ("No longer mourn for me when I am dead"), with its curious defense against the sorrow of loss, anticipates by several centuries Christina Rossetti's Petrarchan sonnet on a similar theme:

REMEMBER

Remember me when I am gone away,
Gone far away into the silent land;
When you can no more hold me by the hand,
Nor I half turn to go, yet turning stay.
Remember me when no more, day by day,
You tell me of our future that you planned:
Only remember me; you understand
It will be late to counsel then or pray.
Yet if you should forget me for a while
And afterwards remember, do not grieve:
For if the darkness and corruption leave
A vestige of the thoughts that once I had,
Better by far you should forget and smile
Than that you should remember and be sad.

1849 CHRISTINA ROSSETTI (1830–1894)

To turn now to some of the variants practiced by Shakespeare's heirs, a good modern example is Yeats' *Leda and the Swan*, in which the classical myth of Leda, whether seducing, or seduced by, Jupiter, is expressed in contemporary idiom with the conventional Shakespearean octave and the climactic Petrarchan sestet, which ends with a question and a consonantal rhyme.

LEDA AND THE SWAN

A sudden blow: the great wings beating still
Above the staggering girl, her thighs caressed
By the dark webs, her nape caught in his bill,
He holds her helpless breast upon his breast.

How can those terrified vague fingers push
The feathered glory from her loosening thighs?
And how can body, laid in that white rush,
But feel the strange heart beating where it lies?

A shudder in the loins engenders there
The broken wall, the burning roof and tower
And Agamemnon* dead.
                                        Being so caught up,
So mastered by the brute blood of the air,
Did she put on his knowledge with his power
Before the indifferent beak could let her drop?

1923 WILLIAM BUTLER YEATS (1865–1939)

Another twentieth-century Shakespearean variant is the following sonnet by Cummings, with its striking use of fractured grammar, its repetition of the *a* rhyme (in consonantal form in the second and third quatrain), and the consonantal uncertainty of the inconclusive couplet:

WHAT FREEDOM'S NOT

what freedom's not some under's mere above
but breathing yes which fear will never no?
measureless our pure living complete love
whose doom is beauty and its fate to grow

shall hate confound the wise?doubt blind the brave?
does mask wear face?have singings gone to say?
here youngest selves yet younger selves conceive
here's music's music and the day of day

are worlds collapsing?any was a glove
but i'm and you are actual either hand
is when for sale?forever is to give
and on forever's very now we stand

nor a first rose explodes but shall increase
whole truthful infinite immediate us

1940 E. E. CUMMINGS (1894–1962)

* **Agamemnon.** A reference to the leader of the Greek armies in the Trojan War. His ancestry included Jupiter, who came to Leda in the form of a swan.

Modern Petrarchan variants are well exemplified in Pound's *A Virginal*, in which the poet, contemplating the virgin beloved, describes the lady deftly in feminine rhymes throughout, as though playing upon that delicate Elizabethan musical instrument, the virginal:

A VIRGINAL

No, no! Go from me. I have left her lately.
I will not spoil my sheath with lesser brightness,
For my surrounding air hath a new lightness;
Slight are her arms, yet they have bound me straitly
And left me cloaked as with a gauze of aether;
As with sweet leaves; as with subtle clearness.
Oh, I have picked up magic in her nearness
To sheathe me half in half the things that sheathe her.
No, no! Go from me. I have still the flavour,
Soft as spring wind that's come from birchen bowers.
Green come the shoots, aye April in the branches,
As winter's wound with her sleight hand she staunches,
Hath of the trees a likeness of the savour:
As white their bark, so white this lady's hours.

1912 EZRA POUND (1885–)

A similar variant on a similar topic occurs in the following poem by Cummings, in which the rhymes not only depart from the Petrarchan scheme but go into the consonantal "frail," "smile," "stole," to end, decisively, on the accurate masculine "into the ragged meadow of my soul":

IF I HAVE MADE

if i have made, my lady, intricate
imperfect various things chiefly which wrong
your eyes(frailer than most deep dreams are frail)
songs less firm than your body's whitest song
upon my mind—if i have failed to snare
the glance too shy—if through my singing slips
the very skillful strangeness of your smile
the keen primeval silence of your hair

—let the world say "his most wise music stole
nothing from death"—
you only will create
(who are so perfectly alive)my shame:
lady through whose profound and fragile lips
the sweet small clumsy feet of April came

into the ragged meadow of my soul.

1926 E. E. CUMMINGS (1894–1962)

On a totally different kind of topic is Robert Lowell's *France*, which picks up the first line and many of the images of a ballade composed by François Villon (1431–*c.* 1463) when he expected to be hanged along with his comrades. At the end, Lowell's poem alludes to the crucifixion of Christ, prefigured by the death of Abel.

FRANCE

(*From the Gibbet*)

My human brothers who live after me,
See how I hang. My bones eat through the skin
And flesh they carried here upon the chin
And lipping clutch of their cupidity;
Now here, now there, the starling and the sea
Gull splinter the groined eyeballs of my sin,
Brothers, more beaks of birds than needles in
The fathoms of the Bayeux Tapestry:
"God wills it, wills it, wills it: it is blood."
My brothers, if I call you brothers, see:
The blood of Abel crying from the dead
Sticks to my blackened skull and eyes. What good
Are *lebensraum* and bread to Abel dead
And rotten on the cross-beams of the tree?

1944 ROBERT LOWELL (1917–)

Twentieth-century poets writing in sonnet sequences of variant patterns include Auden, whose *The Quest* comprises twenty poems, each one different from the others, and each with a title, but showing in the octaves of many a relationship to the conventional Shakespearean forms:

THE PRESUMPTUOUS

They noticed that virginity was needed
To trap the unicorn in every case,
But not that, of those virgins who succeeded,
A high percentage had an ugly face.

The hero was as daring as they thought him,
But his peculiar boyhood missed them all;
The angel of a broken leg had taught him
The right precautions to avoid a fall.

So in presumption they set forth alone
On what, for them, was not compulsory:
And stuck halfway to settle in some cave
With desert lions to domesticity;

13. lebensraum: literally, "room for living," expression used in international politics for the geographical expansion of Germany and other nations to accommodate the needs of their populations.

Or turned aside to be absurdly brave,
And met the ogre and were turned to stone.

W. H. Auden (1907–), *The Quest*, 1941

There is also a second sequence by Auden, *In Time of War*, in which the sonnets are simply numbered (there are twenty-seven). Some appear to be variants on the Petrarchan, others on the Shakespearean, pattern. There are, as in IV, occasional assonantal rhymes, "city," "going," and unusual consonantal variants, from "little" and "cattle" to "simple" and "example," as well as related sounds, "earth," "truth." Line lengths vary from trimeter, "At each domestic wrong" (VII), to hexameter, "But suddenly the earth was full: he was not wanted" (V), in otherwise fourteen-line pentameter sonnets. One sonnet (XII) is entirely in hexameters, reminding the reader of the first in Sidney's *Astrophel and Stella* sequence. The one cited below (XVIII) introduces other variants:

FAR FROM THE HEART OF CULTURE

Far from the heart of culture he was used:
Abandoned by his general and his lice,
Under a padded quilt he closed his eyes
And vanished. He will not be introduced

When this campaign is tidied into books:
No vital knowledge perished in his skull;
His jokes were stale; like wartime, he was dull;
His name is lost for ever like his looks.

He neither knew nor chose the Good, but taught us,
And added meaning like a comma, when
He turned to dust in China that our daughters

Be fit to love the earth, and not again
Disgraced before the dogs; that, where are waters,
Mountains and houses, may be also men.

W. H. Auden (1907–), *In Time of War*, 1945, XVIII

Dylan Thomas' sequence *Altarwise by Owl-Light*, 1939, comprising ten numbered sonnets, retains the fourteen-line pentameter with a wide variety of rhyme patterns and rhyme variants. The sequence is almost impenetrably obscure in content (it has been scrutinized and explicated in several different ways by different commentators), but is clearly sequential in its religious and sexual imagery. No quotation of an isolated sonnet would be useful; the poems must be considered together.*

* See Dylan Thomas, *Collected Poems* (New York: New Directions, 1953).

Three Twentieth-Century Sonnets on a Common Theme

THE SOLDIER

If I should die, think only this of me:
That there's some corner of a foreign field
That is for ever England. There shall be
In that rich earth a richer dust concealed;
A dust whom England bore, shaped, made aware,
Gave, once, her flowers to love, her ways to roam,
A body of England's, breathing English air,
Washed by the rivers, blest by suns of home.
And think, this heart, all evil shed away,
A pulse in the eternal mind, no less
Gives somewhere back the thoughts by England given;
Her sights and sounds; dreams happy as her day;
And laughter, learnt of friends; and gentleness,
In hearts at peace, under an English heaven.

1914 RUPERT BROOKE (1887–1915)

A SOLDIER

He is that fallen lance that lies as hurled,
That lies unlifted now, come dew, come rust,
But still lies pointed as it plowed the dust.
If we who sight along it round the world,
See nothing worthy to have been its mark,
It is because like men we look too near,
Forgetting that as fitted to the sphere,
Our missiles always make too short an arc.
They fall, they rip the grass, they intersect
The curve of earth, and striking, break their own;
They make us cringe for metal-point on stone.
But this we know, the obstacle that checked
And tripped the body, shot the spirit on
Further than target ever showed or shone.

1928 ROBERT FROST (1874–1963)

THE SOLDIER

In time of war you could not save your skin.
Where is that *Ghibelline** whom *Dante* met
On *Purgatory*'s doorstep, without kin
To set up chantries for his God-held debt?

* For the italicized words, consult, as necessary, a standard encyclopedia, a map of Italy, a classical handbook, and a dictionary.

So far from *Campaldino*, no one knows
Where he is buried by the *Archiano*
Whose source is *Camaldoli*, through the snows,
Fuggendo a piedi e sanguinando il piano,
The soldier drowned face downward in his blood.
Until the thaw he waited, then the flood
Roared like a wounded dragon over shoal
And reef and snatched away his crucifix
And rolled his body like a log to *Styx*;
Two angels fought with *bill-hooks* for his soul.

1944 ROBERT LOWELL (1917–)

EXERCISE 48

Analyze the three twentieth-century sonnets given above, using all the techniques you know. Prepare to hand in your analyses. You will note that all represent variants of the standard Shakespearean and Petrarchan forms. In evaluating each sonnet separately consider the effect of the form and the variant on the poem. Rupert Brooke was a soldier who died in World War I, but he was never in combat; he died on the way to the Dardanelles Campaign. Frost was not a soldier. Robert Lowell twice attempted to enlist in World War II, but when he was drafted later, he refused to serve because he believed that his country was in no danger and that the bombing of civilians amounted to murder. He served five months in a federal prison. These biographical facts may, or may not, be relevant to your understanding of the poems. In Frost's poem, as in Shakespeare's *Sonnet 116*, be sure that you understand the figures. Directions about the lance in the octave and the missiles in the sestet are precise; you might try making a rough pencil drawing of each figure. Consider the numerous ALLUSIONS in Lowell's sonnet.

After you have done the analyses and considered the questions above, write a brief essay evaluating the three sonnets.

Special Types of Sonnets and Experimental Sonnets

The first who must be listed among the highly original sonneteers is Edmund Spenser, with his sequence of eighty-nine *Amoretti*, written about his second wife, Elizabeth Boyle. The rhyme scheme, closely followed, is his own (see SONNET, SPENSERIAN); it has not been used by any major poet since the sixteenth century.

8. The line, from Dante (*Purgatorio*, Canto V, l. 99), means "flying on foot and bloodying the plain."

LYKE AS A SHIP

a Lyke as a ship, that through the ocean wyde
b By conduct of some star doth make her way,
a Whenas a storme hath dimd her trusty guyde,
b Out of her course doth wander far astray;
b So I, whose star, that wont with her bright ray
c Me to direct, with cloudes is overcast,
b Doe wander now in darknesse and dismay,
c Through hidden perils round about me plast.
c Yet hope I well that when this storme is past
d My Helice, the lodestar of my lyfe,
c Will shine again, and looke on me at last,
d With lovely light to cleare my cloudy grief.
e Till then I wander carefull, comfortlesse,
e In secret sorrow and sad pensivenesse.

EDMUND SPENSER (1552?–1599), *Amoretti*, 1595, XXXIV

Other major poets besides Spenser are associated with special forms of the sonnet—notably Milton and Wordsworth (see under SONNET: *Miltonic sonnet, caudated sonnet, Wordsworth sonnet*).

A number of experimental sonnets—sonnets in that they consist of fourteen lines of pentameter—have been written in rhyming couplets:

THE FOLLY OF BEING COMFORTED

One that is ever kind said yesterday:
"Your well-belovèd's hair has threads of grey,
And little shadows come about her eyes;
Time can but make it easier to be wise
Though now it seems impossible, and so
All that you need is patience."
Heart cries, "No,
I have not a crumb of comfort, not a grain.
Time can but make her beauty over again:
Because of that great nobleness of hers
The fire that stirs about her, when she stirs,
Burns but more clearly. O she had not these ways
When all the wild summer was in her gaze."

O heart! O heart! if she'd but turn her head,
You'd know the folly of being comforted.

1904 WILLIAM BUTLER YEATS (1865–1939)

ONCE BY THE PACIFIC

The shattered water made a misty din.
Great waves looked over others coming in,
And thought of doing something to the shore
That water never did to land before.
The clouds were low and hairy in the skies,
Like locks blown forward in the gleam of eyes.
You could not tell, and yet it looked as if
The shore was lucky in being backed by cliff,
The cliff in being backed by continent;
It looked as if a night of dark intent
Was coming, and not only a night, an age.
Someone had better be prepared for rage.
There would be more than ocean-water broken
Before God's last *Put out the Light* was spoken.

1928 ROBERT FROST (1874–1963)

A study of STRESSED PROSODY and the use of structural as well as ornamental alliteration* is an introduction to the variations on sonnet form used by Gerard Manley Hopkins in the nineteenth century. His poems, with a preface by him, were published posthumously under the editorship of the English poet laureate Robert Bridges. Although Hopkins devised his own terminology, students will recognize that what he calls SPRUNG RHYTHM is, in fact, the stress principle of Anglo-Saxon verse. But, instead of the Anglo-Saxon four-stress line with a regular pattern of structural alliteration, Hopkins generally uses a five-stress line in his sonnets, and he seems to extend the alliteration through groups of lines in a design of major and minor alliteration. He employs terminal rhyme of various kinds, including many of the experimental types, to complete the structural organization of stanzas and whole poems, as in his sonnets. What he calls "counterpoint" students will recognize as the use of SUBSTITUTION in an established pattern; the number of substitutions in his poetry, as in Donne's, is very high. Hopkins' use of the terminology of classical prosody to describe the patterns of his "sprung rhythm" is a cumbersome, impractical attempt to measure in conventional meters a type of line in which, as he says, the number of syllables is irrelevant and only the stresses should be counted.

NO WORST, THERE IS NONE

No worst, there is none. Pitched past pitch of grief,
More pangs will, schooled at forepangs, wilder wring.
Comforter, where, where is your comforting?
Mary, mother of us, where is your relief?

* See the Glossary, under ALLITERATION, for definitions and examples of *major* and *minor, structural* and *ornamental*, alliteration.

My cries heave, herds-long; huddle in a main, a chief-
woe, world-sorrow; on an age-old anvil wince and sing—
Then lull, then leave off. Fury had shrieked "No ling-
ering! Let me be fell: force I must be brief."
O the mind, mind has mountains; cliffs of fall
Frightful, sheer, no-man-fathomed. Hold them cheap
May who ne'er hung there. Nor does long our small
Durance deal with that steep or deep. Here! creep,
Wretch, under a comfort serves in a whirlwind: all
Life death does end and each day dies with sleep.

1885–87 GERARD MANLEY HOPKINS (1844–1889)

EXERCISE 49

Scan Hopkins' sonnet in two ways: (1) by marking the stresses only, especially those that sound like alliterated stresses; (2) by attempting to mark the poem as if it were written in iambic pentameter with numerous substitutions. These two methods of scansion may also be used for Donne's *"Death, Be Not Proud"* (p. 205), although he did not leave behind any note on his theory of prosody.

Write an essay comparing Donne's sonnet with Hopkins'. The first poem was written in the seventeenth century by a poet who was born a Roman Catholic and became the Anglican Dean of St. Paul's Cathedral in London. The second poem was written in the nineteenth century by an Anglican who became a Roman Catholic priest. The poems reflect the serious religious conflicts of the authors. In your essay, do not neglect the use of CATALOGUE, PARADOX, alliteration, and varieties of rhyme as devices affecting the tone of the poetry.

From the quite regular Petrarchan rhyming of *"No Worst, There Is None,"* Hopkins proceeds in *Pied Beauty* to an alliterative eleven-line structure, known as a *curtal sonnet* (see under SONNET). In this poem (p. 368) an inventory of the variety and beauty of the natural world transmits the impact of the glory of God; it leads back to the Creator, ending with the brief emphatic line "Praise him."

A final group of poems includes works so highly experimental that it is difficult to determine what the form should be called. These poems indicate the possibilities inherent in the basic sonnet structure through the use of line lengths other than the pentameter, stress prosody, and variants in both types and patterns of rhyme.

Hopkins' *Felix Randal* uses a variant on the Petrarchan pattern, *abba, abba, ccd, ccd,* with feminine and minor-accent rhymes predominating. The line length is usually hexameter, but the use of stress and alliteration, both major and minor, makes it difficult to determine exactly how the poem should be read. We know, however, from Hopkins' own Preface that he gave serious consideration to the kinds of prosody and even marked some of the poems with the stresses where he wanted them.

FELIX RANDAL

Felix Randal the farrier, O is he dead then? my duty all ended,
Who have watched his mould of man, big-boned and hardy-handsome
Pining, pining, till time when reason rambled in it and some
Fatal four disorders, fleshed there, all contended?

Sickness broke him. Impatient, he cursed at first, but mended
Being anointed and all; though a heavenlier heart began some
Months earlier, since I had our sweet reprieve and ransom
Tendered to him. Ah well, God rest him all road ever he offended!

This seeing the sick endears them to us, us too it endears.
My tongue had taught thee comfort, touch had quenched thy tears,
Thy tears that touched my heart, child, Felix, poor Felix Randal;

How far from then forethought of, all thy more boisterous years,
When thou at the random grim forge, powerful amidst peers,
Didst fettle for the great grey drayhorse his bright and battering sandal!

GERARD MANLEY HOPKINS (1844–1889)

The next poem in this highly experimental group is Yeats' *High Talk.** Here the fourteen lines are regularly rhymed in end-stopped couplets, but the line length is hexameter (highly substituted in lines 5 and 6, to crowd the lines with spondees as the world is crowded with "poor shows" and demands). In the octave, the circus procession is dominated by the poet, walking on the high stilts, the artifice of his poetry added to his natural height. The last lines are nearly incomprehensible, except in the light of Yeats' own comment, "The past has deceived us; let us accept the worthless present."

HIGH TALK

Processions that lack high stilts have nothing that catches the eye.
What if my great-granddad had a pair that were twenty foot high,
And mine were but fifteen foot, no modern stalks upon higher,
Some rogue of the world stole them to patch up a fence or a fire.
Because piebald ponies, led bears, caged lions, make but poor shows,
Because children demand Daddy-long-legs upon his timber toes,
Because women in the upper storeys demand a face at the pane,
That patching old heels they may shriek, I take to chisel and plane.

13. random: built of irregular stones. **14. fettle:** prepare.
* This discussion is indebted to Janet Sussman's Senior Thesis, Goucher College, 1966.

Malachi Stilt-Jack am I, whatever I learned has run wild,
From collar to collar, from stilt to stilt, from father to child.
All metaphor, Malachi, stilts and all. A barnacle goose
Far up in the stretches of night; night splits and the dawn breaks loose;
I, through the terrible novelty of light, stalk on, stalk on;
Those great sea-horses bare their teeth and laugh at the dawn.

1936–39 WILLIAM BUTLER YEATS (1865–1939)

Frost, too, from the early sonnet *The Oven Bird*, 1916, could and did write experimental poems, differing greatly from the traditional sonnet base. One of these, *The Planners*, works in a series of accurate masculine tercets, until line 10, where the tercet is in feminine rhyme, in correspondence with the syntax and the rhetorical questions asked. The concluding lines are minor-accent, double, and the *t* and *d* are only related sound—an indication of the poet's uncertainty about the planners of a bomb-threatened world.

THE PLANNERS

If anything should put an end to This,
I'm thinking the unborn would never miss
What they had never had of vital bliss.
No burst of nuclear phenomenon
That put an end to what was going on
Could make much difference to the dead and gone.
Only a few of those even in whose day
It happened would have very much to say.
And anyone might ask them who were *they*.
Who *would* they be? The guild of social planners
With the intention blazoned on their banners
Of getting one more chance to change our manners?
These anyway might think it was important
That human history should not be shortened.

1947 ROBERT FROST (1874–1963)

Robert Lowell's *Hart Crane* is another poem which seems to have a sonnet base; the wide variation may be interpreted as a tribute to the experimental work in Crane's own verse, notably *The Bridge*.

The sonnet form is also recognizable in the structure of Dylan Thomas' "*When All My Five and Country Senses See*," an elaborated treatment of the five senses in their relationship to love, in which the rhyme scheme of the first ten lines wanders about in variants of *a*, *b*, and *c*, suggesting that the senses are important, but not of supreme importance. The final four lines alternate, but the concluding rhyme is accurate masculine, in confirmation of the assertion that even when the physical senses are gone, do not "see," "The heart is sensual, though five eyes break."

WHEN ALL MY FIVE AND COUNTRY SENSES SEE

When all my five and country senses see,
The fingers will forget green thumbs and mark
How, through the halfmoon's vegetable eye,
Husk of young stars and handfull zodiac,
Love in the frost is pared and wintered by,
The whispering ears will watch love drummed away
Down breeze and shell to a discordant beach,
And, lashed to syllables, the lynx tongue cry
That her fond wounds are mended bitterly.
My nostrils see her breath burn like a bush.

My one and noble heart has witnesses
In all love's countries, that will grope awake;
And when blind sleep drops on the spying senses,
The heart is sensual, though five eyes break.

1939 DYLAN THOMAS (1914–1953)

This poem recalls a much earlier experimenter, Edmund Spenser, who in the sonnet beginning "Comming to kisse her lyps" (*Amoretti*, LXIV) describes his lady entirely in terms of "dainty odours," from her lips to her breasts, and concludes that, in comparison with all the flowers he has named, "her sweet odour did them all excell."

IX

Narrative Stanzas and Techniques

Besides the ballad stanza and variants of it, which provide the formal pattern for much of the narrative poetry written in rhymed English verse, several complex stanzas have been used for narrative poems of considerable length and distinction.* As in other forms of English verse, wherever terminal rhyme is used as a major device for structural organization, the influence of verse in the Romance languages is reflected. The earliest of these narrative stanzas is the so-called rhyme royal.

RHYME ROYAL

The rhyme scheme of rhyme royal is $ababbcc^5$. Literary legend attributes the name of the stanza to royal use by James I of Scotland in *The King's Quair* ("The King's Book") in the fifteenth century, but the term "royal" may be derived from some of the complicated French forms which also bore the adjective "royal," *e.g.*, the "chant royal." Chaucer, discarding the tetrameter line of his earlier poems for the pentameter, employed rhyme royal in *Troilus and Criseyde*, *c.* 1385, and *The Prioress's Tale*, which was probably written later. The pentameter with its additional foot allows considerably greater freedom

* For further illustration of the stanzas discussed in this chapter, see the Glossary under STANZA.

than the tetrameter, and the odd number, five, preserves the line from a medial cesura coinciding with the end of a foot, at the half line, which in the tetrameter could and did result in the effect of a sequence of dimeter lines (in sound), sometimes called "broken-backed lines." The rhyme pattern of rhyme royal is a demanding one, because of the employment of three *b* rhymes. It is the interlocking of the *b* rhymes in lines 4 and 5 which holds the stanza securely as a unit of seven lines and prevents the separation of the final couplet from the opening quatrain. As the narrative poets employ the stanza, the couplet rarely breaks off with a concluding summary (as it often does in the sonnet), but continues the narrative flow to the end. In this stanza, as in the pentameter couplet, Chaucer must be rated one of the great innovators in the technique of English verse, as well as one of the great craftsmen in this particular form: the 8,000 lines of the *Troilus*, though the poem stands at the beginning of the use of rhyme royal, also mark the highest point in the development of the form. Chaucer's fifteenth-century imitators used the rhyme royal, as did Shakespeare in his nondramatic poem *The Rape of Lucrece* and, in the nineteenth century, the virtuoso of many crafts and techniques, William Morris. Contemporary use of rhyme royal or the other rhymed narrative stanzas in strict form is virtually nonexistent.

Among thise othere folk was Criseyda,
In widewes habit blak; but natheles,
Right as oure firste lettre is now an A,
In beaute first so stood she, makeles.
Hire goodly lokyng gladed al the prees.
Nas nevere yet seyn thyng to ben preysed derre,
Nor under cloude blak so bright a sterre
. . .

From GEOFFREY CHAUCER, *Troilus and Criseyde*, *c.* 1385, I

"O brotel wele of mannes joie unstable!
With what wight so thow be, or how thow pleye,
Either he woot that thow, joie, art muable,
Or woot it nought; it mot ben oon of tweye.
Now if he woot it nought, how may he seye
That he hath verray joie and selynesse,
That is of ignoraunce ay in derknesse?"

Ibid., III

173. prees: multitude. **174. derre:** more dearly.
820. brotel: brittle. **825. selynesse:** happiness.

And on the smale grene twistis sat
The lytil suete nyghtingale, and song
So loud and clere, the ympnis consecrat
Of luvis use, now soft now lowd among,
That all the gardynis and the wallis rong
Ryght of thaire song, and on the copill next
Of thaire suete armony, and lo the text:—
. . .

JAMES I OF SCOTLAND, *The King's Quair*, *c.* 1425, XXXIII

This said, his guilty hand pluck'd up the latch,
And with his knee the door he opens wide.
The dove sleeps fast that this night-owl will catch:
Thus treason works ere traitors be espied.
Who sees the lurking serpent steps aside;
But she, sound sleeping, fearing no such thing,
Lies at the mercy of his mortal sting.

WILLIAM SHAKESPEARE, *The Rape of Lucrece*, 1594

Of Heaven or Hell I have no power to sing,
I cannot ease the burden of your fears,
Or make quick-coming death a little thing,
Or bring again the pleasure of past years,
Nor for my words shall ye forget your tears,
Or hope again for aught that I can say,
The idle singer of an empty day.

From WILLIAM MORRIS, *The Earthly Paradise*, 1868

OTTAVA RIMA

The ottava rima, as its name suggests, is an eight-line stanza of Italian origin, which was introduced into English verse by Sir Thomas Wyatt. It is a pentameter stanza with the rhyme scheme *abababcc*. Because of the use of the *a* and *b* rhymes three times each and the presence of a concluding couplet, the stanza in English suffers from two major difficulties: (1) In continuous narrative the numerous repeated rhymes make heavy demands on a language which, unlike Italian, has relatively few accurate rhyming groups; the tendency to monotony is in part an outgrowth of this difficulty. (2) The concluding couplet, unlinked to the preceding six lines, tends to halt the narrative; unlike

1. twistis: branches. **3. ympnis:** hymns. **6. copill:** stanza.

the rhyme-linked couplet of the rhyme royal, the couplet of the ottava rima in English is abrupt and distracting.

Although Spenser used the ottava rima in one of his minor poems, and Milton used a single stanza in this form to conclude *Lycidas* (which is written in pentameter varied by trimeter, with unpatterned use of rhymes), it remained for Byron, in the nineteenth century, to make of the ottava rima a superb meter for romantic satire, in *Don Juan*, in which the concluding couplet is repeatedly used to drive home the satiric point of the preceding six lines. Byron's earlier work in satire imitates the heroic couplets of his great predecessors of the eighteenth century, notably Pope, but the heroic couplet is a tightly structured meter better suited to classical satire; the freedom of romantic satire is better served by ottava rima. With notable lack of success, Keats attempted to use this Italianate stanza for *Isabella*, a narrative poem based on an Italian plot. Neither the material nor the poet's skill in complex rhyme was equal to the task, and *Isabella* remains an unfortunate attempt by a major poet to use an incompatible meter. It is fair to say that *Don Juan* is the only significant long poem written in English in ottava rima.

She sat, and sewed, that hath done me the wrong
Whereof I plain, and have done many a day;
And, whilst she heard my plaint in piteous song,
Wished my heart the sampler as it lay.
The blind master, whom I have served so long,
Grudging to hear that he did hear her say,
Made her own weapon do her finger bleed,
To feel if pricking were so good indeed.

From SIR THOMAS WYATT, *Of His Love That Pricked Her Finger with a Needle*, c. 1532–41

For at his wonted time in that same place
An huge great serpent, all with speckles pide,
To drench himselfe in moorish slime did trace,
There from the boyling heate himselfe to hide:
He, passing by with rolling wreathed pace,
With brandisht tongue the emptie aire did gride,
And wrapt his scalie boughts with fell despight,
That all things seem'd appalled at his sight.

From EDMUND SPENSER, *Virgil's Gnat*, 1591

Thus sang the uncouth swain to th'oaks and rills,*
While the still morn went out with sandals gray;

254. gride: pierce. **255. boughts:** coils.
* Only the final eight lines of *Lycidas*, here quoted, are in ottava rima.

He touch'd the tender stops of various quills,
With eager thought warbling his Doric lay:
And now the sun had stretch'd out all the hills,
And now was dropt into the western bay;
At last he rose and twitch'd his mantle blue:
Tomorrow to fresh woods, and pastures new.

From John Milton, *Lycidas*, 1638

There was Lorenzo slain and buried in,
There in that forest did his great love cease;
Ah! when a soul doth thus its freedom win,
It aches in loneliness—is ill at peace
As the break-covert blood-hounds of such sin:
They dipp'd their swords in the water, and did tease
Their horses homeward, with convulsed spur,
Each richer by his being a murderer.

From John Keats, *Isabella*, 1820, XXVIII

As boy, I thought myself a clever fellow,
And wished that others held the same opinion;
They took it up when my days grew more mellow,
And other minds acknowledged my dominion:
Now my sere fancy "falls into the yellow
Leaf," and Imagination droops her pinion,
And the sad truth which hovers o'er my desk
Turns what was once romantic to burlesque.

From George Gordon, Lord Byron, *Don Juan*, Canto IV (1819–21), St. 3

Similar to Milton's use of a single ottava rima as the conclusion to his pastoral elegy is the use by Yeats of the same stanza with variant rhymes in two of his best-known poems, *Sailing to Byzantium* and *Among School Children*, in the twentieth century, but neither of these is narrative in type or book-length.

Labour is blossoming or dancing where
The body is not bruised to pleasure soul,
Nor beauty born out of its own despair,
Nor blear-eyed wisdom out of midnight oil.
O chest-nut tree, great-rooted blossomer,
Are you the leaf, the blossom or the bole?
O body swayed to music, O brightening glance,
How can we know the dancer from the dance?

From William Butler Yeats, *Among School Children*, 1928, VIII

SPENSERIAN STANZA

The Spenserian stanza, devised by Spenser for his own use, may have been derived from Chaucer's *Monk's Tale* stanza (*ababbcbc*^{5}), with which it is identical except for the addition of an ALEXANDRINE *c* rhyme. The Spenserian stanza (*ababbcbc*^{5}*c*^{6}) thus consists of nine lines, with interlocking *b* and *c* rhymes: two on *a*, four on *b*, and three on *c*. It seems improbable, however, that a poet capable of so many innovations in technique (the various patterns of *The Shepherd's Calendar*, 1579, the Spenserian form of the sonnet, the *Epithalamion*, etc.) and of such varied accomplishment should have consciously and seriously considered the dismal materials of the Monk's tragedies as a source for a stanza pattern. From a purely theoretical point of view, any technical critic would be justified in discouraging a poet from attempting to write a narrative (comprising features of the epic, the allegory, and the romance) in twelve books of Spenserian stanzas. The fact remains that Spenser achieved six books and a number of stanzas of the seventh in this superlatively difficult form, and, although critical estimates of the work vary, no critic can deny the skill of the prosody of *The Faerie Queene*. The additional foot of the ninth line propels the narrative forward to the next stanza, and, by the difference in line lengths, the effect of a summarizing couplet is successfully avoided. Pope's critical comment on the "needless" alexandrine "that, like a wounded snake, drags its slow length along" is repeatedly contradicted by Spenser's skill. Probably coinciding with the writing of parts of *The Faerie Queene* was the composition of Spenser's sonnet sequence, the *Amoretti*. The relationship between the interlocking rhymes of the Spenserian sonnet (*abab*, *bcbc*, *cdcd*, *ee*) and those of the Spenserian stanza is obvious, but it is probable that the sonnet form was devised later than the stanza. Unlike the Spenserian sonnet, the Spenserian stanza has had a number of practitioners, notably among eighteenth- and nineteenth-century Spenserians, like James Thomson, who attempted to use allegorical materials as well as Spenserian form. Burns and Byron both used the stanza in narrative (*The Cotter's Saturday Night* and *Childe Harold's Pilgrimage*), as did Keats in the short narrative *The Eve of St. Agnes*, in form and style the most Spenserian of the later poems. Keats, despite his difficulties with complex rhyme, in this poem seems to proceed effortlessly, with good effect. Shelley, probably in tribute to Keats' skill in *The Eve of St. Agnes*, chose the Spenserian stanza for his pastoral elegy *Adonais*, a lament on the death of Keats. Since the nineteenth century, no major poet has attempted to write narrative in Spenserian stanza.

A lovely Ladie rode him faire beside,
Upon a lowly asse more white then snow,
Yet she much whiter, but the same did hide
Under a vele, that wimpled was full low,
And over all a blacke stole she did throw,
As one that inly mournd: so was she sad,
And heavie sat upon her palfrey slow:
Seemed in heart some hidden care she had,
And by her in a line a milke white lambe she lad.

From Edmund Spenser, *The Faerie Queene*, Bk. I (*c.* 1590), Canto I, St. 4

Other examples of Spenser's use of this stanza are given in the Glossary (see under STANZA) and in connection with Exercise 37.

A pleasing land of drowsy-hed it was:
Of dreams that wave before the half-shut eye;
And of gay castles in the clouds that pass,
For ever flushing round a summer sky:
There eke the soft delights, that witchingly
Instil a wanton sweetness through the breast,
And the calm pleasures always hover'd nigh;
But whate'er smack'd of noyance, or unrest,
Was far far off expell'd from this delicious nest.

From James Thomson, *The Castle of Indolence*, 1748, Canto I

November chill blaws loud wi' angry sugh;
The short'ning winter-day is near a close,
The miry beasts retreating frae the pleugh,
The black'ning trains o' craws to their repose:
The toil-worn Cotter frae his labour goes,—
This night his weekly moil is at an end,—
Collects his spades, his mattocks, and his hoes,
Hoping the morn in ease and rest to spend,
And weary, o'er the moor, his course does hameward bend.

From Robert Burns, *The Cotter's Saturday Night*, 1785

46. -hed: -ness.

Roll on, thou deep and dark blue Ocean—roll!
Ten thousand fleets sweep over thee in vain;
Man marks the earth with ruin—his control
Stops with the shore; upon the watery plain
The wrecks are all thy deed, nor doth remain
A shadow of man's ravage, save his own,
When, for a moment, like a drop of rain,
He sinks into thy depths with bubbling groan,
Without a grave, unknelled, uncoffined, and unknown.

From George Gordon, LORD BYRON, *Childe Harold's Pilgrimage*, Canto IV, 1818

And still she slept an azure-lidded sleep,
In blanched linen, smooth, and lavender'd,
While he from forth the closet brought a heap
Of candied apple, quince, and plum, and gourd;
With jellies soother than the creamy curd,
And lucent syrops, tinct with cinnamon;
Manna and dates, in argosy transferr'd
From Fez; and spiced dainties, every one,
From silken Samarcand to cedar'd Lebanon.

From JOHN KEATS, *The Eve of St. Agnes*, 1820, XXX

He has outsoared the shadow of our night;
Envy and calumny and hate and pain,
And that unrest which men miscall delight,
Can touch him not and torture not again;
From the contagion of the world's slow stain
He is secure, and now can never mourn
A heart grown cold, a head grown gray in vain;
Nor, when the spirit's self has ceased to burn,
With sparkless ashes load an unlamented urn.

From PERCY BYSSHE SHELLEY, *Adonais*, 1821, XL

A land of streams! some, like a downward smoke,
Slow-dropping veils of thinnest lawn, did go;
And some thro' wavering lights and shadows broke,
Rolling a slumbrous sheet of foam below.
They saw the gleaming river seaward flow
From the inner land; far off, three mountain-tops,
Three silent pinnacles of aged snow,
Stood sunset-flush'd; and, dew'd with showery drops,
Up-clomb the shadowy pine above the woven copse.

From ALFRED, LORD TENNYSON, *The Lotos-Eaters*, 1833

EXERCISE 50

Narrative poetry in the nineteenth and twentieth century has usually been written in blank or free verse, rather than in the strict rhyme patterns of rhyme royal, ottava rima, or Spenserian stanza. All three present problems of interlocking and repeated rhyme. It would be easy to dismiss rhyme, as Milton did in his note on the verse of *Paradise Lost*, as the "invention of a barbarous age" (but he did not begin to write in blank verse until he had succeeded in writing in most of the traditional and complex rhyming forms). It is notable, however, that the major poets represented in the examples succeeded in using these complicated forms in extended major narratives. Minor poets, like Gray, seriously complain of the strictures of rhyme, which Gray felt prevented him from an accurate expression of his thoughts and emotions.

Consider material appropriate for a twentieth-century narrative poem. Write in prose a brief outline of the proposed plot. Select one of the three types of narrative stanza exemplified above and write the opening stanza of your poem in that form. In a page or two, comment on your reasons for selecting the form you chose and the problems you encountered in attempting to write in the form. Do you think you could continue your entire narrative in this form? Would the result be effective? Why?

TWENTIETH-CENTURY NARRATIVE POEMS

In the twentieth century accurately rhymed narrative stanzas such as those described and illustrated in the first part of this chapter have seldom been used in long poems, but it would be rash to conclude that they are too difficult, since the difficulties they present (especially those of repeated rhyme) have been mastered by great poets in earlier centuries, from the fourteenth, in an English noticeably different from our own, through the nineteenth, in an English very close to ours. Perhaps it is true to say that the twentieth century has not produced a poet with either the skill or the patience to master these forms or to vary them, as the sonnet has been varied. There is, however, another argument: the strictly rhymed narrative forms may, indeed, be antiquated and unsuitable for the materials, ideas, and emotions of contemporary verse. Recent experiments, such as the variant rhymes of a basic terza rima (see under STANZA) that MacLeish used in his long poem *Conquistador*, suggest that the future of the rhymed narrative stanza may lie in the deliberate use of approximate rhymes (assonance or consonance, or others) to expand the possibilities of patterned verse as distinct from the resources of free verse, without meter or rhyme.

Not only do the long poems of the contemporary period rarely use strict stanza patterns, few of them could be characterized as "narrative" in the strict sense. The brief chronological survey of significant long poems supplied here (poems from about twenty pages to book length) is for the student who wishes to proceed with the study of longer poems in complex or variant meters:

THOMAS HARDY, *The Dynasts*, 1903–08, an epic drama reflecting the poet's interest in the Napoleonic Wars, in prose, blank verse, some rhyme.

JOHN MASEFIELD, *Dauber*, 1913, a narrative poem about the sea, written in rhyme royal.

E. A. ROBINSON, *Avon's Harvest*, 1921, blank verse narrative of a fearful man and his hatred.

T. S. ELIOT, *The Waste Land*, 1922, a complex poem on the theme of the sterility, in frustration and disillusion, of the twentieth century. The meters vary from tetrameter to hexameter—in some parts, with combinations of pentameter and trimeter; in other parts, notably Section III, with dimeter. There is some rhyming, with particularly complex handling in Section IV, "Death by Water."

E. A. ROBINSON, *Dionysus in Doubt*, 1925, a condemnation of the Eighteenth Amendment (Prohibition), written in irregular-ode form, with lines of varying lengths and rhyming.

EZRA POUND, *Cantos*, 1925——, probably the most complicated poem of the twentieth century. It is still unfinished, although groups of the *Cantos* have been published from time to time. Pound has conceived of the poem as a fugue, as a Human Comedy (in contrast to the work of Dante), and uses, in composition, all his resources as a prosodic technician and experimenter.

ROBINSON JEFFERS, *Roan Stallion, Tamar*, 1926, *The Women at Point Sur*, 1927, *Cawdor*, 1928, *Dear Judas*, 1929, *Thurso's Landing*, 1932: narrative poems usually written on themes of violence, incest, death, in long lines reminiscent of the poetry of Whitman. *Such Counsels You Gave to Me*, 1937, has previously been referred to (p. 102*n*) as an extended psychological interpretation of the popular ballad *Edward*.

STEPHEN VINCENT BENÉT, *John Brown's Body*, 1928, an attempt at narrative epic, on the period of the Civil War. The form is varied, mingling ballad and lyric with blank verse passages and some prose, *e.g.*, "John Brown's Speech" in the courtroom.

Robert Bridges, *The Testament of Beauty*, 1929, a philosophical poem on Beauty as the motivating force in man's life, whether in the time of Plato, Darwin, or twentieth-century socialism. It is written in loose alexandrines, which reflect Bridges' scholarly study of the prosody of Milton.

E. A. Robinson, *Cavender's House*, 1929, a melodramatic narrative exhibiting the poet's negative view of God, the world, and its inhabitants.

Hart Crane, *The Bridge*, 1930, like *The Waste Land* in its complexity, but its opposite in affirmation of the "Myth of America." The poem, which takes its title from the intricate structure of the Brooklyn Bridge, is written in many sections, most of them brief. Each section has its own metrical form, often a variant one. There are pentameter variants and rhyming variants of all kinds ("National Winter Garden"), many quatrain variants, and other stanza patterns (pentameters in eight-line groups). "Southern Cross" employs an elaborate series of complex strophes which should be compared in both form and content with Eliot's "Death by Water" in *The Waste Land.*

Archibald MacLeish, *Conquistador*, 1932, already referred to as a narrative poem written in terza rima, with variant (frequently assonantal) rhyming. The subject matter, as the title suggests, is the discovery and conquest of Mexico and South America by Spanish explorers.

George Barker, *Calamiterror*, 1939, a complicated apocalyptic poem. Stanzas are usually eight lines, but their length varies. Rhyme, when used, is approximate rhyme of various kinds.

W. H. Auden, *The Double Man*, 1941, a modern poem of more than 1,700 lines in tetrameter couplet. Witty, philosophic, and satiric, it may well be compared with Samuel Butler's *Hudibras*, 1663, its seventeenth-century counterpart in style, content, and form (see p. 176).

T. S. Eliot, *Four Quartets*, 1943, a meditative poem, in craftsmanship one of the most interesting in the twentieth century. Each Quartet consists of five parts, each related metrically to its counterparts in the other Quartets. Part I is basically a tetrameter/pentameter with some hexameters, especially in "The Dry Salvages"; Part II begins with a strictly metered and rhymed introduction, followed by a long, reflective, often nearly prosaic passage that is basically tetrameter/pentameter/hexameter; Part III is usually tetrameter/pentameter; Part IV is a strictly patterned brief section, with accurate rhyme (except in "The Dry Salvages") and meter; Part V is, again, tetrameter/pentameter/hexameter, though the basis seems to be pentameter at the beginning and tetrameter at the end. The sound patterns are interwoven with the sophistication of Spenser.

W. H. AUDEN, *For the Time Being*, 1944, comprising "A Christmas Oratorio," in a variety of metrical forms as well as prose, written in the despair of the years of World War II, and "The Sea and the Mirror," a commentary on and re-enactment of Shakespeare's *The Tempest*, in which each character is given a specific metrical form of his own. *The Age of Anxiety*, 1947, not a narrative poem, has already been examined as a modern example of the use of structural alliterative verse (see p. 190).

ROBERT FROST, *A Masque of Reason*, 1945; *A Masque of Mercy*, 1947; both in blank verse; the first, a drama in modern colloquial speech on the problems of Job; the second, a companion piece in which the principal characters are Jesse Bel, Jonah, and Paul.

ROBERT LOWELL, *The Mills of the Kavanaughs*, 1946, a dramatic poem in open pentameter couplets, in which Anne Kavanaugh's reverie is addressed to her dead husband.

WILLIAM CARLOS WILLIAMS, *Paterson*, Books I–V, 1946–58, a study in free verse of the disintegration of modern civilization.

JOHN BERRYMAN, 77 *Dream Songs*, 1959, and *His Toy, His Dream, His Rest*, 1968, two collections, of which the second reflects considerable progress in the development of the major character (Henry) and of the themes established in the earlier book. The stanzas, of varying line lengths, are organized by both rhymes and related sounds. Though the two works are not narrative in the conventional sense, the sections in each are interrelated, and one could construct a conventional linear plot given the "information" contained in the poems.

X

Varieties of Stanza Form and French Forms

Besides the ballad stanzas and quatrain variants (Chapter 6) and the different narrative stanzas (Chapter 9) considered previously, there are innumerable kinds of STANZA patterns. Anyone who is interested in the number and variety of stanzaic forms should consult a collection of Elizabethan lyrics,* the works of such seventeenth-century poets as Donne, Herbert, Traherne, and Crashaw, and the collected poems of Browning and Tennyson in the nineteenth century. In English a stanza is one of two or more groups of lines identical in number of lines and in length and meter of corresponding lines; in rhymed verse—not all stanzaic verse is rhymed: see Collins' *Ode to Evening*, p. 264—the arrangement of rhymes is also identical.

When a poet decides to adopt one of the basic patterns of English verse—ballad, sonnet, etc.—he has the responsibility of choosing what he believes to be an appropriate pattern and then working within its limits. When he begins to select stanzas, he has a much wider choice: R. M. Alden, in his *English Verse*,† examines at least thirty for which he can find examples from early Middle English to late-nineteenth-century work. In making the choice among various stanzas, or in devising his own, the poet assumes even greater responsibility for correspondence between pattern and content from stanza to stanza, since stanzaic pattern is, by definition, a repeated form. Thus the young John Milton

* For example: Norman Ault, *Elizabethan Lyrics* (New York: William Sloane Associates, 1949).
† R. M. Alden, *English Verse* (New York: Henry Holt, 1903).

in his *On the Morning of Christ's Nativity* chose the following pattern for the Hymn section and repeated it twenty-seven times:

a^3 It was the winter wild,
a^3 While the Heav'n-born child,
b^5 All meanly wrapt in the rude manger lies;
c^3 Nature in awe to him
c^3 Had doff't her gaudy trim,
b^5 With her great Master so to sympathize;
d^4 It was no season then for her
d^6 To wanton with the sun, her lusty paramour. approximate rhyme

This elaborate form is used for a variety of quite different effects as Milton's complex tribute to the Incarnate God is developed.

There is no simple way to determine what stanza pattern is appropriate for the poem in the act of creation. There is only the simple requirement that whatever stanza is chosen must work effectively *with* the content throughout the poem, not *against* it, and that the pattern should not appear to control or constrict the content. Perhaps the best example of a conscientious poet working out almost exactly the wrong design for the effect he hoped to achieve is Edgar Allan Poe in *The Raven*. In his essay on the composition of this poem, he describes painstakingly how and why he proceeded as he did in his effort to describe what he believed to be the most moving topic for a poem: the melancholy contemplation of the death of a beautiful woman.

a Once upon a midnight dreary, while I pondered, weak and weary,
b Over many a quaint and curious volume of forgotten lore—
c While I nodded, nearly napping, suddenly there came a tapping,
b As of someone gently rapping, rapping at my chamber door.
b "'Tis some visitor," I muttered, "tapping at my chamber door—
b Only this and nothing more."

From EDGAR ALLAN POE, *The Raven*, 1845

The internal feminine rhymes in lines 1 and 3, the refrain of "more" (in the last stanzas "nevermore"), and the dactylic-trochaic meter all conspire toward a ludicrous effect almost equal to the best efforts at humor by Byron or Ogden Nash.

"French forms" is a general, not wholly accurate term for lyric poems of various types which originated in the Mediterranean areas of Europe during the Middle Ages. Near the close of the eleventh century, two linguistic offshoots of Latin—French, spoken in northern France, and Provençal in southern France —began to develop literatures of their own. Lyric poetry began to appear first in Provençal and then in the dialects of northern France. This poetry was composed and spread by the TROUBADOURS of the south and the TROUVÈRES of the north. Later, about the twelfth century, poetry resembling that of the troubadours began to appear in Spain, Portugal, and Italy, as the troubadours traveled from castle to castle over feudal Europe. Italian assimilation of the troubadour tradition is particularly significant for an English-speaking reader, since the troubadour concept of the lady acting as feudal "lord" in relation to her servile, sighing lover made its way to England several centuries later, first through the French poets, Guillaume de Machaut (*c.* 1300–1377), Eustache Deschamps (*c.* 1340–*c.* 1407), and Jean Froissart (*c.* 1337–*c.* 1410), who influenced Chaucer, and later through François Villon (1431–*c.* 1463). Elizabethan translations of Italian poetry were also influential during the Renaissance.

"Courtly love" is the term given to the mock-feudal, extramarital relationship of romantic love, for writers of the early Middle Ages who depicted this type of affair were patronized by the nobility or members of the court—the only class of people at the time, we assume, wealthy enough for patronage and leisured enough for the slow and elaborate procedures involved in the conduct of a romantic love affair. In the twelfth century Eleanor of Aquitaine, the knowledgeable and sophisticated queen of France and later of England, was one of the most influential patrons of the poets of courtly love.

An equally important indication that troubadour lyrics were written for people with educated tastes is the extreme technical complication of the French forms, in which formal virtuosity, especially in the use of rhyme, can be shown off to glittering advantage. Indeed, by the middle of the twelfth century, Provençal poets—most notably Bernard de Ventadour and Arnaut Daniel—appear to have sought out the most complicated rhyme schemes and the longest and rarest rhyme words possible. These forms are used with almost infinite variation on a severely limited body of material or subject matter, finally satirized by Shakespeare, who sums it up as "a woeful ballad / made to his mistress' eyebrow" (*As You Like It*, II, vii, 148–149) and who begins *Sonnet 130* "My mistress' eyes are nothing like the sun." As a result of the emphasis on technical virtuosity, critics and scholars until the nineteenth and early twentieth centuries have tended to regard the French forms in English as vehicles for technical ingenuity and light, graceful ideas—nothing more.

Recently, however, poets have begun experimenting, with some success, in the use of the French forms for serious ideas. As the student will see from the examples which follow and from technical descriptions of the forms in the Glossary, the FRENCH FORMS involve a considerable amount of carefully patterned repetition, sometimes of single words but often of entire lines. Such a form can lead to a monotony of sound that overshadows the sense, but it can also be an extremely effective link between sound and sense when the *subject* of the poem concerns a recurrent idea or action. In Robinson's *The House on the Hill*, for example (p. 246), the repetitions demanded by the villanelle help emphasize the viewer's frequent futile glances at the empty house, and the finality of its occupants' abandonment.

The *rondeau*, the *triolet*, the *villanelle*, the *ballade*, and the *sestina* are distinguished more by their formal patterns than by their content. In these forms, line length depends on the individual poet's choice, although he is usually consistent within the poem; the essentials of the form are the elaborate rhyme schemes and/or patterns of repetition. Scholars believe that the *rondel* originated as a short dance-song consisting of repetitive parts to be divided between a soloist and a chorus. The triolet and the rondeau were developed in the fourteenth and fifteenth centuries as refinements of the rondel. Although Victorian practitioners of the French forms in English generally chose to imitate the formal pattern quite exactly, modern writers tend to vary the subject matter and to experiment with the use of approximate rather than exact rhymes.

In a poem employing rhyme and composed of stanzas, the convention is to mark the first line of each stanza *a*. Thus, although all lines marked *a* in the same stanza will rhyme, the *a* lines in different stanzas usually will not. Triplets (see under STANZA) would be marked as follows:

a Listen, and when thy hand this paper presses, — feminine rhyme
a O time-worn woman, think of her who blesses
a What thy thin fingers touch, with her caresses.

a O mother, for the weight of years that break thee! — feminine rhyme
a O daughter, for slow time must yet awake thee,
a And from the changes of my heart must make thee!

. . .

a Pause near the ending of thy long migration; — feminine rhyme
a For this one sudden hour of desolation
a Appeals to one hour of thy meditation.

From ALICE MEYNELL (1850–1923), *A Letter from a Girl to Her Own Old Age*

The poem consists of fourteen triplets. The change of rhyme sounds from stanza to stanza is almost universal in English, but in the French forms illustrated below a whole poem of considerable length may be rhymed on two or three sounds.

The conventional system of marking verse forms with repeated lines employs capital letters for the repetitions, as illustrated in the first example of the triolet.

THE TRIOLET

The rhyme scheme of the triolet (see under FRENCH FORMS) is *ABaAabAB*:

A KISS

A Rose kissed me to-day.
B Will she kiss me to-morrow?
a Let it be as it may,
A Rose kissed me to-day.
a But the pleasure gives way
b To a savour of sorrow;—
A Rose kissed me to-day,—
B *Will* she kiss me to-morrow?

AUSTIN DOBSON (1840–1921), *Rose-Leaves*, *c.* 1880

IN HIS ARMS

In his arms thy silly lamb
Lo! he gathers to his breast!
See, thou sadly bleating dam,
See him lift thy silly lamb!
Hear it cry, "How blest I am!"—
"Here is love and love is rest."
In his arms thy silly lamb
Lo! he gathers to his breast!

GEORGE MACDONALD (1824–1905)

WINTER IN DURNOVER FIELD

Scene.—A wide stretch of fallow ground recently sown with wheat, and frozen to iron hardness. Three large birds walking about thereon, and wistfully eyeing the surface. Wind keen from north-east: sky a dull grey.

ROOK Throughout the field I find no grain;
The cruel frost encrusts the cornland!
STARLING Aye: patient pecking now is vain
Throughout the field, I find . . .
ROOK No grain!
PIGEON Nor will be, comrade, till it rain,
Or genial thawings loose the lorn land
Throughout the field.
ROOK I find no grain:
The cruel frost encrusts the cornland!

c. 1900 THOMAS HARDY (1840–1928)

TO A FAT LADY SEEN FROM THE TRAIN

O why do you walk through the fields in gloves,
  Missing so much and so much?
O fat white woman whom nobody loves,
Why do you walk through the fields in gloves?
When the grass is soft as the breast of doves
  And shivering sweet to the touch?
O why do you walk through the fields in gloves,
  Missing so much and so much?

1928 FRANCES CORNFORD (1886–1960)

THE RONDEAU

The rondeau (see under FRENCH FORMS) has the rhyme scheme *Raabba*, *aabR*, *aabbaR*, where *R* stands for the refrain.

RONDEAU

Ra *What, no perdy*, ye may be sure!
a Think not to make me to your lure
b With words and cheer so contrarying,
b Sweet and sour counterweighing.
a Too much it were still to endure.

a Truth is tried where craft is in ure;
a But though ye have had my heartès cure,
b Trow ye I dote without ending?
R *What, no perdy!*

a Though that with pain I do procure
a For to forget that once was pure,
b Within my heart shall still that thing
b Unstable, unsure, and wavering,
a Be in my mind without recure?
R *What, no perdy!*

SIR THOMAS WYATT (1503?–1542)

1. perdy: mild oath, literally "by God." **6. ure:** use.

IN FLANDERS FIELDS

In Flanders fields the poppies blow
Between the crosses, row on row,
That mark our place; and in the sky
The larks, still bravely singing, fly
Scarce heard amid the guns below.

We are the Dead. Short days ago
We lived, felt dawn, saw sunset glow,
Loved, and were loved, and now we lie,
In Flanders fields.

Take up our quarrel with the foe:
To you from failing hands we throw
The torch; be yours to hold it high.
If ye break faith with us who die
We shall not sleep, though poppies grow
In Flanders fields.

c. 1917 JOHN McCRAE (1872–1918)

DEATH OF A VERMONT FARM WOMAN

Is it time now to go away?
July is nearly over; hay
Fattens the barn, the herds are strong,
Our old fields prosper; these long
Green evenings will keep death at bay.

Last winter lingered; it was May
Before a flowering lilac spray
Barred cold for ever. I was wrong.
Is it time now?

Six decades vanished in a day!
I bore four sons: one lives; they
Were all good men; three dying young
Was hard on us. I have looked long
For these hills to show me where peace lay.
Is it time now?

1959 BARBARA HOWES (1914–)

THE VILLANELLE

In the villanelle (see under FRENCH FORMS), the *a* and *b* rhymes are the same *throughout* the poem and the first two *a* lines are repeated alternately. The conventional way of marking the repeated lines is to identify the first as A^1 and the second as A^2.

VILLANELLE OF MARGUERITES

A^1 *"A little, passionately, not at all?"*
b She casts the snowy petals on the air;
A^2 And what care we how many petals fall?

a Nay, wherefore seek the seasons to forestall?
b It is but playing, and she will not care,
A^1 A little, passionately, not at all!

a She would not answer us if we should call
b Across the years; her visions are too fair;
A^2 And what care we how many petals fall!

a She knows us not, nor recks if she enthrall
b With voice and eyes and fashion of her hair,
A^1 A little, passionately, not at all!

a Knee-deep she goes in meadow-grasses tall,
b Kissed by the daisies that her fingers tear:
A^2 And what care we how many petals fall!

a We pass and go: but she shall not recall
b What men we were, nor all she made us bear:
A^1 *"A little, passionately, not at all!"*
A^2 And what care we how many petals fall!

ERNEST DOWSON (1867–1900)

THE HOUSE ON THE HILL

They are all gone away,
  The House is shut and still,
There is nothing more to say.

Through broken walls and gray
  The winds blow bleak and shrill:
They are all gone away.

Nor is there one to-day
  To speak them good or ill:
There is nothing more to say.

Why is it then we stray
  Around the sunken sill?
They are all gone away,

And our poor fancy-play
  For them is wasted skill:
There is nothing more to say.

There is ruin and decay
  In the House on the Hill:
They are all gone away,
There is nothing more to say.

1897 EDWIN ARLINGTON ROBINSON (1869–1935)

VILLANELLE

Time can say nothing but I told you so,
Time only knows the price we have to pay;
If I could tell you, I would let you know.

If we should weep when clowns put on their show,
If we should stumble when musicians play,
Time can say nothing but I told you so.

There are no fortunes to be told, although
Because I love you more than I can say,
If I could tell you, I would let you know.

The winds must come from somewhere when they blow,
There must be reasons why the leaves decay;
Time can say nothing but I told you so.

Perhaps the roses really want to grow,
The vision seriously intends to stay;
If I could tell you, I would let you know.

Suppose the lions all get up and go,
And all the brooks and soldiers run away?
Time can say nothing but I told you so;
If I could tell you, I would let you know.

1937 W. H. AUDEN (1907–)

DO NOT GO GENTLE INTO THAT GOOD NIGHT

Do not go gentle into that good night,
Old age should burn and rave at close of day;
Rage, rage against the dying of the light.

Though wise men at their end know dark is right,
Because their words had forked no lightning they
Do not go gentle into that good night.

Good men, the last wave by, crying how bright
Their frail deeds might have danced in a green bay,
Rage, rage against the dying of the light.

Wild men who caught and sang the sun in flight,
And learn, too late, they grieved it on its way,
Do not go gentle into that good night.

Grave men, near death, who see with blinding sight
Blind eyes could blaze like meteors and be gay,
Rage, rage against the dying of the light.

And you, my father, there on the sad height,
Curse, bless, me now with your fierce tears, I pray.
Do not go gentle into that good night.
Rage, rage against the dying of the light.

1939 DYLAN THOMAS (1914–1953)

THE WAKING

I wake to sleep, and take my waking slow.
I feel my fate in what I cannot fear.
I learn by going where I have to go.

We think by feeling. What is there to know?
I hear my being dance from ear to ear.
I wake to sleep, and take my waking slow.

Of those so close beside me, which are you?
God bless the Ground! I shall walk softly there,
And learn by going where I have to go.

Light takes the Tree; but who can tell us how?
The lowly worm climbs up a winding stair;
I wake to sleep, and take my waking slow.

Great Nature has another thing to do
To you and me; so take the lively air,
And, lovely, learn by going where to go.

This shaking keeps me steady. I should know.
What falls away is always. And is near.
I wake to sleep, and take my waking slow.
I learn by going where I have to go.

1953 THEODORE ROETHKE (1908–1963)

THE BALLADE

The ballade (see under FRENCH FORMS) consists of three stanzas and an envoy, usually an apostrophe. Note that *a*, *b*, and *c* rhymes are the same throughout the poem.

TRUTH

Balade de Bon Conseyl

Flee fro the prees, and dwelle with sothfastnesse,
Suffyce unto thy good, though it be smal;
For hord hath hate, and climbing tikelnesse,
Prees hath envye, and wele blent overal;
Savour no more than thee bihove shal;
Reule wel thyself, that other folk canst rede;
And trouthe thee shal delivere, it is no drede.

Tempest thee noght al croked to redresse,
In trust of hir that turneth as a bal:
Gret reste stant in litel besinesse;
Be war also to sporne ayeyns an al;
Stryve not, as doth the crokke with the wal.
Daunte thyself, that dauntest otheres dede;
And trouthe thee shal delivere, it is no drede.

That thee is sent, receyve in buxumnesse;
The wrastling for this world axeth a fal.
Her is non hoom, her nis but wildernesse:
Forth, pilgrim, forth! Forth, beste, out of thy stal!
Know thy contree, look up, thank God of al;
Hold the heye wey, and lat thy gost thee lede;
And trouthe thee shal delivere, it is no drede.

1. prees: crowd; **sothfastnesse:** truth. **3. tikelnesse:** insecurity. **4. blent:** blinds. **6. rede:** counsel. **7. drede:** doubt. **11. sporne . . . al:** kick against an awl. **13. Daunte:** control. **15. buxumnesse:** humility. **19. contree:** sphere. **20. gost:** conscience.

Envoy

Therfore, thou Vache, leve thyn old wrecchednesse;
Unto the world leve now to be thral;
Crye him mercy, that of his hy goodnesse
Made thee of noght, and in especial
Draw unto him, and pray in general
For thee, and eek for other, hevenlich mede;
And trouthe thee shal delivere, it is no drede.

c. 1390 GEOFFREY CHAUCER (*c.* 1340–1400)

THE BALLAD OF DEAD LADIES

Tell me now in what hidden way is
Lady Flora the lovely Roman?
Where's Hipparchia, and where is Thais,
Neither of them the fairer woman?
Where is Echo, beheld of no man,
Only heard on river and mere,—
She whose beauty was more than human? . . .
But where are the snows of yester-year?

Where's Héloïse, the learned nun,
For whose sake Abeillard, I ween,
Lost manhood and put priesthood on?
(From Love he won such dule and teen!)
And where, I pray you, is the Queen
Who willed that Buridan should steer
Sewed in a sack's mouth down the Seine? . . .
But where are the snows of yester-year?

White Queen Blanche, like a queen of lilies,
With a voice like any mermaiden,—
Bertha Broadfoot, Beatrice, Alice,
And Ermengarde the lady of Maine,—
And that good Joan whom Englishmen
At Rouen doomed and burned her there,—
Mother of God, where are they then? . . .
But where are the snows of yester-year?

Nay, never ask this week, fair lord,
Where they are gone, nor yet this year,
Except with this for an overword,—
But where are the snows of yester-year?

c. 1870 DANTE GABRIEL ROSSETTI (1828–1882),
from the French of FRANÇOIS VILLON, 1450

22. leve: cease. **27. mede:** reward.

THE SESTINA

Arnaut Daniel (*c.* 1180–1210) is credited with the invention of the sestina (see under FRENCH FORMS), a form that depends upon the repetition of the final word in each of the six lines of the first stanza in a particular order which varies with each of the six stanzas. These final words do not have to rhyme, though they generally did in the sestinas of Daniel.

SESTINA

1 In fair Provence, the land of lute and *rose*,
2 Arnaut, great master of the lore of *love*,
3 First wrought sestines to win his lady's *heart*,
4 Since she was deaf when simpler staves he *sang*,
5 And for her sake he broke the bonds of *rhyme*,
6 And in this subtler measure hid his *woe*.

6 "Harsh be my lines," cried Arnaut, "harsh the *woe*
1 My lady, that enthorn'd and cruel *rose*,
5 Inflicts on him that made her live in *rhyme*!"
2 But through the metre spake the voice of *Love*,
4 And like a wildwood nightingale he *sang*
3 Who thought in crabbed lays to ease his *heart*.

3 It is not told if her untoward *heart*
6 Was melted by her poet's lyric *woe*,
4 Or if in vain so amorously he *sang*.
1 Perchance through cloud of dark conceits he *rose*
2 To nobler heights of philosophic *love*,
5 And crowned his later years with sterner *rhyme*.

5 This thing alone we know: the triple *rhyme*
3 Of him who bared his vast and passionate *heart*
2 To all the crossing flames of hate and *love*,
6 Wears in the midst of all its storm and *woe*—
1 As some loud morn of March may bear a *rose*—
4 The impress of a song that Arnaut *sang*.

4 "Smith of his mother-tongue," the Frenchman *sang*
5 Of Lancelot and of Galahad, the *rhyme*
1 That beat so bloodlike at its core of *rose*,
3 It stirred the sweet Francesca's gentle *heart*
6 To take that kiss that brought her so much *woe*
2 And sealed in fire her martyrdom of *love*.

2 And Dante, full of her immortal *love*,
4 Stayed his drear song, and softly, fondly *sang*
6 As though his voice broke with that weight of *woe*;
5 And to this day we think of Arnaut's *rhyme*
3 Whenever pity at the labouring *heart*
1 On fair Francesca's memory drops the *rose*.

2, 5 Ah, sovereign *Love*, forgive this weaker *rhyme*!
4, 3 The men of old who *sang* were great at *heart*,
6, 1 Yet have we too known *woe*, and worn thy *rose*.

Edmund Gosse (1849–1928)

The late-nineteenth-century experiments in the sestina and other French forms were little more than tours de force, but, in 1908, Ezra Pound, in his *Sestina: Altaforte*, indicated the possibilities of this form for twentieth-century verse. Although the PERSONA of Pound's poem is Richard Coeur de Lion, the poem is forceful and contemporary.

An interesting variant on the sestina form is used by T. S. Eliot in *Four Quartets* (1943), where in "The Dry Salvages," II, the six words which end the lines are not themselves repeated in stanzas 2, 3, 4, and 5, but *rhyme* with words in corresponding positions in these stanzas:

Stanza 1	*Stanza 2*
wailing	trailing
flowers	hours
motionless	emotionless
wreckage	breakage
unprayable	reliable
annunciation	renunciation

The line-end words are repeated exactly in stanza 6, but there is no three-line conclusion, as in the traditional form.

A few more recent examples of the sestina follow:

PAYSAGE MORALISÉ

Hearing of harvests rotting in the valleys,
Seeing at end of street the barren mountains,
Round corners coming suddenly on water,
Knowing them shipwrecked who were launched for islands,
We honour founders of these starving cities
Whose honour is the image of our sorrow,

Which cannot see its likeness in their sorrow
That brought them desperate to the brink of valleys;
Dreaming of evening walks through learned cities

They reined their violent horses on the mountains,
Those fields like ships to castaways on islands,
Visions of green to them who craved for water.

They built by rivers and at night the water
Running past windows comforted their sorrow;
Each in his little bed conceived of islands
Where every day was dancing in the valleys
And all the green trees blossomed on the mountains
Where love was innocent, being far from cities.

But dawn came back and they were still in cities;
No marvellous creature rose up from the water;
There was still gold and silver in the mountains
But hunger was a more immediate sorrow,
Although to moping villagers in valleys
Some waving pilgrims were describing islands . . .*

"The gods," they promised, "visit us from islands,
And stalking, head-up, lovely, through our cities;
Now is the time to leave your wretched valleys
And sail with them across the lime-green water,
Sitting at their white sides, forget your sorrow,
The shadow cast across your lives by mountains"

So many, doubtful, perished in the mountains,
Climbing up crags to get a view of islands,
So many, fearful, took with them their sorrow
Which stayed them when they reached unhappy cities,
So many, careless, dived and drowned in water,
So many, wretched, would not leave their valleys.

It is our sorrow. Shall it melt? Ah, water
Would gush, flush, green these mountains and these valleys,
And we rebuild our cities, not dream of islands.

1937 W. H. Auden (1907–)

A MIRACLE FOR BREAKFAST

At six o'clock we were waiting for coffee,
waiting for coffee and the charitable crumb
that was going to be served from a certain balcony,
—like kings of old, or like a miracle.
It was still dark. One foot of the sun
steadied itself on a long ripple in the river.

* The dots are Auden's. The poem has been printed complete.

The first ferry of the day had just crossed the river.
It was so cold we hoped that the coffee
would be very hot, seeing that the sun
was not going to warm us; and that the crumb
would be a loaf each, buttered, by a miracle.
At seven a man stepped out on the balcony.

He stood for a minute alone on the balcony
looking over our heads toward the river.
A servant handed him the makings of a miracle,
consisting of one lone cup of coffee
and one roll, which he proceeded to crumb,
his head, so to speak, in the clouds—along with the sun.

Was the man crazy? What under the sun
was he trying to do, up there on his balcony!
Each man received one rather hard crumb,
which some flicked scornfully into the river,
and, in a cup, one drop of the coffee.
Some of us stood around, waiting for the miracle.

I can tell what I saw next; it was not a miracle.
A beautiful villa stood in the sun
and from its doors came the smell of hot coffee.
In front, a baroque white plaster balcony
added by birds, who nest along the river,
—I saw it with one eye close to the crumb—

and galleries and marble chambers. My crumb
my mansion, made for me by a miracle,
through ages, by insects, birds, and the river
working the stone. Every day, in the sun,
at breakfast time I sit on my balcony
with my feet up, and drink gallons of coffee.

We licked up the crumb and swallowed the coffee.
A window across the river caught the sun
as if the miracle were working, on the wrong balcony.

1946 ELIZABETH BISHOP (1911–)

MR. VIRTUE AND THE THREE BEARS

We hammer out tunes to make bears dance when we long to move the stars.—Flaubert

This morning at his Gas Stand in Lucerne on Route 1, Mr. Virtue was found devoured by his bear. Mr. Virtue left no known relatives.—(Remembered some fifteen years from the Bangor *Daily News.*)

I knew a bear once ate a man named Virtue
All but a mire of clothes, an unlicked bear
Caught, a May cub, to dance for soda pop;
Who when half-grown lumbered before us slowly,
Gurgling and belching in the gas-stand yard,
On a sorry chain, and made rough music there.

A chattel property of Mr. Virtue,
Untaxable and nameless, this black bear,
For some a joke to sell flat soda pop,
For some terror in chains, wove himself slowly
Through foundered postures, till hunger smalled his yard,
And he broke free by eating Virtue there.

If no kin came to claim the clothes of Virtue,
Yet hundreds claimed themselves in that black bear
And drank the upset crate of soda pop,
Kin drinking kin: drinking the stink that slowly,
Like a bear's pavanne, swept the gravel yard
And made of vertigo a music there.

So fell the single hymn to Mr. Virtue:
In rough music that burst from that young bear
When sudden soda in his loins went pop,
All longing and no hope, and he danced slowly,
Rearing and dropping in his chain-swept yard,
Till Mr. Virtue dumped spoiled blueberries there.

—And yet, there move two musics wooing Virtue:
Those of the Great and of the Lesser Bear,
Of the star falling and of new soda pop;
And these two bears dance best when long time slowly,
Overheard, the Dipper spills by inch and yard
The northern lights on us from darkness there.

So praises blew in this bear feast on Virtue.
The greater sprang within the lesser bear
In music wild in the spilled light, to pop,
And by created hunger move, most slowly,
The blacker stars, fast set in their hard yard,
To loose their everlasting shivers there.

Let us in virtue so beseech the bear,
With soda pop, that he may dancing slowly
Move in our yard constellations darkly there.

1951 R. P. Blackmur (1904–1965)

MY GRANDFATHER PLANTED A PEACH ORCHARD

The ruined cabin logs slump, daubed with clay,
The bramble rose bewilders the door stone
Sunk sideways in the thrust of unscythed grass.
South on the hill slope peaches crowd the trees
In Grandfather's orchard that he planted new,
When he was past a hundred, trusting it to bear.

The sweet white freestone fruit it grew to bear
Tastes strangely of his autumn and his clay
This August afternoon, and the warm new
Juice drips on the sumac by the tipped gravestone
Marked with his name. But he stands in the trees
Weighted with peaches, not asleep in grass.

Sold, long ago, his cows that cropped the grass,
His pruning shears, the scythe; the wheels to bear
The Saturday load to town lean on the trees,
Whitewashed. Bright pottery glazed from the grayish clay
Gleams on the summer stand. Neat frame and stone,
The new farmhouse,—even the barn is new.

Manful, the farmer's name is. Nothing new
That matters can be built. The coarse marsh grass
Twists to uproot the level springhouse stone,
And the persistent runnels moss and bear
The softened timbers of the house to clay.
I touch his hands within the loaded trees.

Here once he dug the hollows for his trees,
The naked seedling settled in the new
Field cleared and planted well before the clay
Below the loam wash free, and mustard grass
Be all the glow of gold the land would bear,
After they carved his name across the stone.

Now all he built has toppled, log and stone,
But the stripped withes he trusted grow to trees,
Rounded with ripened peaches that will bear
Him like a promise that the years renew.
His headstone lies half-hidden in the grass,
His name half-covered by the rain-washed clay.

Untended fields will bear thick fruitless grass,
The stone, untended, shift and sink in clay,
Ripe with new seasons, he lives, in his trees.

1951 SARA DEFORD (1916–)

EXERCISE 51

Although the nineteenth-century revival of French forms in English verse produced poems that were chiefly exercises in skill upon trivial subject matter, twentieth-century practice (by Pound, Eliot, Thomas, and others) shows that these forms may appropriately be used for serious material. Choose a subject, preferably a serious subject, and write a villanelle, a rondeau, a ballade, or a sestina. If one of the first three is chosen, the problem of rhyme and repetition is of the utmost importance. Consult a rhyming dictionary (those by J. Walker and Clement Wood are useful; a shorter form appears in the back pages of some ordinary desk dictionaries) before finally determining the rhyme sound, in order to assure yourself that enough rhymes are available in English for the numerous repetitions required in these forms. It is more important, in this exercise, to fulfill the requirements of the form than to say what you wish to say. Ideally, you should be able to do both.

If you wish to write a sestina, rhyme is not necessary (although it is sometimes used), but great care must be applied in the selection of the six (6) words which end the lines. For greater flexibility, choose one or two words usable as different parts of speech, *e.g.*, "bear," which may be a noun or a verb.

In French forms as adapted in English, there is no set rule about length of line; trimeter, tetrameter, pentameter, or combinations have been used. After selecting a line length or arranging a combination, however, you should follow it consistently.

XI

Types of Ode: Variations in Strophe, Line Length, and Rhyming

The term "ode" as commonly used in English is a rather vague one, often applied loosely to any poem addressed "To" someone or something. The Greek ode, from which the English ode, regular and irregular, takes its origin both in subject matter and in form, is an intricate, extended ceremonial poem, closely related to formal chorus (sung or chanted) and dance. In the *regular* or *Pindaric* ODE, as practiced by Pindar (*c.* 522–443 B.C.), the poet was free to determine the rhyme pattern, number of lines, and length of lines for the *strophe*, but once he had chosen these, he was required to adhere to the form for both the strophe and the *antistrophe* throughout the entire poem. For the *epode*, the poet enjoyed similar freedom in determining the form of the *first* epode, but thereafter he was required to repeat that form in every epode throughout the poem.

Over two thousand years later, the interest of Renaissance thinkers in the classics and in classical forms encouraged Ben Jonson to introduce the regular Pindaric ode into English. Jonson, a true classicist, was as careful to follow the rules of the Pindaric ode in verse as he was to obey the requirement of the Aristotelian unities in his dramas. Although in one sense the regular ode in English is a strict form· which requires, beyond meter and rhyme, a certain length, entailing repetition of difficult patterns, it also allows the poet great freedom, for he may originate whatever patterns he wishes, avoiding such restrictions as are imposed by sonnet forms, the various narrative stanzas, and French forms. But if, because of this freedom, the ode can well exhibit the skill of a major poet, it can as conspicuously exhibit the deficiencies of an inept one, deficiencies which might be less obvious in the predetermined patterns of other forms. The regular ode has been little used in English, although Congreve in the eighteenth century revived it, remarking, in *A Discourse on the Pindaric Ode*, which he prefixed to an ode on the victories of the Duke of Marlborough:

> . . . if the reader can observe that the great variation of the numbers* in the third stanza (call it epode, or what you please) has a pleasing effect in the ode, and makes him return to the first and second stanzas with more appetite than he could do if always cloyed with the same quantities and measures, I cannot see why some use may not be made of Pindar's example, to the great improvement of the English ode. There is certainly a pleasure in beholding anything that has art and difficulty in the contrivance, especially if it appears so carefully executed that the difficulty does not show itself till it is sought for.

Following Congreve, in the eighteenth century, Thomas Gray and William Collins interested themselves in constructing regular odes, but Collins began to experiment with the form and wrote his more famous poems as *stanzaic* or *Horatian odes* (see under ODE). The term "ode" for this kind of poem is considered by some scholars to be a misnomer. The form takes its origin from the odes of Horace, and the subject matter tends to be less ceremonious, as the expression is more simply lyrical. Among the most familiar and famous of odes in English are those of Keats, who used the stanzaic form or an approximation of it.

Congreve has been mentioned as "reviving" the regular ode in English in the eighteenth century. It is possible to speak of revival, because in the seventeenth century (between the regular odes of Jonson and those of Congreve, Gray, and Collins), Abraham Cowley, in a volume called *Pindaric Odes, Written in Imitation of the Style and Manner of the Odes of Pindar* (1668), published his own adaptations of the form. Cowley's Preface indicates his intentions in writing when he says of Pindar's Greek odes in translation:

> And lastly (which were enough alone for my purpose), we must consider that our ears are strangers to the music of his numbers, which sometimes (especially in songs and odes), almost without anything else, makes an excellent poet; for though the grammarians and critics have laboured to reduce his verses into regular feet and measures (as they have also those of the Greek and Latin comedies), yet in effect they are little better than prose to our ears.

One result of Cowley's so-called "Pindaric" odes, which are actually *irregular* in form, was to create total confusion in the terminology of the English ode. Cowley's "imitation" of the Greek regular ode produced the highly experimental form in which the regular division of strophe, antistrophe, and

* See Glossary.

epode with their precise patterns disappears (see ODE, IRREGULAR). The "strophes" of the irregular ode are different in length, line lengths, and rhyming patterns each from the other, although definite meter and rhyme, elaborate patterning, and the ceremonial style and subject matter are retained. Even more than the regular ode, the irregular ode gives the poet scope to exhibit his skill or his defects; it is the freest of all the patterned forms in English verse. Cowley proceeds to explain his work in this way:

> It does not at all trouble me that the grammarians perhaps will not suffer this libertine way of rendering foreign authors to be called translation; for I am not so much enamoured of the name "translator" as not to wish rather to be something better, though it want yet a name. . . . Upon this ground, I have in these two odes of Pindar taken, left out, and added what I please; nor make it so much my aim to let the reader know precisely what he spoke, as what was his way and manner of speaking; which has not been yet (that I know of) introduced into English, though it be the noblest and highest kind of writing in verse.

Cowley enjoyed high repute in the seventeenth century as the author of the *Davideis*, an epic based on the career of David, *The Mistress*, a series of poems for which he received the title "metaphysical" (its first use, in Dr. Johnson's *Life of Cowley*), and his "Pindaric" odes. But he has lost his once pre-eminent position as an epic writer to Milton, as a metaphysical poet to Donne and his school, and as a composer of irregular odes to Dryden in his own century and to Wordsworth, Shelley, Tennyson, and others in the eighteenth and nineteenth centuries. Like other minor poets whom we have considered in the study of the formal patterns of English verse, Cowley deserves attention because, although he failed in achieving the forms he attempted, he is one of the great experimenters and innovators. Without his experiments in the irregular ode, we might not have Dryden's odes, or the *Intimations Ode* of Wordsworth, or the form of Arnold's *Dover Beach*.

REGULAR OR PINDARIC ODE

III 1. *The Turn**

a^4 It is not growing like a tree
a^4 In bulk, doth make men better be;
b^5 Or standing long an oak, three hundred year,
b^5 To fall a log at last, dry, bald, and sear:
c^3 A lily of a day
c^3 Is fairer far, in May,

* The terms "turn," "counter-turn," and "stand," which are equivalent to "strophe," "antistrophe," and "epode," refer to the movements of the Greek chorus associated with each of these divisions of the ode (see ODE, REGULAR).

d^4 Although it fall and die that night;
d^4 It was the plant and flower of light.
e^5 In small proportions we just beauties see;
e^5 And in short measures life may perfect be.

III 2. *The Counter-Turn*

a^4 Call, noble Lucius, then for wine,
a^4 And let thy looks with gladness shine;
b^5 Accept this garland, plant it on thy head,
b^5 And think, nay know, thy Morison's not dead.
c^3 He leap'd the present age,
c^3 Possess'd with holy rage,
d^4 To see that bright eternal day
d^4 Of which we priests and poets say
e^5 Such truths as we expect for happy men:
e^5 And there he lives with memory, and Ben.

III 3. *The Stand*

a^5 Jonson, who sung this of him, ere he went,
b^2 Himself, to rest,
a^5 Or taste a part of that full joy he meant
b^2 To have express'd,
c^3 In this bright asterism!—
c^3 Where it were friendship's schism,
$d^{\smile 5}$ Were not his Lucius long with us to tarry,
e^3 To separate these twi-
e^3 Lights, the Dioscuri;
$d^{\smile 4}$ And keep the one half from his Harry.
f^5 But fate doth so alternate the design,
f^5 Whilst that in heav'n, this light on earth must shine.

From BEN JONSON, *To the Immortal Memory and Friendship of That Noble Pair, Sir Lucius Cary and Sir H. Morison*, 1629

I 1. *Strophe*

a^4 Awake, Aeolian lyre, awake,
b^5 And give to rapture all thy trembling strings.
b^4 From Helicon's harmonious springs
a^5 A thousand rills their mazy progress take:
c^4 The laughing flowers, that round them blow,
c^4 Drink life and fragrance as they flow.

73–74. These lines are actually *a* rhymes, but the "Counter-Turn" and the rhyme scheme in the strophes and antistrophes not cited here (I 1 and 2, II 1 and 2, and IV 1 and 2) show that they are intended as *e* rhymes.
91. $d^{\smile 5}$: The symbol for an unstressed syllable, in this position, indicates a feminine rhyme.

d^5 Now the rich stream of music winds along
d^4 Deep, majestic, smooth, and strong,
e^5 Thro' verdant vales, and Ceres' golden reign:
e^4 Now rowling down the steep amain,
f^4 Headlong, impetuous, see it pour:
f^6 The rocks and nodding groves rebellow to the roar.

I 2. *Antistrophe*

a^4 Oh! Sovereign of the willing soul,
b^5 Parent of sweet and solemn-breathing airs,
b^4 Enchanting shell! the sullen Cares,
a^5 And frantic Passions hear thy soft controul.
c^4 On Thracia's hills the Lord of War
c^4 Has curb'd the fury of his car,
d^5 And drop'd his thirsty lance at thy command.
d^4 Perching on the scept'red hand
e^5 Of Jove, thy magic lulls the feather'd king
e^4 With ruffled plumes, and flagging wing:
f^4 Quench'd in dark clouds of slumber lie
f^6 The terror of his beak, and light'nings of his eye.

I 3. *Epode*

a^4 Thee the voice, the dance, obey,
a^4 Temper'd to thy warbled lay.
b^4 O'er Idalia's velvet-green
b^4 The rosy-crowned Loves are seen
a^3 On Cytherea's day
$c^{\sim 4}$ With antic Sports, and blue-eyed Pleasures,
$c^{\sim 4}$ Frisking light in frolic measures;
$d^{\sim 4}$ Now pursuing, now retreating,
e^4 Now in circling troops they meet:
$d^{\sim 4}$ To brisk notes in cadence beating
e^4 Glance their many-twinkling feet.
f^5 Slow melting strains their Queen's approach declare:
a^5 Where'er she turns the Graces homage pay.
f^5 With arms sublime, that float upon the air,
a^5 In gliding state she wins her easy way:
g^5 O'er her warm cheek, and rising bosom, move
$g^{?6}$ The bloom of young Desire, and purple light of Love.

From THOMAS GRAY, *The Progress of Poesy*, 1754

13. Power of harmony to calm the turbulent sallies of the soul (Gray's note). **25.** Power of harmony to produce all the graces of motion in the body (Gray's note). **41.** $g^{?6}$: The question mark, in this position, indicates approximate rhyme probably intended as rhyme.

I 1. *Strophe*

a^4 "Ruin seize thee, ruthless King!
b^4 Confusion on thy banners wait;
a^4 Tho' fann'd by Conquest's crimson wing
b^4 They mock the air with idle state.
c^4 Helm, nor hauberk's twisted mail,
c^5 Nor even thy virtues, Tyrant, shall avail
d^5 To save thy secret soul from nightly fears,
d^4 From Cambria's curse, from Cambria's tears!"
e^5 Such were the sounds, that o'er the crested pride
f^5 Of the first Edward scatter'd wild dismay
e^5 As down the steep of Snowdon's shaggy side
f^5 He wound with toilsome march his long array.
g^5 Stout Glo'ster stood aghast in speechless trance;
g^6 To arms! cried Mortimer, and couch'd his quiv'ring lance.

I 2. *Antistrophe*

a^4 On a rock, whose haughty brow
b^4 Frowns o'er old Conway's foaming flood,
$a?^4$ Robed in the sable garb of woe,
$b?^4$ With haggard eyes the Poet stood
c^4 (Loose his beard, and hoary hair
c^5 Stream'd, like a meteor, to the troubled air),
d^5 And with a master's hand, and prophet's fire,
d^4 Struck the deep sorrows of his lyre.
e^5 "Hark, how each giant-oak, and desert cave,
f^5 Sighs to the torrent's aweful voice beneath!
e^5 O'er thee, oh King! their hundred arms they wave,
$f?^5$ Revenge on thee in hoarser murmurs breathe;
g^5 Vocal no more, since Cambria's fatal day,
g^6 To high-born Hoel's harp, or soft Llewellyn's lay.

I 3. *Epode*

a^3 "Cold is Cadwallo's tongue,
b^3 That hush'd the stormy main;
c^5 Brave Urien sleeps upon his craggy bed;
b^3 Mountains, ye mourn in vain
$a?^3$ Modred, whose magic song
c^5 Made huge Plinlimmon bow his cloud-top'd head.
d^4 On dreary Arvon's shore they lie,
e^4 Smear'd with gore, and ghastly pale;
e^5 Far, far aloof th'affrighted ravens sail;
d^5 The famish'd eagle screams, and passes by.

f^5 Dear lost companions of my tuneful art,
g^5 Dear, as the light that visits these sad eyes,
f^5 Dear, as the ruddy drops that warm my heart,
g^5 Ye died amidst your dying country's cries—
h^4 No more I weep. They do not sleep.* — internal rhyme
i^4 On yonder cliffs, a griesly band,
j^4 I see them sit, they linger yet,* — approximate internal rhyme
i^4 Avengers of their native land:
k^5 With me in dreadful harmony they join,
k^6 And weave with bloody hands the tissue of thy line." — historical rhyme

From THOMAS GRAY, *The Bard*, 1757

STANZAIC OR HORATIAN ODE

ODE TO EVENING

If aught of oaten stop, or pastoral song,
May hope, O pensive Eve, to sooth thine ear,
    Like thy own brawling springs,
    Thy springs, and dying gales,

O Nymph reserv'd, while now the bright-hair'd Sun
Sits in yon western tent, whose cloudy skirts,
    With brede ethereal wove,
    O'erhang his wavy bed:

How air is hush'd, save where the weak-ey'd bat,
With short shrill shriek, flits by on leathern wing,
    Or where the beetle winds
    His small but sullen horn,

As oft he rises 'midst the twilight path,
Against the pilgrim borne in heedless hum:
    Now teach me, Maid compos'd,
    To breathe some soften'd strain,

Whose numbers stealing thro' thy darkning vale,
May not unseemly with its stillness suit,
    As musing slow, I hail
    Thy genial lov'd return!

For when thy folding star arising shews
His paly circlet, at his warning lamp
    The fragrant Hours, and elves
    Who slept in buds the day,

* The pattern of the h^4 and j^4 lines, with their internal rhymes, is repeated in the two other epodes in the poem.

And many a nymph who wreaths her brows with sedge,
And sheds the fresh'ning dew, and lovelier still,
    The pensive Pleasures sweet,
    Prepare thy shadowy car.

Then let me rove some wild and heathy scene,
Or find some ruin 'midst its dreary dells,
    Whose walls more awful nod
    By thy religious gleams.

Or if chill blustring winds, or driving rain,
Prevent my willing feet, be mine the hut
    That from the mountain's side
    Views wilds, and swelling floods,

And hamlets brown, and dim-discover'd spires,
And hears their simple bell, and marks o'er all
    Thy dewy fingers draw
    The gradual dusky veil.

While Spring shall pour his show'rs, as oft he wont,
And bathe thy breathing tresses, meekest Eve!
    While Summer loves to sport,
    Beneath thy ling'ring light,

While sallow Autumn fills thy lap with leaves,
Or Winter, yelling thro' the troublous air,
    Affrights thy shrinking train,
    And rudely rends thy robes:

So long regardful of thy quiet rule,
Shall Fancy, Friendship, Science, smiling Peace,
    Thy gentlest influence own,
    And love thy fav'rite name!

1746 William Collins (1721–1759)

ODE TO A NIGHTINGALE

I

My heart aches, and a drowsy numbness pains
  My sense, as though of hemlock I had drunk,
Or emptied some dull opiate to the drains
  One minute past, and Lethe-wards had sunk:
'Tis not through envy of thy happy lot,
  But being too happy in thine happiness,—
    That thou, light-winged Dryad of the trees,
        In some melodious plot
  Of beechen green, and shadows numberless,
    Singest of summer in full-throated ease.

II

O, for a draught of vintage! that hath been
  Cool'd a long age in the deep-delved earth,
Tasting of Flora and the country green,
  Dance, and Provençal song, and sunburnt mirth!
O for a beaker full of the warm South,
  Full of the true, the blushful Hippocrene,
    With beaded bubbles winking at the brim,
      And purple-stained mouth;
  That I might drink, and leave the world unseen,
    And with thee fade away into the forest dim:

III

Fade far away, dissolve, and quite forget
  What thou among the leaves hast never known,
The weariness, the fever, and the fret
  Here, where men sit and hear each other groan;
Where palsy shakes a few, sad, last gray hairs,
  Where youth grows pale, and spectre-thin, and dies;
    Where but to think is to be full of sorrow
      And leaden-eyed despairs,
  Where Beauty cannot keep her lustrous eyes,
    Or new Love pine at them beyond to-morrow.

IV

Away! away! for I will fly to thee,
  Not charioted by Bacchus and his pards,
But on the viewless wings of Poesy,
  Though the dull brain perplexes and retards:
Already with thee! tender is the night,
  And haply the Queen-Moon is on her throne,
    Cluster'd around by all her starry Fays;
      But here there is no light,
  Save what from heaven is with the breezes blown
    Through verdurous glooms and winding mossy ways.

V

I cannot see what flowers are at my feet,
  Nor what soft incense hangs upon the boughs,
But, in embalmed darkness, guess each sweet
  Wherewith the seasonable month endows
The grass, the thicket, and the fruit-tree wild;

White hawthorn, and the pastoral eglantine;
Fast fading violets cover'd up in leaves;
And mid-May's eldest child,
The coming musk-rose, full of dewy wine,
The murmurous haunt of flies on summer eves.

VI

Darkling I listen; and, for many a time
I have been half in love with easeful Death,
Call'd him soft names in many a mused rhyme,
To take into the air my quiet breath;
Now more than ever seems it rich to die,
To cease upon the midnight with no pain,
While thou art pouring forth thy soul abroad
In such an ecstasy!
Still wouldst thou sing, and I have ears in vain—
To thy high requiem become a sod.

VII

Thou wast not born for death, immortal Bird!
No hungry generations tread thee down;
The voice I hear this passing night was heard
In ancient days by emperor and clown:
Perhaps the self-same song that found a path
Through the sad heart of Ruth, when, sick for home,
She stood in tears amid the alien corn;
The same that oft-times hath
Charm'd magic casements, opening on the foam
Of perilous seas, in faery lands forlorn.

VIII

Forlorn! the very word is like a bell
To toll me back from thee to my sole self!
Adieu! the fancy cannot cheat so well
As she is fam'd to do, deceiving elf.
Adieu! adieu! thy plaintive anthem fades
Past the near meadows, over the still stream,
Up the hill-side; and now 'tis buried deep
In the next valley-glades:
Was it a vision, or a waking dream?
Fled is that music:—Do I wake or sleep?

1820 JOHN KEATS (1795–1821)

IRREGULAR ODE

THE RESURRECTION

I

a^4 Not winds to voyagers at sea,
a^5 Nor showers to earth, more necessary be
b^5 (Heav'n's vital seed cast on the womb of earth
b^4 To give the fruitful year a birth)
c^4 Than verse to virtue, which can do
c^5 The midwife's office, and the nurse's too;
d^5 It feeds it strongly, and it clothes it gay,
e^4 And when it dies, with comely pride
$e?^4$ Embalms it, and erects a pyramid
d^3 That never will decay
d^4 Till Heav'n itself shall melt away,
d^3 And nought behind it stay.

II

a^5 Begin the song, and strike the living lyre;
a^7 Lo how the years to come, a numerous and well-fitted quire,
b^5 All hand in hand do decently advance,
b^6 And to my song with smooth and equal measures dance.
c^5 Whilst the dance lasts, how long so e'er it be,
c^5 My music's voice shall bear it company,
d^4 Till all gentle notes be drown'd
d^4 In the last trumpet's dreadful sound,
e^5 That to the spheres themselves shall silence bring,
e^4 Untune the universal string.
f^4 Then all the wide extended sky,
f^4 And all th'harmonious worlds on high,
f^4 And Virgil's sacred work shall die;
g^5 And he himself shall see in one fire shine
g^6 Rich Nature's ancient Troy, though built by hands divine.

III

a^3 Whom thunder's dismal noise,
b^6 And all that Prophets and Apostles louder spake,
$a?^5$ And all the creatures' plain-conspiring voice,
b^4 Could not, whilst they liv'd, awake,
b^3 This mightier sound shall make
c^2 When dead t'arise,

c^4 And open tombs, and open eyes,
d^5 To the long sluggards of five thousand years.
d^5 This mightier sound shall wake its hearers' ears.
e^5 Then shall the scatter'd atoms crowding come
$e?^3$ Back to their ancient home.
e^4 Some from birds, from fishes some,
f^4 Some from earth, and some from seas,
f^4 Some from beasts, and some from trees.
g^4 Some descend from clouds on high,
g^4 Some from metals upwards fly,
h^6 And where th'attending soul naked and shivering stands,
h^4 Meet, salute, and join their hands,
i^5 As dispers'd soldiers at the trumpet's call
i^3 Haste to their colours all.
j^4 Unhappy most, like tortur'd men,
j^5 Their joints new set, to be new rack'd again,
k^4 To mountains they for shelter pray;
k^7 The mountains shake, and run about no less confus'd than they.

IV

a^5 Stop, stop, my Muse! allay thy vig'rous heat,
$a?^4$ Kindled at a hint so great.
b^5 Hold thy Pindaric Pegasus closely in,
b^3 Which does to rage begin,
c^6 And this steep hill would gallop up with violent course;
c^5 'Tis an unruly and a hard-mouth'd horse,
d^3 Fierce, and unbroken yet,
$d?^4$ Impatient of the spur or bit;
e^6 Now prances stately, and anon flies o'er the place;
e^6 Disdains the servile law of any settled pace;
c^5 Conscious and proud of his own natural force,
f^4 'Twill no unskilful touch endure,
f^6 But flings writer and reader too that sits not sure.

1656 ABRAHAM COWLEY (1618–1667)

A SONG FOR ST. CECILIA'S DAY

November 22, 1687

I

$A\,a^5$ From harmony, from heav'nly harmony
$B\,b^4$ This universal frame began;
c^4 When Nature underneath a heap
d^3 Of jarring atoms lay,

e^{3} And could not heave her head,
$a?^{4}$ The tuneful voice was heard from high,
e^{3} "Arise, ye more than dead."
$a?^{4}$ Then cold and hot and moist and dry
c^{4} In order to their stations leap,
d^{3} And Music's pow'r obey.
Aa^{5} From harmony, from heav'nly harmony
Bb^{4} This universal frame began;
a^{4} From harmony to harmony
b^{5} Through all the compass of the notes it ran,
b^{5} The diapason closing full in Man.

II

Aa^{5} What passion cannot Music raise and quell?
a^{4} When Jubal struck the corded shell,
b^{4} His list'ning brethren stood around,
a^{4} And, wond'ring, on their faces fell
b^{4} To worship that celestial sound.
a^{5} Less than a god they thought there could not dwell
a^{4} Within the hollow of that shell,
a^{4} That spoke so sweetly and so well.
Aa^{5} What passion cannot Music raise and quell?

III

$a\smile^{2}$ The trumpet's loud clangor
b^{2} Excites us to arms
$a\smile ?^{2}$ With shrill notes of anger
b^{2} And mortal alarms.
c^{4} The double, double, double beat
d^{3} Of the thund'ring drum
d^{4} Críes, "Hárk! the fóes cóme;
c^{4} Chárge, chárge, 'tis too late to retreat!"

IV

a^{3} The soft complaining flute
$b\smile ?^{3}$ In dying notes discovers
$b\smile ?^{3}$ The woes of hopeless lovers,
a^{5} Whose dirge is whisper'd by the warbling lute.

V

a^{3} Sharp violins proclaim
$b\smile^{4}$ Their jealous pangs and desperation,
$b\smile^{4}$ Fury, frantic indignation,
$b\smile ?^{4}$ Depths of pains, and height of passion,
a^{4} For the fair, disdainful dame.

VI

a^3 But, oh! what art can teach,
a^3 What human voice can reach
b^3 The sacred organ's praise?
c^4 Notes inspiring holy love,
b^4 Notes that wing their heav'nly ways
c^3 To mend the choirs above.

VII

a^5 Orpheus could lead the savage race,
a^4 And trees unrooted left their place,
b^3 Sequacious of the lyre;
b^5 But bright Cecilia rais'd the wonder high'r;
c^5 When to her organ vocal breath was giv'n,
d^4 An angel heard, and straight appear'd, — approximate internal rhyme
$c?^3$ Mistaking earth for Heav'n.

Grand Chorus

a^4 As from the pow'r of sacred lays
b^3 The spheres began to move,
a^4 And sung the great Creator's praise
$b?^3$ To all the bless'd above;
c^4 So when the last and dreadful hour
c^4 This crumbling pageant shall devour,
d^4 The trumpet shall be heard on high,
d^4 The dead shall live, the living die,
d^4 And Music shall untune the sky.

John Dryden (1631–1700)

EXERCISE 52

Examine carefully the varying line lengths and the rhyming arrangements of Dryden's *Song for St. Cecilia's Day*. Like Spender in *The Express* (p. 11), Dryden is clearly trying to establish a correspondence between the sound of the actual music and the sound of his poem. What is the effect of rhyming tetrameter with trimeter lines? Pentameter with tetrameter? What use is made of short lines, dimeter and trimeter? What is the effect of double or feminine rhymes? Of approximate rhymes? Note the repetition of whole lines and words, as well as the use of alliteration and onomatopoeia.

In commenting upon the various techniques employed to make a musical composition of the verse, through a use of the wide range of devices possible in the irregular ode, do not overlook the argument of the poem: its content. Does the technique add to, or detract from, the ideas Dryden wishes to express? In conclusion, evaluate the effectiveness of the poem as a whole.

ODE:
INTIMATIONS OF IMMORTALITY FROM RECOLLECTIONS OF EARLY CHILDHOOD

I

There was a time when meadow, grove, and stream,
The earth, and every common sight,
        To me did seem
      Apparelled in celestial light,
The glory and the freshness of a dream.
It is not now as it hath been of yore;—
      Turn wheresoe'er I may,
        By night or day,
The things which I have seen I now can see no more.

II

      The rainbow comes and goes,
      And lovely is the rose,
      The moon doth with delight
  Look round her when the heavens are bare,
      Waters on a starry night
      Are beautiful and fair;
  The sunshine is a glorious birth;
  But yet I know, where'er I go,
That there hath passed away a glory from the earth.

III

Now, while the birds thus sing a joyous song,
    And while the young lambs bound
      As to the tabor's sound,
To me alone there came a thought of grief:
A timely utterance gave that thought relief,
      And I again am strong:
The cataracts blow their trumpets from the steep;
No more shall grief of mine the season wrong;
I hear the echoes through the mountains throng,
The winds come to me from the fields of sleep,
      And all the earth is gay;
        Land and sea
    Give themselves up to jollity,
      And with the heart of May
    Doth every beast keep holiday;—
      Thou child of joy,
Shout round me, let me hear thy shouts, thou happy shepherd-boy!

IV

Ye blessèd creatures, I have heard the call
Ye to each other make; I see
The heavens laugh with you in your jubilee;
My heart is at your festival,
My head hath its coronal,
The fullness of your bliss, I feel—I feel it all.
O evil day! if I were sullen
While earth herself is adorning,
This sweet May-morning,
And the children are culling
On every side,
In a thousand valleys far and wide,
Fresh flowers; while the sun shines warm,
And the babe leaps up on his mother's arm:—
I hear, I hear, with joy I hear!
—But there's a tree, of many, one,
A single field which I have looked upon;
Both of them speak of something that is gone;
The pansy at my feet
Doth the same tale repeat:
Whither is fled the visionary gleam?
Where is it now, the glory and the dream?

V

Our birth is but a sleep and a forgetting:
The soul that rises with us, our life's star,
Hath had elsewhere its setting,
And cometh from afar:
Not in entire forgetfulness,
And not in utter nakedness,
But trailing clouds of glory do we come
From God, who is our home:
Heaven lies about us in our infancy!
Shades of the prison-house begin to close
Upon the growing boy,
But he beholds the light, and whence it flows,
He sees it in his joy;
The youth, who daily farther from the east
Must travel, still is Nature's priest,
And by the vision splendid
Is on his way attended;
At length the man perceives it die away,
And fade into the light of common day.

VI

Earth fills her lap with pleasures of her own;
Yearnings she hath in her own natural kind,
And, even with something of a mother's mind,
And no unworthy aim,
The homely nurse doth all she can
To make her foster-child, her inmate man,
Forget the glories he hath known,
And that imperial palace whence he came.

VII

Behold the child among his new-born blisses,
A six years' darling of a pygmy size!
See, where 'mid work of his own hand he lies,
Fretted by sallies of his mother's kisses,
With light upon him from his father's eyes!
See, at his feet, some little plan or chart,
Some fragment from his dream of human life,
Shaped by himself with newly-learnèd art;
A wedding or a festival,
A mourning or a funeral;
And this hath now his heart,
And unto this he frames his song:
Then will he fit his tongue
To dialogues of business, love, or strife;
But it will not be long
Ere this be thrown aside,
And with new joy and pride
The little actor cons another part;
Filling from time to time his "humorous stage"
With all the persons, down to palsied age,
That life brings with her in her equipage;
As if his whole vocation
Were endless imitation.

VIII

Thou, whose exterior semblance doth belie
Thy soul's immensity;
Thou best philosopher, who yet dost keep
Thy heritage, thou eye among the blind,
That, deaf and silent, read'st the eternal deep,
Haunted for ever by the eternal mind,—
Mighty prophet! seer blest!
On whom those truths do rest,

Which we are toiling all our lives to find,
In darkness lost, the darkness of the grave;
Thou, over whom thy immortality
Broods like the day, a master o'er a slave,
A presence which is not to be put by;
Thou little child, yet glorious in the might
O heaven-born freedom on thy being's height,
Why with such earnest pains dost thou provoke
The years to bring the inevitable yoke,
Thus blindly with thy blessedness at strife?
Full soon thy soul shall have her earthly freight,
And custom lie upon thee with a weight,
Heavy as frost, and deep almost as life!

IX

O joy! that in our embers
Is something that doth live,
That nature yet remembers
What was so fugitive!
The thought of our past years in me doth breed
Perpetual benediction: not indeed
For that which is most worthy to be blest—
Delight and liberty, the simple creed
Of childhood, whether busy or at rest,
With new-fledged hope still fluttering in his breast:—
Not for these I raise
The song of thanks and praise;
But for those obstinate questionings
Of sense and outward things,
Fallings from us, vanishings;
Blank misgivings of a creature
Moving about in worlds not realised,
High instincts before which our mortal nature
Did tremble like a guilty thing surprised:
But for those first affections,
Those shadowy recollections,
Which, be they what they may,
Are yet the fountain-light of all our day,
Are yet a master-light of all our seeing;
Uphold us, cherish, and have power to make
Our noisy years seem moments in the being
Of the eternal silence: truths that wake,
To perish never:

Which neither listlessness, nor mad endeavour,
    Nor man nor boy,
Nor all that is at enmity with joy,
Can utterly abolish or destroy!
  Hence in a season of calm weather
    Though inland far we be,
Our souls have sight of that immortal sea
    Which brought us hither,
  Can in a moment travel thither,
And see the children sport upon the shore,
And hear the mighty waters rolling evermore.

X

Then sing, ye birds, sing, sing a joyous song!
    And let the young lambs bound
    As to the tabor's sound!
We in thought will join your throng,
    Ye that pipe and ye that play,
    Ye that through your hearts to-day
    Feel the gladness of the May!
What though the radiance which was once so bright
Be now for ever taken from my sight,
    Though nothing can bring back the hour
Of splendour in the grass, of glory in the flower;
    We will grieve not, rather find
    Strength in what remains behind;
    In the primal sympathy
    Which having been must ever be;
    In the soothing thoughts that spring
    Out of human suffering;
    In the faith that looks through death,
In years that bring the philosophic mind.

XI

And O, ye fountains, meadows, hills, and groves,
Forebode not any severing of our loves!
Yet in my heart of hearts I feel your might;
I only have relinquished one delight
To live beneath your more habitual sway.
I love the brooks which down their channels fret,
Even more than when I tripped lightly as they;
The innocent brightness of a new-born day
      Is lovely yet;
The clouds that gather round the setting sun

Do take a sober colouring from an eye
That hath kept watch o'er man's mortality;
Another race hath been, and other palms are won.
Thanks to the human heart by which we live,
Thanks to its tenderness, its joys, and fears,
To me the meanest flower that blows can give
Thoughts that do often lie too deep for tears.

1802 William Wordsworth (1770–1850)

EXERCISE 53

Wordsworth's *Intimations Ode*, unlike Dryden's ode, is not an attempt to establish a correspondence between an actual physical sound and the sound of the verse. It is, instead, an attempt to use the devices available to verse to correspond with the emotions and ideas of the poem. Read the whole poem closely and carefully, noting Wordsworth's references to the power of nature and to the concept of pre-existence. Scan and annotate the rhyme pattern of strophe V, beginning: "Our birth is but a sleep and a forgetting." In a critical essay evaluate the effect of the techniques used in achieving the total effect of the strophe. Your analysis may be more helpful to you if you consider what might have happened if some lines had been longer, and others shorter; if some of the couplets had been rhymed alternately, and some of the alternating rhymes had been done in couplets instead. In places where you believe the technique ineffective, try to write or to suggest a substitute.

SOME EXPERIMENTS

From Cowley's experiments in the irregular ode, it is only a step to the choruses of Milton's *Samson Agonistes* (see p. 293), which the author described as "of all sorts, call'd by the Greeks *monostrophic*, . . . without regard had to strophe, antistrophe, or epode, which were a kind of stanzas fram'd only for the music." The verse of Milton's poem has been exhaustively studied by Robert Bridges,* who believed it to be based upon the classical principle of QUANTITY. This conclusion may be correct, but, if so, Milton's poem is the sole example of a successful poem in English which employs the quantitative rules exclusively. (For examples by Swinburne and Tennyson, see CLASSICAL PROSODY.) Although Milton's knowledge of the classics was so great that he could have succeeded where other poets failed, he was also a great adapter of poetic forms. It seems more probable that he adapted the forms of Greek dramatic choruses

* R. Bridges, *Milton's Prosody* (Oxford, 1901).

to their equivalents in English sound, just as he adapted the classical dactylic hexameter to give a similar effect in English iambic pentameter for *Paradise Lost*. Some of the choruses of *Samson* are written in a variety of English meters (which involve quantity together with STRESS). Other parts seem to employ the Anglo-Saxon principle of stress (see ANGLO-SAXON PROSODY). And a third group, which seems to be entirely without meter or pattern, may be called FREE VERSE, although the term was unknown in Milton's time and for two centuries more. Free verse may employ rhyme, and some parts of *Samson Agonistes* make use of this device; others do not. The rhythms of *Samson*, by whatever terminology they are interpreted, are effective and exciting, but no major poet undertook this kind of verse again until the nineteenth century, when Shelley employed irregular strophes in *Queen Mab* and the Victorian poets Arnold, Swinburne, Morris, and Henley adopted what appear to be the forms (though not the themes) of the irregular ode, using meter and rhyme, or omitting the rhyme which was characteristic of the ode in English.

Although the poems included in this experimental group are usually not titled "Ode" by their authors, the type of strophe with varying line lengths and occasional, but not strictly patterned, rhyme is clearly a prosodic development in the form, if not the subject matter, of the irregular ode.

DOVER BEACH

The sea is calm to-night,
The tide is full, the moon lies fair
Upon the Straits;—on the French coast, the light
Gleams, and is gone; the cliffs of England stand,
Glimmering and vast, out in the tranquil bay.
Come to the window, sweet is the night air!
Only, from the long line of spray
Where the ebb meets the moon-blanch'd sand,
Listen! you hear the grating roar
Of pebbles which the waves suck back, and fling,
At their return, up the high strand,
Begin, and cease, and then again begin,
With tremulous cadence slow, and bring
The eternal note of sadness in.

Sophocles long ago
Heard it on the Aegean, and it brought
Into his mind the turbid ebb and flow
Of human misery; we
Find also in the sound a thought,
Hearing it by this distant northern sea.

The sea of faith
Was once, too, at the full, and round earth's shore
Lay like the folds of a bright girdle furl'd;
But now I only hear
Its melancholy, long, withdrawing roar,
Retreating to the breath
Of the night-wind down the vast edges drear
And naked shingles of the world.

Ah, love, let us be true
To one another! for the world, which seems
To lie before us like a land of dreams,
So various, so beautiful, so new,
Hath really neither joy, nor love, nor light,
Nor certitude, nor peace, nor help for pain;
And we are here as on a darkling plain
Swept with confused alarms of struggle and flight,
Where ignorant armies clash by night.

1867 MATTHEW ARNOLD (1822–1888)

THE HOUND OF HEAVEN

I fled Him, down the nights and down the days;
  I fled Him, down the arches of the years;
I fled Him, down the labyrinthine ways
  Of my own mind; and in the mist of tears
I hid from Him, and under running laughter.
          Up vistaed hopes I sped;
          And shot, precipitated,
Adown Titanic glooms of chasmèd fears,
  From those strong Feet that followed, followed after.
          But with unhurrying chase,
          And unperturbèd pace,
     Deliberate speed, majestic instancy,
          They beat—and a Voice beat
          More instant than the Feet—
     "All things betray thee, who betrayest Me."

          I pleaded, outlaw-wise,
By many a hearted casement, curtained red,
  Trellised with intertwining charities
(For, though I knew His love Who followèd,
          Yet was I sore adread
Lest, having Him, I must have naught beside);

But, if one little casement parted wide,
The gust of His approach would clash it to:
Fear wist not to evade as Love wist to pursue.
Across the margent of the world I fled,
And troubled the gold gateways of the stars,
Smiting for shelter on their clangèd bars;
Fretted to dulcet jars
And silvern chatter the pale ports o' the moon.
I said to Dawn: Be sudden—to Eve: Be soon;
With thy young skiey blossoms heap me over
From this tremendous Lover—
Float thy vague veil about me, lest He see!
I tempted all His servitors, but to find
My own betrayal in their constancy,
In faith to Him their fickleness to me,
Their traitorous trueness, and their loyal deceit.
To all swift things for swiftness did I sue;
Clung to the whistling mane of every wind.
But whether they swept, smoothly fleet,
The long savannahs of the blue;
Or whether, Thunder-driven,
They clanged his chariot 'thwart a heaven,
Plashy with flying lightnings round the spurn o' their feet:—
Fear wist not to evade as Love wist to pursue.
Still with unhurrying chase,
And unperturbèd pace,
Deliberate speed, majestic instancy,
Came on the following Feet,
And a Voice above their beat—
"Naught shelters thee, who wilt not shelter Me."

I sought no more that after which I strayed
In face of man or maid;
But still within the little children's eyes
Seems something, something that replies,
They at least are for me, surely for me!
I turned me to them very wistfully;
But just as their young eyes grew sudden fair
With dawning answers there,
Their angel plucked them from me by the hair.
"Come then, ye other children, Nature's—share
With me" (said I) "your delicate fellowship;

Let me greet you lip to lip,
Let me twine with you caresses,
Wantoning
With our Lady-Mother's vagrant tresses,
Banqueting
With her in her wind-walled palace,
Underneath her azured daïs,
Quaffing, as your taintless way is,
From a chalice
Lucent-weeping out of the dayspring."
So it was done:
I in their delicate fellowship was one—
Drew the bolt of Nature's secrecies.
I knew all the swift importings
On the wilful face of skies;
I knew how the clouds arise
Spumèd of the wild sea-snortings;
All that's born or dies
Rose and drooped with; made them shapers
Of mine own moods, or wailful or divine;
With them joyed and was bereaven.
I was heavy with the even,
When she lit her glimmering tapers
Round the day's dead sanctities.
I laughed in the morning's eyes.
I triumphed and I saddened with all weather,
Heaven and I wept together,
And its sweet tears were salt with mortal mine:
Against the red throb of its sunset-heart
I laid my own to beat,
And share commingling heat;
But not by that, by that, was eased my human smart.
In vain my tears were wet on Heaven's grey cheek.
For ah! we know not what each other says,
These things and I; in sound *I* speak—
Their sound is but their stir, they speak by silences.
Nature, poor stepdame, cannot slake my drouth;
Let her, if she would owe me,
Drop yon blue bosom-veil of sky, and show me
The breasts o' her tenderness:
Never did any milk of hers once bless
My thirsting mouth.

Nigh and nigh draws the chase,
With unperturbèd pace,
Deliberate speed, majestic instancy;
And past those noisèd Feet
A Voice comes yet more fleet—
"Lo! naught contents thee, who content'st not Me."

Naked I wait Thy love's uplifted stroke!
My harness piece by piece Thou hast hewn from me,
And smitten me to my knee;
I am defenceless utterly.
I slept, methinks, and woke,
And, slowly gazing, find me stripped in sleep.
In the rash lustihead of my young powers,
I shook the pillaring hours
And pulled my life upon me; grimed with smears,
I stand amid the dust o' the mounded years—
My mangled youth lies dead beneath the heap.
My days have crackled and gone up in smoke,
Have puffed and burst as sun-starts on a stream.
Yea, faileth now even dream
The dreamer, and the lute the lutanist;
Even the linked fantasies, in whose blossomy twist
I swung the earth a trinket at my wrist,
Are yielding; cords of all too weak account
For earth with heavy griefs so overplussed.
Ah! is Thy love indeed
A weed, albeit an amaranthine weed,
Suffering no flowers except its own to mount?
Ah! must—
Designer infinite!—
Ah! must Thou char the wood ere Thou canst limn with it?
My freshness spent its wavering shower i' the dust;
And now my heart is as a broken fount,
Wherein tear-drippings stagnate, spilt down ever
From the dank thoughts that shiver
Upon the sighful branches of my mind.
Such is; what is to be?
The pulp so bitter, how shall taste the rind?
I dimly guess what Time in mists confounds;
Yet ever and anon a trumpet sounds

From the hid battlements of Eternity;
Those shaken mists a space unsettle, then
Round the half-glimpsèd turrets slowly wash again.
But not ere him who summoneth
I first have seen, enwound
With glooming robes purpureal, cypress-crowned;
His name I know, and what his trumpet saith.
Whether man's heart or life it be which yields
Thee harvest, must Thy harvest-fields
Be dunged with rotten death?

Now of that long pursuit
Comes on at hand the bruit;
That Voice is round me like a bursting sea:
"And is thy earth so marred,
Shattered in shard on shard?
Lo, all things fly thee, for thou fliest Me!
Strange, piteous, futile thing!
Wherefore should any set thee love apart?
Seeing none but I makes much of naught" (He said),
"And human love needs human meriting:
How hast thou merited—
Of all man's clotted clay the dingiest clot?
Alack, thou knowest not
How little worthy of any love thou art!
Whom wilt thou find to love ignoble thee,
Save Me, save only Me?
All which I took from thee I did but take,
Not for thy harms,
But just that thou might'st seek it in My arms.
All which thy child's mistake
Fancies as lost, I have stored for thee at home:
Rise, clasp My hand, and come!"
Halts by me that footfall:
Is my gloom, after all,
Shade of His hand, outstretched caressingly?
"Ah, fondest, blindest, weakest,
I am He Whom thou seekest!
Thou dravest love from thee, who dravest Me."

1890 FRANCIS THOMPSON (1859–1907)

THE LOVE SONG OF J. ALFRED PRUFROCK

S'io credesse che mia risposta fosse
A persona che mai tornasse al mondo,
Questa fiamma staria senza piu scosse.
Ma perciocche giammai di questo fondo
Non torno vivo alcun, s'i'odo il vero,
*Senza tema d'infamia ti rispondo.**

Let us go then, you and I,
When the evening is spread out against the sky
Like a patient etherised upon a table;
Let us go, through certain half-deserted streets,
The muttering retreats
Of restless nights in one-night cheap hotels
And sawdust restaurants with oyster-shells:
Streets that follow like a tedious argument
Of insidious intent
To lead you to an overwhelming question . . . †
Oh, do not ask, "What is it?"
Let us go and make our visit.

In the room the women come and go
Talking of Michelangelo.

The yellow fog that rubs its back upon the window-panes,
The yellow smoke that rubs its muzzle on the window-panes
Licked its tongue into the corners of the evening,
Lingered upon the pools that stand in drains,
Let fall upon its back the soot that falls from chimneys,
Slipped by the terrace, made a sudden leap,
And seeing that it was a soft October night,
Curled once about the house, and fell asleep.

And indeed there will be time
For the yellow smoke that slides along the street,
Rubbing its back upon the window-panes;
There will be time, there will be time
To prepare a face to meet the faces that you meet;
There will be time to murder and create,
And time for all the works and days of hands
That lift and drop a question on your plate;
Time for you and time for me,

* "If I thought my answer were to one who could ever return to the world, this flame should shake no more, but since, if what I hear be true, none ever did return alive from this depth, without fear of infamy, I answer thee."—Dante, *Inferno*. The speaker is one damned, encircled in flame.
† The ellipsis marks here and below are Eliot's. The poem is given in full.

And time yet for a hundred indecisions,
And for a hundred visions and revisions,
Before the taking of a toast and tea.

In the room the women come and go
Talking of Michelangelo.

And indeed there will be time
To wonder, "Do I dare?" and, "Do I dare?"
Time to turn back and descend the stair,
With a bald spot in the middle of my hair—
[They will say: "How his hair is growing thin!"]
My morning coat, my collar mounting firmly to the chin,
My necktie rich and modest, but asserted by a simple pin—
[They will say: "But how his arms and legs are thin!"]
Do I dare
Disturb the universe?
In a minute there is time
For decisions and revisions which a minute will reverse.

For I have known them all already, known them all:—
Have known the evenings, mornings, afternoons,
I have measured out my life with coffee spoons;
I know the voices dying with a dying fall
Beneath the music from a farther room.
  So how should I presume?

And I have known the eyes already, known them all—
The eyes that fix you in a formulated phrase,
And when I am formulated, sprawling on a pin,
When I am pinned and wriggling on the wall,
Then how should I begin
To spit out all the butt-ends of my days and ways?
  And how should I presume?

And I have known the arms already, known them all—
Arms that are braceleted and white and bare
[But in the lamplight, downed with light brown hair!]
Is it perfume from a dress
That makes me so digress?
Arms that lie along a table, or wrap about a shawl.
  And should I then presume?
  And how should I begin?

. . . . .

Shall I say, I have gone at dusk through narrow streets
And watched the smoke that rises from the pipes
Of lonely men in shirt-sleeves, leaning out of windows? . . .

I should have been a pair of ragged claws
Scuttling across the floors of silent seas.

. . . . .

And the afternoon, the evening, sleeps so peacefully!
Smoothed by long fingers,
Asleep . . . tired . . . or it malingers,
Stretched on the floor, here beside you and me.
Should I, after tea and cakes and ices,
Have the strength to force the moment to its crisis?
But though I have wept and fasted, wept and prayed,
Though I have seen my head [grown slightly bald] brought in upon a platter,
I am no prophet—and here's no great matter;
I have seen the moment of my greatness flicker,
And I have seen the eternal Footman hold my coat and snicker,
And in short, I was afraid.

And would it have been worth it, after all,
After the cups, the marmalade, the tea,
Among the porcelain, among some talk of you and me,
Would it have been worth while,
To have bitten off the matter with a smile,
To have squeezed the universe into a ball
To roll it toward some overwhelming question,
To say: "I am Lazarus, come from the dead,
Come back to tell you all, I shall tell you all"—
If one, settling a pillow by her head,
  Should say: "That is not what I meant at all.
  That is not it, at all."

And would it have been worth it, after all,
Would it have been worth while,
After the sunsets and the dooryards and the sprinkled streets,
After the novels, after the teacups, after the skirts that trail along the floor—
And this, and so much more?—
It is impossible to say just what I mean!
But as if a magic lantern threw the nerves in patterns on a screen:
Would it have been worth while
If one, settling a pillow or throwing off a shawl,
And turning toward the window, should say:
  "That is not it at all,
  That is not what I meant, at all."

. . . . .

No! I am not Prince Hamlet, nor was meant to be;
Am an attendant lord, one that will do

To swell a progress, start a scene or two,
Advise the prince; no doubt, an easy tool,
Deferential, glad to be of use,
Politic, cautious, and meticulous;
Full of high sentence, but a bit obtuse;
At times, indeed, almost ridiculous—
Almost, at times, the Fool.

I grow old . . . I grow old . . .
I shall wear the bottoms of my trousers rolled.

Shall I part my hair behind? Do I dare to eat a peach?
I shall wear white flannel trousers, and walk upon the beach.
I have heard the mermaids singing, each to each.

I do not think that they will sing to me.

I have seen them riding seaward on the waves
Combing the white hair of the waves blown back
When the wind blows the water white and black.

We have lingered in the chambers of the sea
By sea-girls wreathed with seaweed red and brown
Till human voices wake us, and we drown.

1917 T. S. ELIOT (1888–1965)

EXERCISE 54

A contemporary critic has pointed out that the themes of *Dover Beach* and *Prufrock* are similar. Consider the effect of the publication of Charles Darwin's *Origin of Species* (1859), with its theory of evolution, on the religious faith of Matthew Arnold. Consider the effect of this theory and the world tensions of 1914–1918 on the sensibilities of Eliot.

Scan both poems, using all the techniques you know. Note carefully the correspondence you find between the poetic devices used and the content of the lines or strophes in which they appear; for example, examine the movement of Arnold's lines describing the sea, the movement of Eliot's lines as "they" walk in the opening strophe. What is the effect of the use of the sea as metaphor in Arnold's poem?

Consider the allusions in Eliot's poem, notably to Michelangelo, and those in the strophe which begins "No! I am not Prince Hamlet." To what effect are these allusions used?

After you have considered the questions above and done the analysis, write a critical essay, comparing and evaluating the two poems.

ODE TO THE CONFEDERATE DEAD

Row after row with strict impunity
The headstones yield their names to the element,
The wind whirrs without recollection;
In the riven troughs the splayed leaves
Pile up, of nature the casual sacrament
To the seasonal eternity of death;
Then driven by the fierce scrutiny
Of heaven to their election in the vast breath,
They sough the rumour of mortality.

Autumn is desolation in the plot
Of a thousand acres where these memories grow
From the inexhaustible bodies that are not
Dead, but feed the grass row after rich row.
Think of the autumns that have come and gone!—
Ambitious November with the humors of the year,
With a particular zeal for every slab,
Staining the uncomfortable angels that rot
On the slabs, a wing chipped here, an arm there:
The brute curiosity of an angel's stare
Turns you, like them, to stone,
Transforms the heaving air
Till plunged to a heavier world below
You shift your sea-space blindly
Heaving, turning like the blind crab.

  Dazed by the wind, only the wind
  The leaves flying, plunge

You know who have waited by the wall
The twilight certainty of an animal,
Those midnight restitutions of the blood
You know—the immitigable pines, the smoky frieze
Of the sky, the sudden call: you know the rage,
The cold pool left by the mounting flood,
Of muted Zeno and Parmenides.
You who have waited for the angry resolution
Of those desires that should be yours tomorrow,
You know the unimportant shrift of death
And praise the vision
And praise the arrogant circumstance
Of those who fall
Rank upon rank, hurried beyond decision—
Here by the sagging gate, stopped by the wall.

Seeing, seeing only the leaves
Flying, plunge and expire

Turn your eyes to the immoderate past,
Turn to the inscrutable infantry rising
Demons out of the earth—they will not last.
Stonewall, Stonewall, and the sunken fields of hemp,
Shiloh, Antietam, Malvern Hill, Bull Run.
Lost in that orient of the thick-and-fast
You will curse the setting sun.

Cursing only the leaves crying
Like an old man in a storm

You hear the shout, the crazy hemlocks point
With troubled fingers to the silence which
Smothers you, a mummy, in time.

The hound bitch
Toothless and dying, in a musty cellar
Hears the wind only.

Now that the salt of their blood
Stiffens the saltier oblivion of the sea,
Seals the malignant purity of the flood,
What shall we who count our days and bow
Our heads with a commemorial woe
In the ribboned coats of grim felicity,
What shall we say of the bones, unclean,
Whose verdurous anonymity will grow?
The ragged arms, the ragged heads and eyes
Lost in these acres of the insane green?
The gray lean spiders come, they come and go;
In a tangle of willows without light
The singular screech-owl's tight
Invisible lyric seeds the mind
With the furious murmur of their chivalry.

We shall say only the leaves
Flying, plunge and expire

We shall say only the leaves whispering
In the improbable mist of nightfall
That flies on multiple wing;
Night is the beginning and the end
And in between the ends of distraction
Waits mute speculation, the patient curse

That stones the eyes, or like the jaguar leaps
For his own image in a jungle pool, his victim.

What shall we say who have knowledge
Carried to the heart? Shall we take the act
To the grave? Shall we, more hopeful, set up the grave
In the house? The ravenous grave?

Leave now
The shut gate and the decomposing wall:
The gentle serpent, green in the mulberry bush,
Riots with his tongue through the hush—
Sentinel of the grave who counts us all!

1932, rev. 1947 ALLEN TATE (1899–)

KILROY*

Also Ulysses once—that other war.
(Is it because we find his scrawl
Today on every privy door
That we forget his ancient role?)
Also was there—he did it for the wages—
When a Cathay-drunk Genoese set sail.
Whenever "longen folk to goon on pilgrimages,"
Kilroy is there;
he tells The Miller's Tale.

At times he seems a paranoic king
Who stamps his crest on walls and says "My Own!"
But in the end he fades like a lost tune,
Tossed here and there, whom all the breezes sing.
"Kilroy was here"; these words sound wanly gay,
Haughty yet tired with long marching.
He is Orestes—guilty of what crime?—
For whom the Furies still are searching;
When they arrive, they find their prey
(Leaving his name to mock them) went away.
Sometimes he does not flee from them in time:
"Kilroy was—"
with his blood a dying man
Wrote half the phrase out in Bataan.

* "An example of an unfaked epic spirit emerging from [World War II] was the expression 'Kilroy was here,' scribbled everywhere by American soldiers and implying that nothing was too adventurous or remote."—Louis Untermeyer

Kilroy, beware. "HOME" is the final trap
That lurks for you in many a wily shape:
In pipe-and-slippers plus a Loyal Hound
    Or fooling around, just fooling around.
Kind to the old (their warm Penelope)
But fierce to boys,
        thus "home" becomes that sea,
Horribly disguised, where you were always drowned—
    (How could suburban Crete condone
The yarns you would have V-mailed from the sun?)—
And folksy fishes sip Icarian tea.

One stab of hopeless wings imprinted your
    Exultant Kilroy-signature
Upon sheer sky for all the world to stare:
    "I was there! I was there! I was there!"

God is like Kilroy. He, too, sees it all;
That's how He knows of every sparrow's fall;
That's why we prayed each time the tightropes cracked
On which our loveliest clowns contrived their act.
The G. I. Faustus who was
                everywhere
Strolled home again. "What was it like outside?"
Asked Can't, with his good neighbors Ought and But
And pale Perhaps and grave-eyed Better Not;
For "Kilroy" means: the world is very wide.
    He was there, he was there, he was there!

And in the suburbs Can't sat down and cried.

1948 PETER VIERECK (1916–)

XII

Free Verse and Some Twentieth-Century Experiments

The development of FREE VERSE as we think of it today originated in France in the nineteenth century, but the first modern practitioner of English verse "free" of meter and based solely on rhythm and CADENCE was Walt Whitman (1819–1892). The verse of Whitman is characterized by long lines and extended rhythmical patterns employing frequent rhetorical PARALLELISM to correspond with the broad statements and inclusive subject matter which the poet preferred. Those who question whether verse so free can be considered "poetry" in form will realize that the relationship between elaborately designed rhythmical prose and free verse is very close. Both rely on rhythm, cadence, diction, and subject matter, rather than metrical pattern, for their effects, and it is futile to attempt absolute distinctions between the two. Although rhyme is an available device for writers of free verse (as it is not, for writers of prose), in practice it is very infrequently used, with the result that many people regard free verse as verse without meter *or* rhyme.

The experiments of the nineteenth century with variants of the irregular ode form and with free verse retained the elevated subject matter and diction of much traditional poetry and especially of the ode. Lofty themes and diction, however, were not compatible with the principles of the Imagist poets, who published free verse in the early decades of the twentieth century. The original Imagist group (Richard Aldington, H. D., John Gould Fletcher, F. S. Flint, D. H. Lawrence, and Amy Lowell, with Ezra Pound as their sponsor) called for "the language of common speech" and "absolute freedom in the choice of subject"; and although they did not "insist upon 'free-verse' as the only method of writing poetry," they believed that "the individuality of a poet may often be better expressed in free-verse than in conventional forms. In poetry, a new cadence means a new idea."*

Free verse and freedom of subject matter and diction are now accepted ways of writing poetry, but experiments both in patterned and in free verse continue. The freedom of verse, as more than one critic has had occasion to observe, is dangerous to the unskilled, and free verse has too often seemed to the uninformed easier to write than the patterned forms. It is certainly easier to write badly, but it is the most difficult of all forms to write well. Robert Hillyer describes the results achieved by those who have undistinguished prose printed in the style of verse:

Free verse
Is prose
Cut up
To look
Like this.

Although it is impossible to define the limits of prose and poetry absolutely, there is obviously more to the artistic achievement of fine prose or poetry than cutting up sentences for arrangement on the printed page.

It is beyond the scope of this book to discuss advanced experimentation, and the present chapter can do little more than touch on a few suggestive current trends. Some historic examples of free verse, from Milton to the Imagists, are cited below, by way of introduction.

HISTORIC EXAMPLES OF FREE VERSE

Chorus: O, how comely it is and how reviving
To the spirits of just men long oppress'd,
When God into the hands of their deliverer
Puts invincible might,
To quell the mighty of the earth, th'oppressor,
The brute and boist'rous force of violent men,
Hardy and industrious to support
Tyrannic power, but raging to pursue
The righteous, and all such as honour truth.

From JOHN MILTON, *Samson Agonistes*, 1640–70

* See pp. 42–43 for the body of the Preface to *Some Imagist Poets*, from which these phrases are quoted, and for a brief account of Imagist poetry, with some other examples besides those given below.

I HEAR AMERICA SINGING

I hear America singing, the varied carols I hear,
Those of mechanics, each one singing his as it should be blithe and strong,
The carpenter singing his as he measures his plank or beam,
The mason singing his as he makes ready for work, or leaves off work,
The boatman singing what belongs to him in his boat, the deckhand singing on the steamboat deck,
The shoemaker singing as he sits on his bench, the hatter singing as he stands,
The woodcutter's song, the plowboy's on his way in the morning, or at noon intermission or at sundown,
The delicious singing of the mother, or of the young wife at work, or of the girl sewing or washing,
Each singing what belongs to him or her and to none else,
The day what belongs to the day—at night the party of young fellows, robust, friendly,
Singing with open mouths their strong melodious songs.

c. 1860 WALT WHITMAN (1819–1892)

ALBA

As cool as the pale wet leaves
of lily-of-the-valley
She lay beside me in the dawn.

EZRA POUND (1885–)

Maine knows you,
Has for years and years;
New Hampshire knows you,
And Massachusetts
And Vermont.
Cape Cod starts you along the beaches to Rhode Island;
Connecticut takes you from a river to the sea.
You are brighter than apples,
Sweeter than tulips,
You are the great flood of our souls
Bursting above the leaf-shapes of our hearts,
You are the smell of all Summers,
The love of wives and children,
The recollection of the gardens of little children,
You are State Houses and Charters
And the familiar treading of the foot to and fro on a road it knows.
May is lilac here in New England,
May is a thrush singing "Sun up!" on a tip-top ash-tree,
May is white clouds behind pine-trees

Puffed out and marching upon a blue sky.
May is a green as no other,
May is much sun through small leaves,
May is soft earth,
And apple-blossoms,
And windows open to a South wind.
May is a full light wind of lilac
From Canada to Narragansett Bay.

Lilacs,
False blue,
White,
Purple,
Color of lilac,
Heart-leaves of lilac all over New England,
Roots of lilac under all the soil of New England,
Lilac in me because I am New England,
Because my roots are in it,
Because my leaves are of it,
Because my flowers are for it,
Because it is my country
And I speak to it of itself
And sing of it with my own voice
Since certainly it is mine.

From Amy Lowell, *Lilacs*, 1925

PEAR TREE

Silver dust,
lifted from the earth,
higher than my arms reach,
you have mounted,
O, silver,
higher than my arms reach,
you front us with great mass;

no flower ever opened
so staunch a white leaf,
no flower ever parted silver
from such rare silver;

O, white pear,
your flower-tufts
thick on the branch
bring summer and ripe fruits
in their purple hearts.

1915–17 H. D. (1886–1961)

EVENING

The chimneys, rank on rank,
Cut the clear sky;
The moon,
With a rag of gauze about her loins,
Poses among them, an awkward Venus—
And here am I looking wantonly at her
Over the kitchen sink.

1915 RICHARD ALDINGTON (1892–1962)

EXERCISE 55

Read Whitman's poem aloud, putting stress marks where you believe they fall, naturally, in a meaningful reading of the poem. Do the same for H. D.'s poem *Heat*, p. 43. Note the length of Whitman's lines in comparison with H. D.'s. What is the difference, if any, in effect? Is there a significant difference in the way the two poems *look* as printed on the page, as distinct from the way they sound when read aloud? Do you see any relationship between these poems and the rhythmical prose of Chapter I? What effect on the poems is achieved by the freedom from meter and rhyme? Would anything be gained, or lost, by the use of a conventional meter and/or rhyme? Comment on these poems as successful or unsuccessful achievements in verse.

EXERCISE 56

Following the directions of the Imagist Preface, p. 42, write ten (10) lines or more in free verse. In a brief prose paragraph, explain what effects you hoped for. What problems did you encounter? To what extent did you succeed in solving them? Do you think your poem would be more or less successful if you had used conventional meter and/or rhyme? Why?

VISUAL PROSODY

The term "visual prosody," borrowed from Harvey Gross,* applies to verse lacking exact meter or a strictly organized pattern of accents—in short, lacking any ascertainable prosodic system except the way the poem looks on the page. (Calling such a piece of writing a poem seems heresy to the prosodist who insists that every poem must be read aloud before one does anything else with it.) Though Puttenham and George Herbert (as Gross points out) were

* Harvey Gross, *Sound and Form in Modern Poetry* (Ann Arbor: University of Michigan Press, 1964).

designing poems in shapes in the sixteenth and seventeenth centuries, the recent prominence of visual prosody seems due to the Imagists. An important part of their doctrine was that the image is the poem's reason for existence; one must not "dull the image," in the words of Pound's essay *A Few Don'ts by an Imagiste*. Pound meant by this, as he explains in the same essay, that the poet should "go in fear of abstractions," but many Imagist imitators extended the idea to mean that the reader should *see* as literally as the poet. In other words, many post-Imagist writers felt that the poem was a *thing*, to be apprehended as immediately by the reader's vision as a painting or a vase.

William Carlos Williams did much for the theory of visual prosody. In most of his prosodic statements (in his *Autobiography* and letters) he stresses "organic form" and the "thinginess" of poetry. The subject matter of many of his poems concerns the singularity, delight, and philosophic importance of direct, unintellectualized sensory experience. A poem like the following might stand as the Poetry-as-Thing Manifesto.

THE RED WHEELBARROW

so much depends
upon

a red wheel
barrow

glazed with rain
water

beside the white
chickens

William Carlos Williams (1883–1963)

"Let the writing be of words," says Williams in one of his poems, reiterating Pound's "beware of abstractions." Undoubtedly, in *The Red Wheelbarrow*, the configuration of the words on the page, in little darting expanding and contracting lines—even the very shortness of the poem—visually helps express the meaning. Yet it is important to remember that the poem's visual appearance *underscores* what the terse, hard diction actually *says*. Williams does not advocate relying solely on "how it looks on the page"; he is interested in the experience of all the senses.

Cummings won much notoriety by his insistence on the visual; and certainly his poem on the moon depends for its effect almost entirely on the reader's visual perception of the roundness, the "mooniness," of the O's.

MOON

mOOn Over tOwns mOOn
whisper
less creature huge grO
pingness

whO perfectly whO
flOat
newly alOne is
dreamest

oNLY THE MooN o
VER ToWNS
SLoWLY SPRoUTING SPIR
IT

1935 E. E. CUMMINGS (1894–1962)

On the other hand, metrical experimenter that he was, Cummings, like Williams, wrote relatively few poems which could be said to depend on visual effects to the total exclusion of all other forms of organization. Even some of the typographically more spectacular ultra-moderns generally employ other devices as well, if only devices of grammar or reiteration. By way of example, Lawrence Ferlinghetti, generally classified as one of the "beat" poets (though he himself rejects the appellation) is guilty of writing a piece of verse in which the last sixteen lines consist of "Death" and "Death Death" scattered across a page. The meaning is apparently supposed to lie in the spacing, the visual pattern. The device is ineffective. Yet much of Ferlinghetti's verse is literate, leavened by a sense of humor, and genuinely lyrical, as in the following visually *and* audibly constructed piece:

Dove sta amore*
Where lies love
Dove sta amore
Here lies love
The ring dove love
In lyrical delight
Hear love's hillsong
Love's true willsong
Love's low plainsong
Too sweet painsong
In passages of night

* Italian for "Where is love."

Dove sta amore
Here lies love
The ring dove love
Dove sta amore
Here lies love

From LAWRENCE FERLINGHETTI, *A Coney Island of the Mind*, 1955–58, Sec. 28

It might be added, in defense of visual prosody, that the old conception of poet as bard, as speaker rather than writer, has been undermined by several centuries in which most people first met poetry as an experience in reading, on the silent printed page of a textbook.

DURATIONAL PROSODY

The term "durational prosody" may refer to one of two kinds of duration: first, QUANTITY, as applied in classical prosody, a system of ordering verse on the basis of the length of time required to pronounce a syllable; second, "duration of breath," or oral phrasing, as a means of governing line length.

It would be a mistake to say flatly that no one uses quantity in this century, for, if our discussion of rhythm in Chapter I is valid, all meter in English verse is related to the length of time demanded by various sounds. Nevertheless, quantity in its classical sense, as the actual basis, not just a component, of prosody, is being employed little if at all. A few modern poets hint that they believe in quantitative prosody. Charles Olson, for example, states: "the syllable . . . is the king and pin of versification, what rules and holds together the lines, the larger forms, of a poem."* Neither from his prosodic statements nor from his poetry, however, can one tell whether he means the duration of the syllable, which would imply genuine quantity, or the number of syllables per line, which would, of course, signify another prosodic form altogether.

We are left, then, with the other kind of duration: the time span between breaths allowing the speaking of a phrase. Allen Ginsberg, the chief writer of the San Francisco school, states: "Ideally each line of *Howl* is a single breath unit."† Such a conception of how to limit the line fits in with the bardlike image of the poet as orator-preacher, or at least as oral reader, which Ginsberg and many of his followers have helped to revive. The "breath-duration" prosodic theory is not really new, of course, for there is something else, considerably

* Charles Olson, "Projective Versus Non-Projective Verse," in Donald Allen (ed.), *The New American Poetry 1945–1960* (New York: Grove Press, Inc., 1960), p. 388.
† Allen, *op. cit.*, p. 416.

older than Ginsberg, which is also based on the duration of human breath: English syntax. Thus this type of prosody might as accurately be called "syntactical prosody," for it is a verse system in which lines and/or strophes, instead of being ordered in patterned meter, are organized in grammatical units (sentences, series of phrases, etc.) that correspond roughly to the intervals between natural "breathing points."

A number of poets are as impassioned in their defense of this kind of prosody as if it were really brand-new. Says LeRoi Jones in an essay called "How You Sound??": "all this means that we want to go into a quantitative verse . . . the 'irregular foot' of Williams . . . the 'Projective Verse' of Olson. Accentual verse, the regular metric of rumbling iambics, is dry as slivers of sand. Nothing happens in that frame anymore."* Jones' *One Night Stand* tells us something about his method. The poem is written in "tercets" of approximately the same line length. Though most of the lines are longer than a single breath unit (see the first line quoted below), they are articulated by syntactically logical stops, "breathing points," *e.g.*, the end of a sentence or clause, occurring near the midpoint or at the end of a line. But all regularity of line length, line grouping, and syntactic arrangement breaks down at the very end, leaving "is cool" exposed and alone:

> We *are* foreign seeming persons. Hats flopped so the sun
> can't scald our beards; odd shoes, bags of books & chicken.
> We have come a long way, & are uncertain which of the masks
> is cool.

From LeRoi Jones (1934–), *One Night Stand*

The whole point of the poem lies in the flowing "beat" rhetoric, undercut and made just a little comic by the vulnerability of the hitchhiking bards' search for what "is cool."

Jones' *One Night Stand* also serves to illustrate how awkward it is to speak of "duration" or "syntax" as a self-contained prosody, for surely the ironic contrast between the very small "is cool" and the very expansive preceding rhetoric is seen as much as heard. Thus, though durational prosody would seem at first to be the very opposite of the visual prosody discussed earlier, it actually is not. As we noted before, one also *hears* in a visually organized poem such as Cummings' "*Moon*." In short, visual prosody and durational prosody are not very good categories; but the one under discussion—organization according to the duration of the human breath—is one which many modern poets insist they actually use.

As noted earlier, Ginsberg says that "ideally" he makes line lengths correspond to breath units. His *A Supermarket in California*, however, is clearly arranged not in single breaths (read it aloud and see!) but in paragraphs:

* Allen, *op. cit.*, p. 425.

A SUPERMARKET IN CALIFORNIA

What thoughts I have of you tonight, Walt Whitman, for I walked down the sidestreets under the trees with a headache self-conscious looking at the full moon.
In my hungry fatigue, and shopping for images, I went into the neon fruit supermarket, dreaming of your enumerations!
What peaches and what penumbras! Whole families shopping at night! Aisles full of husbands! Wives in the avocados, babies in the tomatoes!—and you, Garcia Lorca, what were you doing down by the watermelons?

I saw you, Walt Whitman, childless, lonely old grubber, poking among the meats in the refrigerator and eyeing the grocery boys.
I heard you asking questions of each: Who killed the pork chops? What price bananas? Are you my Angel?
I wandered in and out of the brilliant stacks of cans following you, and followed in my imagination by the store detective.
We strode down the open corridors together in our solitary fancy tasting artichokes, possessing every frozen delicacy, and never passing the cashier.

Where are we going, Walt Whitman? The doors close in an hour. Which way does your beard point tonight?
(I touch your book and dream of our odyssey in the supermarket and feel absurd.)
Will we walk all night through solitary streets? The trees add shade to shade, lights out in the houses, we'll both be lonely.
Will we stroll dreaming of the lost America of love past blue automobiles in driveways, home to our silent cottage?
Ah, dear father, graybeard, lonely old courage-teacher, what America did you have when Charon quit poling his ferry and you got out on a smoking bank and stood watching the boat disappear on the black waters of Lethe?

1955 ALLEN GINSBERG (1926–)

The poem has a purely syntactical organization, and a much simpler one than Whitman himself uses: Ginsberg depends for form entirely on the stringing together of paragraphs that do not have much rhythmic similarity to each other, whereas Whitman generally echoes grammatical structures from line to line, and balances very long lines with shorter ones.

Other current poets follow Ginsberg's idea of organization by breath units much more closely than Ginsberg: Gregory Corso is a good example. In his comic and wistful *Marriage*, of which strophe 4 is quoted below, nearly every line halts where syntax makes it feasible to take a breath: ends of sentences, before appositives (*e.g.*, lines 3–4), before participial phrases (lines 6–7), before prepositional phrases (lines 14–15), before quotations (lines 17–18), and so on.

But I should get married I should be good
How nice it'd be to come home to her
and sit by the fireplace and she in the kitchen
aproned young and lovely wanting my baby
and so happy about me she burns the roast beef
and comes crying to me and I get up from my big papa chair
saying Christmas teeth! Radiant brains! Apple deaf!
God what a husband I'd make! Yes, I should get married!
So much to do! like sneaking into Mr. Jones' house late at night
And cover his golf clubs with 1920 Norwegian books
Like hanging a picture of Rimbaud on the lawnmower
Like pasting Tannu Tuva postage stamps
all over the picket fence
Like when Mrs. Kindhead comes to collect
for the Community Chest
grab her and tell her There are unfavorable omens in the sky!
And when the mayor comes to get my vote tell him
When are you going to stop people killing whales!
And when the milkman comes leave him a note in the bottle
Penguin dust, bring me penguin dust, I want penguin dust—

From GREGORY CORSO, *Marriage*, 1959

Corso makes further use of syntactical organization when he parallels grammatical structures, as in lines 11, 12, and 14–16, which form a series of verbal phrases ("Like hanging . . .," "Like pasting . . .," "Like when Mrs. Kindhead . . ."), and in lines 17–19, with their series of "when" clauses.

SYLLABLE-COUNTING VERSE AND OTHER TRENDS

Where shall we place the syllable-counting or SYLLABIC VERSE of Marianne Moore? Surely in still another category, for it is a prosody wholly different from "traditional," "visual," or "durational." Although its use can hardly be considered a major modern trend, since few contemporary poets appear to employ it as a main device, syllabic verse in the English language raises a significant point, and one which we have touched upon, frequently and unavoidably, in this chapter and others: the tendency of all our categories to overlap.

Syllable counting overlaps with traditional meter: a regular iambic pentameter is usually a decasyllabic line, though the English-accustomed ear hears the "fiveness" of it more than the "ten." Syllable counting also overlaps with our other categories, "visual" and "durational." How is the reader first alerted to the fact that one of Miss Moore's poems (see p. 376 for an example) does not simply sprawl over the page, but is written in formally organized stanzas that recur in a very definite pattern? By the way it looks on the page! Visually alerted, he *then* takes pencil in hand and begins counting. On the other hand, what does he *hear* in that same poem: 9–8–2–2–1? Probably not; he hears phrases and clauses and sentences, uttered (through her diction as well as her rhythms) in Miss Moore's quick-breathed, keen-edged feminine voice.

Our discussion has aimed at providing the reader with a few categories that may be of some use in the difficult job of examining a body of poetry which is still so close to us that we cannot see it clearly. But if anything has been proved, it is that many poems are, like Marianne Moore's, impossible to place in a single pigeonhole. In the estimation of mid-century modern poets, to be uncategorizable appears to be of major importance.

Glossary

PROSODIC SYMBOLS

Short and/or unstressed syllable	◡
Long syllable	—
Stressed syllable	´
Long stressed syllable	—́
Light or secondary stress	`
Foot mark	|
Light pause	/
Heavy pause	//
Rest or metrical pause	∧

abstract noun: a noun that expresses a quality or condition without specific reference to any particular object: "blackness," "joy," "life." Its opposite is CONCRETE NOUN.

accent: the emphasis or STRESS on a syllable. A *primary accent* is the emphasis that in normal speech falls on the most heavily stressed syllable of a word, as in "mis táke." Some words also contain a syllable that is lightly stressed, called the *secondary accent.* Metrical stress usually falls upon the primary accent. Thus a word like "ĕtérnĭtỳ," containing primary and secondary stresses as well as unstressed syllables, would ordinarily be scanned "ĕtérnĭtў."

accentual verse: see STRESS PROSODY.

alba: see FRENCH FORMS.

alcaics: see CLASSICAL PROSODY.

alexandrine: in English, a twelve-syllable iambic line owing its name to its use in an Old French romance on Alexander the Great. The French alexandrine, which became the meter for classical French tragedy, is characterized by the regularity of its twelve syllables and its strong medial pause, or CESURA. In a French alexandrine, there are accents on the sixth and twelfth syllables, but the other accents occur at random intervals, since accent plays a relatively small part in French verse:

> Elles gaignent au piéd; tous les fleuves s'abaissánt.
> La mer rentre en prisón; les montagnes renaissánt.
>
> From GUILLAUME DU BARTAS, *La Première Semaine,* 1579

The English alexandrine depends to a much greater extent on the regular alternation of accents created by its iambic meter; in its basic pattern it is generally a six-stress as well as a twelve-syllable verse. An example is the following line from Byron's *Childe Harold's Pilgrimage* (IV):

What I | can ne'er | express, | yet can|not all | conceal.|

allegory: a literary form in which abstract terms such as "Virtue," "Temptation," and the like are given the qualities of people or places, as a way of dramatizing and making concrete the author's interpretation of these abstractions as they interact with one another. In Guillaume de Lorris' medieval allegory *Le Roman de la Rose*, each emotional attribute of a young maiden falling in love becomes a separate character, and we see, for example, "Daunger" (her wish to remain aloof) conflicting with "Bialacoil" (*bel accueil:* the natural cordiality resulting from her good breeding). Thus we also see, in *The Pilgrim's Progress*, "Christian" in danger of being mired in the "Slough of Despond." In a sense, allegory is the direct opposite of symbolism, since in allegory abstract ideas are given concrete forms, whereas in symbolism a concrete thing, place, or person takes on abstract significance (see SYMBOL).

alliteration: the repetition of sounds, usually consonant sounds, in a sequence of words: "Peter Piper picked a peck of pickled peppers." The repetition of the initial sound in stressed syllables constitutes *major alliteration.* The repetition of sounds in unstressed syllables—that of the internal *p*'s in "Piper" and "peppers," for example—constitutes *minor alliteration.*

structural alliteration: major alliteration used as a principal organizing device in a poem; a specifically prescribed element of the poem's form. Structural alliteration is characteristic of all verse written in Old English, in which two to four of the stressed syllables in each line are alliterative (see ANGLO-SAXON PROSODY). *The Pearl*, a Middle English poem, uses structural alliteration as well as rhyme:

a The dubbemente of tho derworth depe
b Wern bonkez bene of beryl bryght.
a Swangeande swete the water con swepe,
b Wyth a rownande rourde raykande aryght.

ornamental alliteration: alliteration used as a sound effect in a poem relying for its structure primarily on devices other than alliteration, such as terminal rhyme and meter. Thus even in a heavily alliterated passage like the one below, in which the alliteration clearly plays an important part in producing the total effect, the term "ornamental alliteration" (rather than "structural alliteration") applies, since the stanza depends for its form on a particular rhyme and metric scheme, and since the alliteration does not occur at prescribed rhythmic intervals as it would in Old English verse. In the quoted passage, both major and minor alliteration are employed:

Right in the middest of that Paradise,
There stood a stately mount, on whose round top
A gloomy grove of mirtle trees did rise,
Whose shadie boughes sharpe steele did never lop,
Nor wicked beasts their tender buds did crop,
But like a girlond compassèd the hight,
And from their fruitfull sides sweet gum did drop,
That all the ground with precious deaw bedight,
Threw forth most dainty odours, and most sweet delight.

From EDMUND SPENSER, *The Faerie Queene*, Bk. III, Canto VI, St. 43

allusion: an indirect or undeveloped reference to a familiar personage or event or, frequently, to a well-known character, object, or phrase in literature. An allusion is a means to conciseness, for by drawing on the reader's knowledge of literature, mythology, events past and present, it may convey what could otherwise be conveyed only by elaborate exposition or description.

Mythological allusions are common:

I Tiresias, though blind, throbbing between two lives,
Old man with wrinkled female breasts . . .

From T. S. ELIOT, *The Waste Land*

Topical allusions, glancing references to persons and events of current importance, are also found throughout literature, as in *The Dunciad*, in which Pope refers thus to Sir George Thorold, Lord Mayor of London, 1720:

'Twas on the day, when Thorold rich and grave,
Like Cimon, triumph'd both on land and wave

Veiled allusion is a term applied to references made without actually naming the person or thing to which the writer is alluding; *e.g.,* Sidney's mention of Cupid, in *Astrophel and Stella*, as "that murth'ring boy." Sometimes the grammatical structure and diction of a phrase or sentence constitutes a veiled allusion; *e.g.,* a critic's saying of Donne, "He wears his Petrarch with a difference," recalling Ophelia's wearing her rue with a difference.

ambiguity: words or situations admitting of dual or multiple interpretations. Donne's *The Canonization* contains the following lines:

Observe his honour, or his grace,
Or the King's reall, or his stampèd face
Contemplate, . . .

Here Donne sets up a deliberate ambiguity by permitting the context to justify interpreting the second line in the quotation as (1) the king's real face as opposed to his portrait stamped on a coin, or (2) simply the coin of the realm, which the term "reall," a corruption of "royal," denoted at that time.

amphibrach: see CLASSICAL PROSODY.

anacrusis: the presence, at the beginning of a line of trochaic or dactylic verse, of one or more unstressed syllables which are not considered part of the meter, as in Shelley's *To a Skylark:*

> Frŏm | ráinbŏw | clóuds thĕre | flów nŏt|

anapest: a metrical FOOT consisting of two short unstressed syllables followed by one long stressed syllable.

Anglo-Saxon prosody: a form of verse based on stress and on structural ALLITERATION, rather than on meter. Each line is composed of two half lines (hemistichs) separated by a cesura. In each hemistich are two stressed syllables, making four to a line. In each line, at least two stressed syllables are alliterated; in some lines, three or even four of the stressed syllables alliterate. Anglo-Saxon poets based the alliterative sound on that occurring in the third stressed syllable of the line. *Piers Plowman,* written during the fourteenth-century revival of alliterative verse, usually follows the basic rules of Anglo-Saxon prosody:

> I śhope me in śhroudes . as I a śhepe ẃere,
> In h́abite as an h́eremite . unh́oly of ẃorkes,
> Went ẃyde in this ẃorld . ẃondres to h́ere.
>
> B-text, ll. 2–5

For the "rules" of Anglo-Saxon prosody see pp. 184–85.

antistrophe: see ODE, REGULAR.

antithesis: a rhetorical device used in both verse and prose. It is very much like PARALLELISM in that groups of words similar in grammatical construction are juxtaposed; in antithesis, however, the juxtaposed parts are contrasting rather than parallel in sense.

> A generation goes, and a generation comes,
> but the earth remains for ever.
> The sun rises and the sun goes down,
> and hastens to the place where it rises.
> The wind blows to the south,
> and goes round to the north;
> round and round goes the wind,
> and on its circuits the wind returns.
>
> *Ecclesiastes* 1:4–6 (Rev. Standard Version)

apostrophe: a figure of rhetoric in which an address is made to someone not present, or to an abstraction:

> If aught of oaten stop, or pastoral song,
> May hope, O pensive Eve, to sooth thine ear,
>
> From WILLIAM COLLINS, *Ode to Evening*

argument: a statement of the main idea of a poem, generally in prose. Spenser, for example, introduces his eclogues with a prose summary of each poem. Coleridge's marginal notes to *The Rime of the Ancient Mariner* (p. 105) similarly summarize the central ideas or arguments presented in groups of stanzas.

arsis: see THESIS.

assonance: according to ordinary technical usage, the deliberate repetition of stressed vowel sounds in a line or group of lines:

> But as the riper should by time decease,
> His tender heir might bear his memory.
>
> From WILLIAM SHAKESPEARE, *Sonnet 1*

More subtle effects are obtained by varying the vowel sounds, without obvious and exact repetition:

> With how sad steps, O Moon, thou climb'st the skies!
>
> From SIR PHILIP SIDNEY, *Astrophel and Stella*, XXXI

> This lunar beauty
> Has no history
> Is complete and early;
>
> From W. H. AUDEN, *"This Lunar Beauty"*

Terminal assonance may be used to replace or to vary accurate RHYME:

> The County Roland, seeing his peers lie dead,
> And Oliver, who was his dearest friend,
> Begins to weep for ruth and tenderness.
>
> From *The Song of Roland*, laisse 164, trans. Dorothy L. Sayers

As a type of terminal rhyme, assonance was systematically employed in French verse, as in the original of the lines quoted above in translation:

> Li quens Rollant, quant il veit mort ses pers
> E Oliver, qu'il tant poeit amer,
> Tendrur en out, cumencet a plurer.

Here, in place of terminal rhyme, is the repetition of the short-*e* sound. The use of terminal assonance as a substitute for full end rhyme is not, however, effective in English.

A comparison between the terminal assonance from *The Song of Roland* given in translation above ("dead," "friend," "tenderness") and an example of approximate rhyme (such as "resume" and "June" in the Dickinson lines cited under RHYME, APPROXIMATE) will show that the terms are sometimes equivalent. "Terminal assonance," however, is generally employed when the sound device is employed consistently, with obvious structural intent, throughout a major portion of a poem. "Approximate rhyme" is a much broader term, since it comprehends repetition of consonant sounds as well as of vowel sounds.

aubade: see FRENCH FORMS.

ballad: a piece of narrative verse consisting of several stanzas. The typical form of the ballad stanza is either $a^4 b^3 c^4 b^3$ (*ballad meter*) or $a^4 b^4 a^4 b^4$ (*long meter*), although a number of well-known ballads are written in variant forms of these basic patterns.

popular ballad (*folk ballad*): an anonymous ballad, composed to be sung, that has undergone variations as a result of being passed on from generation to generation, in different localities, before being written down. The subject matter of the popular ballad is generally violence, death, love, work, or supernatural occurrences. Occasionally a popular ballad is deliberately humorous. The stories are told abruptly, beginning in the midst of the spectacular events, with little attention to the motivations behind them. Rhymes may be approximate; WRENCHED ACCENTS occur; a REFRAIN, either as the closing line in the regular stanza or between stanzas, is common, as are REPETITION and INCREMENTAL REPETITION. Some ballads are partially or wholly in the form of dialogue, with little identification of speaker.

literary ballad: an author's deliberate imitation of the folk ballad form. In *The Ballad of the Goodly Fere* (p. 151), Ezra Pound has tried to approximate the form, tone, subject matter, and casualness of rhyme of the folk ballad. William Butler Yeats, in such poems as *The Ballad of Father Gilligan*, also closely approximates the characteristics of the popular ballad but develops "inner meaning" to a somewhat greater extent:

"And is the poor man dead?" he cried.
"He died an hour ago."
The old priest Peter Gilligan
In grief swayed to and fro.

"When you were gone, he turned and died
As merry as a bird."
The old priest Peter Gilligan
He knelt him at that word.

"He who hath made the night of stars
For souls, who tire and bleed,
Sent one of His great angels down
To help me in my need.

"He who is wrapped in purple robes,
With planets in His care,
Had pity on the least of things
Asleep upon a chair."

ballade: see FRENCH FORMS.

bard: originally, the composer and singer of Celtic poems honoring heroes and their feats. Although the term has now become synonymous with "poet," such usage (referring to Shakespeare as "the Bard of Avon," to Robert Frost as "the New England bard") is considered "elegant variation" and undesirable in critical writing.

blank verse: unrhymed verse, usually in iambic pentameter. Not to be confused with FREE VERSE, it is called "blank" only because of the absence of terminal rhyme. Its most famous uses are probably Milton's in such works as *Paradise Lost* and Shakespeare's in his dramas:

> Oh, I could play the woman with mine eyes
> And braggart with my tongue!—But, gentle heavens,
> Cut short all intermission; front to front
> Bring thou this fiend of Scotland and myself;
> Within my sword's length set him; if he 'scape,
> Heaven forgive him, too! . . .
>
> *Macbeth*, IV, iii

broken rhyme: see RHYME.

burden: see REFRAIN.

cadence: the pattern of stressed and unstressed syllables between two pauses. In FREE VERSE, the arrangement of cadences may be the principal sound effect. In metric verse, cadences are means of achieving variety in sound effects within the set metrical pattern; they may repeat, rearrange, or reverse the established metrical pattern. An example of reversal occurs in

> Tŏ bé,| ŏr nót | tŏ bé,|/ thát ĭs | thĕ qués|tĭon:

in which the position of the pause after "not to be" makes the second half of the line sound trochaic.

canto: one of the major divisions of a long poem; as in Dante's *Divine Comedy*, which consists of 100 cantos, or Spenser's *Faerie Queene*.

canzo: see FRENCH FORMS.

canzone: see FRENCH FORMS.

catalexis: the omission of a light syllable at the end of a trochaic line, or the omission of one or both light syllables at the end of a dactylic line. See also INITIAL TRUNCATION.

catalogue: a list in poetry of related objects, as in T. S. Eliot's *Gerontion*: "Rocks, moss, stonecrop, iron, merds."

cesura: a PAUSE in the reading of a line of verse. It is dictated by the sense of the passage and may be indicated by punctuation, though logical pauses may occur where there is no punctuation. It is analogous to the pause for breath at the close of a musical phrase. The term is properly used only for pauses within the line. The pauses—designated by a single slant line if they are short, by a double slant line if they are longer—may occur either at the end or in the middle of a foot:

> Sénd mĕ | nów,/ ănd | Í shăll | gó; ∧ |//
> Cáll mĕ,|// Í shăll | héar yŏu | cáll; ∧ |

From A. E. HOUSMAN, *"Say, Lad, Have You Things to Do?"*

chanson de geste: an Old French poem portraying heroes and events of French history and legend. Believed to have been composed to be sung, not recited, it consists of stanzas of uneven line length (*laisses*) instead of the rhymed couplets of religious and subsequent court poetry. Some scholars consider the chanson de geste a true epic, while others regard it as a step in the development of the French epic form.

Chaucerian stanza: see STANZA: *rhyme royal.*

choriamb: see CLASSICAL PROSODY.

cinquain: a piece of verse consisting in its entirety of five lines, of two, four, six, eight, and two syllables respectively. The form was originated by Adelaide Crapsey as an attempt at the conciseness of the Japanese HAIKU or waka:

THE WARNING

> Just now,
> Out of the strange
> Still dusk . . . as strange, as still . . .
> A white moth flew. Why am I grown
> So cold?

ADELAIDE CRAPSEY (1878–1914)

classical: (1) pertaining to works produced in ancient Greece and Rome; (2) "neoclassical"—the work of certain eighteenth-century poets ("Augustans"), led by Pope, who consciously strove to imitate classical poetry; (3) pertaining to writing of any period which resembles that of the ancients in clarity of structure, simplicity of style, and restraint of tone. See also ROMANTIC.

classical prosody: the verse structures and patterns used by the ancient Greeks and Romans. The basis of classical versification is the length of time required to pronounce a syllable (see QUANTITY), rather than, as in English verse, accentuation of syllables.

Of the classical feet, several have been adapted to the requirements of English prosody, notably the iamb, the trochee, the anapest, the dactyl, and the spondee (see FOOT). Where the classical foot uses a quantitatively long syllable, the corresponding English foot uses a stressed syllable, which is nearly always experienced as longer than an unstressed syllable. The following classical feet are only rarely found in English verse:

amphibrach: a foot composed of three syllables, of which the first is short, the second long, and the third short: ∪ — ∪. In English verse, satisfactory scansion can usually be achieved without this foot.

choriamb: a four-syllable foot: — ∪ ∪ —. Choriambics have been imitated by Rupert Brooke, and by Swinburne in the following:

> Love, what | ailed thee to leave | life that was made | lovely, we thought,|
> with love?|
> What sweet | visions of sleep | lured thee away,| down from the light | above?|
> . . .
> Ah, thy | luminous eyes!| once was their light | fed with the fire | of day;|
> Now their | shadowy lids | cover them close,| hush them and hide | away.|

From ALGERNON CHARLES SWINBURNE, *Choriambics*

An almost identical pattern—initial foot and closing foot circumscribing three choriambs—is repeated throughout this poem.

ionic: a foot of four syllables, two long (spondee) and two short (pyrrhic): — — ∪ ∪ or ∪ ∪ — —.

paeon: a foot consisting of four syllables, one long and three short, in which the position of the long syllable varies. A rare example in English verse is a phrase of Hopkins' which contains a paeon with the long syllable first:

> Glory be to | God . . .

Some of the following terms used in classical prosody describe verse forms occasionally attempted in English.

alcaics: a metrical pattern originated by the Greek poet Alcaeus and later used with slight variations by the Roman poet Horace; see ODE, HORATIAN for an example in translation. It was imitated in English verse by Tennyson, who in his *Experiments* tried out several of the classical verse forms (see also below):

> Where | some re|fulgent | sunset of | Indi|a ∧ |
> Streams | o'er a | rich am|brosial | ocean | isle, ∧ |
> And | crimson-|hued the | stately | palmwoods|
> Whisper in | odorous | heights of | even.|

From ALFRED, LORD TENNYSON, *Milton*

dimeter: a line composed of four feet or two dipodies. In English verse a dimeter is a line composed of *two* feet; see METER.

dipody: a measure composed of two feet.

dithyramb: originally, a choral hymn to Dionysus; later, a lyric similar to such a hymn in its highly emotional tone and irregular structure.

elegiacs: a verse form made up of distichs, where the first line is in classical *hexameter* and the second in classical *pentameter* (see below). Tennyson imitated the form and also commented on its crabbedness in English:

ON TRANSLATIONS OF HOMER
(Hexameters and pentameters)

These lame | hexame|ters the | strong-wing'd | music of | Homer !|
No—but a | most bur|lesque ∧ | barbarous | experi|ment. ∧ |
When was a | harsher | sound ever | heard, ye | Muses, in | England?|
When did a | frog coar|ser ∧ | croak upon | our Heli|con? ∧ |
Hexame|ters no | worse than | daring | Germany | gave us,|
Barbarous | experi|ment, ∧ | barbarous | hexame|ters. ∧ |

ALFRED, LORD TENNYSON (1809–1892)

The scansion marked on the lines above is the traditional pattern of elegiac meter, but it should be noted that this abstract pattern does not conform, in many feet, to the rhythmic pattern one actually hears. Thus it is not a true scansion in the modern English sense of the word. Scholars have theorized that Tennyson deliberately set his wording flagrantly at odds with the elegiac pattern in order to reinforce the main point of the selection: that translations of Homer which attempt to use the classical meter cannot be other than "barbarous."

hendecasyllable: an eleven-syllable line, seen primarily in classical verse, especially that of Catullus; imitated by Tennyson, as in the following:

O you chorus of indolent reviewers (11)
Irresponsible, indolent reviewers, (11)
Look, I come to the test, a tiny poem (11)
All composed in a metre of Catullus, (11)

hexameter: the meter of the Greek and Latin epics; a six-foot line in which the first four feet may be dactyls or spondees, the fifth is usually a dactyl, and the sixth is a spondee. Saintsbury in his *Historical Manual of English Prosody* cautions that the term "hexameter" is properly applied only to this meter and to attempts at imitating it in English, and never to the ALEXANDRINE.

logaoedics: lines of verse combining iambs and anapests or trochees and dactyls. The line length in such verse is from two to four feet.

pentameter: the second line in an elegiac distich. Although five feet may be counted in the line (*e.g.*—in the second line cited under *elegiacs*—a dactyl, two spondees, and two anapests), the classical pentameter is actually scanned as two half hexameters, each lacking a final syllable. For the English pentameter see METER.

sapphics: a stanza of four lines in a meter associated with the Greek poet Sappho. It has been imitated both in Latin and in English. A stanza from Swinburne's *Sapphics* helps illustrate the metrical pattern, the exact abstract structure of which is marked above Swinburne's syllables. The few deviations from the classical pattern are marked by italic type.

All with|drew long | since, and the | land was | barren,|
Full of | fruit*less* | women and | music | only.|
Now per|chance, *when* | winds are as|suaged at | sunset,|
Lulled at the | dewfall,|

From ALGERNON CHARLES SWINBURNE, *Sapphics*

common measure: a stanza whose pattern is $a^4 b^3 a^4 b^3$ or $a^4 b^3 c^4 b^3$. Sometimes called *common hymn meter* because of its frequent use in hymns, it is exactly like the BALLAD stanza except that it is usually more regular in meter and in rhyme. The following is a typical example:

THE LORD BE WITH US

The Lord be with us as we bend
His blessing to receive;
His gift of peace on us descend
Before his courts we leave.

The Lord be with us as we walk
Along our homeward road;
In silent thought, or friendly talk,
Our hearts be near to God.

The Lord be with us till the night
Enfold our day of rest;
Be He of every heart the light,
Of every home the guest.

The Lord be with us through the hours
Of slumber calm and deep,
Protect our homes, renew our powers,
And guard his people's sleep.

JOHN ELLERTON (1801–1873)

See LONG MEASURE and SHORT MEASURE for comparison.

compensation: the balancing-out of metrical substitutions within a segment of verse. In the following lines from Marlowe's *Faustus*, the spondaic substitutions (first and third feet) compensate for the anapest in "perpetual day" and help in avoiding the skipping effect which an anapest often produces:

Fair Nature's eye, rise, rise again, and make
Perpetual day; . . .

conceit: a figure of speech in which the comparisons or relationships suggested are highly developed and ingeniously worked out to show a number of points of contact between the objects being related. An example is Edward Taylor's *Huswifery*, in which each part of a spinning wheel is made to correspond in function to some attribute of the human mind and soul; or Sir Philip Sidney's seventh sonnet in *Astrophel and Stella*, in which he praises his lady's dark eyes by exploring the wide variety of uses and connotations of black coloring.

metaphysical conceit: a trademark of the "metaphysical poets" of the seventeenth century. Its chief characteristics are the following:

1. The relationships between the things compared are extremely intricate and detailed; Taylor's *Huswifery*, for example, is a carefully elaborated analogy, not a mere series of similes.

2. There is frequent use, for purposes of comparison, of objects or concepts drawn from "nonpoetic" areas, such as mechanics, mathematics, and astronomy; as when Donne in *Hymn to God, My God, in My Sickness* draws upon cartography, heightening the intricacy of the conceit by punning on the two meanings of "straits," on "west" and "waste," etc.

> Whilst my physicians by their love are grown
> Cosmographers, and I their map, who lie
> Flat on this bed, that by them may be shown
> That this is my south-west discovery
> *Per fretum febris*, by these straits to die,
> I joy, that in these straits, I see my west;

Some of the "Metaphysicals," Donne and George Herbert in particular, also drew heavily on classical philosophy and on Christian theology as interpreted by the Latin Fathers in constructing their conceits. The first of the following excerpts from Donne, for instance, deals with the idea of the Church as the spouse of Christ; the second, with the ancient concepts of "humors" and of the imperfect, fluctuating state of the sublunary world:

> Betray, kind husband, thy spouse to our sights,
> And let mine amorous soul court thy mild Dove,
> Who is most true, and pleasing to thee, then
> When she's embrac'd and open to most men.

From JOHN DONNE, *Holy Sonnets*, XVIII

> Oh, to vex me, contraries meet in one:
> Inconstancy unnaturally hath begot
> A constant habit; that when I would not
> I change in vows, and in devotion.
> As humorous is my contrition
> As my profane Love, and as soon forgot:

From JOHN DONNE, *Holy Sonnets*, XIX

3. A third characteristic is a tendency toward the fantastic or grotesque, as in the above excerpt from Donne ("Betray, kind husband"), in which a plea for Christ to vouchsafe his Holy Spirit is expressed as a request for a husband to turn panderer, or as in the following gory piece:

UPON THE INFANT MARTYRS

To see both blended in one flood,
The mothers' milk, the children's blood,
Makes me doubt if Heaven will gather
Roses hence or lilies rather.

RICHARD CRASHAW (1613?–1649)

A metaphysical conceit may, as in Taylor's *Huswifery*, resemble a complicated extended metaphor, but it need not. The complexity of many metaphysical poems lies in the close interweaving of a number of conceits:

Our eye-beams twisted, and did thread
  Our eyes, upon one double string;
So to'entergraft our hands as yet
  Was all the means to make us one,
And pictures in our eyes to get
  Was all our propagation.
As 'twixt two equal armies, Fate
  Suspends uncertain victory,
Our souls, which to advance their state,
  Were gone out, hung 'twixt her and me.
And whilst our souls negotiate there,
. . .

From JOHN DONNE, *The Ecstasy*

Here there are at least three interlocking conceits. Two in the first six lines are drawn from seventeenth-century optics: the suggestion that the convergence of the lovers' lines of vision, when diagrammed, would resemble a sort of double-stringed cat's cradle; and the observation that each of the lovers causes a miniature reflection ("eye-babies") in the other's lenses. Next is a conceit in which a comparison of souls with army generals who leave behind their troops (the lovers' bodies) to parley, each hoping for terms favorable to his state in a neutral area between, is complicated by the theological notion that when the soul is *out* of the body it is in a more "advanced state" than when it is imprisoned within the body.

See also METAPHYSICAL POETRY.

concrete noun: a noun having specific application to a thing or being. It designates the objects of immediate sensory experience, not the abstract or ideal, and directly evokes that which is physically perceptible: "tar," "bluebird," "kitchen." Its opposite is ABSTRACT NOUN. All poetic IMAGES employ concrete nouns; however, not all concrete nouns, taken singly, constitute imagery. For example, "girl" is concrete, as opposed to the abstract "femininity," even though the word "girl" does not in itself suggest a specific sensory experience.

connotation: the "overtones" of a word; the associations called forth by a word, as opposed to its specific dictionary meaning or DENOTATION. For example, both "odor" and "fragrance" mean "smell"; but, because "odor" may have unpleasant connotations and "fragrance" has uniformly pleasant connotations, one would not ordinarily speak of the odor of a delicate perfume or the fragrance of garbage. The connotations of a word may be highly personal and emotional: "night" might connote, for a child, goblins and the distasteful procedure of going to bed; moonbeams and romance to a teen-age girl; death to the inmate of an old people's home. Connotations may also be partially dictated by tradition: *e.g.,* E. E. Cummings' use of the phrase "goat-footed balloonman" to add overtones of sexuality to an otherwise seemingly childlike poem.

consonance: see RHYME, CONSONANTAL.

couplet: a pair of lines that, linked by the same rhyme sound, form a unit.

open couplet: two lines of rhyming iambic pentameter in which neither line has a heavy terminal pause. The second line commonly runs on into the next couplet to complete the sense of the passage. Most of *The Canterbury Tales* is written in open couplets.

> Whan Zephirus eek with his sweete breeth
> Inspired hath in every holt and heeth
> The tendre croppes, and the yonge sonne
> Hath in the Ram his halve cours yronne,

From GEOFFREY CHAUCER, *The Canterbury Tales, General Prologue*

closed couplet (*heroic couplet*): two lines of rhyming iambic pentameter in which the first line is end-stopped with a brief pause, while the second is end-stopped with a heavy pause. Although examples of this couplet may be found as early as Chaucer, Pope brought the form to its highest development.

dactyl: a three-syllable metrical FOOT in which the first syllable is long and stressed and the remaining two are short and unstressed.

decasyllabic verse: a term derived from French prosody for lines consisting of ten syllables each. In English verse, a decasyllabic line usually produces the effect of a five-stress line, or of iambic pentameter. See METER: *pentameter.*

denotation: the specific, standard signification of a word, as opposed to the associations or CONNOTATIONS a word may have in addition to its actual meaning. For example, "charwoman" and "custodian" denote a person who cleans a building, though "custodian" may have more dignified connotations.

diction: the choice of words in a poem. See also POETIC DICTION and Chapter II.

didactic verse: verse in which the author's intent to teach takes precedence over purely aesthetic values; as in *The New England Primer* (1727):

In Adam's Fall
We sinned all.

Zaccheus he
Did climb the Tree
Our Lord to see.

dimeter: see CLASSICAL PROSODY; METER.

dipody: see CLASSICAL PROSODY.

dirge: see ELEGY.

distich: a pair of lines sufficiently similar in meter and self-contained in sense to produce the effect of a couplet, *e.g.*, these lines from *The Distichs of Cato*, a famous medieval text:

> Si deus est animus, nobis ut carmina dicunt,
> Hic tibi praecipue sit pura mente colendus.
>
> (If God a spirit is as poets sing,
> With mind kept pure make thou thy offering.)

distributed stress: the kind of accentuation that occurs when either of two consecutive syllables may take the stress. It is sometimes called *hovering accent*. In the line from Marlowe's *Faustus* given below, strong accents "hover" over both "Now" and "hast," "one" and "bare":

> Nów hást thóu bŭt óne báre hóur tŏ líve,

dithyramb: see CLASSICAL PROSODY.

doggerel: a deprecatory term applied to verse of trivial or overinflated sense or of slipshod construction. The term is sometimes also used for verse in which these characteristics are present as deliberate burlesque. An example of doggerel in the sense of inept verse is the following stanza:

> At first, happy news came, in gay letters moil'd
> With my kisses,—of camp-life and glory, and how
> They both lov'd me; and, soon coming home to be spoil'd,
>   In return would fan off every fly from my brow
>   With their green laurel-bough.
>
> From ELIZABETH BARRETT BROWNING, *Mother and Poet: Turin, After News from Gaeta, 1861*

Despite the poet's probable attempt at combining homeliness and symbolism in the concluding two lines of the stanza, there remains the unfortunate image of a bug-infested mother being vigorously swatted at by her boys.

dramatic irony: a term applied to a situation in which a speaker is less fully aware of the meaning of what he is saying than his listeners are. Originally the term was applied primarily to drama; in *Oedipus Rex*, for example, when Oedipus describes his intention of stamping out the evil plaguing Thebes, only the audience knows that Oedipus himself embodies that evil. Dramatic irony may also be present in nondramatic literature, as in Robert Browning's *My Last Duchess*, in which the speaker unwittingly reveals horrors within himself while describing the faults of his late wife.

eclogue: a pastoral poem generally consisting of a dialogue between two herdsmen, *e.g.,* Spenser's "April Eclogue" in *The Shepherd's Calendar*, in which Thenot and Hobbinoll discuss the lovesickness of one of their friends.

elegiacs: see CLASSICAL PROSODY.

elegy: originally, a classical poem composed in elegiacs; now, a poem of mourning or of serious contemplation, of any form; *e.g.,* Gray's *Elegy in a Country Churchyard*, Shelley's *Adonais*, Tennyson's *In Memoriam*. The ***dirge*** and ***threnody*** are also mourning songs, but they generally emphasize grief less than the elegy, stressing meditation instead.

elision: a term whose strict classical meaning is the combination of two unstressed syllables in order to regularize the meter of a line when a vowel at the end of a word comes before a vowel at the beginning of the next word. The term was later extended to apply also to the omission of an unstressed syllable within a word. Both kinds of elision are illustrated in the following lines from Pope's *The Rape of the Lock*:

> A livid paleness spreads o'er all her look;
> She sees, and trembles at th'approaching ill,

See also HIATUS.

end-stopped line: a line which has a pause at the end. This pause is usually indicated by a colon, semicolon, exclamation point, question mark, or period. Heavily end-stopped lines, which contrast with the verse paragraphing of Milton and of Shakespeare's later plays, are characteristic of the blank verse of Marlowe and the heroic couplets of Dryden and eighteenth-century poets. See also COUPLET, CLOSED.

enjambement: a term taken from the French, meaning the "crossing-over," the running-on without pause, of a phrase or sentence from one line to the next. See RUN-ON LINE.

envoy: see FRENCH FORMS: *ballade*.

epic: a long narrative poem, usually dealing with the adventures of a single hero such as Aeneas in Virgil's *Aeneid* or Beowulf in the Anglo-Saxon poem of that name, but having some lasting universal significance beyond the particular hero and plot. In *Beowulf*, for example, which has undergone a continuing process of reinterpretation by critics, some have seen the succession of monsters slain by the hero as symbolic of Evil recurrent in human life.

epigram: a brief, generally barbed poem, such as the following by Coleridge:

Sir, I admit your general rule,
That every poet is a fool,
But you yourself may serve to show it,
That every fool is not a poet.

epistle: a letter, especially a highly formalized one. The *verse epistle* is exemplified by Donne's *Heroical Epistle: Sappho to Philaenis*. Other poems by Donne, such as *Of the Progress of the Soul*, are prefaced by prose epistles.

epithalamion: a term of Greek origin for a marriage poem, generally fairly long and meditative. Spenser's famous *Epithalamion*, imitative of the classical form in its invocation to the gods, also describes in detail the bride's preparations, the events of the nuptial day, and the speaker's hopes for the success of the marriage.

epode: see ODE, REGULAR.

eye rhyme: see under RHYME.

false rhyme: see RHYME, APPROXIMATE.

feminine ending (*light ending*): an unstressed syllable at the end of an iambic or anapestic line, which would not ordinarily have such a syllable.

Our rev|els now | are end|ed. These | our act|*ors*,

From WILLIAM SHAKESPEARE, *The Tempest*, IV, i

The feminine ending is not counted as part of the meter.

figurative language: language composed of figures of speech.

figure of speech: generic term, roughly synonymous with *trope* as used in classical rhetoric, for groups of words designed to indicate a relationship among unlike things. The relationship may be based on the discovery of similarities, or on contrast. For specific kinds of figures of speech, see CONCEIT; KENNING; METAPHOR; METONYMY; PERSONIFICATION; SIMILE; SYMBOL; SYNECDOCHE.

foot: the basic unit of METER, roughly equivalent to a measure of music. The feet used in English verse, which derive from classical prosody, consist of particular sequences of stressed and unstressed syllables. The following are the most common in English prosody:

Name of foot	*Ajective form*	*Scansion*
iamb (*or* iambic)	iambic	◡ ⊥
trochee	trochaic	⊥ ◡
anapest	anapestic	◡ ◡ ⊥
dactyl	dactylic	⊥ ◡ ◡

The symbols indicate the combination of stressed (⊥) and unstressed (◡) syllables characteristic of each foot. An iamb, for example, consists of an unstressed syllable followed by a stressed one. In this book the double mark $\acute{-}$ is generally used for a stressed syllable, because in English verse a stressed syllable is nearly always experienced as long. Divisions between feet are marked by a short straight line: |. For examples of lines of poetry written in each of the above feet, see Exercise 3 (p. 9).

Note that when a line of verse is referred to as iambic, say, what is generally meant is that it consists predominantly of iambs: it may include other types of feet as well.

Two other feet are encountered in English verse: the *pyrrhic* and the *spondee*. The pyrrhic, also called a pyrrhus, consists of two unstressed syllables (◡ ◡). The spondaic foot, or spondee, is made up of two syllables, both long (— —), whose effect is sometimes that of two consecutive stresses. Both these feet are used only in SUBSTITUTION for other feet in regular metrical patterns.

See also SCANSION.

fourteener: a line of seven iambic feet. See METER: *heptameter.*

free verse: verse which has no meter. Free verse depends on diction, rhythmical patterns, and the arrangement of CADENCES for its effects; see also PARALLELISM, STROPHE. It may be rhymed or unrhymed. The following poem is an example:

A DECADE

When you came, you were like red wine and honey,
And the taste of you burnt my mouth with its sweetness.
Now you are like morning bread,
Smooth and pleasant.
I hardly taste you at all, for I know your savor;
But I am completely nourished.

AMY LOWELL (1874–1925)

French forms: verse patterns developed by the Provençal TROUBADOURS, which appeared in England in the fourteenth century. These forms are chiefly characterized by their extremely elaborate patterns of rhyme and repetition.

alba: a name derived from the Provençal word meaning "dawn" for a lyric whose theme is lovers' parting at dawn. "Ah God, ah God, the dawn, it comes how soon" is the refrain of one of the most typical albas.

aubade (*aube*): a song identical in subject matter with the Provençal *alba* of southern France, but composed by the TROUVÈRES of northern France.

ballade: a verse form of French origin, comprising three stanzas and an *envoy* or *coda*. Customarily the stanza consists of eight lines using three rhyme sounds. The envoy is a dedication to an important person or an invocation of a personified abstraction, a deity, or the like.

This wrecched worldes transmutacioun,
As wele or wo, now povre and now honour,
Withouten ordre or wys discrecioun

Governed is by Fortunes errour.
But natheles, the lak of hir favour
Ne may nat don me singen, though I dye,
"Jay tout perdu mon temps et mon labour";
For fynally, Fortune, I thee defye!

Lenvoy de Fortune

Princes, I prey you, of your gentilesse,
Lat nat this man on me thus crye and pleyne,
And I shal quyte you your bisinesse
At my requeste, as three of you or tweyne;
And, but you list releve him of his peyne,
Preyeth his beste frend, of his noblesse,
That to som beter estat he may atteyne.

From GEOFFREY CHAUCER, *Fortune: Balades de Visage sanz Peinture*, St. 1 and envoy

The *double ballade* and *chant royal* are expansions of the ballade form.

canzo: a name, Italian in origin, applied to any love song in the style of the troubadours.

canzone: a term applied to the words of a Provençal or Italian song, especially a song praising love or beauty; an Italian derivative of the Provençal *chanso*. Though the arrangement of rhymes and the number of stanzas vary, certain patterns seem preferred; for example, a stanza often opens with an *abc abc* rhyme order. The canzone usually ends with an envoy known as a *comiato*, which may take the form of an invocation to the poem itself.

rondeau: a name for a French form similar to (and originally synonymous with) the *rondel*. The rondeau is composed of thirteen lines, divided into three stanzas employing two rhyme sounds, and of an unrhymed refrain to the second and third stanzas formed from the opening words of the first line. The refrain frequently contains a pun and has the effect of a punch line. The first and last stanzas contain five lines, and the second stanza three. The meter is generally tetrameter, though not in the following example, which illustrates the pattern of rhymes and repetitions (*R* stands for the refrain).

LET US BE DRUNK

Ra Let us be drunk, and for a while forget,
a Forget, and, ceasing even from regret,
b Live without reason and despite of rhyme,
b As in a dream preposterous and sublime,
a Where place and hour and means for once are met.

a Where is the use of effort? Love and debt
a And disappointment have us in a net.
b Let us break out, and taste the morning prime . . .
R Let us be drunk.

a In vain our little hour we strut and fret,
a And mouth our wretched parts as for a bet:
b We cannot please the tragicaster Time.
b To gain the crystal sphere, the silver clime,
a Where Sympathy sits dimpling on us yet,
R Let us be drunk!

William Ernest Henley (1849–1903)

An alternative form of rondeau consists of ten lines plus refrain, arranged *abbaabR, abbaR.*

rondeau redoublé: a much more elaborate form of the *rondeau.* It consists of five quatrains on two alternating rhymes. Throughout there is a pattern of recurring lines. The first half of the initial line is repeated as an unrhymed tail to the last stanza. Each line in the first quatrain becomes, in order, the last line of the four succeeding quatrains. The last stanza is linked with the first by the tail and the rhyme scheme. The pattern is *ABA′B′, abaB, babA′, abaB′, babaA*, in which *A* indicates a repeated line with *a* rhyme, and *A′* indicates a second repeated line with *a* rhyme, etc.

rondel: a fourteen-line poem utilizing two rhymes with a refrain. The first two lines of the initial quatrain return at the end of the second quatrain and at the end of the sestet which concludes the poem. The meter and rhyme scheme vary, but a pattern frequently used is *ABba, abAB, abbaAB.*

roundel: originally the Chaucerian spelling of *rondel*, now applied primarily to Swinburne's variant on the traditional rondel. This variant consists of three tercets on two rhymes, with a refrain taken from the opening of the first line and rhyming with the second line in the pattern *abaR, bab, abaR* (*R* signifying the rhymed refrain).

sestina: a complicated verse form originated in Provence by Arnaut Daniel (*c.* 1180–1210) and used in Italian and in English verse. It is made up of six six-line stanzas and a concluding tercet. Instead of end rhyme as a structural device, there is repetition of the end *words* of each line in each stanza in a set order which varies from stanza to stanza. The six end words also recur in the final tercet, three in the middle and three as the end words of the lines. With the numbers 1, 2, 3, 4, 5, 6 representing the end words of the initial stanza, and each line representing a stanza, the scheme may be set down thus:

1, 2, 3, 4, 5, 6
6, 1, 5, 2, 4, 3
3, 6, 4, 1, 2, 5
5, 3, 2, 6, 1, 4
4, 5, 1, 3, 6, 2
2, 4, 6, 5, 3, 1

The arrangement of the key words in the last three lines is optional.

sirvente: a Provençal poem, without fixed form, satirizing public affairs. The twelfth-century sirvente by Bertran de Born of which the first stanza is given below (translated by Barbara Smythe) is written in eight-line stanzas:

D'un sirventes no'm chal far lonhor guanda
Tal talan ai que'l diga e que l'espanda,
Quar n'ai razo tan novela e tan granda
De'l jove rei qu'a fenit sa demanda
So frair Richart, puois sos pairs lo comanda;
    Tan es forzatz!
Puois n'Aenrics terra no te ni manda,
    Sia reis de'ls malvatz.

(I care not to delay longer over making a sirvente,
such desire have I to say and to spread it;
for I have such a new and such a great reason
in the Young King, who has given up his claim
on his brother Richard, since his father wishes it,
so bullied is he!
Since Sir Henry does not hold or command land,
let him be King of the dastards!)

triolet: a short verse form related in structure to the *rondel.* It consists of a pair of quatrains using two rhyme sounds. The first line is repeated as the fourth and seventh, and the second line is repeated as the last. The following example illustrates the form as well as the generally light tone of the triolet in English:

"URCEUS EXIT"

A I intended an Ode,
B   And it turn'd to a Sonnet.
a It began *à la mode,*
A I intended an Ode;
a But Rose cross'd the road
b   In her latest new bonnet;
A I intended an Ode;
B   And it turn'd to a Sonnet.

AUSTIN DOBSON (1840–1921), *Rose-Leaves*

villanelle: a verse form consisting of nineteen lines on two rhymes. It is divided into six stanzas: five tercets and a concluding quatrain. The structure is based upon repetition: the first and third lines of the initial tercet recur alternately as the end lines of the succeeding tercets, and recur together as the last two lines of the quatrain at the end. See pp. 246–49 for examples.

virelai: a verse form based upon interlocking rhyme and alternating long and short lines. Within a stanza, short lines rhyme together and long lines rhyme together, with the rhyme sound of the short lines becoming the rhyme sound of the long lines in the next stanza. Apart from these rules, the structure of the virelai varies, but it can be illustrated by a series of five-line stanzas in which the second and fourth lines are the short ones: *ababa, bcbcb, cdcdc, dadad.* Note that in the final stanza the short-line rhyme sound is the long-line rhyme sound of the first stanza. This form is seldom used in English verse.

genre: French term meaning "species," which has passed into English usage and come to mean a distinctive category in literature or art comprising works of a particular style or form. Examples of poetic genre are the CHANSON DE GESTE, EPITHALAMION, and PASTORAL.

haiku: a Japanese poem consisting of three lines, of five, seven, and five syllables respectively. In translation, the exact syllable count is often only approximated. Characterized by delicate juxtaposition of images to produce an emotion or feeling, Japanese haiku are also designed to afford spiritual insights frequently connected with Zen Buddhism. For example, the following haiku by Issa, translated by R. H. Blyth, is said by its translator to have been intended not only to set forth two sharp taste images and a feeling of motherly love, but also to show a human version of the kind of love reaching perfection in Buddha:

> Wild persimmons,
> The mother eating
> The bitter parts.

head rhyme: an alternative name (seldom used) for ALLITERATION.

headless line: see INITIAL TRUNCATION.

hemistich: a half line of verse. See also ANGLO-SAXON PROSODY.

hendecasyllable: see CLASSICAL PROSODY.

heptameter: a seven-foot line. See also under METER.

heroic couplet: in English verse, a closed COUPLET in rhyming iambic pentameter. In CLASSICAL PROSODY, the heroic line is dactylic hexameter, without rhyme.

hexameter: see CLASSICAL PROSODY.

hiatus: the coming together of two vowel sounds, with no intervening consonant, as in "the empyreal Heaven." The hiatus is avoided by ELISION of one of the vowels: "th'empyreal Heaven." This kind of elision may be more disturbing to the reader than the hiatus. Both hiatus and elision are considered outmoded in twentieth-century verse.

hokku: alternative and now less preferred spelling of HAIKU.

Horatian ode: see ODE.

hymn stanza: see COMMON MEASURE.

iamb: a metrical FOOT consisting of two syllables, the first short and unstressed, the second long and stressed. See also METER.

ictus: the metrical or rhythmical stress on a syllable; ordinarily indicated by ′.

idyl: a poem presenting an idealized picture of rustic life; sometimes used as a synonym for PASTORAL. An example is Tennyson's *The Gardener's Daughter*:

> . . . The fields between
> Are dewy-fresh, browsed by deep-udder'd kine,
> And all about the large lime feathers low—
> The lime a summer home of murmurous wings.
> In that still place she, hoarded in herself,
> Grew, seldom seen; not less among us lived
> Her fame from lip to lip. Who had not heard
> Of Rose, the Gardener's daughter? . . .

The aspects of rustic life most often emphasized in an idyl are simplicity and harmony growing out of intimacy with nature. In Tennyson's *Idylls of the King*, in which King Arthur's kingdom comes to ruin through man's violation of the natural order, the use of the word "idyl" is somewhat ironic.

image: a word or group of words designed to appeal to one or more of the senses. Although imagery is the raw material of poetic figures of speech, the use of images need not involve comparison, symbolism, or any complex kind of utterance. The following lines exemplify images that appeal to the respective senses:

Sight:

> There, on beds of violet blue,
> And fresh-blown roses washed in dew,

From JOHN MILTON, *L'Allegro*

Sound:

> The ice was all around:
> It cracked and growled, and roared and howled,

From SAMUEL TAYLOR COLERIDGE, *The Rime of the Ancient Mariner*, I

Smell:

> . . . the rose
> Blendeth its odour with the violet,—
> Solution sweet: . . .

From JOHN KEATS, *The Eve of St. Agnes*, XXXVI

Taste:

And every tongue, through utter drought,
Was withered at the root;
We could not speak, nor more than if
We had been choked with soot.

From COLERIDGE, *The Rime of the Ancient Mariner*, II

Touch:

Not a softness anywhere about me,
Only whalebone and brocade.

From AMY LOWELL, *Patterns*

Kinesthesia (muscular tension and relaxation):

That I may rise and stand, o'erthrow me and bend
Your force to break, blow, burn and make me new.

From JOHN DONNE, *"Batter My Heart"*

Temperature:

It was a miracle of rare device,
A sunny pleasure-dome with caves of ice!

From COLERIDGE, *Kubla Khan*

An image may, of course, appeal to more than one of the senses; the mouthful of soot in *The Rime of the Ancient Mariner* is to be felt as well as tasted; the rigidity of the lady's garments in *Patterns* can be seen as well as felt; and so on.

imagism: a movement in poetry which originated in America about the beginning of World War I, with the publication of a volume called *Some Imagist Poets.* According to the Preface, the poets' aim was "to produce poetry that is hard and clear," "to present an image," for "poetry should render particulars exactly and not deal in vague generalities" (see p. 42). The six poets represented in the book were Richard Aldington, H. D. (Hilda Doolittle), John Gould Fletcher, F. S. Flint, D. H. Lawrence, and Amy Lowell. Ezra Pound had helped to bring these poets together and to spark the movement, but was only temporarily a part of it.

incremental repetition: lines or phrases in a poem repeated with slight alterations in such a way as to help develop the subject matter of the poem. Incremental repetition thus differs from simple REPETITION or from a REFRAIN, which, while its wording may change slightly from stanza to stanza, does not advance the "story." The anonymous ballad *Edward,* of which the first three stanzas are cited below, contains many kinds of repetition; the incremental repetition is identified by italics:

"Why dois your brand sae drap wi bluid?
Edward, Edward?
Why dois your brand sae drap wi bluid?
And why sae sad gang yee, O?"

> "*O, I hae killed my hauke sae guid,*
> Mither, mither,
> O, I hae killed my hauke sae guid,
> And I had nae mair bot hee, O."
>
> "Your haukis bluid was nevir sae reid,
> Edward, Edward,
> Your haukis bluid was nevir sae reid,
> My deir son I tell thee, O."
> "*O, I hae killed my reid-roan steid,*
> Mither, mither,
> O, I hae killed my reid-roan steid,
> That erst was sae fair and frie, O."
>
> "Your steid was auld, and ye hae gat mair,
> Edward, Edward,
> Your steid was auld, and ye hae gat mair,
> Sum other dule ye drie, O."
> "*O, I hae killed my fadir deir,*
> Mither, mither,
> O, I hae killed my fadir deir,
> Alas, and wae is mee, O!"

initial rhyme: a seldom-used alternative term for ALLITERATION.

initial truncation (*headless line*): the omission of light syllables at the beginning of an iambic or anapestic line.

inversion: a rearrangement of normal word or sentence order in prose or verse. When well used, inversion serves to emphasize rhetorically important words, *e.g.*, the key word "born" at the beginning of Milton's *On the Morning of Christ's Nativity*:

> This is the month, and this the happy morn
> Wherein the Son of Heaven's Eternal King
> Of wedded Maid and Virgin Mother born,

Normal word order in English is basically subject, verb, direct object, indirect object, with adjectives preceding nouns. Normal word order in the preceding passage would be "born of wedded Maid and Virgin Mother."

In the tradition of English verse, inversion has been misused to simplify the problems of rhyme and meter, as in the following portion of Thomas Gray's *Sonnet on the Death of Richard West*:

> A different object do these eyes require;
> My lonely anguish melts no heart but mine;
> And in my breast the imperfect joys expire;

Yet morning smiles the busy race to cheer,
And new-born pleasure brings to happier men;
The fields to all their wonted tribute bear;
To warm their little loves the birds complain.
I fruitless mourn to him that cannot hear,
And weep the more because I weep in vain.

irony: the use of words whose implication is the opposite of their literal meaning; as when Donne, in *The Dream*, remarks "For thou lovest truth" as an aside to a woman whose moral and intellectual qualities he holds in low esteem. Irony may also take more complex forms than clear-cut sarcasm. It may be implicit mockery or subversion of an established tradition, as when Edna St. Vincent Millay says in *Spring* that "April/Comes like an idiot, babbling and strewing flowers." It may also take the form of a result or conclusion strikingly different from the expected, as in Donne's *Song: "Go and Catch a Falling Star"* when the speaker, after two stanzas implying that he would give a king's ransom to meet an honest woman, concludes:

If thou find'st one, let me know,
  Such a pilgrimage were sweet;
Yet do not, I would not go,
  Though at next door we might meet;
Though she were true when you met her,
And last till you write your letter,
    Yet she
    Will be
False, ere I come, to two or three.

Sometimes an author's whole approach to a subject may be ironic or different from the expected; in Donne's *Woman's Constancy*, the speaker (ungallantly betraying considerable experience with ladies like the one he is with now) anticipates in detail all the excuses she may make for future unfaithfulness—and then puts his stamp of approval on them:

Now thou hast lov'd me one whole day,
Tomorrow when thou leav'st, what wilt thou say?
Wilt thou then antedate some new-made vow?
  Or say that now
We are not just those persons which we were?
. . .
Vain lunatic, against these scapes I could
  Dispute and conquer, if I would,
  Which I abstain to do,
For by tomorrow, I may think so too.

A modern example of an ironic approach is Dorothy Parker's terse

Résumé of various means of suicide and their attendant discomforts: "You might as well live," she concludes.

See also DRAMATIC IRONY.

jongleur: a wandering musician who performed the compositions of the TROUBADOURS.

kenning: a figurative phrase used in Anglo-Saxon poetry, such as, in *Beowulf*, "swan-road" for sea. Like the Greek epithet, it is used as a poetic convention, but while in Homer a single epithet is regularly linked with a given person or thing, as "rosy-fingered" is with Dawn, a wide variety of kennings name the same person or thing. For example, Grendel, one of the monsters in *Beowulf*, is "the lonely prowler," "exile accurst," "slaughterous fiend," and so on; Hrothgar, the Danish king, may be referred to as "the Scyldings' Friend" or, as in the following lines, by his ancestry:

> Thus boiled with care the breast of Hrothgar;
> Ceaselessly sorrowed the son of Healfdene.

Though apparently much admired in Anglo-Saxon poetry, this practice of "elegant variation" to avoid repeating a name is considered bad form in modern English.

lay: a simple lyric or short narrative poem, originally one intended to be sung. Among the most famous are the *Lais* of Marie de France (*c.* 1170). Later poets use the term primarily as a deliberate archaism, as Sir Walter Scott does in *The Lay of the Last Minstrel.*

light ending: see FEMININE ENDING.

light stress: a metrical stress that falls on a word which, in ordinary speech, would not be accented; usually indicated ˋ.

> She doth tell me where to borrow
> Comfort in the midst of sorrow:
> Mákes thĕ désŏlàtĕst pláce
> To her presence be a grace.

From GEORGE WITHER, *The Shepherd's Hunting,* Eclogue 4

limerick: two three-stress lines followed by two two-stress lines and another three-stress line, with an *aabba* rhyme scheme. Edward Lear, the famed "nonsense" poet, wrote scores of limericks:

> There was an old man of Dumbree
> Who taught little owls to drink tea;
> For he said, "To eat mice
> Is not proper or nice,"
> That amiable man of Dumbree.

There was an old person of Putney
Whose food was roast spiders and chutney,
Which he took with his tea,
Within sight of the sea,
That romantic old person of Putney.

line length: the number of feet in a single VERSE; or, in SYLLABIC VERSE, the number of syllables.

L.M.: abbreviation for LONG MEASURE.

long measure: a form of hymnal stanza: $a^4a^4b^4b^4$ or $a^4b^4a^4b^4$. It is "long" by comparison with COMMON MEASURE and SHORT MEASURE. The hymn from which one stanza is given below is written in long measure.

a^4 Courage, brother, do not stumble,
b^4 Though thy path be dark as night;
a^4 There's a star to guide the humble,—
b^4 Trust in God and do the right!

From NORMAN MACLEOD, *"Courage, Brother"*

lyric: originally, verse composed to be sung to the accompaniment of a lyre; now, a poem characterized by its "singing" or musical quality, whether it is intended to be sung or not, and by its emphasis on the speaker's personal emotions rather than on outward incidents or events. The melodious quality of the lyric is exemplified by an anonymous Middle English poem called *Alysoun*, whose refrain goes:

An hende hap I have i-hent,
I wot from hevene it is me sent;—
From alle wommen my love is lent
And light on Alysoun.

Elizabethan lyrics, like the following, are noted for their singing quality:

CORINNA

When to her lute Corinna sings,
Her voice revives the leaden strings,
And doth in highest notes appear
As any challenged echo clear.
But when she doth of mourning speak,
E'en with her sighs the strings do break.

And as her lute doth live or die,
Led by her passion, so must I.
For when of pleasure she doth sing,
My thoughts enjoy a sudden spring;
But if she doth of sorrow speak,
E'en from my heart the strings do break.

THOMAS CAMPION (1567?–1619)

masculine ending: the conclusion of a line, usually an iambic or anapestic line, on a stressed syllable:

> My wits | be wea|ry and | my eyes | are dim,|
>
> From GEORGE GASCOIGNE, *The Steel Glass*

Compare FEMININE ENDING.

measure: an alternative term, now archaic, for foot. The terms LONG MEASURE, SHORT MEASURE, and COMMON MEASURE refer to specific stanza patterns. Occasionally "measure" is applied to rhythm in general: "Sing to me in merry *measure*."

metaphor: language that, by suggesting some significant point of contact between things ordinarily perceived as being unlike, heightens the reader's perception of one or both of them. See also what can be considered special forms of the metaphor: METONYMY; PERSONIFICATION; SIMILE; SYNECDOCHE.

The subject to which a metaphor refers is known as its ***tenor***; the metaphoric term itself—the figurative language by which implicit reference to the subject is made—is the ***vehicle***. For example, "a bucket-full of gold" is the vehicle by which Edna St. Vincent Millay evokes the rising sun (here the tenor). In the following lines the tenor is fog and the vehicle is a waiflike apparition:

> What grave has cracked and let this frail thing out,
> To press its poor face to the window-pane,
>
> From LIZETTE WOODWORTH REESE, *Fog*

simple metaphor: an implied comparison: "cobalt sky," "street lights blooming on long green stalks," "ranked trees in an armed host."

complex metaphor: one in which the relationship between the linked things is more subtle than, for example, that between "rows of trees" and "ranked troops" in the simple metaphor just quoted. A complex metaphor can be quite simple in expression. The statement "I am become a name" in Tennyson's *Ulysses* is a complex metaphor because what is suggested is not merely a comparison between man and name, but the notion that this man of fame and power now scarcely exists except in the renowned name still on people's lips. Similarly, in the following lines by Hilda Conkling, there is no direct comparison being made:

> When moonlight strikes the water
> I cannot get it into my poem.

Keats uses a complex metaphor when he refers to the Grecian urn as "thou foster-child of silence and slow time." Obviously there is an implicit comparison here: the urn has been cared for like a foster-child (its "natural" parent being the artisan who made it) by "silence and slow time"; but this comparison does not explain the whole metaphor—for example, why "silence" has been a preservative factor. The metaphoric weight of that word is not developed until the next stanza, in which Keats presents the idea that "Heard melodies are sweet, but those unheard/ Are sweeter," because they are not subject to natural decay.

extended metaphor: one in which the same relationship or comparison is developed throughout an entire poem, or a significant portion of a poem, as in Carl Sandburg's *Prayers of Steel,* which depends entirely on the linkage between the speaker and a piece of unshaped steel:

> Lay me on an anvil, O God.
> Beat me and hammer me into a crowbar.
> Let me pry loose old walls.
> Let me lift and loosen old foundations.

functional (or ***organic***) ***metaphor:*** a metaphor that is an organic part of the poem's structure and meaning, rather than merely a decorative rhetorical device. In the following poem by the Tudor poet Sir Thomas Wyatt, the imagery of the first section—that of wild, shy forest creatures that briefly became semitamed—becomes, in context, a metaphor expressing memorably the nature and course of a dying love affair:

THEY FLEE FROM ME

They flee from me that sometime did me seek,
With naked foot stalking in my chamber.
I have seen them gentle, tame, and meek
That now are wild, and do not remember
That sometime they put themselves in danger
To take bread at my hand. And now they range,
Busily seeking with a continual change.
Thanked be fortune, it hath been otherwise
Twenty times better; but once in special,
In thin array, after a pleasant guise,
When her loose gown from her shoulders did fall,
And she me caught in her arms long and small,
Therewith all sweetly did me kiss
And softly said, "Dear heart, how like you this?"
It was no dream; I lay broad waking.
But all is turn'd through my gentleness
Into a strange fashion of forsaking.
And I have leave to go of her goodness,
And she also to use newfangleness.
But since that I so kindely am served,
I would fain know what she hath deserved.

Sir Thomas Wyatt (1503?–1542)

On the other hand, when Elizabeth Barrett Browning, in her famous sonnet *"How Do I Love Thee,"* writes

> I love thee freely, as men strive for Right;

the metaphor is not functional or organic. The vaguely political overtones of "as men strive for Right" are not consistent with other imagery in the poem. Though men striving for Right may be possessed of powerful emotion, that emotion is not necessarily the passionate love of woman for man explored by the rest of the poem, nor is it necessarily true that men strive for right "freely."

mixed metaphor: one in which the implied relationships are not harmonious, and the metaphor as a whole is consequently ineffectual, or humorous; as in the following notorious sentence: "Dante stood with one foot in the grave of the Middle Ages; with the other he waved a salute to the rising dawn of the Renaissance."

dead metaphor: one so frequently used that it has become more idiomatic than metaphoric: "the brink of danger," "blood red."

metaphorical and figurative language: language that associates dissimilar objects in order to produce a vivid and exact perception of one of them—essentially the METAPHOR and particular forms of the metaphor: METONYMY; PERSONIFICATION; SIMILE; SYNECDOCHE.

metaphysical poetry: a name applied to a type of poetry written in the seventeenth century by authors such as John Donne, Richard Crashaw, Thomas Traherne, George Herbert, and Andrew Marvell, and, in America, Edward Taylor. The somewhat misleading term "metaphysical" was apparently first suggested for this school of poetry by John Dryden, who, in 1693, took Donne to task for writing love poetry that "perplexes the minds of the fair sex" with matters of metaphysics when "he should engage their hearts." Alexander Pope later wrote that "Cowley . . . borrowed his metaphysical style from Donne." The first, however, to use the term "metaphysical poet" was Samuel Johnson, in his *Life of Cowley* (1779). He wrote: "The metaphysical poets were men of learning, and to show their learning was their whole endeavour."

Most characteristic of metaphysical poetry is the CONCEIT, a device suited to its highly intellectual cast and its frequently paradoxical turns of thought. Many of the metaphysical poets were also noted for their metrical experimentation, which often produced a harsh and abrupt sound pattern that pre-twentieth-century critics tended to ascribe to the authors' inability to count out a smooth meter. Contemporary critics, however, view the crabbedness of rhythm in some metaphysical poetry as a deliberate sound device paralleling the uncertainties and irresolutions which form the subject matter of many metaphysical poems. A number of twentieth-century critics, particularly the "New Critics," who are credited with rediscovering the Metaphysicals, consider both the harsh sound and complicated structure of much metaphysical poetry a symptom of a seventeenth-century Age of Anxiety caused by the decay of Elizabethan social concepts, the demise of the earth-centered Ptolemaic theory of the universe, and a general collapse of the optimistic values of the Renaissance. T. S. Eliot is among the critics who note a desperate urgency, a sense of the minuteness of human time, in Andrew Marvell's *To His Coy Mistress*, though on the surface, the poem appears to be simply another love poem on the theme of "Gather ye rosebuds":

Had we but world enough, and time,
This coyness, lady, were no crime.
We would sit down, and think which way
To walk, and pass our long love's day.
Thou by the Indian Ganges' side.
Should'st rubies find: I by the tide
Of Humber would complain. I would
Love you ten years before the Flood,
And you should, if you please, refuse
Till the conversion of the Jews.
My vegetable love should grow
Vaster than empires, and more slow.
An hundred years should go to praise
Thine eyes, and on thy forehead gaze;
Two hundred to adore each breast;
But thirty thousand to the rest;
An age at least to every part,
. . .

In addition to helping reawaken interest in seventeenth-century metaphysical poets such as Marvell, Eliot in his own poems drew on certain qualities of metaphysical poetry: its preoccupation with the discords within the human personality, its willingness to make heavy demands on the reader's intellect by complicated allusions to diverse literary, philosophical, and theological writings. Eliot's *The Waste Land* is undoubtedly the best example of neometaphysical writing, but his shorter poem *The Love Song of J. Alfred Prufrock* (p. 284) can also be considered "metaphysical" in its exposure of the fragmented and out-of-harmony self.

meter: a category of RHYTHM characterized by regular, measurable patterns of stressed or long and unstressed or short syllables, representing nearly equivalent time intervals. Each of these patterns is called a FOOT; the foot constitutes the basic metrical unit. Unlike rhythmical patterns, metrical patterns, which properly occur only in verse, are repeated regularly or continuously (see Chapter I).

English verse, which evolved from the Latin, Anglo-Saxon, and French prosodic systems, as well as from imitation of Italian forms, might be termed quantitative-accentual-syllabic verse. Essentially, English prosody depends on the number of ACCENTS or stressed syllables in a line and the number of unstressed syllables accompanying them—the particular combination of stressed and unstressed syllables constituting the metrical feet. Stress partly determines QUANTITY in English verse: a stressed syllable is generally felt to be long, an unstressed syllable to be short.

A meter is often described by type of foot and LINE LENGTH. Thus iambic pentameter is a meter in which most of the feet are iambs and the line consists of five feet. It is not necessarily a meter in which the lines each contain *five* iambs, for the SUBSTITUTION of other types of feet for the foot predominantly used is very common in English verse. A meaningful, unforced reading of a poem will show that the actual pattern of stressed and unstressed syllables frequently deviates from an abstract scheme based on the strict repetition of one type of foot. Both the abstract or exact metrical pattern and the actual pattern can be discovered by SCANSION. By an emphatically rhythmic reading of lines like the following from William Cowper's *A Comparison*, the reader can find an abstract pattern in which each foot consists of a short syllable preceding a long one:

The lapse | of time | and riv|ers is | the same,|
Both speed | their jour|ney with | a rest|less stream;|
The si|lent pace,| with which | they steal | away,|
No wealth | can bribe,| no prayers | persuade | to stay.|

He can then reread the poem, relying on word accent, and see that the abstract scheme above underlies a less exact pattern:

The lapse | of time | and riv|ers is | the same,|
Both speed | their jour|ney with | a rest|less stream;|
The si|lent pace,| with which | they steal | away,|
No wealth | can bribe,| no pray|ers persuade | to stay.|

Despite the substitutions in certain feet, these lines are classified as iambic pentameter.

English verse owes much of its flexibility to the free use of substitution. And it draws on many other means of variation upon the basic metrical patterns: ANACRUSIS; CADENCE; CATALEXIS; COMPENSATION; FEMININE ENDING.

The various line lengths commonly employed in English verse derive their names from classical prosody.

monometer: a line consisting of only one foot. Monometer lines sometimes occur within a poem employing longer lines elsewhere; the concluding single anapest in each stanza of Austin Dobson's *The Song of the Sea Wind* is an example:

How it sings again, and whistles
As it shakes the stout sea-thistles—
    How it sings!

A few pieces of verse written entirely in monometer do exist, however, including the following, which uses not only one-foot lines but also one-syllable feet:

THE AERONAUT TO HIS LADY

I
Through
Blue
Sky
Fly
To
You.
Why?

Sweet
Love
Feet
Move
So
Slow.

FRANK SIDGWICK (1879–1939)

dimeter: a line consisting of two feet, such as the first, second, fourth, and fifth lines in the following poem:

A WORD

A word | is dead|
When it | is said,|
Some say.
I say | it just|
Begins | to live|
That day.

EMILY DICKINSON (1830–1886)

trimeter: a line consisting of three feet, as in the following:

NO SPOUSE BUT A SISTER

A bach|elor | I will|
Live as | I have | liv'd still,|
And nev|er take | a wife|
To cru|cify | my life:|
But this | I'll tell | ye too,|
What how | I mean | to do;|
A sis|ter (in | the stead|
Of wife) | about | I'll lead;|
Which I | will keep | embrac'd,|
And kiss,| but yet | be chaste.|

ROBERT HERRICK (1591–1674)

tetrameter: a line consisting of four feet, frequently with a medial pause (see CESURA). Verse using this line ranges from lyrics to long narrative works. Lord Byron's "*She Walks in Beauty,*" of which the first four lines of the first stanza are quoted, illustrates the use of tetrameter:

She walks | in beau|ty, like | the night|
Of cloud|less climes | and star|ry skies;|
And all | that's best | of dark | and bright|
Meet in | her as|pect and | her eyes:|

pentameter: a line consisting of five feet. The five-foot *iambic* line, a derivative of the French decasyllabic line, came into use in English through Chaucer. This line, iambic pentameter, has become the most widely used in English-language verse. It owes much of its popularity to its suitability for "large" forms such as long narratives, drama, and epic, though it is also the requisite meter of the sonnet and is used in many other short poetic forms. The following iambic pentameter lines are from Shakespeare's *The Merchant of Venice* (V, i):

How sweet | the moon|light sleeps | upon | this bank!|
Here will | we sit,| and let | the sounds | of mu|sic
Creep in | our ears:| soft still|ness and | the night|
Become | the touch|es of | sweet har|mony.|
Sit, Jes|sica:| look, how | the floor | of heav|en
Is thick | inlaid | with pat|ines of | bright gold;|
There's not | the small|lest orb | which thou | behold'st|
But in | his mo|tion like | an an|gel sings,|
Still quir|ing to | the young-|eyed cher|ubins;|
Such har|mony | is in | immor|tal souls;|
But, whilst | this mud|dy ves|ture of | decay|
Doth gross|ly close | it in,| we can|not hear | it.

hexameter: a term properly used only in CLASSICAL PROSODY for a particular type of quantitative six-foot line.

alexandrine: in English verse, a six-foot iambic line. See ALEXANDRINE.

heptameter: a seven-foot line, also known as a *septenary* and a *fourteener.* The latter name refers to the fourteen syllables of which the seven-foot line was commonly composed in the time of the early Elizabethan poets; some scholars believe that the ballad stanza $a^4b^3c^4b^3$ was originally a pair of fourteeners. The following lines from a poem by Surrey are written in alternating alexandrines and heptameters, a type of verse known as POULTER'S MEASURE:

When sum|mer took | in hand | the win|ter to | assail,|
With force | of might | and vir|tue great | his storm|y blasts | to quail,|
And when | he cloth|ed fair | the earth | about | with green|
And ev|ery tree | new gar|mented,| that pleas|ure was | to seen,|

octometer: an eight-foot line, generally dactylic, as in Tennyson's *Kapiolani*:

> Whén frŏm thĕ | térrŏrs ŏf | Nátŭre ă | péoplĕ hăve | fáshiŏn'd ănd | wórshĭp ă |
> Spírĭt ŏf | Évĭl,|
> Bléssed bĕ thĕ | Vóice ŏf thĕ | Téachĕr whŏ | cálls tŏ thĕm |
> "Sét yŏursĕlves | frée!" ∧ |

metonymy: a figure of speech in which, instead of naming a particular object or person, the poet substitutes a term associated with the thing to be named; *e.g.,* Shakespeare's "The crown will find an heir," in which "crown" stands for "king."

minnesinger: one of the German lyric poets and singers active from about 1150 to about 1350. See also TROUBADOUR.

mixed metaphor: see METAPHOR.

monometer: a line consisting of only one foot; rarely used. See METER.

Muse: one of the Greek goddesses of the arts and sciences. Four were in charge of poetry: Calliope of the epic, Euterpe of the lyric, Erato of love poetry, and Polyhymnia of sacred poetry. The term is also used to personify poetic inspiration, as when Shakespeare invokes "a Muse of fire, that would ascend/ The brightest heaven of invention!" Such usage is now considered overblown, though occasionally a modern writer employs the term or the concept for a particular effect; Robert Graves prefaces a volume of his verse with a poem called *To Calliope*, which ends:

> No: nothing reads so fresh as I first thought,
> Or as you could wish—
> Yet must I, when far worse is eagerly bought,
> Cry stinking fish?

near-rhyme: see RHYME, APPROXIMATE.

neoclassical: see CLASSICAL.

numbers: a loose and now archaic term that can mean metrical feet, meter, or, simply, verse. Pope wrote that he "lisp'd in numbers, for the numbers came," apparently using the term to refer to metrical organization in general. On the other hand, Thomas Campion, writing "of our English Numbers in general" (*Observations in the Art of English Poesy,* 1602), discusses specific types of feet.

occasional poetry: verse composed to commemorate a particular event, *e.g.,* Gerard Manley Hopkins' *The Wreck of the Deutschland* ("To the happy memory of five Franciscan Nuns, exiles by the Falk Laws, drowned between midnight and morning of December 7th, 1875"); William Butler Yeats' *Among School Children,* inspired by his inspection of Irish primary schools; Milton's

On the Death of a Fair Infant Dying of a Cough. Occasional poetry is sometimes commissioned, *e.g.*, James Russell Lowell's Harvard Commemoration Ode and certain works of the British poet laureates. Some of the best-known poems in English are occasional—the following, for example:

TO LUCASTA, GOING TO THE WARS

Tell me not, sweet, I am unkind
  That from the nunnery
Of thy chaste breast and quiet mind
  To war and arms I fly.

True, a new mistress now I chase,
  The first foe in the field;
And with a stronger faith embrace
  A sword, a horse, a shield.

Yet this inconstancy is such
  As thou too shalt adore;
I could not love thee, dear, so much,
  Lov'd I not honour more.

RICHARD LOVELACE (1618–1658)

octave: (1) A poem or stanza of eight lines. The following is the second in a series by E. A. Robinson, called, simply, *Octaves*:

Tumultuously void of a clean scheme
Whereon to build, whereof to formulate,
The legion life that riots in mankind
Goes ever plunging upward, up and down,
Most like some crazy regiment at arms,
Undisciplined of aught but Ignorance,
And ever led resourcelessly along
To brainless carnage by drunk trumpeters.

(2) The first eight lines of a sonnet, after which, especially in a Petrarchan sonnet, there is some shift in the direction of the ideas. See SONNET, PETRARCHAN.

octometer: an eight-foot line, generally dactylic. See METER.

octosyllabic verse: verse consisting of eight-syllable lines.

ode: originally a Greek term meaning, simply, a song; applied later to a lyric of exalted tone and elaborate design.

regular ode (*Pindaric ode*): a form which imitates the triumphal odes of the Greek poet Pindar. It is composed of (1) a strophe followed by (2) an antistrophe of identical structure and (3) an epode of different structure; the whole pattern may be repeated. The structure of all the parts is optional with the poet.

1. *strophe:* from the Greek "turning"—the first part of a Greek ode was

sung as the chorus moved to one side. In the ode, a STROPHE is a grouping of lines for which neither metrical pattern nor number of lines in the group is prescribed.

2. *antistrophe:* from the Greek "counterturn"—at this point in the classical Greek ode the chorus would move to the other side. Structurally, in the regular ode, meter and number of lines are an exact repetition of the strophe.
3. *epode:* from the Greek "stand"—during this part of the Greek ode, the chorus stood still.

For an example of the regular ode in English, see Thomas Gray's *Progress of Poesy*, pp. 261–62.

Horatian ode, also called *stanzaic ode*: a form, named for the Roman poet Horace, consisting of a series of formal stanzas and lacking an epode. The following translation of an ode by Horace exemplifies the form. It is written in an approximation of alcaics (see CLASSICAL PROSODY):

LOOK HOW THE SNOW

Look how the snow lies deeply on glittering
Soracte. White woods groan and protestingly
Let fall their branch-loads. Bitter frost has
Paralysed rivers: the ice is solid.

Unfreeze the cold! Pile plenty of logs in the
Fireplace! And you, dear friend Thaliarchus, come,
Bring out the Sabine wine-jar four years
Old and be generous. Let the good gods

Take care of all else. Later, as soon as they've
Calmed down this contestation of winds upon
Churned seas, the old ash-trees can rest in
Peace and the cypresses stand unshaken.

Try not to guess what lies in the future, but,
As Fortune deals days, enter them into your
Life's book as windfalls, credit items,
Gratefully. Now that you're young, and peevish

Grey hairs are still far distant, attend to the
Dance-floor, the heart's sweet longings; for now is the
Right time for midnight assignations,
Whispers and murmurs in Rome's piazzas

And fields, and soft, low laughter that gives away
The girl who plays love's games in a hiding-place—
Off comes a ring coaxed down an arm or
Pulled from a faintly resisting finger.

HORACE, *Odes*, Bk. I, 9, trans. James Michie

The Horatian ode in English is exemplified by Keats' *Ode on a Grecian Urn* and William Collins' *Ode to Simplicity*, of which the first three stanzas are quoted below:

O thou by Nature taught,
To breathe her genuine thought,
In numbers warmly pure and sweetly strong:
Who first on mountains wild,
In Fancy, loveliest child,
Thy babe, or Pleasure's, nurs'd the pow'rs of song!

Thou, who with hermit heart
Disdain'st the wealth of art,
And gauds, and pageant weeds, and trailing pall:
But com'st a decent maid
In Attic robe array'd,
O chaste unboastful Nymph, to thee I call!

By all the honey'd store
On Hybla's thymy shore,
By all her blooms, and mingled murmurs dear,
By her, whose love-lorn woe
In ev'ning musings slow
Sooth'd sweetly sad Electra's poet's ear:
. . .

irregular ode: a form consisting of a series of STROPHES. There may be any number of strophes or groupings of lines in the poem, and no two strophes are necessarily the same in line length, number of lines, or metrical pattern. The irregular strophes approximate in verse the paragraph in prose. Among the most famous irregular odes in English is William Wordsworth's *Ode: Intimations of Immortality from Recollections of Early Childhood*, p. 272.

stanzaic ode: see *Horatian ode*, above.

off-rhyme: see RHYME, APPROXIMATE.

onomatopoeia: the use of words or combinations of letters to imitate a sound, as in Alfred Noyes' *The Highwayman*, in which the hoofbeats of a galloping horse become "tlot, tlot." Many common words are onomatopoeic: "crash," "shriek," "cough," "rip," "murmur," and the like.

open couplet: see COUPLET, OPEN.

organic metaphor: see METAPHOR, FUNCTIONAL.

ottava rima: see STANZA.

paeon: see CLASSICAL PROSODY.

pantoum: from *pantun*, a Malayan verse form initiated primarily by the French, and similar to the *villanelle* (see FRENCH FORMS). It consists of a series of quatrains in which the second and fourth lines of each quatrain recur as the first and third lines of the next; the second and fourth lines of the final stanza repeat the first and third lines of the first stanza. Brander Matthews wrote the following pantoum, *En Route*:

Here we are riding the rail,
  Gliding from out of the station;
Man though I am, I am pale,
  Certain of heat and vexation.

Gliding from out of the station,
  Out from the city we thrust;
Certain of heat and vexation,
  Sure to be covered with dust.

Out from the city we thrust:
  Rattling we run o'er the bridges;
Sure to be covered with dust,
  Stung by a thousand of midges.
. . .

The stanzas continue until, in the final one, the original first line recurs as the last line:

Ears are on edge at the rattle,
  Man though I am, I am pale,
Sounds like the noise of a battle,
  Here we are riding the rail.

paradox: statement which, on the surface, appears self-contradictory but which more careful examination may reveal to be true. In Gilbert and Sullivan's *H. M. S. Pinafore*, the chorus sings, "A paradox! A paradox!" as it transpires that the hero, supposedly twenty-one years of age, has had only four birthdays —since he was born on February 29. In John Donne's famous *"Batter My Heart"* (*Holy Sonnets*, XIV), the closing lines are paradoxical:

Take me to you, imprison me, for I,
Except you'enthrall me, never shall be free,
Nor ever chaste, except you ravish me.

parallelism: a device used in both verse and prose consisting in the juxtaposition of phrases closely similar in structure or sense. Biblical translators have attempted to preserve the parallelism of Hebrew poetry, *e.g.*, in Psalm 68:

But let the righteous be joyful;
let them exult before God;
let them be jubilant with joy!

Revised Standard Version

The structure of much primitive verse depends largely on parallelism. For example, a song of the Pueblo Indians of the American Southwest goes:

O our Mother the Earth, O our Father the Sky,
Your children are we, and with tired backs
We bring you the gifts that you love.
Then weave for us a garment of brightness;
May the warp be the white light of morning,
May the weft be the red light of evening,
May the fringes be the falling rain,
May the border be the standing rainbow.
Thus weave for us a garment of brightness,
That we may walk fittingly where birds sing,
That we may walk fittingly where grass is green,
O our Mother the Earth, O our Father the Sky.

Trans. H. J. Spinden

A hymn ascribed to St. Patrick, who lived in the fifth century, uses parallelism in a manner reminiscent of heathen Anglo-Saxon charms:

I arise to-day
Through God's strength to pilot me:
God's might to uphold me,
God's wisdom to guide me,
God's eye to look before me,
God's ear to hear me,
God's word to speak for me,
God's hand to guard me,
God's way to lie before me,
God's shield to protect me,
God's host to save me
From snares of devils,
From temptations of vices,
From every one who shall wish me ill,
Afar and anear,
Alone and in a multitude.

Translation from Kuno Meyer ed.

A much later hymn, *The Song of the Creatures,* by St. Francis of Assisi (1182–1226), makes similar use of parallelism; as translated by Matthew Arnold, six of its eighteen lines begin, "Praised be my Lord . . . ," slight variations of this phrase occurring in several other lines.

Parallelism appears frequently as an incidental rhetorical or aural device throughout poetry in traditional meters, as in William Collins' *"How Sleep the Brave"*:

By fairy hands their knell is rung;
By forms unseen their dirge is sung;

Parallelism as a structural device, however, more often appears in modern free verse, as in Walt Whitman's *Song of Myself*:

> I celebrate myself, and sing myself,
> And what I assume you shall assume,
> For every atom belonging to me as good belongs to you.
>
> I loafe and invite my soul,
> I lean and loafe at my ease observing a spear of summer grass.
> . . .
> Tenderly will I use you, curling grass.
> It may be you transpire from the breasts of young men,
> It may be if I had known them I would have loved them;
> It may be you are from old people, and from women, and from offspring
> taken soon out of their mothers' laps.
> And here you are the mothers' laps.

See also ANTITHESIS.

Parnassus: the name of a mountain which, in ancient Greece, was sacred to Apollo and the Muses; hence, a symbol of the arts, particularly poetry.

pastoral: a poem or other work evoking rural life. Though the term is sometimes used as a synonym for IDYL—a poem presenting a happy picture of rustic life—a pastoral generally includes serious reflection, often culminating in the view that the city is evil; country life is romanticized by the pastoral poet, who is usually a city dweller. Theocritus, a Greek poet of the third century B.C., and his younger contemporaries Bion and Moschus established the pastoral form. The Roman poet Virgil imitated the Greek pastoral, but departed from his Greek models in that he presented somewhat more idealized pictures of the country, included formal mythology, and dwelled on more general and significant themes. Later writers frequently merged the stock figures of the classical pastoral with Christian symbolism, particularly the image of Christ as shepherd.

The following excerpt from a pastoral by the Elizabethan poet Samuel Daniel refers to an Edenlike "golden age":

> O happy golden age,
> Not for that rivers ran
> With streams of milk, and honey dropp'd from trees,
> Not that the earth did gauge
> Unto the husbandman
> Her voluntary fruits, free without fees,
> Not for no cold did freeze
> Nor any cloud beguile

Th'eternal-flow'ring spring,
Wherein liv'd everything,
. . .

Famous examples of the pastoral in English are, in verse, Spenser's *The Shepherd's Calendar*, Milton's *Lycidas*, Shelley's *Adonais*; in prose, Sir Philip Sidney's *Arcadia*; in drama, Shakespeare's *As You Like It.*

pathetic fallacy: a critical term originated by Ruskin, meaning the attribution of human feelings to nature—to animals, atmospheric conditions, landscape, and so on; as in the following lines from Wordsworth's *To a Sky-Lark*:

Joyous as morning,
Thou art laughing and scorning;
Thou hast a nest for thy love and thy rest,
And, though little troubled with sloth,
Drunken Lark! thou would'st be loth
To be such a traveller as I.

Most frequently the feelings ascribed to nature either parallel the feelings of the speaker in the poem (*e.g.*, the despondent speaker sees "weeping" skies) or are strikingly in opposition to them (*e.g.*, "happy" bird songs "mock" the speaker's despondency).

pause: a temporary stop or rest in the reading of a line. Though some poets have experimented with using pauses as part of the meter, as measured rests are used in music, pauses are more frequently dictated by the sense of the passage. A *terminal pause* occurs at the end of a line of verse (see END-STOPPED LINE). A *medial pause* comes in the middle of a line (see CESURA). Occasionally there may be a *midfoot pause*. The following lines from E. A. Robinson's sonnet *Thomas Hood* exemplify all three kinds of pause (a single slant line indicates a shorter pause, a double slant line a longer one):

We laugh,| and crown | him;// but | anon | we feel| — midfoot
A still | chord sor|row-swept,|/ —a weird | unrest;|// — medial, terminal
And thin | dim shad|ows home | to mid|night steal,|/ — terminal
As if | the ver|y ghost | of mirth | were dead—|// — terminal

pentameter: a line of verse consisting of five feet. See METER; also CLASSICAL PROSODY.

perfect rhyme: see under RHYME.

persona: the speaker in a poem, when the poet assumes a role or a point of view other than his own. The term derives from the name given to the masks traditionally worn by the actors in classical drama. Browning's *My Last Duchess*, spoken throughout by a duke, and all the poems in Edgar Lee Masters' *Spoon*

River Anthology, from which the first five lines of *Lucinda Matlock* are quoted here, make conspicuous use of personae:

> I went to the dances at Chandlerville,
> And played snap-out at Winchester.
> One time we changed partners,
> Driving home in the moonlight of middle June,
> And then I found Davis.

The student should remember that poets frequently use personae, probably more often than not. In fact, he should always be wary of assuming, without careful study of a poem in conjunction with other poems by the same author, that the poet is *not* using this device. John Donne's *Break of Day*, of which the first and last stanzas are quoted below, is often badly misread on an assumption that the speaker is Donne. Actually, the last lines of the poem reveal that for once Donne has assumed a female persona:

> 'Tis true, 'tis day; what though it be?
> O wilt thou therefore rise from me?
> Why should we rise, because 'tis light?
> Did we lie down, because 'twas night?
> Love which in spite of darkness brought us hether,
> Should in despite of light keep us together.
> . . .
> Must business thee from hence remove?
> Oh, that's the worst disease of love,
> The poor, the foul, the false, love can
> Admit, but not the busied man.
> He which hath business, and makes love, doth do
> Such wrong as when a married man doth woo.

Current critics and scholars generally prefer to say, "The *speaker* in such and such a poem says (or feels or thinks) . . . ," rather than, "The *poet* says . . ." This wording helps avoid misreadings, and it also puts the student or critic on guard against making unwarranted assumptions, on the basis of a single poem, about what the *poet* thinks, or what his "philosophy" is.

personification: the attributing of certain human characteristics to nonhuman things; sometimes, by extension, the attribution to inanimate objects of the qualities of living beings:

> The sea creeps to pillage,
> She leaps on her prey,

From Elinor Wylie, *Sea Lullaby*

. . . Morning sought
Her eastern watch-tower, and her hair unbound,
Wet with the tears which should adorn the ground,
Dimmed the aerial eyes that kindle day;

From Percy Bysshe Shelley, *Adonais*, XIV

The fog comes
On little cat feet.

From Carl Sandburg, *Fog*

poesy: an archaic term meaning poetry or the writing of poetry.

poetic diction: the use of certain kinds of words and the avoidance of others (frequently technical or "unbeautiful") on the theory that the language of poetry should be different from the language of prose. See Chapter II.

poetic license: a departure from normal pronunciation, grammar, or diction in order to fit an idea to the rhyme or meter. George Puttenham, in *The Art of English Poesy* (1589), cautions: "our maker must not be too licentious in his concords, but see that they go even, just, and melodious in the ear. . . . For a licentious maker is in truth but a bungler and not a poet." Nevertheless, many well-known poets have been "licentious makers" to the extent of using false rhymes (*e.g.*, Wordsworth, when he links "spell" and "terrible") and eye rhymes, such as "love" and "prove," which conclude the opening lines spoken by Marlowe's Passionate Shepherd (see *approximate rhyme* and *eye rhyme* under RHYME); ELISION, derided by Pope but also much used by him; elaborate grammatical INVERSION; words such as "eke" (also), "lo," and the like, or "do" and "did" as auxiliary verbs, to "eke out" a line metrically. Liberties of this kind for the sake of meter and rhyme are not acceptable in modern poetry. Variations in meter and in types of rhyme, however, are admired today when they fit the context and do not seem merely the result of structural demands. See METER; RHYME; SUBSTITUTION.

Poetic license may also refer to a bending of the facts, such as occurs whenever a writer puts words into the mouths of historical figures, as Michael Drayton does in his ballad *Agincourt*:

And turning to his men,
Quoth our brave Henry then:
"Though they to one be ten
  Be not amazèd!"

Here, whether from motives of patriotism or for the sake of the rhyme, Henry V himself seems to indulge in some poetic license, for at the Battle of Agincourt the French outnumbered the English four to one, not ten to one.

poetics: a piece of writing expounding a theory of the art of poetry; *e.g.*, Aristotle's *Poetics*.

poulter's measure: a type of verse, popular with the early Elizabethan poets, composed of alexandrines and fourteeners (see METER: *heptameter*) in alternate lines. A poem of Surrey's, for example, is composed in sets of lines like the following:

> "Abroad," quoth my desire, "assay to set thy foot
> Where thou shalt find the savour sweet, for sprung is every root,"

According to George Saintsbury, in his authoritative work on English prosody, the name is "said to be derived from the practice of poulter[ers] in giving twelve to the dozen in one case and thirteen or fourteen in another."

primary accent: see ACCENT.

prosodic symbols: signs used in the SCANSION of verse. See list on p. 307; also CESURA, FOOT, ICTUS, PAUSE, VIRGULE.

prosody: the system by which verse is organized; a generic term including such aspects of versification as rhythm and/or meter, stanzaic pattern, accentuation, syllable count, and the like. The chief organizing factor in a particular type of versification is usually taken as the name of that type: *e.g.,* STRESS PROSODY.

pyrrhic: a FOOT consisting of two short or unstressed syllables. See also SUBSTITUTION.

quantitative verse: verse in which the meter is governed by the time required to pronounce a syllable, rather than by accentuation. In quantitative verse the feet are composed of long and short syllables, the long syllable being given a duration equivalent to that of two short syllables. Classical prosody is based upon QUANTITY. There are few successful examples of quantitative verse in English (see CLASSICAL PROSODY), since English pronunciation relies heavily on accentuation.

quantity: a term used in Greek and Latin prosody for the time required to pronounce a syllable. A *long syllable*, in classical prosody, is one containing either a long vowel or a short vowel followed by two or more consonants not conveniently pronounced as part of the next syllable. A *short syllable* is one containing a short vowel separated from the vowel of the next syllable by not more than one consonant; two short syllables count as equal to one long syllable.

Quantity, the governing factor in classical prosody, is subordinate to stress in English verse; see METER. QUANTITATIVE VERSE has, however, been imitated in English; for specific examples, see CLASSICAL PROSODY.

quatrain: a STANZA consisting of four lines.

refrain, also called *burden*: phrases or lines repeated in every stanza, either within the stanza or at the end. They do not necessarily rhyme with any other line, nor do they have to be repeated exactly. While a refrain may consist in simple REPETITION of a significant phrase in the poem, perhaps of a line or part of a line appearing in the opening stanza (see FRENCH FORMS), it is often extraneous to the thematic and metrical development of the poem. In the examples below, though the refrains contribute to the mood of the poems, they have no obvious connection with the "story." The second and fourth line in Shakespeare's song are repeated in every stanza:

When that I was and a little tiny boy,
  With hey, ho, the wind and the rain,
A foolish thing was but a toy,
  For the rain it raineth every day.

But when I came to man's estate,
  With hey, ho, the wind and the rain,
'Gainst knaves and thieves men shut their gate,
  For the rain it raineth every day.

From WILLIAM SHAKESPEARE, *Twelfth Night*, V, i

It was Lilith the wife of Adam:
    (*Eden bower's in flower.*)
Not a drop of her blood was human,
But she was made like a soft sweet woman.

Lilith stood on the skirts of Eden;
    (*And O the bower and the hour!*)
She was the first that thence was driven;
With her was hell and with Eve was heaven.

In the ear of the Snake said Lilith:—
    (*Eden bower's in flower.*)
"To thee I come when the rest is over;
A snake was I when thou wast my lover.

"I was the fairest snake in Eden:
    (*And O the bower and the hour!*)
By the earth's will, new form and feature
Made me a wife for the earth's new creature."

From DANTE GABRIEL ROSSETTI, *Eden Bower*

repetition: the use of precisely the same wording within a stanza or in different stanzas. In the folk ballad *Edward*, cited under INCREMENTAL REPETITION, there is repetition of the question and answer in each stanza. The recurrent "Edward, Edward" and "Mither, mither" are instances of *parallel repetition.* See also REFRAIN.

rest: a pause in a line of verse that takes the place of a light syllable, as in Tennyson's

> Bréak, ∧ | bréak, ∧ | bréak, ∧ |

rhyme: the repetition at recognizable intervals of similar or identical sounds, as a means of emphasis, unification, or ornamentation. In English verse, rhyme is generally taken to mean *accurate masculine rhyme* (see below).

accurate masculine rhyme (*full rhyme*): the repetition of a stressed syllable, where the vowel sound and any following consonant sounds are duplicated exactly but the preceding consonant sounds are different, as in "bat," "cat." Other examples:

> Fair nymphs and well-dressed youths around her shóne,
> But every eye was fixed on her alóne.
>
> From ALEXANDER POPE, *The Rape of the Lock*

> The willows, and the hazel copses gréen,
> Shall now no more be séen,
>
> From JOHN MILTON, *Lycidas*

alternating rhyme: rhyme in which the rhyming sounds occur in every other line, *abab*. See example under *end rhyme*.

approximate rhyme (*off-rhyme*): near-rhyme; the use of rhyme words similar rather than identical in sound. Such rhyming is sometimes identified by a question mark. In the following lines from the old ballad *Barbara Allan*, the approximate rhyming is probably not deliberate:

> *a* It was in and about the Martinmas time,
> *b* When the green leaves were a-*falling*,
> *c* That Sir John Graeme in the West Country
> *b*? Fell in love with Barbara *Allan*.

For modern poets, however, approximate rhyme can be an effective device to produce a deliberately loose or uncertain sound pattern. Emily Dickinson, quoted below, was one of the innovators in approximate rhyme used in this way:

> I felt a Funeral, in my Brain,
> And Mourners to and *fro*
> Kept treading—treading—till it seemed
> That Sense was breaking *through*—
> . . .
> And then a Plank in Reason, broke,
> And I dropped down, and *down*—
> And hit a World, at every Crash—
> And Got through—knowing—*then*—

The approximate rhymes employed in the second and fourth lines of the second stanza might also be called *consonantal rhyme* (see below), since the final consonants are the same but the vowels differ. In the following stanza, Emily Dickinson's approximate rhyme can be equated with ASSONANCE, since the vowel sound is the same in both words but the final consonants differ:

> These are the days when skies re*sume*
> The old—old sophistries of *June*—
> A blue and gold mistake.

Approximate rhyme differs from ***false rhyme*** chiefly in connotation. False rhyme is the use of an approximate rhyme which, in context, seems accidental, awkward, or unjustified by the sense of the passage:

> And beast and bird that from the spell
> Of sleep took import terrible;—
>
> From WILLIAM WORDSWORTH, *Memorials of a Tour in Scotland*, 1814, VII

assonantal rhyme: see ASSONANCE.

broken rhyme (*split rhyme*): end rhyme in which, because the rhyming syllable is not the last syllable of a word, the remainder of the word must be continued at the beginning of the following line; as in E. E. Cummings'

> . . . education snakeoil vac
> uumcleaners terror strawberries democ
> [racy] . . .

or

> thoroughly bretish
> they scout the inhuman
> itarian fetish
> that man isn't wuman

consonantal rhyme (*consonance*): linkage of sounds in which the final consonant sounds agree but the preceding vowels do not; *e.g.*, "bard" and "heard." Consonance may also be a variety of rhyme in which *both* the preceding and the terminal consonant sounds of the stressed syllable agree, but the vowel sounds do not:

> Let the boy try along this bayonet-blade
> How cold steel is, and keen with hunger of blood;
> Blue with all malice, like a madman's flash;
> And thinly drawn, with famishing for flesh.
>
> From WILFRED OWEN, *Arms and the Boy*

See also *approximate rhyme; half rhyme.*

double rhyme: see *feminine rhyme.*

end rhyme (*terminal rhyme*): rhyme that occurs at the end of a line of verse, as in Wordsworth's

A slumber did my spirit seal;
  I had no human fears;
She seemed a thing that could not feel
  The touch of earthly years.

The contrasting term is *internal rhyme*.

eye rhyme: the use of words that look as though they would rhyme, because their endings are spelled similarly, but that do not, because they are pronounced differently; *e.g.,* "lies" and "phanta*sies*" in Keats' *The Eve of St. Agnes*. Since rhyme is a sound effect, eye rhyme does not really qualify as a type of rhyme.

false rhyme: see *approximate rhyme*.

feminine rhyme (*double rhyme*): rhyme in which a rhyming stressed syllable is followed, in each of the rhyme words, by an identical unstressed syllable. A feminine rhyme is sometimes identified by the symbol for an unstressed syllable, as shown:

a˘ That wee bit heap o' leaves an' stibble
a˘ Has cost thee monie a weary nibble!

From Robert Burns, *To a Mouse*

Feminine rhyme is just one of the many types of rhyming which Ogden Nash exploits with great skill for comic effects:

MY DREAM

Here is a dream.
It is my dream,
My own dream,
I *dreamt it.*
I dreamt that my hair was kempt,
Then I dreamt that my true love un*kempt it.*

Ogden Nash (1902–   )

Of course, the poem depends for its sound effect not only on the here italicized feminine rhymes (in "punch-line" positions), but also on the internal rhymes, "dreamt" and "kempt," in lines 5 and 6. See *internal rhyme*.

full rhyme: see *accurate masculine rhyme*.

half rhyme: a form of approximate rhyme in which the vowel sounds differ but the consonant sounds, those at the beginning of the rhyme syllable as well as the terminal ones, are the same. Thus half rhyme is a form of *consonantal rhyme* (see above). Half rhyme is employed as a major structural device in Wilfred Owen's *From My Diary, July 1914*, of which the opening lines are:

Leaves
    Murmuring by myriads in the shimmering trees.
Lives
    Wakening with wonder in the Pyrenees.
Birds
    Cheerily chirping in the early day.
Bards
    Singing of summer scything thro' the hay.

historical rhyme: the occurrence of words which, though they were full rhymes at the time they were written, no longer rhyme because of changes in pronunciation; *e.g.,* Pope's "join" and "twine."

interlocking rhyme: repetition of a rhyme sound to connect different parts of a rhyme-patterned verse form; not to be confused with *alternating rhyme*. Interlocking occurs in a stanza like rhyme royal (see under STANZA), in which the *a* and *b* of the *abab* alternate, but the *b* of the *bcc* picks up, and interlocks with, the *b*'s in *abab*. Similar interlocking occurs in the Petrarchan sonnet, in the Spenserian stanza and sonnet, and in the *In Memoriam* stanza, in which the *a*'s lock in the *b*'s. Interlocking also occurs in a sequential form like terza rima (see under STANZA), in which the *b*'s of the second tercet interlock with the *b* of the first, the *c*'s of the third tercet interlock with the *c* of the second, etc.

internal rhyme: rhyme that occurs within a line; *e.g.,* Tennyson's

"Spanish ships of war at *sea*! we have sighted fifty-*three*!"

See also *leonine rhyme* and the example given for *triple rhyme*.

Though internal rhyme is often thought of as an old-fashioned or comic device, Archibald MacLeish, in *The Fall of the City*, uses it for modern subject matter with dead-serious intent:

In the day of con*fusion* of reason when all is de*lusion*:
In the day of the *tyr*ants of tongues when the truth is for *hire*:
In the day of de*ceit* when ends *meet*:
Turn to your gods!
In the day of di*vision* of nations when hope is de*rision*:
In the day of the *supp*ing of hate when the soul is cor*rupt*ed:
In the day of de*spair* when the heart'*s bare*:
Turn to your gods!

leonine rhyme: a form of recurrent internal rhyme; originally, the occurrence of rhyme sounds in the third and sixth foot of a medieval Latin hexameter line.

masculine rhyme: see *accurate masculine rhyme*.

minor-accent rhyme: rhyme in which the rhyme sound occurs on a syllable that receives only a secondary, or light, stress, as in the following lines:

Then by the bed-side, where the faded moon
Made a dim, silver twilight, soft he set
A table, and, half anguish'd, threw thereon
A cloth of woven crimson, gold, and *jet*:—
O for some drowsy Morphean amu*let*!

From JOHN KEATS, *The Eve of St. Agnes*, XXIX

The term "minor-accent rhyme" also applies to an occurrence of the rhyme sound on a syllable which, according to word accent, is not stressed at all, as in the rhyming of "sing" and "lingering." Rhymes in which the rhyme sound does not fall on an accented syllable in *either* word (*e.g.*, trilo*gy* and horri*bly*) also constitute minor-accent rhyme.

off-rhyme: see *approximate rhyme.*

perfect rhyme (*rime riche*): a form of rhyme considered desirable in French verse but, since 1400, seldom used to good effect in English verse. In this type of rhyme, the rhyming words or syllables are exactly the same in sound, though they may differ in sense; *e.g.,* "Criseyde" and "seyde" (said) in Chaucer's *Troilus and Criseyde.*

slant rhyme: see *consonantal rhyme.*

split rhyme: see *broken rhyme.*

terminal rhyme: see *end rhyme.*

triple rhyme: rhyme in which a stressed syllable is followed by two unstressed syllables; now generally used for comic effect, as in the following:

Blue-Beard, the Monday *following*, his jealous feelings *swallowing*,
Packed all his clothes together in a leather-bound valise,
Then, feigning repre*hensibly*, he started out os*tensibly*,
By traveling to learn a bit of Smyrna and of Greece.

From GUY WETMORE CARRYL, *How the Helpmate of Blue-Beard Made Free with a Door*

rhyme royal: see STANZA.

rhythm: the general pattern manifest in any extended series, particularly (for the purposes of this book) a series of sounds. In poetry as in music, this pattern is sometimes measurable in "beats," but the terms "beat" and "rhythm" are not interchangeable. "Rhythm" is much broader, indicating the whole shape and arrangement of a sound pattern and thus, too, the broad distinguishing features of that pattern: the characteristic flow of a particular prose writer's sentence structure, the habitual speedings-up and slowings-down of a person's speech, the CADENCES of free verse.

Rhythm, both in artistic prose and in verse, may be defined as a recognizable pattern of stressed and unstressed syllables, with *roughly* equivalent time intervals between the stresses. "Pattern," of course, implies repetition; in prose, the pattern rarely occurs more than three times in succession, while in verse it may be extended indefinitely.

METER is a category of rhythm. The term refers to a nearly regular pattern in which the beats occur at measurable time intervals. Many metric sound patterns occur spontaneously, as in breathing, the beating of the heart, the dripping of a faucet, nervous pencil-tapping. It is therefore erroneous to suggest, as is often done, that whereas rhythm is a product of accident or nature, meter is intentional or willed. Both rhythm and its special category meter may occur either as natural phenomena or as deliberate devices. See Chapter I.

rime royal: see STANZA.

romance: a tale, originally in the medieval Romance dialects, later written in other languages as the chivalric traditions spread to other areas of the world. These tales recounted knightly and/or amorous adventures, generally in verse. Chrétien de Troyes, a French troubadour of the twelfth century, helped develop and popularize the form. In many of his romances, Chrétien focuses upon love adventures unfolding against a backdrop of Arthurian legend. Lancelot, for example, and Lancelot's affair with Guinevere, which became a staple in the story of Arthur, seem to have been Chrétien's invention.

Chaucer's tale of *Sir Thopas* in *The Canterbury Tales*, of which one stanza is given here, parodies the romance tradition:

He spurred his way through forest fair
Where many a monster has its lair,
  Such as the hare and buck;
And as he went by east and north,
I tell you, and was riding forth
  He met with evil luck.

Trans. Nevill Coghill

romantic: a term used to characterize poetry in which the sensibilities and emotions of the writer override the restraint of tone, formality of structure, and intellectualization of content distinguishing classical verse. The *Romantic* poets of the nineteenth century, of whom Wordsworth, Coleridge, Shelley, Byron, and Keats are the most famous representatives in English, tended to find their subject matter in archaic legends, exotic locales, supernatural occurrences, and their own emotional response to the beauties of nature and to personal incidents.

The following excerpts exemplify the romantic tone:

No, no, go not to Lethe, neither twist
  Wolf's-bane, tight-rooted, for its poisonous wine;
Nor suffer thy pale forehead to be kiss'd
  By nightshade, ruby grape of Proserpine;
Make not your rosary of yew-berries,
  Nor let the beetle, nor the death-moth be
    Your mournful Psyche, nor the downy owl
A partner in your sorrow's mysteries;
  For shade to shade will come too drowsily,
    And drown the wakeful anguish of the soul.

From JOHN KEATS, *Ode on Melancholy*

Come, be happy!—sit near me,
Shadow-vested Misery;
Coy, unwilling, silent bride,
Mourning in thy robe of pride,
Desolation—deified!

Come, be happy!—sit near me:
Sad as I may seem to thee,
I am happier far than thou,
Lady, whose imperial brow
Is endiademed with woe.

From PERCY BYSSHE SHELLEY, *Invocation to Misery*

In Xanadu did Kubla Khan
A stately pleasure-dome decree:
Where Alph, the sacred river, ran
Through caverns measureless to man
Down to a sunless sea.
. . .
And from this chasm, with ceaseless turmoil seething,
As if this earth in fast thick pants were breathing,
A mighty fountain momently was forced:
Amid whose swift half-intermitted burst
Huge fragments vaulted like rebounding hail,
Or chaffy grain beneath the thresher's flail:
And 'mid these dancing rocks at once and ever
It flung up momently the sacred river.

From SAMUEL TAYLOR COLERIDGE, *Kubla Khan*

The term "romantic," however, can be applied not only to members of the nineteenth-century romantic movement, but also to any work of verse or prose which shows similar characteristics. In twentieth-century English verse,

Dylan Thomas, for example, is considered a romantic poet. In the poem from which the following stanza is taken, the speaker identifies with nature:

> The force that through the green fuse drives the flower
> Drives my green age; that blasts the roots of trees
> Is my destroyer.
> And I am dumb to tell the crooked rose
> My youth is bent by the same wintry fever.

rondeau: see FRENCH FORMS.

rondel: see FRENCH FORMS.

roundel: see FRENCH FORMS.

runes: originally, the letters of the early Teutonic alphabet; but, since these letters were used in incantations, "rune" has come to mean a poem embodying a magic spell. The term is sometimes used as a deliberate archaism, as in Kipling's *The Runes on Weland's Sword.*

run-on line: one in which ENJAMBEMENT occurs, *i.e.*, in which the sense of the line continues into the succeeding line without a pause. The first line of a couplet is said to be run-on when the sense runs over, without end-stopping, to the next line. A couplet is said to be run-on when the sense of the *second* line must be completed in a succeeding couplet. See also COUPLET, OPEN; END-STOPPED LINE; VERSE PARAGRAPH.

satire: writing designed to expose human follies, social evils, and the like, generally through the use of wit, sarcasm, travesty, or parody. John Donne, in the fourth of his series of *Satires*, writes:

> Well; I may now receive, and die; my sin
> Indeed is great, but I have been in
> A purgatory, such as fear'd hell is
> A recreation to, and scarce map of this.
> My mind, neither with pride's itch, nor yet hath been
> Poison'd with love to see, or to be seen,
> I had no suit there, nor new suit to show,
> Yet went to court; . . .

Pope's *The Rape of the Lock*, parodying in mock-heroic terms the sumptuous triviality of eighteenth-century high society, makes an epic battle of a card game and a religious ceremony of Belinda's primping; see p. 16.

scald: a Scandinavian BARD.

scansion: close analysis of a poem's metrical pattern, by use of a system of symbols to indicate the stressed and unstressed syllables which make up the metrical feet, and to indicate the pauses. Because scansion is a purely inductive process, the stresses are marked *where they naturally occur* and *then* the whole is examined to see what pattern has emerged. Scansion does *not* mean forcing the words of a poem into a pre-established pattern.

In a poem using any of the traditional English meters, scansion will reveal a basic pattern that can be expressed in terms of the kind and number of feet in a line; *e.g.*, Tennyson's *Ulysses* is said to be in iambic pentameter, because each line contains five metrical feet of which the most frequently used is the iamb, even though in a meaningful reading only one of the quoted lines (the last) is purely iambic:

> It lit|tle prof|its that | an i|dle king,|
> By this | still hearth,| among | these bar|ren crags,|
> Matched with | an ag|ed wife,| I mete | and dole|
> Une|qual laws | unto | a sav|age race,|
> That hoard,| and sleep,| and feed,| and know | not me.|

In attempting to establish the basic metrical pattern, it is sometimes helpful, before marking the stresses as they are dictated by the sense of the selection, to read a passage in an exaggeratedly rhythmic manner:

> Matched with | an ag|ed wife,| I mete | and dole|

No worthwhile poem, however, actually follows the basic metrical pattern exactly, syllable by syllable, throughout. To avoid monotony and prevent the meaning of the poem from being dominated by metronomically accurate rhythm, a poet deliberately allows variations to occur in some feet, as Tennyson does by his use of a spondaic foot in the second line quoted above. Because variations or SUBSTITUTIONS are used, and because the variations are frequently related to the sense of the line, scansions of the same poem may differ among individual readers according to their interpretation of its meaning.

See also METER; PROSODY.

scop: an Anglo-Saxon poet, such as the one who might have composed *Beowulf.* See also BARD; SCALD.

secondary accent: see ACCENT.

septenary: a line consisting of seven feet. See METER: *heptameter.*

sestet: (1) A poem or stanza consisting of six lines; *e.g.,* the following complete poem by Tennyson:

> Flower in the crannied wall,
> I pluck you out of the crannies,
> I hold you here, root and all, in my hand,
> Little flower—but *if* I could understand
> What you are, root and all, and all in all,
> I should know what God and man is.

(2) The second part (last six lines) of a sonnet; applies particularly to the Petrarchan sonnet, in which the rhyme scheme sets off these lines as a unit. See SONNET, PETRARCHAN.

sestina: see FRENCH FORMS.

short measure: a variant hymn stanza. It is "short" by comparison with COMMON MEASURE (usually $a^4 b^3 c^4 b^3$) and LONG MEASURE (usually $a^4 b^4 a^4 b^4$). The arrangement of rhymes and beats in short measure is $a^3 b^3 c^3 b^3$ or $a^3 b^3 a^3 b^3$. There are no four-stress lines. The following poem is written in short measure:

IS MY TEAM PLOUGHING

"Is my team ploughing,
  That I used to drive
And hear the harness jingle
  When I was man alive?"

Aye, the horses trample,
  The harness jingles now;
No change though you lie under
  The land you used to plough.

"Is football playing
  Along the river shore,
With lads to chase the leather,
  Now I stand up no more?"

Aye, the ball is flying,
  The lads play heart and soul;
The goal stands up, the keeper
  Stands up to keep the goal.

"Is my girl happy,
  That I thought hard to leave,
And has she tired of weeping
  As she lies down at eve?"

Aye, she lies down lightly,
  She lies not down to weep:
Your girl is well contented.
  Be still, my lad, and sleep.

"Is my friend hearty,
  Now I am thin and pine;
And has he found to sleep in
  A better bed than mine?"

Aye, lad, I lie easy,
  I lie as lads would choose;
I cheer a dead man's sweetheart.
  Never ask me whose.

A. E. HOUSMAN (1859–1936)

simile: a figure of speech in which an overt comparison is made between two fundamentally unlike things on the basis of some quality they both possess. What distinguishes the simile from other METAPHORICAL LANGUAGE is the presence of a definite comparative word: "My luve is *like* a red, red rose"; "folk dance *like* a wave of the sea"; "as merry *as* a bird."

sirvente: see FRENCH FORMS.

Skeltonic verse: a form of verse used by John Skelton, an early Tudor poet who was the tutor of Henry VIII and later became poet laureate under him. This verse form relies for its structure on stress, alliteration, and rhyme, rather than on syllabic count or feet. Skeltonic verse is one form of TUMBLING VERSE; what distinguishes it from other tumbling verse, which is mostly four-stress, is the frequent use of two- and three-stress lines rhyming in couplets. The following lines from Skelton's *Colin Clout* exemplify the form:

For though my rhyme be raggèd,
Tattered and jaggèd,
Rudely rain-beaten,
Rusty and moth-eaten,
If ye take well therewith,
It hath in it some pith.

S.M.: abbreviation for SHORT MEASURE.

sonnet: term sometimes used by early Elizabethan poets for any short poem concerned with a single thought, generally a reflection on love; now properly applied only to a poem of fourteen lines in iambic pentameter, with any one of several prescribed rhyme schemes. The various sonnet forms take their names from the type of rhyme scheme employed. The following are the most important:

Petrarchan sonnet: named for the Italian poet Petrarch, who perfected it; sometimes called *Italian sonnet*. Its OCTAVE is rhymed *abba abba*; the SESTET is on either two or three other rhymes, often, but by no means invariably, *cd cd cd* or *cde cde*. This pattern of rhyming sharply separates the sestet from the octave; consequently, in the Petrarchan sonnet, the octave frequently takes the form of a meditation on some subject from one point of view, the sestet then reflecting a distinct change of tone or attitude. Two examples of the Petrarchan sonnet in English are given below. The first is taken from Sir Philip

Sidney's SONNET SEQUENCE *Astrophel and Stella.* The second, by Sir Thomas Wyatt, illustrates a frequently used modification of the Petrarchan form by concluding with a couplet.

YOU THAT DO SEARCH FOR EVERY PURLING SPRING

You that do search for every purling spring
Which from the ribs of old Parnassus flows,
And every flower, not sweet perhaps, which grows
Near thereabouts into your poesy wring;
Ye that do dictionary's method bring
Into your rhymes, running in rattling rows;
You that poor Petrarch's long-deceased woes
With new-born sighs and denizen'd wit do sing;
You take wrong ways; those far-fet helps be such
As do bewray a want of inward touch,
And sure at length stol'n goods do come to light.
But if, both for your love and skill, your name
You seek to nurse at fullest breasts of Fame,
Stella behold, and then begin to indite.

SIR PHILIP SIDNEY (1554–1586), *Astrophel and Stella*, XV

UNSTABLE DREAM

Unstable dream, according to the place,
Be steadfast ones or else at least be true.
By tasted sweetness make me not to rue
The sudden loss of thy false feigned grace.
By good respect in such a dangerous case
Thou broughtest not her into these tossing seas,
But madest my sprite to live, my care t'encrease,
My body in tempest her delight t'imbrace.
The body dead, the sprite had his desire.
Painless was th'one, the other in delight.
Why, then, alas! did it not keep it right,
But thus return to leap into the fire?
And where it was at wish, could not remain?
Such mocks of dreams do turn to deadly pain.

SIR THOMAS WYATT (1503?–1542)

The following twentieth-century sonnet adheres to one of the conventional Petrarchan rhyme schemes (*abba abba, cde cde*) more strictly than the two earlier sonnets above.

PURITAN SONNET

Down to the Puritan marrow of my bones
There's something in this richness that I hate.
I love the look, austere, immaculate,
Of landscapes drawn in pearly monotones.
There's something in my very blood that owns
Bare hills, cold silver on a sky of slate,
A thread of water, churned to milky spate
Streaming through slanted pastures fenced with stones.
I love those skies, thin blue or snowy gray,
Those fields sparse-planted, rendering meager sheaves;
That spring, briefer than apple-blossom's breath;
Summer, so much too beautiful to stay;
Swift autumn, like a bonfire of leaves;
And sleepy winter, like the sleep of death.

ELINOR WYLIE (1885–1928)

Shakespearean sonnet (*English sonnet*): a form consisting of three quatrains and a final couplet: *abab*, *cdcd*, *efef*, *gg*. Since in the Shakespearean sonnet the quatrains remain more or less distinct, the form lends itself particularly to a series of variations on a single theme, with the final couplet as a climactic summary:

SONNET 6

Then let not winter's ragged hand deface
In thee thy summer, ere thou be distill'd:
Make sweet some vial; treasure thou some place
With beauty's treasure, ere it be self-kill'd.
That use is not forbidden usury
Which happies those that pay the willing loan;
That's for thyself to breed another thee,
Or ten times happier, be it ten for one;
Ten times thyself were happier than thou art,
If ten of thine ten times refigured thee:
Then what could death do, if thou shouldst depart,
Leaving thee living in posterity?
Be not self-will'd, for thou art much too fair,
To be death's conquest and make worms thine heir.

WILLIAM SHAKESPEARE (1564–1616)

Spenserian sonnet: a form developed by Edmund Spenser and seldom employed by any other poet. Its scheme is *abab*, *bcbc*, *cdcd*, *ee*. Because of the linkage in the rhyme scheme, the sharp break between octave and sestet of the Petrarchan sonnet and the distinct quatrains of the Shakespearean sonnet are absent, the only outstanding break occurring between the first twelve lines and the concluding couplet. The following sonnet by Spenser exemplifies the form:

MY LOVE IS LYKE TO YSE

My love is lyke to yse, and I to fyre:
How comes it then that this her cold so great
Is not dissolvd through my so hot desyre,
But harder growes the more I her intreat?
Or how comes it that my exceeding heat
Is not delayd by her hart frosen cold:
But that I burne much more in boyling sweat,
And feele my flames augmented manifold?
What more miraculous thing may be told,
That fyre, which all things melts, should harden yse:
And yse, which is congeald with sencelesse cold,
Should kindle fyre by wonderfull devyse?
Such is the powre of love in gentle mind,
That it can alter all the course of kynd.

EDMUND SPENSER (1552?–1599), *Amoretti*, XXX

The following are some variations on the major sonnet forms:

Miltonic sonnet: a term applied by some critics to a sonnet which retains the Petrarchan rhyme scheme, but which, because of enjambement between lines 8 and 9, has no division of thought between octave and sestet. Moreover, the Miltonic sonnet, at least as practiced by Milton himself, is often concerned not with traditional themes such as love and death, but with subjects like current politics, public figures, and moral and philosophical problems. An example of the Miltonic form and Miltonic subject matter is the following:

TO THE LORD GENERAL CROMWELL

Cromwell, our chief of men, who through a cloud
Not of war only, but detractions rude,
Guided by faith and matchless fortitude
To peace and truth thy glorious way hast plough'd,
And on the neck of crowned Fortune proud
Hast rear'd God's trophies, and His work pursu'd,
While Darwen stream with blood of Scots imbru'd
And Dunbar field resounds thy praises loud,
And Worcester's laureate wreath; yet much remains
To conquer still; peace hath her victories
No less renown'd than war, new foes arise
Threat'ning to bind our souls with secular chains:
Help us to save free conscience from the paw
Of hireling wolves whose gospel is their maw.

JOHN MILTON (1608–1674)

caudated (tailed) sonnet: also developed by Milton, and exemplified by his twenty-line *On the New Forcers of Conscience*, in which the scheme of the sestet is *cdedec* and that of the "tail," or added lines, *cfffgg*.

Wordsworth sonnet: one containing any one of several variants that Wordsworth made on the Petrarchan form, such as the use of *acca* in the second half of the octave, and *cdcddc* or *cddccd* in the sestet.

curtal sonnet: variant developed by Gerard Manley Hopkins that begins with a sestet (*abcabc*), which is followed by a quatrain and tail (*dbcdc* or *dcbdc*). *Pied Beauty* is the most famous example of this form:

PIED BEAUTY

Glory be to God for dappled things—
For skies of couple-colour as a brinded cow;
For rose-moles all in stipple upon trout that swim;
Fresh-firecoal chestnut-falls; finches' wings;
Landscape plotted and pieced—fold, fallow, and plough;
And all trades, their gear and tackle and trim.

All things counter, original, spare, strange;
Whatever is fickle, freckled (who knows hcw?)
With swift, slow; sweet, sour; adazzle, dim;
He fathers-forth whose beauty is past change:
Praise him.

GERARD MANLEY HOPKINS (1844–1889)

sonnet sequence: a gathering of sonnets by one author, often, but not necessarily, arranged by him in an order that reflects a progression of moods, the development of a love affair, or the like. The sonnet sequence was a common Elizabethan form, used by many poets, including Shakespeare. Among the most famous sonnet sequences is Sir Philip Sidney's *Astrophel and Stella*, modeled to some extent on Petrarch's sonnet sequence in praise of Laura. Elinor Wylie is the author of a twentieth-century sonnet sequence.

spondee: a FOOT consisting of two syllables, both long. See also SUBSTITUTION.

sprung rhythm: a term originated by Gerard Manley Hopkins for the effect produced by STRESS PROSODY, *i.e.,* verse in which the structure of the line is based on the number of stresses, each stress coinciding with a stress in natural speech. Hopkins used the term to point up the contrast between this type of verse and the more smoothly flowing traditional English meters. The following lines by Hopkins from *God's Grandeur* exemplify sprung rhythm:

Génerátions have tród, have tród, have tród;
And áll is séared with tráde; bléared, sméared with tóil;
And wéars man's smúdge and sháres man's sméll: the sóil
Is báre now, nor can fóot féel, béing shód.

stand: an alternative name for *epode.* See ODE.

stanza: lines of verse grouped to compose a pattern distinguishable by the number of lines, the system of stresses or feet within each line, and any other organizing device such as rhyme or assonance. The formal structure of a poem consists of the repetition of this pattern.

Stanzaic structure is generally indicated by use of the same lower-case letter to stand for each line ending with the same rhyme sound, and a raised Arabic numeral next to each letter to mark the number of feet or stresses in that line. If a sequence of lines containing the same number of feet appears, the numeral is generally given only with the last of those lines. The letter x is sometimes used to indicate the lack of any rhyme sound at the end of a particular line. Lines repeated as a whole are indicated by capital letters (see FRENCH FORMS). The term "stanza" is correctly used only when a particular pattern is repeated throughout the poem. When each pattern is different (as in the irregular ode), the correct term is STROPHE. The following stanzas are shown marked with the appropriate designation before each line:

a^4 "Oh father, oh father, a little of your gold,
b^3 And likewise of your fee!
x^4 (or c^4) To keep my body from yonder grave,
b^3 And my neck from the gallows-tree."

From *The Maid Freed from the Gallows*, anonymous ballad

a^4 The world's great age begins anew,
b^3 The golden years return,
a^4 The earth doth like a snake renew
b^3 Her winter weeds outworn:
c^5 Heaven smiles, and faiths and empires gleam,
c^4 Like wrecks of a dissolving dream.

From PERCY BYSSHE SHELLEY, *The World's Great Age*

Many important and widely used stanza forms have no individual titles. Some, however, have acquired names as a result of association with a particular poet or poem, or because of some outstanding structural feature:

In Memoriam stanza: an iambic quatrain made famous by Tennyson's famous elegy. Its form is $abba^4$:

I sometimes hold it half a sin
To put in words the grief I feel;
For words, like Nature, half reveal
And half conceal the Soul within.

From ALFRED, LORD TENNYSON, *In Memoriam*, V

Monk's Tale stanza: used by Chaucer in the narrative of that name in *The Canterbury Tales*. This stanza is identical with the Spenserian stanza except for the omission of the concluding alexandrine. Its pattern is $ababbcbc^5$.

ottava rima: a stanza consisting of eight iambic pentameter lines, with the following rhyme scheme: $abababcc^5$. One of the most noted uses of this stanza is by Byron in *Don Juan*:

> Man's love is of man's life a thing apart,
> 'Tis woman's whole existence; man may range
> The court, camp, church, the vessel, and the mart;
> Sword, gown, gain, glory, offer in exchange
> Pride, fame, ambition, to fill up his heart,
> And few there are whom these cannot estrange;
> Men have all these resources, we but one,
> To love again, and be again undone.

From George Gordon, Lord Byron, *Don Juan*, Canto I, St. 194

quatrain: a stanza consisting of four lines, characteristic of the BALLAD and hymn (see COMMON MEASURE).

rhyme royal: a French stanza, $ababbcc^5$, which Chaucer made a part of English verse by his use of it, especially in *Troilus and Criseyde*:

> Criseyde was this lady name al right.
> As to my doom, in al Troies cite
> Nas non so fair, for passynge every wight
> So aungelik was hir natif beaute,
> That lik a thing inmortal semed she,
> As doth an hevenyssh perfit creature,
> That down were sent in scornynge of nature.

From Geoffrey Chaucer, *Troilus and Criseyde*, Bk. I

This stanza pattern is now also known as the *Chaucerian stanza.* The term "rhyme royal" may have arisen because King James I used the form in a piece of verse called *The King's Quair* (p. 229).

Spenserian stanza: the stanza of Spenser's *The Faerie Queene*; later used by Byron, Keats, and other poets. Its structure, resembling an abbreviated form of the Spenserian sonnet (see under SONNET), is characterized by an interlocking rhyme scheme and a concluding alexandrine, $ababbcbc^5c^6$:

> The noble hart, that harbours vertuous thought,
> And is with child of glorious great intent,
> Can never rest, untill it forth have brought
> Th'eternall brood of glorie excellent:
> Such restlesse passion did all night torment
> The flaming corage of that faery knight,
> Devizing, how that doughtie turnament
> With greatest honour he atchieven might;
> Still did he wake, and still did watch for dawning light.

From Edmund Spenser, *The Faerie Queene*, Bk. I, Canto V, St. 1

tail-rhyme stanza: a variant stanza characterized primarily by the inclusion of a shorter line that forms a "tail" to a group of lines and rhymes with another short line. Among many variations on the tail-rhyme stanza made by individual poets is the *Burns stanza*, $a\,a\,a^4\,b^2\,a^4\,b^2$:

Wee, modest, crimson-tipped flow'r,
Thou's met me in an evil hour;
For I maun crush amang the stoure
    Thy slender stem:
To spare thee now is past my pow'r,
    Thou bonie gem.

From ROBERT BURNS, *To a Mountain Daisy*

In many of his *Songs and Sonnets*, John Donne uses stanzas in which the short rhyming lines occur consecutively:

    Let me pour forth
My tears before thy face, whilst I stay here,
For thy face coins them, and thy stamp they bear,
And by this mintage they are something worth,
    For thus they be
    Pregnant of thee;
Fruits of much grief they are, emblems of more,
When a tear falls, that thou fallst which it bore,
So thou and I are nothing then, when on a diverse shore.

From JOHN DONNE, *A Valediction: Of Weeping*

Donne (as well as other poets, such as Pope in *Ode on Solitude*) also frequently rhymes the short line or "tail" with one of the long lines rather than with another "tail":

Who ever guesses, thinks, or dreams he knows
Who is my mistress, wither by this curse;
   His only, and only his purse
   May some dull heart to love dispose,
And she yield then to all that are his foes;
May he be scorn'd by one whom all else scorn,
Forswear to others what to her he hath sworn,
With fear of missing, shame of getting, torn.

From JOHN DONNE, *The Curse*

Except in a tail-rhyme stanza, the "tail" need not rhyme with any other line; see REFRAIN.

tercet: three lines of verse forming a group in the general rhyme scheme. These lines frequently form part of a larger group and are not necessarily set off as a separate stanza; they may or may not be all on the same rhyme. The sestet of a Petrarchan sonnet often consists of two tercets:

c The poetry of earth is ceasing never:
d On a lone winter evening, when the frost
e Has wrought a silence, from the stove there shrills
c The Cricket's song, in warmth increasing ever,
d And seems to one in drowsiness half lost
e The Grasshopper's among some grassy hills.

From JOHN KEATS, *On the Grasshopper and Cricket*

terza rima: a series of tercets with interlocking rhyme: *aba, bcb, cdc,* etc.; the verse form of Dante's *The Divine Comedy*. With variant rhymes, this is the meter of Archibald MacLeish's *Conquistador*, a long narrative poem published in 1932. English terza rima also occurs in short poems. For example, Shelley, in *Ode to the West Wind*, uses a pattern consisting of four tercets followed by a couplet (*aba, bcb, cdc, ded, ee*), the fourteen lines forming a structural unit repeated through the poem:

O wild West Wind, thou breath of Autumn's being,
Thou, from whose unseen presence the leaves dead
Are driven, like ghosts from an enchanter fleeing,

Yellow, and black, and pale, and hectic red,
Pestilence-stricken multitudes: O thou,
Who chariotest to their dark wintry bed

The winged seeds, where they lie cold and low,
Each like a corpse within its grave, until
Thine azure sister of the Spring shall blow

Her clarion o'er the dreaming earth, and fill
(Driving sweet buds like flocks to feed in air)
With living hues and odours plain and hill:

Wild Spirit, which art moving everywhere;
Destroyer and preserver; hear, oh, hear!

W. H. Auden, in *"The Strings' Excitement,"* varies the strict terza rima by varying the rhymes:

The strings' excitement, the applauding drum
Are but the initiating ceremony
That out of cloud the ancestral face may come.

And never hear their subaltern mockery,
Graphiti writers, moss-grown with whimsies,
Loquacious when the watercourse is dry.

A complex and interesting variant on terza rima, with repetition, is Wallace Stevens' *Sea Surface Full of Clouds*.

triplet: a form of tercet in which the three lines forming the unit are linked by rhyme. The following poems are series of triplets:

PARADISE

I bless Thee, Lord, because I grow
Among thy trees, which in a row
To Thee both fruit and order owe.

What open force, or hidden charm,
Can blast my fruit, or bring me harm,
While the inclosure is thine arm?

Inclose me still for fear I start;
Be to me rather sharp and tart,
Than let me want thy hand and art.

When Thou dost greater judgments spare,
And with thy knife but prune and pare,
Ev'n fruitful trees more fruitful are:

Such sharpness shows the sweetest friend,
Such cuttings rather heal than rend,
And such beginnings touch their end.

GEORGE HERBERT (1593–1633)

UPON JULIA'S CLOTHES

Whenas in silks my Julia goes,
Then, then, methinks, how sweetly flows
The liquefaction of her clothes.

Next, when I cast mine eyes, and see
That brave vibration, each way free,
O, how that glittering taketh me!

ROBERT HERRICK (1591–1674)

stave: an alternative term, now archaic, for STANZA.

stress: emphasis placed upon a syllable in normal speech. It is marked ´ in SCANSION. See ACCENT; ICTUS; METER.

stress prosody (*accentual verse*): verse structure depending on the number of accented syllables in a line, rather than on the total number of syllables, the time required to pronounce the syllables, or organization into feet. Sir Walter Scott uses stress prosody in *The Lay of the Last Minstrel* (Canto II):

If thóu would'st viéw fair Mélrose arígh,
Go vísit ít by the pále móonlight;
For the gáy beáms of líghtsome dáy
Gíld, but to flóut, the rúins gréy.

See also ANGLO-SAXON PROSODY; METER; SKELTONIC VERSE; SPRUNG RHYTHM; TUMBLING VERSE.

Anglo-Saxon prosody is based upon stress, with the stressed syllables reinforced by alliteration. Duncan Spaeth's translation of the Anglo-Saxon epic *Beowulf* maintains the major elements of the prosodic system used in the original:

> In the d́arkness d́welt a d́emon-śprite,
> Whose h́eart was f́illed with f́ury and h́ate,
> When he h́eard each ńight the ńoise of ŕevel
> Ĺoud in the h́all, ĺaughter and śong.

See also the excerpt from *Beowulf* on p. 185.

strophe: in English, lines of verse arranged in a grouping which may or may not have a distinct metrical pattern and rhyme, and which, unlike the STANZA, is not repeated within the poem. The strophe corresponds roughly to the paragraph in prose. Examples of the English strophe are found in the irregular ode (see ODE, IRREGULAR) and in FREE VERSE, in which divisions may be based more on thought or emotional development than on formal structure:

GRASS

> Pile the bodies high at Austerlitz and Waterloo.
> Shovel them under and let me work—
>   I am the grass; I cover all.
>
> And pile them high at Gettysburg
> And pile them high at Ypres and Verdun.
> Shovel them under and let me work.
> Two years, ten years, and passengers ask the conductor:
>   What place is this?
>   Where are we now?
>
>   I am the grass.
>   Let me work.

CARL SANDBURG (1878–1967)

The classical strophe, found in the regular ode (see ODE, REGULAR), is rarely used in English except in imitations of the classical form.

substitution: the poet's use of a foot other than that normally required by the basic metrical pattern of his poem. Substitutions are revealed by SCANSION, when the scanning is done properly so that the stressed and unstressed syllables are marked exactly as they are dictated by the sense of the words—according to the reader's interpretation of them—rather than by a predetermined or "normal" metrical pattern.

The following are some frequently used substitutions for the iambic foot, the one most commonly employed in English-language poetry:

1. A trochee in the first foot, to give an emphatic start to a line or to a whole poem:

> *Loving* in truth, and fain in verse my love to show,
>
> From Sir Philip Sidney, *Astrophel and Stella*, I, 1

2. A pyrrhic foot within a line, to correspond with the normal flow of speech, particularly when prepositions, articles, possessive pronouns, and the like occur together (see the fifth foot marked in the quoted line); and sometimes, through repeated use, to create an effect of lightness or weakness.

> That she, dear she, might take some pleas*ure of* my pain,
>
> From *Astrophel and Stella*, I, 2

3. A spondaic foot, especially for emphasis (see the second foot of the previously quoted line).
4. Anapests or dactyls within a line, sometimes for a deliberately light effect or to suggest skipping movement; sometimes simply because of normal de-emphasis of certain words or syllables.

> Or lose thyself in the contin*uous woods*
>
> From William Cullen Bryant, *Thanatopsis*

The basic metrical pattern of a poem will nearly always be varied by substitution. For example, scansion shows that Ben Jonson's *Of Life and Death*, written fundamentally in iambic pentameter, includes a considerable number of substitutions:

> The ports | of death | are sins,| of life,| good deeds,|
> Through which | our mer|it leads | us to | our meeds.|
> How wil|ful blind | is he,| then, that | would stray|
> And hath | it in | his pow|ers to make | his way!|

Some of these substitutions would be marked in any meaningful reading of the lines; for instance, to scan line 3 of the above excerpt as

> How wil|ful blind | is he,| then, that | would stray|

would destroy the meaning. Often, however, scansion of irregular or "substituted" lines depends upon individual interpretation. In the last line of Donne's famous *"Death Be Not Proud"* (*Holy Sonnets*, X), probably no one would demolish the sense by an absolutely regular scansion:

> And death | shall be | no more;| Death, thou | shalt die.|

But one reader might find in the last half of the line the solemn death knell of two spondees,

> Death, thou | shalt die.|

whereas another might prefer to emphasize the irony of the line, giving prominence to "Death, *thou*" by reading "shalt die" as a regular iamb:

> Death, thou | shalt die.|

syllabic verse (*syllable-counting verse*): verse whose meter is based upon the total number of syllables in each line, regardless of accentuation or duration. Just as quantity is fundamental to classical Greek and Latin poetry, syllable counting is fundamental to French poetry, in which word accent has little structural importance. Each stanza of Lamartine's *Le Lac*, for example, is organized upon a pattern of three twelve-syllable lines with a fourth line of six syllables:

> Ainsi, toujours poussés vers de nouveaux rivages,
> Dans la nuit éternelle emportés sans retour,
> Ne pourrons-nous jamais sur l'océan des âges
>   Jeter l'ancre un seul jour?

Some poets, such as Tennyson (see CLASSICAL PROSODY: *hendecasyllable*), have imitated syllabic verse to the extent of writing lines containing a precise number of syllables; but because of the stresses inherent in English pronunciation, such verse generally tends to fall into an accentual pattern. Thus Tennyson's hendecasyllabics sound like lines of traditional iambic pentameter with a feminine ending in each. The contemporary poet Marianne Moore, however, writes syllabic verse in which syllable counting is clearly the prime metrical device, as the following two stanzas from *The Fish* show. (Stresses as well as numbers are given to point up the irrelevance of stress in this poem's formal structure.)

> 1 Wade
> 3 through black jade
> 8 Of the crow-blue mussel shells, one
> 1 keeps
> 6 adjusting the ash heaps;
> 9 opening and shutting itself like
>
> 1 an
> 3 injured fan.
> 8 The barnacles which encrust the
> 1 side
> 6 of the wave, cannot hide
> 8 there for the submerged shaft of the
> . . .

The entire poem follows this pattern, each stanza comprising lines of 1, 3, 8, 1, 6, and 8 (9) syllables. Among other twentieth-century poets who have experimented with syllabic verse are Robert Bridges and W. H. Auden.

symbol: in its simplest form, a sign or object which represents something larger or more complex than itself; *e.g.*, a ring, signifying marriage; a flag, signifying a nation. In poetry, a symbol is a word or image carrying, in addition to its denotation, a wider significance, which may be specified by tradition or may be highly individual, lending itself to a variety of interpretations. Traditional symbols are Shakespeare's mention of Romeo's brooding beneath a sycamore tree—the sycamore being an accepted Elizabethan symbol of melancholy and foreboding—and Emerson's reference to God as "the great Planter" in *Waldeinsamkeit.*

In the broad category of private symbols are the "tiger burning bright" in Blake's famous poem; the "noiseless patient spider" in Whitman's poem by that name; the "four lean hounds crouched low and smiling" throughout a poem by E. E. Cummings (p. 191); etc. There are, of course, widely varying degrees of explicitness within the category of individualized symbols. While the context of the Whitman poem makes it fairly clear that the spider symbolizes the striving human soul, the underlying meaning of Blake's "tiger" is still an unsolved critical problem; E. E. Cummings, with his "hounds," may be interweaving traditional symbolism (hound as symbol of hunting and of hunger) with personal symbolism (hound as symbol of sexual desire).

symbolism: the use of symbols; also, the name of a late-nineteenth-century movement in French poetry whose chief exponent was Mallarmé.

synecdoche: substitution of a part for the whole, as in the ballad *Edward*, in which the mother refers to her son's castle as "your towirs and your hall." Substitution of the whole for a part may also be classified as synecdoche; Cleopatra's referring to herself as "Egypt" in Shakespeare's *Antony and Cleopatra* is an example. As a conscious rhetorical device, synecdoche is seldom systematically employed in modern writing.

synesthesia: the association of an image perceived by one of the senses with an image perceived by another. For Arthur Rimbaud each vowel sound evoked a definite color. Charles Baudelaire, in the sonnet *Correspondances*, links colors, sounds, and fragrances. Many modern poets make use of such associations; they occur in Dylan Thomas' *Fern Hill*, in which he speaks of "the tunes from the chimneys," linking a sound with the visual image of curling smoke; in William Carlos Williams' *Winter Trees*, in which the phrase "the liquid moon" links sight with touch; in Wallace Stevens' *Domination of Black*, in which sound, touch, and sight are associated in "the loud fire."

tail: see SONNET, CAUDATED; STANZA, TAIL-RHYME.

tanka or **waka:** a five-line Japanese poem consisting of 31 syllables, unrhymed, in a pattern of 5, 7, 5, 7, 7 syllables. Originally, the HAIKU was the three-line beginning of the tanka.

tenor: see METAPHOR.

tercet: see STANZA.

terza rima: see STANZA.

tetrameter: a line of verse consisting of four feet. See METER.

thesis and **arsis:** the longer and the shorter part, respectively, of a metrical foot. The thesis is the place where the ICTUS, or stress, falls; or it may refer to the ictus mark itself. Derived from the Greek, thesis and arsis are not useful terms in English because prosodists have inadvertently reversed their meanings: thesis may refer to the shorter as well as the longer part of a foot; arsis may refer to the longer as well as the shorter part of a foot.

threnody: see ELEGY.

tone: the attitude of the poet to his theme and to his audience, as revealed by his choice of words and rhythms, the level of language, the observance or breach of conventions of technique and idea, and so on. In Sir Walter Raleigh's *The Lie*, terse trimeter rhythm, parallelism, and antithesis help create the embittered tone:

Go, Soul, the Body's guest,
  Upon a thankless arrant;
Fear not to touch the best;
  The truth shall be thy warrant:
Go, since I needs must die,
And give the World the lie.

Say to the Court, it glows
  And shines like rotten wood.
Say to the Church, it shows
  What's good, and doth no good:
If Court and Church reply
Then give them both the lie.
. . .
Tell Zeal it wants devotion;
  Tell Love it is but lust;
Tell Time it is but motion;
  Tell Flesh it is but dust:
And wish them not reply,
For thou must give the lie.

The tone of a poem need not remain the same throughout; shifts in tone in the course of a poem are a distinguishing feature in much of the work of the Metaphysicals and the "New Metaphysicals." Andrew Marvell's *To His Coy*

Mistress (see METAPHYSICAL POETRY) begins apparently as a traditional love lyric and darkens in tone—becomes increasingly serious—as it proceeds. In Donne's sonnet cited below, the tone becomes more urgent and vehement with the sestet, where the imagery alters from that of tears, which are to drown or wash the "little world" (himself), to that of destroying and purifying fires:

I AM A LITTLE WORLD

I am a little world made cunningly
Of elements and an angelic sprite,
But black sin hath betray'd to endless night
My world's both parts, and (oh) both parts must die.
You which beyond that heaven which was most high
Have found new spheres, and of new lands can write,
Pour new seas in mine eyes, that so I might
Drown my world with my weeping earnestly,
Or wash it if it must be drown'd no more:
But oh, it must be burnt! Alas, the fire
Of lust and envy have burnt it heretofore,
And made it fouler. Let their flames retire,
And burn me, O Lord, with a fiery zeal
Of thee and thy house, which doth in eating heal.

JOHN DONNE (1572–1631), *Holy Sonnets*, V

tribrach: a foot consisting of three syllables, all short or unstressed.

trimeter: a three-foot line. See METER.

triolet: see FRENCH FORMS.

triplet: see STANZA.

trisyllabic foot: a metrical foot consisting of three syllables. Unlike the TRIBRACH, which consists of three unstressed syllables, a trisyllabic foot may consist of any grouping of stressed and unstressed syllables. In English, the ANAPEST and the DACTYL are trisyllabic feet.

trochee: a metrical FOOT consisting of two syllables, the first long and stressed, the second short and unstressed.

trope: another term for FIGURE OF SPEECH.

troubadour: a wandering medieval poet-musician who composed lyrics in Provençal and other Romance languages, performing these compositions in Spain, southern France, and Italy. The troubadours originated and developed the very elaborate verse patterns now generally known as FRENCH FORMS. From the tradition of courtly love that the lyrics of the troubadours embodied came the conventions of Renaissance love poetry, imported into Elizabethan England through the Italian poet Petrarch and the French poets of the fourteenth century.

Later these conventions, parodied and satirized, provided a springboard for the metaphysical conceit and the irony of much seventeenth-century poetry. Thus the influence of the troubadour compositions transcended by many miles and several centuries the place and time of their originators.

trouvère: northern French imitator of the TROUBADOUR, writing in French.

truncation: see CATALEXIS; INITIAL TRUNCATION.

tumbling verse: accentual verse, usually rhymed and generally, but not invariably, containing four stresses per line. See also SKELTONIC VERSE; STRESS PROSODY.

variable syllable: a syllable which, according to the rhetorical structure of the phrase or sentence in which it appears, may be long or short, stressed or unstressed; it is marked $\underline{\smile}$ or $\bar{\smile}$. See also DISTRIBUTED STRESS.

vehicle: see METAPHOR.

verse: (1) One line of poetry, used especially in reference to a poem with a formal structure. "Verse" is not a synonym for "stanza." (2) A piece of writing, or a body of writing, which conforms to some system of prosody. "Verse" in this sense is synonymous with "poetry," except that it does not carry evaluative connotations and, consequently, can be more widely applied. "Verse" may be trivial or important in content, competent or incompetent in execution. The term "poetry," on the other hand, is generally applied to verse in which sound pattern, figures of speech, tone, diction, and all other technical aspects, as well as many indefinable elements, have combined to form a cohesive whole of considerable artistic value.

verse paragraph: a passage of iambic pentameter blank verse so arranged that most of the significant pauses occur medially (as cesuras) and the heavy terminal pause does not occur until the end of the passage or "paragraph." A verse paragraph, therefore, exhibits a high proportion of RUN-ON LINES:

  So cheer'd he his fair spouse, and she was cheer'd,
But silently a gentle tear let fall
From either eye, and wip'd them with her hair;
Two other precious drops that ready stood,
Each in their crystal sluice, he ere they fell
Kiss'd as the gracious signs of sweet remorse
And pious awe, that fear'd to have offended.
  So all was clear'd, and to the field they haste.
But first from under shady arborous roof
. . .

From JOHN MILTON, *Paradise Lost*, Bk. V

versification: the craft of writing verse; the technical or practical, rather than theoretical, aspects of verse.

villanelle: see FRENCH FORMS.

virelai: see FRENCH FORMS.

virgule: a slanting line (/) used to indicate a pause in scansion or a division between lines of verse when the quotation is consecutive, as in the following two lines quoted from George Meredith: "Sure of her haven, O like a dove alighting,/ Arms up, she dropped; . . ."

vowel rhyme: an alternative term for ASSONANCE.

waka: see TANKA.

weak ending: a light syllable at the end of a line. The syllable may be part of a foot, or it may be a FEMININE ENDING.

wit: term with a lengthy history of alterations in meaning, derived from an Anglo-Saxon verb meaning "to know." In the present century alone, its meanings range from the very general one of "mental faculties" ("keep your wits about you") to "humor" or "comic ability." Writers during the eighteenth century, probably the period when this word received the greatest amount of critical attention, applied the term primarily to aptness of expression. Dryden, in 1677, wrote: "The definition of wit . . . is only this: that it is a propriety of thought and words; or in other terms, thought and words elegantly adapted to the subject." Locke considered wit "lying most in the assemblage of ideas, and putting those together with quickness and variety." In 1704, Pope laid down what became the definitive eighteenth-century dictum concerning wit: "True wit, I believe, may be defined a justness of thought, and a facility of expression." Later he re-expressed this idea in a much-quoted couplet: "True wit is nature to advantage dress'd;/ What oft was thought, but ne'er so well express'd."

word accent: the accent given a word in normal speech. Correct word accent may be determined by consulting a dictionary.

wrenched accent: the displacement of normal word accent through metrical stress. Wrenched accents occur frequently in the old folk ballads, as in the following stanza from *The Wife of Usher's Well*, in which the italicized syllable is accented, though it would not be in ordinary speech:

> And she has made to them a bed,
>   She's made it large and wide,
> And she's taen her mantle her about,
>   Sat down at the bed-*side*.

Indeed, wrenched accent is so distinctly a characteristic of the popular ballad that imitators often deliberately use it to lend a "folk" quality to literary ballads. Notice, in *A Ballad of Marjorie* by Dora Sigerson, the wrenched accent, demanded by rhythm and rhyme, in the last line:

"What ails you that you look so pale,
    O fisher of the sea?"
"'Tis for a mournful tale I own,
    Fair maiden Marj*orie*."

Index

Index of Authors, Titles, and First Lines

Author entries (**boldface**) refer the reader to both text commentary and works cited. Title and first-line entries refer him only to the work cited. First lines are given for poems known by them and poems cited in their entirety or from the beginning.

The cover photograph, of the Salle des Chevaliers at Mont-Saint-Michel, was provided by courtesy of the French Government Tourist Office.